GEORGE L. MOSSE SERIES
IN MODERN EUROPEAN CULTURAL AND
INTELLECTUAL HISTORY

Advisory Board

Carl Schmitt and the Jews

The "Jewish Question," the Holocaust, and German Legal Theory

Raphael Gross

Translated by
JOEL GOLB

Foreword by
PETER C. CALDWELL

THE UNIVERSITY OF WISCONSIN PRESS

This work was published with the assistance of a translation grant from the Goethe-Institut and support from the George L. Mosse Program at the University of Wisconsin–Madison.

The University of Wisconsin Press
1930 Monroe Street, 3rd Floor
Madison, Wisconsin 53711-2059

www.wisc.edu/wisconsinpress/

3 Henrietta Street
London WC2E 8LU, England

Originally published as *Carl Schmitt und die Juden: Eine deutsche Rechtslehre*
© 2000 Suhrkamp Verlag Frankfurt am Main

Translation and foreword copyright © 2007
The Board of Regents of the University of Wisconsin System
All rights reserved

Printed in the United States of America

Library of Congress Cataloging-in-Publication Data
Gross, Raphael.
[Carl Schmitt und die Juden. English]
Carl Schmitt and the Jews : the "Jewish question,"
the Holocaust, and German legal theory /
Raphael Gross ; translated by Joel Golb ; foreword by Peter C. Caldwell.
p.   cm.—(George L. Mosse series in modern European cultural and
intellectual history)
Includes bibliographical references and index.
ISBN 0-299-22240-3 (cloth: alk. paper)
1. Schmitt, Carl, 1888–1985.   2. Political theology—Germany.
3. Antisemitism.   I. Title.
JC263.S34G75813   2007
323.1192´4043—dc22   2006031771

For

LILLY and THOMAS GROSS

CONTENTS

PART 4. ACCELERATION: KATECHON AND
ANTICHRIST

PART 5. SELF-STYLIZATIONS

FOREWORD

PETER C. CALDWELL

Raphael Gross's well-researched and carefully argued book on the role of antisemitism in Carl Schmitt's thought made great waves when it appeared in its original German in 2000. Bringing antisemitism, indeed Nazism, together with Carl Schmitt was not in itself controversial; Schmitt's involvement with the Nazis, especially between 1933 and 1936, is well known. What grabbed the attention of the scholarly and general public was Gross's claim that antisemitism not only played a role in Schmitt's scholarly career but also structured Schmitt's very thinking.

Beyond challenging assessments of Schmitt the person, Gross's reading has challenged attempts to make use of Schmitt's thoughts without reference to his personal history. Readings of Schmitt, even when critical, have tended to separate Schmitt's ideas from his personal beliefs. Schmitt's former student Otto Kirchheimer as well as Franz Neumann and Ernst Fraenkel drew upon Schmitt's political writings under the Nazis to try to comprehend German fascism as a modern phenomenon—and as a primarily *political* phenomenon rather than one structured by racism and antisemitism.[1] Similarly, Jürgen Habermas's discussion of the rise and fall of democratic republicanism and the "public" made use of both Schmitt's history of the concept of representation and his assessment of what happens when interest groups occupy and structure public discussion. While Habermas was certainly aware of Schmitt's personal involvement with Nazism, Schmitt's antisemitic worldview played no role in Habermas's analysis.[2] Leading constitutional scholars of the Federal Republic, such as Justice Ernst-Wolfgang Böckenförde of the Federal Constitutional Court, translated Schmitt's ideas into more moderate language that expressed the problems of liberal democracy and no longer implied a radical alternative to it.[3] Reinhart Koselleck's highly influential work on the history of concepts, which culminated in the grand, multivolume *Foundational Historical Concepts (Geschichtliche Grundbegriffe)*, similarly sought to expand upon Schmitt's approach to the history of political thought, without raising the key issue of what its function was in Schmitt's political thought.[4] Was an essential part of Schmitt lost with the rhetoric—and did that essence involve antisemitism? Finally, Giorgio Agamben has made use of Schmitt's doctrine of sovereignty to suggest the ongoing importance of the "state of the exception" in modern politics. Schmitt's involvement with the Nazis is important to Agamben: here is where Schmitt's doctrine of sovereignty met up with the "immediate coincidence of fact and law," here is where Schmitt's prophetic ruminations on the changing nature of the state took on real form as the Führer took "the decision on bare life by which the German biopolitical body is made actual."[5] But even here the specificity of antisemitism disappears: for Agamben, Schmitt was above all a reflective intellectual and an active participant in a movement that pointed to the political destiny of the West in general.[6]

Gross's arguments appeared at the end of a decade that had seen a significant reevaluation of Schmitt in Germany. In 1991 Carl Schmitt's journals from the period 1947–51 appeared in print.[7] The content came as a shock. Even years after the fall of the Nazi regime, Schmitt's private writings evidenced a crude antisemitism. Schmitt, the brilliant theorist of Weimar democracy and the unofficial master of political theory in the early Federal Republic, was also a representative of Germany's unmastered past.

The *Glossarium* raised the problem of Schmitt's antisemitism on several different levels. On one level, it remained the crude paranoia of a leading intellectual of defeated Germany: in an odd inversion, Jews were not victims, but victors, and the "Isra-Elites" were the only elites left on the planet after World War II.[8] On another level, Jews seemed to be for Schmitt the cause of Germany's misfortune; they were the people who "introduced themselves among us," the Germans, when "we came to be at odds," who exploited and deepened national differences for their own ends.[9] Perhaps most disturbing for those who had read Schmitt as a serious political thinker, Schmitt's very political thought seemed to take on racial tones. A major thinker like Spinoza was reduced to the embodiment of a race. Spinoza, he writes, was "the first" to surreptitiously introduce himself among the Germans;[10] instead of working out the philosophical problem of Spinoza's famous statement implying the identity of God and nature, "Deus sive natura" (God, or nature) Schmitt writes: "Deus Spinozistikus sive Spinozistika Natura" (Spinozian God, or Spinozian nature).[11] Spinoza's nature, which Schmitt had already in 1938 reduced to Judaism, explained his notion of divinity.[12] Did Schmitt as historian of political philosophy intend to reduce philosophical arguments to what Jakob Taubes called a "racist theozoology," a religio-biological essence?[13] On a third level, the *Glossarium* seemed to reveal Schmitt's deep, personal prejudices. In the mid-1930s, after the Nazis had come to power, Schmitt's antisemitism had served to further his career. Schmitt's infamous 1936 conference on "Jews in Legal Scholarship," though certainly horrible, could make sense as an opportunist career move, while his own ideas remained intact. After 1945 these ideas could in no way help his career. They furthermore appeared in the private context of writing that he did not intend to reach the public during his lifetime. Schmitt's own private writing challenged any attempts to read him as a "normal" political thinker. It was now difficult to focus on the stimulating, stylistically brilliant texts he had written outside of their political context. To put it bluntly, the *Glossarium* raises the question of whether Schmitt's antisemitism provided the structure and indeed impetus for Schmitt's thought.

Gross's book intervenes into a huge, complicated literature. Schmitt was always a controversial and fascinating figure. Work on Schmitt has always faced the question of how to relate his brilliant theory to his often-dismal political practice, and whether he is inserting brilliant insights into modern politics or simply providing justifications for an authoritarian political position. His work before 1933 represented one of the first attempts to work out the paradoxes of "constitutional democracy" under the new Weimar Constitution; it still poses challenges to all-too-complacent defenses of democracy today.[14] One can read the same work, however, as a strategic attempt to reach a practical goal by means of theoretical arguments in light of Schmitt's decision at the end of the republic to support an authoritarian presidentialism. That, he believed, would sustain the core of a state threatened with dissolution by the pluralistic world of mass parties, federalism, and corporatism.[15] Schmitt's work has both a theoretical and a practical orientation, placing the historian of intellectuals before an especially difficult task. Did Schmitt's theoretical understanding of democracy lead him to endorse antidemocratic politics at the end of Weimar? Or were his actions to support an authoritarian end to pluralistic democracy the impetus for his theoretical critique of democracy? Or were Schmitt's theories and his practice unrelated?

In the case of Schmitt's Weimar-era writings, one could argue that even if Schmitt himself used theoretical arguments chiefly for practical ends, the theory still provides important insights beyond Schmitt's own intentions: insights may not be reducible to the intentions of their authors. It is far harder to make such an argument about Schmitt's work in the service of the Nazi state. After Hitler took power, Schmitt moved quickly to the center of the Nazi legal establishment. He provided early, scholarly defenses of the *Gleichschaltung* of the German *Länder,* the suspension of civil rights, and of the concentration of powers of legislature, judiciary, and executive in the hands of the Führer. Beyond merely defending dictatorship, Schmitt helped to radicalize the theoretical debate on the nature of Nazism. As part of the dismantlement of the *Rechtsstaat,* he proclaimed that the Führer embodied the race. And in 1936, he called a national legal conference on the role of Jews in German jurisprudence, at which he sought to exorcise the "Jewish spirit" from German law. Schmitt's theoretical contributions from 1933 to 1936 were minimal, his point was practical: to shape the Nazi agenda.[16] After being "deposed" as crown jurist in an internal dispute of 1936, Schmitt apparently pulled back into political philosophy. But his political theory continued to have aspects that fit within Nazism. His 1938 interpretation of Hobbes provided insight into his own grand conception of historical decline; it did not break, however, from the fundamental anti-semitism. And his critique of Anglo-American universalism and human rights foreshadowed later criticism of American hegemony; like the Japanese "Marxists" who turned to nationalism in the 1930s and lent their support to Japanese imperialism, however, Schmitt's anti-American rhetoric ultimately served to justify Nazi foreign policy.[17]

After 1945 Schmitt was banned from returning to university teaching. He assumed a marginal position, outside of the academy, but at the same time became a key conversation partner for an entire generation of political thinkers, from far left to liberal center to far right.[18] His own occasional publications were the works of a Cassandra, one who questioned the stability of the Federal Republic and indeed of the post-1945 world order. He questioned whether morality could actually play a role in law, taking on the jurisprudence of the new German Constitutional Court and postwar natural law doctrine in an important and still under-researched article of 1960.[19] He sketched a view of the new post–World War II organization of the world that provided critical insight into the development of a grand, liberal-democratic empire.[20] And as doctrines of revolutions on the Left were driving toward ever more nationalist positions in the aftermath of Mao and decolonization, Schmitt examined the role of guerrillas in the new proxy wars of the late twentieth century and the implications for state sovereignty and the rules of war.[21] Many of Schmitt's harshest critics make use of these ideas.[22]

How does one relate the critical, compelling, penetrating Schmitt who produced five decades of fascinating scholarship to the Schmitt of the *Glossarium*? As Gross argues, if one holds that Schmitt merits close attention as a coherent political thinker, then it is not adequate to treat him as a free-floating and uncommitted intellectual or to focus on various facets of his work rather than asking what lies at its core. But finding Schmitt's core, what makes him an organic, integral thinker, is not an easy task. Schmitt himself poses the challenge with one of the central ideas he sets forth in an important contribution to the history of political thought, his famous essay on "Political Theology." There he writes that "all significant concepts of the state are secularized theological concepts."[23] He makes a strong argument that the ultimate foundations of all political concepts lie in *Weltanschauung* rather than reason. Schmitt thereby raises a question that goes to the heart of political theory, as Heinrich Meier has shown: *is* there a rational basis to political theory and thus politics? And if not, then what *does* provide the foundation for political thought? This question also applies to Schmitt himself: his political theory may provide a series of interesting logical statements, but if his statement on "political theology" is correct, then the foundation of Schmitt's theory is not rational. This problem of the status of Schmitt's own "political theology" has fueled three generations of German scholarship on Schmitt.

In 1935 Karl Löwith undertook a short analysis of Carl Schmitt's understanding of political theology as part of an attempt to grasp the deeper motivations of conservative intellectuals like Schmitt and Heidegger, with whom he had been close, and the Nazi regime, which had driven him into exile. Schmitt was not an opportunist, Löwith contended. He was a European nihilist; while he argued that political concepts had a theological basis, Schmitt himself did not find a foundation for politics in either the theology of the sixteenth century or the humanitarianism of the eighteenth. The basis for a political decision in Schmitt, Löwith argued, was simply the decision. Schmitt's "political theology" was a void; all that mattered was political order, of whatever kind happened to prevail. For Löwith, Schmitt's political theory was first and foremost about power; antisemitism played a secondary role.[24] Löwith's analysis foreshadowed Schmitt's own work on Hobbes in 1938, which read Hobbes as advocating order over disorder in the face of the collapse of authentic, religious legitimacy.[25]

Heinrich Meier continued this line of argument in his work of the 1980s.[26] On the basis of a careful reading of Schmitt and his Jewish former student Leo Strauss, Meier finds in Schmitt a negation of the very possibility of political philosophy. At the heart of politics is not rationality but faith, based on not reason but revelation. Meier finds in Schmitt a sense of historical decline from legitimacy to legality, from foundations to lack of faith. Meier furthermore finds in Schmitt the suspicion that what looks like order may in fact be disorder. On what basis are we to determine that a given leader does the work of the Lord? This is the secret message of Schmitt, the search for the one who can resist the Antichrist. Revelation has to serve as the foundation of this insight. Meier thus rejects an ultimately empty "occasional decisionism" that Löwith had found at Schmitt's core and argues that for Schmitt a concrete revelation grounds faith. Meier leaves the content of this revelation open, although he clearly sees a role for antisemitism in it.

Löwith and Meier together present, then, the following propositions. First, the notion of "political theology" stands at the center of Schmitt's thinking and asserts that rationality does not found political order, but rather faith does. Second, "political theology" is based on explicit and specific statements of faith, and ultimately on revelation. If these propositions are correct, and if Carl Schmitt was subject to the same rules that he applied to political philosophy in general, then the next step must be to ask what his faith consisted of. That next step involves speculation about the content of a thinker, about the specific items that impelled him to take positions. And this is where Gross's study begins.

Gross's strong argument is that antisemitism is not incidental to Schmitt but pervades his thoughts on law and state. Schmitt's political work is marked by a series of oppositions, between the abstract norm and the concrete decision, legality and legitimacy, positive law and substantive order, the state as mechanism and the state as authentic order. All of these oppositions find their parallels in antisemitic thinking. Positivism reflects an allegedly positivistic model of law in the Old Testament; the German critical tradition, including many of the Young Hegelians, opposed the inward truth of Christian law to this "external" law. Universalist concepts are driven by the particular interests of Jews seeking a foothold in a non-Jewish community; universalism masks arcane intent, while the concrete order makes substantive distinctions to maintain the homogeneity and substance of the community. The mechanistic state grants all subjects citizenship regardless of their nature; juxtaposed to it is the Christian state (or, in the work of the Young Hegelian Bruno Bauer, the post-Christian state) capable of drawing critical distinctions among citizens. Some of the most important theoretical arguments in Schmitt's corpus take on a new meaning in Gross's reading.

At stake in the debate on legal positivism, for example, was not just a legal methodology that screened out issues of legitimacy and factual order, but a destructive "political theology" that ultimately undermined the state. Gross's book maintains that again and again the key to Schmitt's critique of politics in modernity is not the theory but rather the concrete enemy. Again and again Schmitt finds that enemy in individuals like Hans Kelsen: secular, positivist, relativistic, a defender of liberal democracy—and an assimilated Jew ultimately driven from Germany. The theoretical is political and also highly personal.

Gross's work on Schmitt is a significant work of scholarship for several reasons, then. At a methodological level, it poses the central problem of intellectual history: how to relate text and context. A thinker's ideas deserve clear and careful examination on their own merits; but what if the thinker has himself indicated the presence of an arcane message embedded in his writing? As a study of Schmitt, Gross's book raises questions that demand consideration even by Schmitt's strongest defenders. At the very least, Schmitt's antisemitism cannot any longer be reduced to an unfortunate episode. Last but certainly not least, Gross's work poses the problem of what antisemitism was and how it functioned in twentieth-century Germany, and how it operated in a specific and essential discipline of the modern state: law. The problem of Carl Schmitt and the Jews cannot be set aside; it must be confronted. For, as George Mosse wrote some decades ago, "German antisemitism is a part of German intellectual history. It does not stand outside of it."[27]

ACKNOWLEDGMENTS

Without constant intellectual, financial, and emotional support over many years by friends, teachers, academic institutions, and foundations, my research on Carl Schmitt would never have been finished. At the University of Essen, Dan Diner was a dissertation advisor who offered me a great deal more intellectual aid and personal encouragement than can be reflected in footnotes. My knowledge of both specific questions of Schmitt-research and general problems of German—and German-Jewish—history was enriched by our many intensive discussions regarding a thinker who greatly concerned us both. Over a long time-span and from considerable distance, Jonathan Steinberg (at the time in Cambridge, England) likewise encouraged me to continue my work, supplementing that support with generous recommendations. And such recommendations were kindly offered as well by the late George Mosse (also from Cambridge), Jacques Picard (Basel), and the late Gerhard Riegner (Geneva).

A range of legal, political, and philosophical factors inform the theme of Carl Schmitt and the Jews. It was thus important for me to discuss various aspects of my work in different forums with colleagues from various disciplines. I was able to present my initial ideas in Bielefeld, Germany, in a colloquium led by Jörn Rüsen, and in Freiburg in a seminar led by Ingeborg Villinger. Later I received useful critiques in a research colloquium organized by Dirk Blasius and Wolfgang Horn in Essen. Blasius was then generously willing to serve as second doctoral-committee assessor when I submitted this book's first version to the history department of Essen University in 1997.

I was able to present parts of my work to the Wiener Library in Tel Aviv on two occasions, one of these in the framework of an international conference on Hans Kelsen and Carl Schmitt organized by Dan Diner and Michael Stolleis. On a number of occasions I was able to discuss aspects of the work with fellows of the Franz Rosenzweig Center in Jerusalem, directed by Stéphane Moses (1992) and Paul Mendes Flohr (1993). I would like to thank members and fellows of the center for many at times intense conversations we had during the two very pleasant and productive years of my fellowship. In addition, I had the opportunity to participate in many graduate seminars on German Jewish history organized by the German Working Group of the Leo Baeck Institute and hosted by the Werner-Reimers Foundation, Bad Homburg. I thank the students who participated between 1992 and 1997, and the working-group's director, Reinhard Rürup, for many useful questions and suggestions. In the same period, I was fortunate to have a grant from the Axel Springer Foundation partly covering the costs of my research in Germany; I would also like to thank foundation-board member Ernst Cramer for his interest in my project. The closing stages of my dissertation were furthered by a grant from the Institute of Social Research in Hamburg. I warmly thank both institute-director Jan Reemtsma and research-director Ulrich Bielefeld for their support and interest.

I was likewise able to discuss various stages of my work in colloquia and conferences organized by Michael Stolleis (Max Plank Institute for European Legal Studies, Frankfurt am Main), Friedrich Stadler (Institute for the Study of the Vienna Circle, Vienna), Herfried Münkler (Humboldt University, Berlin), Bernd Weisbrod (Göttingen), and Norbert Frei (Jena). In addition, Norbert Frei read the manuscript's last version and offered much needed encouragement regarding publication. Before the writing process began, I learned a great deal about Carl Schmitt through conversations with Reinhard Mehring (Humboldt University). The late Reinhart Koselleck (Bielefeld) kindly took the time to discuss difficult questions related to my theme. He encouraged me to work through its complexities, while furnishing valuable help in gaining access to important archives. Nicolaus Sombart (Berlin), who like Koselleck knew Schmitt personally, was not only a stimulating interlocutor but was always an amiable host. I benefited as well from a number of conversations with Jean-Pierre Faye (Université Européenne, Paris) regarding his impressions of the work and person of Schmitt.

I shared many hours in libraries with Peter C. Caldwell (Rice University, Houston) during our research time in Bielefeld and Berlin. I learned a great deal about legal history and theory from both Caldwell and our mutual friend Christoph Schönberger (Berlin). Dirk van Laak (Jena) not only offered his support during my work in Carl Schmitt's archives in Düsseldorf but encouraged me over some years to finish the project, which he knew well and most of which he had read. The legal scholars Clemens Jabloner (president of Vienna's Upper Administrative Court), Bernd Rüthers (Constance), and Yitzhak Englard (judge on Israel's Supreme Court) read and commented on different versions of this book, for which I thank them warmly. In addition, I was able to maintain a long and detailed correspondence with Judge Englard concerning questions of law and religious studies.

Josef Kaiser (Freiburg) kindly offered me full access to the Carl Schmitt archives.

In the course of my research and writing, I received support from many friends. Among these, I would particularly like to mention Julia Albrecht (Berlin), Andrea Büttner (London), Birgit Erdle (London), Miriam Gebhardt (Munich), Katharina Hacker (Berlin), Katharina Kollmann (Frankfurt am Main), Werner Konitzer (Frankfurt/Oder), Alexander Lohse (Berlin), Thomas Lüttenberg (Bielefeld), Eva Peters (Berlin), Annette Vowinckel (Berlin), and Daniel Wildmann (Zurich). A number of friends and acquaintances also helped in various editorial revisions of the text, in particular Johanna Drobnig (Hamburg) and Christian Jansen (Bochum). But I would like to especially mention my friend Joel Golb (Berlin and New York), who offered many suggestions regarding the argumentative organization of this book's German version, along with a careful editorial reading of the manuscript, before its submission to the Suhrkamp Verlag. Golb then undertook fresh editorial labor in the course of preparing his present translation of the book; the revisions made for this first English-language edition reflect that labor, and a process of close consultation between translator and author.

Publication of the book's original German version was made possible by the financial support of the Irène Bollag Herzheimer Foundation. I would like to thank Sander Gilman for pointing me toward the Mosse Program at the University of Wisconsin–Madison, which generously contributed to the costs of this translation. And my warm thanks as well to the Goethe Institut for offering its own subsidy for this purpose.

CARL SCHMITT AND THE JEWS

Introduction

Carl Schmitt is famous. Possibly the most-discussed German jurist of the twentieth century, he is certainly the most controversial. A great many political scientists, theologians, literature professors, and historians in Germany, the United States, France, Italy, and elsewhere have written on him at considerable length. Compiling a bibliography of the work on Schmitt over just the last five years would require a book of its own. Together the bibliographies prepared by Piet Tommissen in 1959, 1968, and 1978 contain more than 1,600 entries—and this before the actual "Schmitt Renaissance" had begun.[1]

Schmitt's most well-known texts are *Political Romanticism* (*Politische Romantik*, 1919); *On Dictatorship* (*Die Diktatur*, 1921); *Political Theology* (*Politische Theologie*, 1922); *Roman Catholicism and Political Form* (*Römischer Katholizismus und politische Form*, 1923); *Constitutional Theory* (*Verfassungslehre*, 1928); *The Concept of the Political* (*Der Begriff des Politischen*, 1932); *Legality and Legitimacy* (*Legalität und Legitimität*, 1932); *Leviathan* (*Der Leviathan*, 1938); *The Nomos of the Earth* (*Der Nomos der Erde*, 1952); and *Theory of the Partisan* (*Theorie des Partisanen*, 1963).[2] None of these books and brochures was greeted with unmitigated enthusiasm, but often the striking conceptual combinations of their titles would have their own careers. In general, what made Schmitt's texts attractive was not so much any consistent theory as his polarizing concepts: friend and enemy, discussion and decision, legality and legitimacy, nomos and law, land and sea, Katechon and Antichrist. Schmitt's reputation as a brilliant thinker and pregnant formulator is owed to these basic concepts. Interestingly, the aura emanating from his work and person for many readers is not at all nourished by a clarity of ideas. To the contrary: his special powers of attraction rested much more strongly on a downright provocative pseudoclarity of concepts open to all kinds of interpretations, and in the impenetrability of his person. Schmitt promises mystery. Similarly to the seventeenth- and eighteenth-century political theory he intensely admired, his work transmits what he would term an *arcanum*.[3]

The extraordinary impact of Schmitt's writings has not been lessened by either his Nazi or antisemitic engagement. Not even his tireless efforts on behalf of the conference he organized and chaired called "Judaism in Legal Studies," sponsored by the Reich Group of University Teachers in the National Socialist Association of Legal Guardians, has diminished the spread of his arguments and concepts. (The conference's title itself evoked Richard Wagner's notorious essay "Judaism in Music.") The same can be said for the antisemitic outbursts in Schmitt's notes covering the 1947–51 period, published posthumously in 1993 under the title *Glossarium*.

Until the appearance of this book's first German-language edition in 2000, little attention had been paid to the relationship between Schmitt's lifelong preoccupation with the Jews and "the Jewish," on the one hand, and his work, on the other. This situation had several sources, the most prominent of these certainly being the attitude of Schmitt and his students. Carl Schmitt did not consider himself an antisemite. After World War II, the jurist insisted that his earlier statements and arguments had in no way been antisemitic. When the reproach of antisemitism was nonetheless raised, he parried it by, for instance, replacing the term *antisemitisch* with *judenkritisch*—"critical of the Jews."[4]

Schmitt's most faithful students have always stressed his integrity. In doing so, they have principally used two strategies. The first has involved citing Schmitt's personal friendships. And indeed, the manifold nature of his personal relations with Jews has impressed many readers. In that context all people who in Schmitt's eyes were Jewish have been designated as such, which is to say also individuals of Jewish origin who converted to Christianity; the following pages will maintain the same approach. The "Judaism" of these individuals did not, in fact, prevent Schmitt from having friendly ties with some of them. This is demonstrated by the following list, which also offers a sense of the wealth of his intellectual contacts: Schmitt dedicated his *Constitutional Theory* (1928) to his friend Fritz Eisler, fallen in the Great War; Schmitt was also—so it has always seemed[5]—a close friend of Eisler's brother Georg, with whom he restored contact after 1945.[6] He maintained a correspondence going far beyond business matters with Ludwig Feuchtwanger (brother of the author Lion Feuchtwanger), who had been director of the Duncker & Humblot publishing house since 1915, and who would publish Schmitt's most important books until 1932. He also had friendly relations with the economist Moritz Julius Bonn,[7] to whom he owed his appointment to Berlin's Handelshochschule in 1928; with the writer Hermann Broch; and with the legal scholar, journalist, and early theorist of fascism Waldemar Gurian.[8]

In addition, in the 1920s Schmitt was in contact with the important Social Democratic legal theorist Hermann Heller, reflected in a brief correspondence, first friendly, then increasingly distanced.[9] After the Nazi takeover, he wrote a letter on behalf of his Jewish colleague Erwin Jakobi, meant to protect Jakobi from the new antisemitic "Law for the Restoration of the Civil Service";[10] a year earlier, as mentioned, he and Jakobi had together defended the dissolution of the Prussian government by Reich Chancellor von Papen before the constitutional court.[11] Further, Schmitt cultivated friendly ties with the jurists Albert Hensel[12] and Gerhard Lassar;[13] ties with the conservative jurist Erich Kaufmann and—above all—the jurist and legal philosopher Hans Kelsen, who would be his most important opponent, were of special biographical and intellectual significance. Schmitt cultivated esteem for Gerhard Leibholz, eventually a judge on West Germany's constitutional court.[14] Also noteworthy are Schmitt's relations with, for instance, Karl Löwith,[15] Karl Mannheim,[16] and, following World War II, Francis Rosenstiel,[17] Raymond Aron,[18] Alexander Kojève, and the philosopher of religion Jakob Taubes.[19] Finally, Schmitt's students and admirers included Walter Benjamin, Leo Strauss, Otto Kirchheimer (the Frankfurt School's leading jurist), and Franz Neumann.[20] After the Nazi defeat, Schmitt did not hesitate to use such friendships when he could to promote his rehabilitation.

In the same postwar period, most of Schmitt's interpreters had great difficulty distinguishing these disparate social ties from his and their own apologetic intentions. The most well-known example of this difficulty involved a reversal of the usual pattern, as it reflected a condemnation of Schmitt and an effort to protect Walter Benjamin from association with the jurist: Theodore Adorno's excision of those passages in Benjamin's *Origins of German Tragic Drama* that positively refer to Schmitt. Inversely, after initially being passed over by Benjamin's editors, the only known letter of Benjamin to Schmitt—a short letter written in 1930—has been cited in various ways meant to show a supposed closeness between the two thinkers; eventually the letter was referred to by Jacques Derrida as part of an actually nonexistent Schmitt–Benjamin "correspondence."[21]

One rather more direct way of avoiding the question of Carl Schmitt and the Jews was apparent in *Complexio oppositorum*, a volume of conference proceedings published in 1988 in connection with the jurist's hundredth birthday. The volume, whose title evoked Schmitt's characterization of the Roman Catholic church, contained articles on his work by twenty-eight authors. At the start of this huge essay collection, the editor, Helmut Quaritsch, placed a notice titled "On the Approach to the Person and Work of Carl Schmitt." What followed was a flat assertion that any charges of antisemitism were entirely irrelevant, in no way touching on the core of Schmitt's thinking: "What . . . would it mean for the 40 books and 200 articles written between 1910 and 1978," Quaritsch asked, "if he were [in fact] an antisemite?" In response to his own question, he then steered the reader away from the topic through a set of "guiding principles" for the "proper" study of Carl Schmitt. He countered the especially delicate question of Schmitt's *openly* antisemitic writings by condemning it as inquisitorial tactlessness, by way of an anecdotal reference to the self-defined "arch Jew" Jacob Taubes, one of Schmitt's most often-cited admirers. For Quaritsch, the political scientist Kurt Sontheimer committed an indecent act in raising Schmitt's antisemitism with Taubes.[22]

In general, those critical of Schmitt in this and related respects have been quickly subject to violent and emotional attack in the prominent German journal *Der Staat,* a long-standing organ for Schmitt's champions and defenders.[23] In this and other ways, Schmitt and his students have been adept at influencing his work's reception. For a long time, the adeptness was decisively bolstered by widespread West German mechanisms for coping with the Nazi past. As has by now become well known, the early years of the new German democracy were marked in a basic way by a consensual sociolegal process of denial and silence.[24] To be sure, there were many public pronouncements of regret and disgust at the corpse-heaps; but beyond the most abstract moral condemnations, reticence took over. This was most pronouncedly the case, perhaps, in the academic world: when it came to any look at the concrete antisemitic statements and actions of German professors under Nazism, and indeed at the broader phenomenon of the German intellectual elite's Nazi and anti-Jewish activities from the Weimar Republic onward, West German academia was largely marked by an unstated, quasi-religious ban.[25]

In other words, there was a persistent willingness to condemn what was considered primitive *Radauantisemitismus*—that is, Jew-hatred of the vulgar, rabble-rousing sort—and its consequences. But for a long time, there was very little willingness to confront the causes and significance of the "less primitive" form of Jew-hatred motivating the juridical-bureaucratic elite of the SS and SD.[26] Following Martin Broszat, we can thus understand West Germany's official blanket-apologies for Nazi atrocities as both a compensation and cover-up in face of an inadequate investigation of individual guilt and complicity: the failure to prosecute a huge number of former Nazi criminals, many professionally integrated into the young West German state after World War II.[27]

In this context, it is worth recalling Freud's famous theory of the meaning and function of taboos. This theory has, in fact, great value for understanding the social mechanisms at work in postwar West Germany's collective effort to cope with a widespread sense of guilt. For Freud, the taboo gains its meaning from two opposing sources. On the one hand, it is supplied with an "aura of the holy" and consecrated; on the other hand it is uncanny, forbidden, and impure. In the context of such primal ambivalence, the taboo is meant to offer protections against danger associated with contact with corpses.[28] Freud's interpretive schema would seem to apply powerfully to the postwar West German situation. As Freud describes it, the taboo on the dead reveals that something other than the usual mourning for, say, a lost friend is present: the anxiety at contact is based on the death of the dead individual having been either unconsciously desired or indeed brought about by the anxious parties.

However close or distant one may feel from Freud's particular conceptual vocabulary, it remains clear that such emotional ambivalence was very much part of West Germany's dynamic of guilt and restitution in the years following 1945. But on a separate level, a process of *democratization* was taking place: a process with special resonance in the ex-Nazi and conservative milieu in which Schmitt's thinking was most warmly embraced. With the turn toward democracy imposed by the occupying powers, old images of the enemy were preserved. Hence in that milieu, a familiar trio was now defined as the key to the triumph in Germany of Hitler and Nazism: modernism, mass society, secularization.[29] In a historical irony that continues to have great resonance, the battle against modernism, positivism, secularization, and parliamentarianism unfolding in the Weimar Republic was now turned retroactively against Nazism, in the name of *democracy*. In this way, the political-moral defeat of Nazism could be acknowledged without basic positions being called into doubt. Strikingly, within this context the theme of antisemitism was fully deleted. It was thus possible for a Nazi Party "comrade" such as Carl Schmitt to now emerge, reinterpreted, as the conservative guardian of the Weimar constitution—a figure who had always struggled against precisely the evil culminating in the Nazi catastrophe.

This metamorphosis took place very quickly. It would turn out to be enduring.

No one would seriously maintain that the German Federal Republic amounted to a continuation of Nazi Germany. But alongside the break with the past, there were indeed important continuities. The simplest reason for this was, in Heinz Bude's words, the "continuity of societal personnel."[30] Some representative political offices excepted, everywhere the same people were present—particularly in the universities, commerce, and industry—who had steered Nazi Germany between its early victories and final defeat. On an institutional level, that naturally rendered difficult any scholarly examination of the antisemitism of the German elite.[31]

To a large extent, the history of Nazism's aftermath has yet to be written. This is particularly the case in the realm of intellectual history, where a particular tendency of human memory is especially apparent. In the framework of his controversy with Martin Broszat, Saul Friedländer has pointed to this tendency as follows: "It prefers the normal to the abnormal, the comprehensible to what is hard to comprehend, the comparable to what is hard to compare, the bearable to the unbearable."[32] In our context, the philosophical, sociological, psychoanalytical, juridical, and historiographical developments mirroring this tendency have not yet been researched in depth; the fields of legal studies and history would be especially important here.[33] Nevertheless, it seems clear that a sober look at the case of Carl Schmitt has been stymied by certain aspects of postwar West German intellectual life: developments in legal studies and especially the renaissance of natural law in the immediate postwar period; the ways in which antisemitism and the "final solution" was approached by both historians from the Hitler Youth generation and their teachers.

Various personal, academic-strategic, and historical motives thus led to the "sensitive" theme of Carl Schmitt and the Jews being neglected for many decades. At the same time, as mentioned, the literature devoted to the jurist has steadily expanded. Over recent years, alongside his major works and collections of essays, both his early efforts at literary criticism and personal notations have been published.[34] His correspondence with Franz Blei (unfortunately only Blei's letters), Ernst Robert Curtius, Ernst Jünger, and the journalist Armin Mohler along with other Schmitt students has been made accessible to researchers, as has a range of interviews; publication of other correspondence, including letter exchanges with Hans Barion, Ernst-Wolfgang Böckenförde, and

Ernst Forsthoff, is being negotiated.[35] Comparatively oriented studies of Schmitt are increasingly appearing, including studies of Schmitt and Hegel, Juan Donoso Cortés, Max Weber, Karl Barth, Helmuth Plessner, Karl Jaspers, Jürgen Habermas, Walter Benjamin, and Leo Strauss.[36] A number of historical works devoted to Schmitt himself have also appeared. Among these, several are based on material from the extensive Schmitt archives: books by Andreas Koenen and Dirk van Laak are especially noteworthy; on the other hand, the first German-language biography of Schmitt, by Paul Noack, offers little information going beyond what was already offered by Joseph Bendersky—the first purely biographical study of Schmitt, itself strongly under the influence of the jurist's personality.[37]

Until the German publication of the present book, Nicolaus Sombart had offered the most detailed account of Schmitt's attitude toward the Jews and Judaism. In his memoirs of his youth, Sombart describes the question of the meaning of the Jews for European history as occupying the center of Schmitt's thinking.[38] In his important book *German Men and Their Enemies,* a book focused on Schmitt, he explores this connection from a cultural and psychological-historical perspective. Here, Sombart is less interested in Schmitt's confrontation with the Jews than in exploring an opposition between matriarchy and patriarchy in order to explain the pathological conceptual structures of "German men." For Sombart, as he already indicates in the earlier memoirs, the fatefully decisive question for Schmitt and his generation was the "primal phenomenon of human bisexuality"; using psychoanalytic categories, he constructs an idiosyncratic interpretation of Schmitt's antisemitism. Whatever criticisms one may have of some of its aspects, the book needs to be recognized as an important contribution: it not only comments in detail on the explicitly antisemitic ideas Schmitt formulated between 1933 and 1945 but also on the *structurally* antisemitic potential of his pre-1933 texts.[39] Sombart's book thus points the way to one of the basic problems explored in the following chapters.

Biographical, historical, and intellectual-historical elements inform Schmitt's confrontation with the Jews and "the Jewish." The history of his terms and ideas illuminates the foundations of his thinking and is thus the single most important element. But a sense of Schmitt biography is also needed, if we are to understand the genealogy of his obsessions. Schmitt was born in 1888 in Plettenberg, in a region of northern Germany, the Sauerland. He was raised in a middle-class Catholic family. In his own words, looking back after World War II: "For me, the

Catholic faith is the religion of my forefathers. I am not only confessionally a Catholic but one through historical origin—if I may say so, of race."[40] But although the immediate environment was piously Catholic, the surroundings were strongly Protestant. While after departure from Plettenberg the Catholic "diaspora" would serve to strengthen Schmitt's sense of inner identity,[41] Protestantism, and especially its canon of *Bildung* (education and self-formation), undoubtedly left a strong mark on his character. As a secondary school student, he developed a strong interest in the critique of religion that had emerged from German Protestantism. This eventually forced him to leave the church-supported Catholic dormitory: he had been caught with a copy of David Friedrich Strauss's *Life of Jesus* (a work of liberal Protestantism made famous through Nietzsche's devastating critique in *Untimely Meditations*).[42] At this time, he was also reading texts by the anarchist philosopher Max Stirner, one of the circle of Young Hegelians around Bruno Bauer.

Schmitt's later preoccupation with the "Jewish question" needs to be examined against both his Catholic and Protestant backdrop. In his political theory, he would draw on various concepts from Catholic theology.[43] The picture he drew of Judaism and Jewry, however, appears less stamped by academic theology than by the worldview of Germany's nineteenth- and early-twentieth-century *political* Catholicism. Schmitt was here in debt to prejudices and resentments tied to his socialreligious origins: feelings radicalized by his sense of living a second-class existence as a Catholic. As a result of nineteenth-century legal and political secularization, the Catholic situation in Germany was in fact difficult; the secularization process had led to a confiscation of the wealth of the Catholic Church, hence to an educational catastrophe among German Catholics. For this reason, the Protestant culture of *Bildung* sparked considerable resentment within the Catholic minority. Precisely as a reaction to the weakening of the Catholic universities, educated Catholics now tended to lay special stress on their independence vis-à-vis modern Protestant culture. In these circumstances, the Catholic relationship with the economically and academically more successful Jewish minority, which appeared to be moving much more successfully into the Protestant world, became palpably tense.[44] A defensive contempt for Protestant-Jewish *Bildung* is apparent in the writing of the young Carl Schmitt— dramatically so in his *Silhouettes (Schattenrisse)* of 1913, written under the pseudonym Johannes Negelinus.[45] This book can, in fact, be read as a satire on the Protestant-Jewish canon of *Bildung*—the pseudonym itself likely stemming from the so-called *Judenbücherstreit* (controversy over

Jewish books) between Johannes Reuchlin ("Magister Petrus Negelinus," the humanist-champion of such Jewish literature) and Ulrich von
Hutten.

From the Catholic perspective, Judaism had come to occupy terrain
in close proximity to modern institutions and ways of thinking. (The in-
dustrialist and planning minister Walther Rathenau, theorist of a de-
centralized, democratic social order for a modernized Germany, was a
figure with particularly symbolic value in this respect; in the years before
his assassination by right-wing and antisemitic army officers in 1922,
he would also be an especially detested figure for Schmitt.) The genuine
affinity, on a certain level, between Judaism and modernism was here
crudely distorted on a popular level; the result was a Judaism standing
out in sharp contrast to a Catholic skepticism regarding modern life and
culture.[46] The most open expression of the church's antisemitism had
been the so-called *Syllabus Errorum* (1864) and the following infallibility-
dogma (1870).[47] Nevertheless, there would be no open embrace of racist
antisemitic positions—from a Catholic perspective racism was itself
viewed as a product of modernity.

Since the church encountered racist antisemitism with reserve, Catholic antisemitism took on its own tenor, mobilizing traditional forms of
anti-Judaism instead. To be sure, a *functionalization* of racist stereotypes
aimed at "Jewish modernism" was in the end accepted. As a result, forms
of differentiation and secularization considered dire from a tradition-
alist viewpoint were aligned with the particular social group Christianity had rejected throughout its history. This was the new form of an old,
deep-seated prejudice, designed to neutralize complexity while ascrib-
ing guilt.[48]

Frequent accusations of both deicide and ritual murder here
conjured up the idea of a Jewish rejection of traditional Christian-
Occidental values. It is today a little-known fact that between 1873 and
1900, thirteen ritual-murder trials against Jews were held in Germany.[49]
What ritual murder symbolized on a "micro" level was imagined as
"rule of the modern Jewish spirit" on a "macro" level.[50] At the center of
that theme stood the idea—frequently evoked in Germany's Catholic
areas—of a Jewish conspiracy to "Judaize" the world through allegedly
Jewish concepts like liberalism, communism, and freemasonry.[51] And
this sense of a Jewish conspiracy was always tied to a belief in a special
Jewish secret, often even a secret Jewish knowledge: a fiction emerging
from a Christian anti-Jewish tradition that had already formed by the
twelfth century.[52] For centuries before then, Christian criticism had

been leveled at the supposed "instability and rigidity of the Jewish national consciousness." (The phrase was Bruno Bauer's mid-nineteenth-century contribution to an old theme.) This rigidity, it was felt, was expressed as a rejection of the New Testament and the idea of Jesus as savior. But around the twelfth century, Judaism's *historical development* itself, as most clearly expressed in the Talmud, became the object of Christian anti-Jewish arguments.[53] From this new perspective, the Jews only *seemed* to define themselves as bearers of the Old Testament, remaining faithful to it "to the letter." In reality, they had created a secret law: the Talmud, a new heresy that they furtively followed while outwardly continuing to maintain their traditional belief and practices.[54]

In later centuries, the idea of malevolent Jewish secrets—secrets aimed at the surrounding Christian order—made its way into the Christian perception of the Kabbala. Theological disapproval was mixed with a certain fascination at the uncanny mysteriousness of secret Jewish knowledge:[55] a contradictory blend of concepts that would henceforth cling to the fantasies of antisemitic authors. In this way, the secret, conspirative moment became a fixed element of anti-Jewish polemics. In the nineteenth and twentieth centuries, German Catholicism could thus draw on a long tradition to instrumentalize this most attractive image of the enemy—to tie the modern institutions and ideologies it opposed to the *secret influence of the Jews.*

Elements of this way of thinking are present in Schmitt's work, running through his multileveled struggle against the Jews. The reproach of spiritless, literal Jewish interpretation is a fixed element in his battle against normativism; he likewise assigns an important role to the idea of an *arcanum,* in the context of a "scientification" of the realm of politics amounting to a detheologization.[56] Over the nineteenth century, "the Jews" increasingly served as a metaphor in Germany—as they had already in France because of the Dreyfus affair—so that in the end, what Schmitt would call "the Jewish" did not have to be tied to the Jews. The concept could even be applied to non-Jewish Germans associated, in the words of Dan Diner, "with images of abstraction and dynamic social change," or in the words of Schmitt himself, with *acceleration.* The concept thus stood, depending on circumstances, for "social mobility, the not-immediately-graspable, 'secret things,' abstraction."[57] And it stood for persons representing such qualities and forces: freemasons, intellectuals, leftists and liberals, those steering politics and the economy behind the scenes.

This is the backdrop for understanding Schmitt's obsession with the Jews, as directly and indirectly expressed throughout his writings. Consequently, the first part of this book discusses Schmitt's directly expressed opinions regarding the Jews during his Nazi years, along with his related activities. Nazism as a form of political biology here emerges as a central idea for Schmitt and like-minded colleagues. The three parts that follow explore different concepts around which this "biologistically" oriented antisemitic engagement crystallized: universalism, particularism, and acceleration. A last part looks at Schmitt's relevant statements during the postwar period.

One concern that will emerge in the following pages is illuminating Schmitt's basic ideas against their social-historical background. This will involve moving past isolated examples of his antisemitism to consider the open assault he embarked on after Hitler's advent to power. This meant a concretizing of a specific image of the enemy—an image against which he formed the contours of what he termed his "good German law."[58] In order to understand Schmitt's critique of universalism and its ties to his assault on Judaism, it will be necessary to examine his Roman Catholic background. This stands in the context of Catholic counterrevolutionary political theory—the focus of part 2, chapter 5. Schmitt embraced broad aspects of this counterrevolutionary tradition. Within it, for the first time in history the Jews became symbols of revolution, emancipation, and universalism. But this French-Catholic background has an equally important Protestant-German, Young Hegelian counterpart, the focus of part 3. The Young Hegelians offered Schmitt the idea that because of an innate, insurmountable particularism, the Jews could not be integrated into the modern state. This idea can be clarified with an examination of Schmitt's theological metaphors, the focus of part 4. The jurist made frequent use of New Testament ideas and images in order to interpret history as eschatology. Within this theologically imbued understanding of history, he ascribed "the Jews" with a perpetually unchanging function: whatever the historical circumstances, they served for Schmitt as accelerators.

The theme of Carl Schmitt and the Jews is not fairly treated through a list of the jurist's accomplishments or his real or imaginary "good Jewish friends." Instead, the consequences for both Schmitt and legal theory of his battle against "the Jews" and "the Jewish" needs to be analyzed. That is the basic goal of this book.

PART I

NAZISM: POLITICAL BIOLOGY

1

The Jews in Schmitt's Early Work

Over the past decades German scholars have mainly explained Schmitt's antisemitic activism in a way that harmonizes with the post–World War II social and political tendencies described in the introduction. They have argued that the political circumstances of the 1933–45 period led to a purely opportunistic embrace of an anti-Jewish position;[1] that in 1933 Schmitt had indeed written antisemitic texts out of opportunism but later felt defensive about this (the year 1936, when Schmitt was forced to give up many honorary posts, is stressed here as the breaking point); and that afterwards he tried to intellectually defend a position that had in fact only been opportunistically motivated.[2] In light of various statements Schmitt made after the war, and of the failure to raise even the possibility that the heavily antisemitic Catholic milieu in which he grew up may have affected his adult ideas, this construction seems to rest on flimsy foundations. It seems, in fact, to have been a maneuver meant to suppress doubt.[3] As a result of the construction, the entire question of Carl Schmitt and the Jews could be almost completely ignored by the Schmitt scholars for many years—or the question was conveniently left to either Jacob Taubes or the academic outsider Nicolaus Sombart. Authors such as Bendersky and George Schwab relied on the presumed fact that Schmitt made no antisemitic pronouncements before or after the Nazi period.

With the publication of Schmitt's diary for the years 1947–51, it has become clear that after the war Schmitt suffered from extreme antisemitic resentment. Reflecting the nature of prejudice in general, he did not himself define his feelings in those terms, seeing himself rather as simply *judenkritisch*, or "critical of the Jews," and feeling himself willfully misunderstood. In the notebooks, however, Schmitt refers to the Jews as "the true enemy," and the theme clearly stands at the center of his reflections on a number of topics.[4] In reading such entries it becomes

clear that in his postwar writings Schmitt *hid* all his antisemitic observations through an encoding process, sharing them more openly with both
the diary and pen pals with similar leanings. Beyond this, we can observe how intensely concerned he was with confronting the Jews, although nothing appears explicitly in this regard in his published work of
the time. Despite his own sense of being treated unjustly, he himself indicates awareness of such an obsession, and at least verbally moves toward freeing himself from it: "first of all enough with these so-important
Judaeis!"[5]

In this manner, the widely held notion of Schmitt's "opportunism"
collapses. For the idea that Schmitt was preoccupied with the Jews from
1933 until the end of his life (but not before) is unconvincing. Even
before publication of the diaries, critical observers like Sombart and
Taubes observed that—in Taubes's words—"the Jewish problem pursued Carl Schmitt for his entire life." Taubes indicates, significantly, that
Schmitt saw 1936 as

> simply an occasion to take a position in a "timely" manner regard-
> ing a problem that for him had entirely other depths. He was a
> Christian from among the Gentiles, who looked with hate and
> envy at those who "are descendents of Israel, chosen to be God's
> sons; theirs is the glory of the divine presence, theirs the covenants,
> the law, the temple worship, and the promises. The patriarchs are
> theirs, and from them through natural descent came Christ." [Ro-
> mans 9:4–5[6]] . . . For Schmitt Christianity was "Judaism for the
> Gentiles, he always longed to stand up against its power."[7]

Taubes's interpretation of Schmitt's grappling with the "Jewish problem" itself places far too much emphasis on the Christian motif emerging in Schmitt's work after the war. Nevertheless, Taubes is correct in
stressing the lifelong importance for Schmitt of a question possessing
"entirely other depths." On this level the presence or absence of *personal*
prejudice on Schmitt's part toward individual Jews is not the decisive
factor.

There is a simpler and more likely explanation than pure opportunism for Schmitt's behavior. The absence of comments on the "Jewish
question" before 1933 can be explained on the same social grounds as
his public silence after 1945. To have publicly voiced antisemitic views in
his position during the Weimar Republic years would have been extremely unwise. It was not only after 1945 that *crude* antisemitic remarks
were taboo in many circles of German Catholicism—this was especially
the case in cultivated circles and among followers of "Reich Theology"

to whom Schmitt was close.[8] The outspoken antisemites could not shed the reputation of being crude and primitive, which meant that a great many Catholics wanted nothing to do with them.[9] In addition, Schmitt was ambitious; he wished to be part of Weimar's academic establishment. With so many of his colleagues being Jewish, he quite obviously would *not* have wished to seriously damage his reputation as a jurist through reckless honesty. In any case, early on he already had plenty of possibilities for making his "critical" feelings clear to those of a similar persuasion through hints and pointers. One strategy for accomplishing this involved a polemic use of names, itself part of a specifically antisemitic tradition: Schmitt would invent names for various "Jewish jurists." (The quotation marks here indicate that many of these figures had no such understanding of themselves as outsiders.) These names were associated with specific themes characterized as Jewish within the masked worldview that Schmitt would later openly affirm. Such use of names as widely understood code words made clumsy direct attacks unnecessary.[10]

A series of additional factors strengthens the suspicion that Schmitt's desire to confront Judaism and the Jews began long before 1933. We need to pay some attention to these factors—without viewing them as in themselves persuasive, for reasons explained below: In the ironic and parodic *Silhouettes*, German Jews form a constant theme, the text repetitively playing with aspects of the German-Jewish relationship. The book begins with a "systematic table" offering Walther Rathenau as the only entry located under the rubric "non-German."[11] "In his room," we read, "threads" of power come together, threads guided with the same hand that has just ended "the chapter on India rubber and thranscendence [*Thranszendenz*]"[12]—the last word's spelling an obvious play on an East European Jew's German accent. At the satire's end, "rhyme-rules for the fully uneducated" (or "the fully uncultivated"—"Reimregeln für ganz Ungebildete") conclude with the (rhymed) words "Es passt hierher nicht ganz genau / Der Kaufmann Walther Rathenau" (the businessman Walther Rathenau does not entirely fit in here).[13] The frequent passages of this sort reveal a humor that, while now rather unpleasant, was widespread and accepted at the time. We thus find the caricature of a "receiver and board-member" named "Ewald Oskar Kohn," who refers in slightly broken German to his "swindle with water from the Jordan" and bankrupt "children's crusade."[14] There are also "silhouettes" of the German-Jewish philosopher Fritz Mauthner (1849–1923) and the non-Jewish French novelist Anatole France (1844–1924).[15] The latter of these is more interesting in our context, Schmitt placing the following words in France's mouth: "And it is a fact that many Jews no longer have themselves circumcised, not even when they are more mature. Oh republic that I've loved so tenderly! Even the Affair only gave me four volumes. . . ."[16] The "Affair" is of course the Dreyfus Affair; Schmitt's sarcasm is aimed at Anatole France's position in that historically momentous episode. The novelist had been the first signatory of Émile Zola's famous manifesto, *J'Accuse,* condemning the false indictment for treason of Jewish army captain Alfred Dreyfus. He had then protested strongly against Zola's exclusion from the Legion of Honor, to which he himself belonged, following publication of *J'Accuse.* In a not especially subtle manner, Schmitt here first suggests France is ignorant of Jewish ritual, then insinuates that he only took Dreyfus's side for financial reasons.[17]

Despite the constant anti-Jewish passages and the fact that at the same time Schmitt was writing for the openly antisemitic *Bayreuther Blätter,*[18] the *Silhouettes* cannot be counted among the period's vehemently antisemitic publications. The text does seem, however, to reveal a remarkably strong interest in "the Jews"—an impression confirmed by diary entries for the 1913–15 period; located in the Schmitt estate, these were only recently published.[19] The tone maintained in these intimate entries reveals a consistently anti-Jewish stance. In his limited free time, Schmitt indicates, he reads "Solovjeff on the Jews"—an apparent reference to the Russian philosopher and poet Vladimir Sergejevitch Solovyev's "Short Story about the Antichrist."[20] His comment on the distinguished Jewish theater critic Alfred Kerr (1867–1948) is less cryptic: "Kerr gets on my nerves horribly and makes me suspicious. Capricious, insolent, coveting pleasure. A repulsive fellow. But among the Jews, probably the most sober, i.e., the one [Jew] who still has a need for intellectual labor."[21]

It is very possible that Schmitt himself did not view such defamatory remarks as antisemitic. This, however, would simply underscore his deeply anti-Jewish perspective. Olaf Blaschke has aptly characterized the attitude toward the Jews widespread in Schmitt's Catholic circles as "we're no antisemites, but . . ."—a bad "anti-Christian" antisemitism here being juxtaposed with a "good, Catholic" variety.[22] An unsigned letter to Schmitt from a certain Georg Schmitt (no relation) illuminates the general attitude toward the Jews in the jurist's most intimate personal circle. The letter was written in Göttingen on 2 February 1920; in contrast to the remarks cited previously, it thus does not stem from the Wilhelminian period but rather from the early years of the Weimar

Republic, marked by a "right-wing wave" accompanied by the rise of a radical political antisemitism.[23] "The antisemitic German National stream [*deutschnationale Strömung*]," Georg Schmitt writes, "is naturally very powerful here in the ancestral castle of the corps, and although in a certain way like every Christian I can't especially love a Jew, this disagreeable stupid fuss [*dieses widerwärtige dumme Getue*] has gotten on my nerves."[24] The "disagreeable stupid" antisemitic fuss most likely displeased Carl Schmitt as much as it did Georg Schmitt; it is also quite clear that as a Christian Carl Schmitt, as well, could not "especially love a Jew." Another letter, written in 1932 to mark the new year and congratulate Schmitt on his successful move from Berlin's *Handelshochschule* to Cologne University, makes clear how little "love" was involved here at the end of the Weimar Republic: "First I'd like to wish you a very merry New Year! Hopefully the Cologne Jews will please you more than those of the capital of the Reich!"[25] Schmitt knew the Berlin Jews starting in his student days in the city. The "Cologne Jews" meant above all Hans Kelsen, chased from the University of Vienna by antisemitic students; his Cologne appointment in 1929 had been greeted with very little enthusiasm in the circles surrounding Schmitt. To be sure, German Catholicism's generally anti-Jewish mood in both the Kaiserreich and the Weimar Republic did allow some "Jewish exceptions": within certain limits, Georg and Fritz Eisler were part of Schmitt's social circle; but— as the 1915 diaries strongly suggest—such exceptions were present *despite* what amounted to fundamental social rejection.[26]

Such examples may seem ordinary. Nonetheless, they convey a picture strikingly different from that of a "sudden" opportunistic antisemitic conversion. Banalizing in its effect, that picture still prevails in European intellectual circles, among American "cultural critics," and within the value system of many German jurists. At the same time, these examples show that initially Schmitt's antisemitism hardly extended beyond his everyday Catholic surrounding. The sort of resentment he expressed was widespread among his intellectual contemporaries, Catholic and Protestant; some of his remarks could have easily stemmed from the young Thomas Mann, or even from German Jews sharing common stereotypes of the time regarding "the Jews" and matters Jewish.[27] In this regard, it is notable that Schmitt, in fact, may well have written the *Silhouettes* together with his Jewish friend Fritz Eisler.[28] On such grounds alone, Schmitt's position can hardly be reduced to the "private myth" Günter Meuter speaks of in his essay on Schmitt's antisemitism.[29] Deeply rooted in Wilhelminian society and culture and seeing itself at a great distance from its vulgar or "rowdy" counterpart, the ordinary antisemitism Schmitt revealed before his Nazi years intensified in vehemence after World War I. Within our historical framework, what matters is that such antisemitism formed a basis for Schmitt's later, radically antisemitic stance—a stance that in the face of all apologies was both authentic and passionately held. Acknowledging this does not call into question that fact that Schmitt's virulently antisemitic engagement after 1933 cannot be derived in a simple causal way from the statements he made in earlier years. Rather, deeply rooted both cognitively and emotionally, the passion invested in this engagement is far less puzzling than those wishing to admire Schmitt would have it.

2

Schmitt's Position in 1933

The basic ideological principles underpinning Nazi rule included the "Führer-principle" or absolute leadership, the rejection of political pluralism, the insistence on the necessity of maintaining a one-party system, and "the idea of race."[1] But these concepts do not amount to a consistently constructed theory of public law, applicable throughout the Nazi period.[2] Such a unified legal doctrine could never have generated the structural dynamics of the Nazi movement.[3] Nevertheless, there were repeated efforts to develop a Nazi theory of law and state: sharp conflicts over the grounding of a Nazi legal system already emerged in the first weeks after Hitler's accession to power. Public and criminal law were at the center of these quarrels, and Schmitt, a professor of public law, would contribute many brochures and articles in both areas.[4]

The absence of a coherent body of Nazi legal doctrine naturally does not imply any scarcity of jurists sympathetic with Nazism. This was nevertheless a conclusion often drawn in postwar Germany, either with apologetic intentions or through inadequate insight into the power-structure of the Nazi state. Figures defended in this framework would often be juxtaposed with "real Nazis," without, however, explaining what was meant by this term. It is in any case a historical fact that more than a few German jurists struggled to gain power and influence and spread their National Socialist legal concepts within both the older legal organizations and the newer ones created under the Nazis.[5] Carl Schmitt belonged to this group of guiding lights and commentators within Nazi legal policy and theory. But he also did *not* belong, since in his international renown and intellectual stature he towered over his Nazi colleagues.[6]

It is important to gain an accurate idea of the position Schmitt occupied in the Nazi state, since this has basic implications concerning both Nazism and Schmitt's life and writing. For various reasons, however, this task is a difficult one. In the first place, as has become clear in the debate about the extent and nature of Heidegger's Nazism, the position of intellectuals in the Nazi hierarchy has not been adequately explored. It is well known that Hitler often made disparaging pronouncements about intellectuals. But at the same time, as Marlis Steinert has emphasized, he depended on many of them—and especially on the same jurists he hated.[7] Consequently, their power inside and outside the bureaucracy should not be underestimated. They played an especially important role in steering the process of dispossessing, expelling, and exterminating the Jews, in all its decisive stages.[8] Above all, extensive collaboration by the bureaucratic elite was a basic factor in the unprecedented mass murder of Europe's Jews. The starting point for this collaboration was one particular question the bureaucracy felt called on to answer: "Who is a Jew"?

A further difficulty in fixing Schmitt's role in the Nazi state results from the strong influence his self-interpretation has had on the research about him.[9] When it comes to getting the facts straight, the situation has changed since the appearance of Andreas Koenen's book on Schmitt. On the basis of systematic archival research, Koenen describes the individual stages of power and influence involved in Schmitt's rise to "crown jurist of the Third Reich." Nevertheless, the book offers no explanation of the basis for Schmitt's decision to serve the Nazi state and wholeheartedly support its antisemitic policies. Despite his fresh evaluation of the historical evidence, Koenen himself interprets Schmitt's antisemitism more or less in harmony with the jurist's self-understanding.[10]

As a first step in a break with that understanding, let us look at the historical context in which the jurist confronted his self-chosen friends and enemies.

The Expulsion of the Jewish Jurists

One of the factors facilitating Schmitt's speedy ascent within various Nazi legal organizations was the academic expulsion on racist grounds of many Jewish legal scholars who had gained renown in the Weimar Republic. Younger Jewish jurists were naturally also affected; more than 30 percent of Germany's jurists who received their academic qualification (the *Habilitation*) in 1931—Gertrud Rapp has named them the "dissidents among the constitutional theorists"—had already left Germany by the end of 1933.[11] In addition, on either moral or political grounds a handful of important non-Jewish jurists preferred to keep their distance from Nazism and suffer the consequences.[12] Gerhard Anschütz, a distinguished commentator on the Weimar constitution, handed in an obviously politically motivated application for early retirement and was removed from his official duties at the University of Heidelberg on 1 April 1933.[13] Gustav Radbruch, former Social Democratic minister of justice, was dismissed from the same university for political reasons on 29 April.[14] Hermann Heller, Hans Kelsen, Erich Kaufmann, and many other jurists of Jewish origin had to flee or were expelled and persecuted.[15] Hermann Heller, who was a veteran of World War I, did not return from a trip to Spain, losing his hard-won professorship in public law at the University of Frankfurt in September.[16]

Even in exile Heller was subject to virulent personal and political attacks by Schmitt's friend Wilhelm Stapel in the February, April, and September 1933 issues of the notorious Hamburg cultural journal that Stapel directed, *Deutsches Volkstum*. In a letter written on 28 August 1933 Stapel informed Schmitt, with obvious pride, about the following protest received from Heller after the first two contributions:

> You have—characteristically enough, after January 30 [the date Hitler took power]—not only attacked me in an unjustified manner, but beyond this, in [the framework of] my [only partially published] response of 4/2/33, revealed such a degree of conscious mendacity and baseness, that in view of the weapons you have decided to use I declare myself beaten as a Jew and deeply ashamed as a German—which despite everything I am and remain.[17]

In his letter to Schmitt, Stapel announced that "I'll hurt this rascal once again" by publishing "this exhibition of his rage." "I believe," he added, "that when you make such guys say such things you've earned a place in heaven." Hence Stapel represented his antisemitic smearing of Heller as a heroic Christian deed. Stapel seems to have counted on Schmitt's approval. Heller had meanwhile mailed Schmitt an ironic congratulation following the latter's appointment as *Staatsrat:* "Hermann Heller felicitates you on the exceedingly well-earned honor accorded you by Herr Minister Goering."[18]

Schmitt and his disciples did not simply participate in the mistreatment and expulsion of Jewish scholars. Rather, they directly profited from the now-open positions. For instance, Ernst Forsthoff—Schmitt's student, and son of Heinrich Forsthoff, a Mülheim pastor, German Christian activist, and friend of Schmitt—profited in this way from Heller's expulsion from his chair in Frankfurt.[19] This is the context in which Schmitt refused to sign a resolution in support of Hans Kelsen, who had just been dismissed from his professorship at Cologne University. Schmitt had precisely Kelsen to thank for his own recent appointment to Cologne. The refusal can thus be interpreted as either a sign of Schmitt's limitless opportunism or as a sign of a new Nazi sensibility.[20] Probably, it was a combination of both.

But the situation was far more serious regarding Schmitt's behavior toward Erich Kaufmann, his former colleague in Bonn. In this case he displayed industry, successfully using an antisemitic attack to prevent Kaufmann's further academic employment. In an undated letter from 1934 to the Ministry of Culture he explained that for "German feelings" *(deutsches Empfinden)*, "such a [form of] existence [*Existenz*], aimed solely at concealing origins and at disguise" *(auf Verschweigung der Abstammung und auf Tarnung)*, was only "understandable with difficulty"; were the National Socialist state to now furnish an "especially pronounced form of the Jewish assimilated type" *(besonders ausgesprochenen Typus jüdischen Assimilantentums)* with the chance to work at Germany's greatest university, this would not only result in "dreadful confusion" *(eine schlimme Verwirrung)* but also in "spiritual damage" to German students.[21]

Clearly, Schmitt's antisemitic pronouncements should not be brushed off as public "lip service to the terminology of National-Socialist propaganda" by an erstwhile Young Conservative author.[22] Schmitt formulated his letter in the knowledge that the culture ministry was prepared to transform antisemitic ideology into practice. The letter is a contribution to the realization of Nazi policies, and to interpret its contents as "nonsensical servility" *(nonsens proskynese)* or "silly celebrating" *(Narrenjubel)*, as does Helmut Quaritsch,[23] is consequently not merely wrong but actually a crude form of whitewashing. After 1933 Schmitt was thoroughly serious about his engagement for Nazism and thoroughly sincere in his antisemitism. His ideological zeal is not called into question by the fact that after 1933 he tried to shield one Jewish colleague, Erwin Jakobi, his ally in the crucial "Prussia vs. the Reich" trial (in which Prussia tried to prevent itself from being ruled by the Reich), from the effects of the "Aryan clauses" in the Nazi civil-service law.

It is thus possible to sharpen our understanding of the role opportunism actually played in Schmitt's career. For the post-1933 period, a reproach of that sort should be leveled only with considerable caution. But Schmitt's behavior *before* 1933 can appropriately be termed opportunistic, in that he refrained from publicly engaging in antisemitic attacks. Instead, he profited from the help of Jewish friends—soon, virtually without exception, to be renounced for the sake of long-standing inner principles. Or, to reformulate once again, Schmitt's career in-deed reveals a consistent opportunism—an opportunism that precisely does *not* explain his antisemitic pronouncements while the Third Reich reigned.

The Nazi Jurists

Although once the Nazi Party came to power Schmitt displayed an avid willingness to cooperate with it, this does not necessarily mean that before 1933 he hoped the Nazis would triumph and worked to that end. We here need to distinguish between exploring questions of intellectual genealogy on the one hand, and understanding the complicated factors that determine how an intellectual behaves in the field of practical politics on the other hand. Scholars have convincingly shown that Schmitt only opted for the party after Hitler became German chancellor. There are no direct expressions of opposition to the Nazis in Schmitt's Weimar Republic writings; but he also has nothing positive to say about them. We can in fact assume some opposition, since in the republic's final phase he spoke up for the presidential dictatorships of Brüning, Papen, and Schleicher—but not for the Nazis. There are also indications that Schmitt was initially not enthusiastic about Hitler's appointment as Schleicher's successor.[24] In this sense, the year 1933 can indeed be understood as a caesura.

As indicated, Schmitt's quick professional ascent under the Nazis was facilitated by an elimination from the scene of much of the competition. Nevertheless, during the Third Reich's first weeks he found himself in a politically difficult position: he had lent much support to the experiment of basing a dictatorship on Article 48 of the Weimar constitution, and the experiment had failed. Likewise, he had devised a "plan for winning time," meant to bypass the sixty-day deadline for new Reichstag elections set in Article 25 of the constitution.[25] (After the war, he possibly tied the plan to his discovery in the 1940s of the notion of the Katechon, or agent of eschatological delay.[26]) The plan failed to function. By 1932 Hitler's popularity was already far greater than that of Schleicher or any other representatives of the old elite.[27] The elite itself sensed this, drawing closer to Hitler in its turn. Hitler seemed to be an authentic spokesman for German youth and the German masses; he was moving toward specific radical goals as leader of a modern revolution.[28] Schmitt, the intellectual, did not view Hitler as an especially sympathetic character. But in face of the state of emergency and the threat posed by the communists, he considered him as at least the lesser evil. Still, if his basic views had stood fundamentally opposed to Hitler's, than he certainly would never have been willing or able to take on the role of intellectual interpreter of the new regime.

If we consider the biographies of other jurists who did not have to fear for their jobs and lives because of Jewish origins or an overtly anti-Nazi stance, then the impression that Schmitt was facing grave danger in 1933 needs some correction. With the exceptions of Otto Koellreuter and Arnold Köttgen, not a single professor of public law supported the Nazis before 1933.[29] Similarly with other juridical groups, such as the judiciary: of around seven thousand Prussian judges, only thirty openly belonged to the Nazi Party before 1933.[30] The main reason for this lack of support was the threat of dismissal from state service. Hence there were clandestine party memberships, revealing themselves in the belated receipt of low membership numbers. Helmut Quaritsch's explanation of Schmitt's passionate embrace of Nazism in terms of his supposed status as a "National Socialist neophyte" *(NS-Konvertit)* is thus not convincing. Most German jurists serving the new regime, and nearly all professors, were formally "neophytes."[31] Jurists just beginning their careers such as Ernst Forsthoff, Reinhard Höhn, Ernst Rudolf Huber, and Theodor Maunz—for the most part in chairs previously occupied by the expelled Jewish professors—were themselves not "old fighters" in the Nazi Party, and so their position was no easier than Schmitt's. Höhn had been active for a long time in Arthur Mahraun's Jungdeutscher Orden, and both Ernst Forsthoff and Huber had published diligently in Young Conservative journals.[32] In fact, if they were to have careers these younger jurists needed to demonstrate far more identification with Nazism than their established older counterparts;[33] when the occasion arose, the new men in power, who cared about the views held abroad of German legal studies and political science, would find it far easier to get rid of such lesser-known figures than an academic like Carl Schmitt, with his international reputation. (Höhn, a member of the SD, would contribute substantially to Schmitt's fall from grace in the Nazi hierarchy in 1936, only to be forced out of the SD himself shortly after.)[34] Especially in the first phase of the Third Reich's consolidation, the nature and scope of Schmitt's writing on the "new legal scholarship" was politically significant.[35] Even if we assume that his possibilities for exerting direct political influence were slim, as the most important of the "converts," his engagement for the Nazis had great symbolic meaning.[36]

Antisemitism and Nazism

Schmitt was less of an outsider within the space defined by his juridical colleagues than in the space defined by the Nazi elite. In their world, he was isolated as a jurist and thinker. He was nevertheless part of a large group of intellectuals deeply committed to the Nazi cause and actively engaged in shaping Nazi policy.[37] As was the case for some of these other intellectuals, Schmitt's most important tie with the Nazis—in practical respects certainly the most consequential tie—was his strongly pronounced antisemitism.

Contrary to a view long cherished in postwar Germany, Schmitt's perspective was here in harmony with that of large portions of the German non-Jewish population. Approval of Hitler's policies was especially high in the upper levels of the educated middle class, including the academic leadership.[38] It is important to note that this majority did not favor the "rowdy antisemitism" of someone like *Stürmer*-founder Julius Streicher. Rather, it favored an inestimably more dangerous "antisemitism of reason" with a Hitlerian stamp.[39] Schmitt in fact nurtured a widespread resentment. His commentators have overlooked this reality because of a form of inverted logic: from a presumed absence of antisemitism on Schmitt's part, they have concluded that he kept at least an inner (if not always outer) distance from the "Nazi *Weltanschauung*." Schmitt's biographer Joseph Bendersky thus flatly maintains that the jurist's antisemitic statements during the Nazi period did not reflect his own convictions but had tactical purposes.[40] Correspondingly, he interprets the large and ambitious antisemitic conference of jurists Schmitt organized in 1936 as an effort at self-protection by someone who felt highly vulnerable because of his earlier friendships with Jews.[41] Bendersky lists a series of compromises Schmitt made during these years, each drawing him further into the maw of the Nazi leviathan: "Now he found himself articulating ideas about race and the Jews which he thought were truly absurd."[42]

In the world of Schmitt scholarship, Bendersky's argument has continued to receive widespread approval.[43] That notwithstanding, it flies in the face of three facts. First, even after Schmitt's fall from favor engineered by the SD (the Nazi security services) in 1936, he continued to promulgate antisemitic ideas in *many* texts between 1937 and 1945. Second, after 1945 he did not retract a single one of these ideas. Third, during his interrogation by Robert Kempner in Nuremberg in 1947, he directly defended the ideas as being formulated toward "scientific" ends.[44]

As already shown by his letter concerning Kaufmann, during the Nazi period Schmitt tried to concretely realize his antisemitic ideas. Nazism supplied him with an opportunity to apply those ideas, which he entertained, as political currency, before his Nazi engagement—no other conclusion makes logical sense.

Racism and Antisemitism

Nazi Jew-hatred is often defined as racial antisemitism. This is meant to express the fact that it has a Social Darwinist or pseudoscientific rather than a religious basis: that it involves a "biologization" falsely suggesting that nature itself generates value judgments.

Nevertheless, the theory of a categorical break between traditional, religiously grounded antisemitism (often denoted as anti-Judaism) and Nazi "Aryan" mythology falls short. This can be seen in the political-religious dimension of Nazi propaganda, representing Hitler as an "instrument of divine will" and stigmatizing "the Jews" as (to cite Goebbels) "Antichrist."[45] The Jews are not the "natural" victims of any racial theory. Rather, in their historical development, the various theories have revealed a wide range of typologies and hierarchical categories. This suggests that another reason must exist for one such theory focusing the way it did on the Jews: in other words, for the struggle against "non-Aryans" being perceived first and foremost as a struggle against the Jews.[46]

It is well known that the biologization of anti-Jewish metaphors had its source in the eighteenth- and nineteenth-century proliferation of concepts emerging from the natural sciences. This process transformed the *theological* opposition between Jews and Christians into an apparently *scientific* opposition. Nazism's racist hostility to the Jews was a product of this transformation. Thus, to move beyond the level of Nazism's own claims, we need to pinpoint the specific character of its ideology of history: the deeply embedded religious roots of the polar opposition, formulated in Social Darwinist terms, between biologically superior Aryans and inferior (albeit menacing and malevolent) Semites.[47] Notably, despite all their biological metaphors and pseudoscientific rhetoric, the Nazi executors of racial law confronted a basic problem—that of the absence of any concrete biological determinant for who was a Jew and who an Aryan, or for what, exactly, distinguished Aryan from Jewish blood.[48] For this reason, under the Nazis the juridical definition of Jewishness was, in fact, *not* biological-racial but rather religious. This is even the case for State Secretary Wilhelm Stuckart's commentary on this question, despite his insistence that the Nazi state viewed the Jews as forming not a religious but a "blood-determined" body.[49] Thus a merger of racial and older, Christian forms of antisemitism is evident even in the specifically anti-Christian portion of the Nazi movement.

Already before 1933, both Nazi and "German National" politicians (themselves not known for anti-Christian views) maintained that specific discriminatory laws had to be imposed on Germany's Jews. With few exceptions, the non-Nazi right wing was hardly less antisemitic than the Nazis.[50] This state of affairs was reflected in Franz von Papen and his followers offering no objections to legal discrimination against Jews after Hitler's rise to power. To properly understand Schmitt's antisemitism in the framework of Nazi ideology, we need to keep in mind the broad-based existence of such Christian-conservative anti-Jewish feelings. The connection between Schmitt's racist texts and this context of anti-Jewish hatred in general, Christian antisemitism in particular has been ignored in the literature on Schmitt: doubtless a result of explaining away those texts as mere camouflage for ordinary "anti-Judaism" by an intellectual outsider.[51] The frequently drawn distinction between "moderate" and "radical" antisemites is here carried over to a distinction between Christian and racial antisemitism.[52] But at least from a functionalist perspective, the distinction is questionable, since until World War II it played absolutely no role in the German state's legal discrimination against the Jews.[53]

For Schmitt, Nazi antisemitism had theological, political, and legal functions. He did his best to make use of Nazi antisemitism in all its functions. Whether he was at war with the *Jews* on account of their allegedly normative thinking or, inversely, was at war with *normativism* as a specific product of "the Jewish," is an occasionally irritating interpretive problem. The same applies to the question of the relation between "the Jews" and the ideational complex of positivism, liberalism, and Marxism. Since Schmitt himself was often unsure about the basis for what he referred to as a "situatively" applied "declaration of enmity," we can set this problem aside. Once we have done so, a general picture begins to emerge of the role played by the Jews in Schmitt's ideas.

3

Schmitt's Assault on the "Jewish Legal State"

Equality of Kind instead of Equality

Schmitt's early Nazi articles already reveal an unusual radicalism. On 12 March 1933, twelve days after his official admission into the Nazi Party, he published an article titled "The Good Law of the German Revolution" ("Das gute Recht der deutschen Revolution") in the *Westdeutsche Beobachter*, an official party organ. The article makes clear the central role Schmitt assigned the struggle against Judaism in the framework of the "national revolution"; in one way or another, he connects practically all the problems addressed in the article to the "Jewish question." The connection is made possible through polemic use of the term *Gleichartigkeit*, translatable as "being of the same kind." At a later point he would replace the term with another, *Artgleichheit*, used mainly in biology to denote identity of species but translatable here as "equality of kind."[1] In Schmitt's words, "Many concepts only emerge into daylight through repeated sallies and circumambulations."[2]

Schmitt sees the concept of *Gleichartigkeit* as above all the key to the "entire legislative work at hand," that is, to the "Law for the Restoration of the Civil Service" ("Gesetz zur Wiederherstellung des Berufsbeamtentums"), meant to "purify" public life of "non-Aryan elements of a foreign kind [*fremdgeartet*]."[3] Schmitt comments in his article that "a people [*Volk*] awakens into consciousness of its own kind [*Art*] and reflects on itself and its equals [*seinesgleichen*]." In this "intimate process of growth," no people "of a foreign kind" are meant to mix in, since they would create a "damaging and dangerous" disturbance, even with "perhaps" good intentions. The concept of growth and the related concept, employed by Schmitt later, of the "folk-soul" *(Volksseele)* are tied to a set of quasi-idealist, quasi-romantic ideas with which Schmitt stood on intimate terms at least since his *Romanticism* book of 1919.[4] In order to understand the atmosphere and intellectual environment into which such ideas were now being injected, it is useful to glance at the journal issue containing "The Good Law of the German Revolution." Directly next to Schmitt's article is a piece on the "Restoration of the Civil Service" and especially on the new law's "so-called Aryan clauses." Following that article we find a transcript, under the heading "Against the Un-German Spirit!" ("Wider den undeutschen Geist!"), of "the fireside maxims delivered at the midnight burning of un-German literature at sites of higher education" *(die Feuersprüche bei der mitternächtlichen Verbrennung undeutschen Schrifttums an den Hochschulorten).*

Importantly, the motif of *Gleichartigkeit* also appears in another work by Schmitt:

> Someone who is *artfremd* [a biological term signifying "alien to the species," here translatable literally as "someone alien to one's own kind"] may behave as critically and strive as keenly as he wishes, may read books and write books, [but still] he thinks and understands in another way, because he is of another kind, and in every decisive train of thought remains within the existential conditions of his own kind. That is the objective reality of "objectivity" [*sic*].[5]

In differing yet related fashions, both the Aryan clauses and the book burnings on the one hand and Schmitt's concept of *Gleichartigkeit* on the other are radical attacks on fundamental bourgeois principles stemming from the Enlightenment and French Revolution; Schmitt's concept represents, in fact, a polemical attack on the bourgeois-liberal idea of *Gleichheit*—equality.

More concretely, Schmitt's concept represents an undermining of the idea enshrined in Article 109 of the Weimar Constitution: equality before the law, regardless of origins, religion, or nationality.[6] In this respect, Schmitt could make use of a tradition, represented for example in the writings of Paul de Lagarde, that understood itself as both *völkisch* and Christian. Against supposedly heathen principles of freedom, equality, and fraternity, Lagarde proposed another conceptual triad, understood as Christian: "the right to become what God has charged us with becoming; inequality [*Ungleichheit*], which alone makes possible a polyphonic phrase [*Satz*]; being a child to God."[7] Schmitt's friend Wilhelm Stapel had criticized "application of the concept of equality to the political sphere" as "a violation by means of mathematical competence."

Schmitt disqualified the demand for "equality for everyone before the law" as "empty and formal"; he defined it as a tool and weapon of "strangers and swindlers" and their "strange, hostile legality." Against this demand, Schmitt put forward the "objective" *(sachlich)* and substantive concept of *Gleichartigkeit.*[8]

In thus pushing aside the equality principle of the constitutional state, he was removing the main obstacle to establishing a body of special, discriminatory laws aimed at the Jews. Here we can recognize the difficulties in distinguishing means and ends within Schmitt's argumentation. It is no longer very easy to distinguish his polemic against the constitutional state from his polemic against "the Jews" and "the Jewish"; the constitutional state has become an expression of Jewish legislative ideas—as it were, a *"Jewish* constitutional state." In his "New Guiding Principles for Legal Practice" ("Neue Leitsätze für die Rechtpraxis"), appearing in various journals in December 1933, Schmitt counters the concept of the *Rechtsstaat,* the constitutional state, with the following words, appearing beneath numeral five: "The National Socialist State Is a Just State" *(Der nationalsozialistische Staat ist ein gerechter Staat).*[9]

In the book by Günther Krauss and Otto von Schweinichen *Disputation over the Constitutional State (Disputation über den Rechtsstaat),* which Schmitt edited, the ties between the *Rechtstaat* and Judaism are spelled out by Krauss:

> In truth, declaring faith in the constitutional state and its legality is senseless at present, after the seizure of power. The entire question has an instructive analogy in the quarrel about circumcision of the heathen Christians in the old church, if using such analogies will be allowed. After Christ's resurrection Jewish legal thinking [*das jüdische Gesetzesdenken*] and the Jewish ceremonial precepts could hardly be recognized; similarly, following the seizure of power the National Socialist state can hardly submit to the rules at work in the earlier idea of the state.[10]

The transition from the constitutional state to the Nazi state is here compared with Christianity's superseding of Judaism; the oft-scorned "Jewish Republic" has been overcome by the Nazi state.

Issued on 28 February 1933, the "Decree of the President of the Reich for the Protection of *Volk* and State" formed the backdrop to Schmitt's discarding of constitutional legality. Schmitt welcomed this so-called Reichstag-fire decree, which declared the death penalty for those who carried out the arson, thus throwing out the constitutional principle of *nulla poena sine lege* (no punishment without a law).[11] Whenever this principle is denied, in order, for instance, to justify arbitrary political measures, one has moved outside the bounds of the civil constitutional state. Schmitt was fully aware of this fact. He thus now confronted the defender of the "liberal constitutional state," for whom "a mark was in fact simply a mark, and baptized was simply baptized," with the "true law" emerging from a "just and German" cause.[12]

The linkage of antiliberal and antisemitic polemics is one of Nazism's basic features. Although in his article and elsewhere Schmitt chose to not explicitly mention the Jews, he quite clearly assumed that enough hints were present for readers to understand exactly what he meant. The identity of those benefiting from the scorned liberal-constitutional state and the legal equality it guaranteed would have been entirely clear to these readers: "Thousands of strangers were allowed to change the names that had made them recognizable; they received official permission to deceive harmless Germans with names which sparked trust. That was a legal administrative step of the authorities and justified a person's [ostensibly] well-earned right to the name."[13] Later, in the major conference Schmitt organized in October 1936 called "Judaism in Legal Studies," he would return to the problem of Christianized, once-"Jewish" names. The problem had special importance for Schmitt, since the challenge of Jewish invisibility was at its core. Beyond this, it opened Schmitt's key question of how to distinguish friend from enemy when the enemy was no longer recognizable. Since Schmitt viewed the ability to make such a distinction as the deciding premise for political unity, an "invisible," assimilated enemy represented the greatest provocation for his political concept. Such unity could be achieved only through exclusion of what was different; *substantive homogeneity* thus served for Schmitt as the basis of the democratic state.[14]

Schmitt used his political concept in support of the Nazi effort to create *völkisch* homogeneity through a radical definition of enmity. He wielded the concept in the struggle to produce a homogeneous *Volk*—in his untranslatable phrase, an *eigenvölkische Art*—for the "coming German generations" *(die kommenden deutschen Geschlechter)*. In this way the difference between those who were *gleichartig* and those who were *artfremd* now emerged for Schmitt as the embodiment of political thinking: "We are learning once more to distinguish. We are above all learning to properly distinguish friend from enemy."[15] Schmitt here appears intoxicated at the thought of connecting the central thesis of his 1932 book, *Der Begriff des Politischen (The Concept of the Political)*, with the concept of *Gleichartigkeit*. In 1933 he published an essentially altered edition of the book. In this respect, despite Heinrich Meier's argument in the course of his close examination of the "dialogue of absent parties" between Schmitt and Leo Strauss,[16] it is quite unlikely that a main concern of Schmitt in the new edition was answering Strauss. (In fact, he no longer bothered responding to Strauss's personal letters.) Rather, it seems to me that the important question is that of the *political effect* Schmitt was aiming at with his alterations, in the context of his Nazi engagement—an effect announced in the switch from the bourgeois-conservative publisher Duncker & Humblot to the Nazi publisher Hanseatische Verlagsanstalt. (Backed up with massive advertising, the new edition was published at very high volume and a rock-bottom price.[17])

In this edition, Schmitt ties his biologistic terminology—itself manifestly racist in its underlying meaning—with political concepts, without to be sure exploring their political context:

> The alien individual of another nature [*der Fremde und Andersgeartete*] may present himself as strictly "critical," "objective," "neutral," "purely scientific," and infiltrate his alien judgments through similar types of camouflage [*Verschleierungen*]. His objectivity is either simply political camouflage [*Verschleierung*] or a complete absence of connection [*Beziehungslosigkeit*], lacking everything essential. In political decisions, even the mere possibility of proper recognition and understanding, hence the authority to have one's say and judge, rests only on existential partaking and participation, only on authentic *participatio*. For this reason, the case of extreme conflict can only be constituted by the participants themselves; in particular, each one of them can only decide for himself whether the otherness of the alien [*das Anderssein des Fremden*] signifies, in the concrete case of conflict that is at hand, the negation of one's own type of existence [*der eigenen Art Existenz*] and thus must be fended off or fought against in order to save one's own type of life, a life corresponding to one's own being.[18]

The rhetoric of defense was always present in the Nazi assault upon the Jews. In their commentary on Nazi legislation, Wilhelm Stuckart and Rolf Schiedermair declared a "solution to the Jewish Question" to be an "imperative of *völkisch* self-preservation and self-defense."[19] As the quoted passage indicates, in the new edition of Schmitt's book, the concept of the alien or stranger is superimposed on the earlier concept of the enemy; and the earlier friend-enemy schema is replaced by an equally polarized distinction between those who are similar and those who are alien to one's kind: *artgleich* and *artfremd*.[20] Correspondingly, we can observe Schmitt's earlier *decision*-centered thinking now making way for a radically Manichean *distinction*-centered view of the world.

In his article in the *Westdeutsche Beobachter,* Schmitt addresses what he considers another essential evil at work in the liberal idea of equality:

> This sort of liberal constitutional state finally managed to render the penal code into a big "safe-conduct letter for criminals"; in line with this, the constitution became a safe-conduct letter for high treason. German judges were helpless in face of the impudence of racially alien pettifoggers [*die Dreistigkeiten fremdrassiger Rabulisten*]: the "constitutional state" would have been endangered if anyone had energetically tried to resist it.

One might conclude from this formulation that Schmitt is trying to defend his pre-1933 reticence in the "Jewish question." It is more likely, however, that he wishes to once again underscore his role in the so-called *Preussenschlag*—the legal "strike against Prussia" on 20 July 1932 that deposed the state's legitimate government. But now, Schmitt describes the trial as part of a struggle against the "Jewish pettifoggers" (Hermann Heller, Hans Nawiaski, and others).[21]

Schmitt concludes his article by linking remarks on a pair of ideas he considers central, legality and legitimacy, to the question of *Gleichartigkeit*. Once more, his views concur with those of the most radical admirers of Nazi rule. He declares that the "national revolution" need not be justified as having "respected the legality of the Weimar system and its constitution," as some conservative advocates of the Nazi seizure of power had hoped. In that way, he indicates, one would simply be trying, insultingly, to correct the "German revolution" with "the concepts of its deadly enemy." At this time, Schmitt was still tying the concept of revolution to the nation, and not to Nazism. The "national revolution," he indicates, is not concerned at all with preserving the old legality; its goals are in fact entirely different: "Presently we are first of all creating the necessary *Gleichartigkeit;* only then can a rational and just equality [*Gleichheit*] rule; only then can formal norms containing a sensible legality again take their course. The German revolution will not allow itself to be trapped in the snare of an alien and hostile legality." A few years later, the writer Franz Blei, an erstwhile friend of Schmitt, pointed to the circular reasoning involved here: the jurist's need to create the same *Gleichartigkeit* that he already assumes to exist.[22] For Schmitt the inherent nature of Weimar "legality" stood in opposition to the *Gleichartigkeit* that had to be created. In his article, the juncture between formal equality and Judaism is only implied; it possesses mainly political-polemical thrust. Later, he would expound on it at greater length. With the article, the biologization of Schmitt's political metaphors began.

Schmitt would develop the biologistic idea tied to the conception of *Gleichartigkeit* over the coming months; it was now that he would start to speak of *Artgleichheit*.[23] On 3 October 1933, at the German Conference of Jurists, he delivered a talk in which he elevated the new term to what he called a "central concept," meant to be applied to both state and administration.[24] The conference was held in Leipzig from 30 September to 3 October, under the motto "Through National Socialism German Law for the German People." Approximately twelve thousand jurists participated in what was termed a jurists' "deployment" or "march-up" *(Juristen-Aufmarsch)*.[25] In contrast to his *Westdeutsche Beobachter* article, in his talk Schmitt linked the *Artgleichheit* that has emerged from *Gleichartigkeit* to the idea of leadership, *Führerschaft*:

> To lead is not the same as dictatorship. Leading is something that rests on an *Artgleichheit* between the leader [*Führer*] and those who follow him [*Gefolgschaft*]. . . . Leadership [*Führung*] only exists between *Artgleichen* [those of the same kind], and this concept of *Artgleichheit* is an indispensable central concept—indeed even juridically and systematically indispensable—of present-day state and administrative legal thinking. But in its essentials this concept is itself clear and has prevailed.[26]

Schmitt here conjures up a clarity that is by no means present. Although he makes frequent use of biologistic metaphors, he avoids defining the concept of *Artgleichheit* in a concretely biologistic manner. He in fact evades any substantial statement concerning the nature of this *Artgleichheit*, something such a definition would require. The concept thus remain indistinct, just as was the case with the concept of *Gleichartigkeit;* it can be wielded as a tool that is both extremely political and extremely polemic. In this respect, Schmitt does establish a referential network offering his audience and readers an idea of the goal tied to his vague conceptualizations: On the one hand, he once again suggests a linkage to the concept of legality, which "in its narrowest confines must be true to both its nature and its kind [*wesens- und artgetreu*]. For this reason we created the [particular] legality of our own National Socialist state. We do not need to let ourselves be instructed in this matter by those who think differently and have a different disposition [*Andersdenkenden und Andersgesinnten*]."[27] On the other hand, he links "kind" *(Art)* with "thinking"

(Denken). It is clear that those who are *artfremd* cannot think in a German way; as "those who think differently and have a different disposition," they represent another form of legality and can be true neither to German kind nor German nature.

At the end of his talk, Schmitt introduced a new, important concept:

> We will not allow ourselves to be misled by the sophisticated antithesis of politics and law and law and power: the will of the Führer is law [*der Wille des Führers (ist) Recht*]. As Heracleitus told us, to follow the Führer's will is likewise a nomos. . . . But in repeatedly speaking of leadership [*Führertum*] and the Führer concept, we do not mean to forget that authentic leaders take part in this struggle [*Kampf*], and that our struggle would be hopeless if they were not there for us. We have them, and for this reason I close my talk by naming two names: Adolf Hitler, the Führer of the German *Volk*, whose will is presently the nomos of the German *Volk*, and Hans Frank, the Führer of our German legal front [*Rechtsfront*], the pioneer [*Vorkämpfer*] of our good German law, the model for our National Socialist German jurists. Heil![28]

Albeit only obscurely and in hymnic Nazi prose, the "nomos" is here announced in a prominent venue. The nomos—an idea already present in debates unfolding in adjacent circles—will be Schmitt's vehicle for replacing the alien, "Jewish" legal understanding characterizing the constitutional state, along with the idea of legitimacy connected to it.

In his first extensive programmatically Nazi text, treating "the tripartite division of political unity," Schmitt characterizes the "*Artgleichheit* of the unified German *Volk*" as the indispensable premise and foundation for the new idea of political leadership.[29] As in both of the essays from 1933, here he takes an outspokenly Nazi line. He refers to *Führertum* and *Artgleichheit* as "basic concepts of National Socialist law," and to the "Law for the Restoration of the Civil Service" as having "purified German officialdom from alien [*fremdgeartete*] elements." He does not hesitate to treat Hegel and Göring in the same breath.[30] As in the other texts, here as well Schmitt leaves it open how, precisely, the *Volk* is to reflect "on itself and its equals"—here as well he presumes that "today" equality must "first of all" be created.[31] Through the negative category of the alien, he moves methodologically toward a legal concept he views as German and true to one's kind *(arteigen)*; he will consistently juxtapose this concept with what he terms formalistic superstition regarding the law as *Gesetz (formalistischer Gesetzesaberglauben)*.[32] And he directly transfers his notion of political sovereignty into the judicial realm, declaring that everything depended "on the kind and type [*Art und . . . Typus*] of our judges and officials. At no point beforehand has the question *quis judicabit* [who will do the judging?] been endowed with such all-deciding significance." Schmitt then proposes a concept of legality suitable for the "new jurisprudence":

> We are searching for a tie that is more reliable, more alive, and deeper than the deceptive tie to the malleable letters of a thousand legal clauses. Where else could it be located than in ourselves and our own kind [*unserer eigenen Art*]? Here too . . . all questions and answers flow into the prerequisite of *Artgleichheit*, without which a total Führer-state [*ein totaler Führerstaat*] cannot exist for a day.[33]

In the context of his concept of *Artgleichheit*, Schmitt asserts that as a political unit each *Volk* possesses its own sense of law:

> We know, not only through our feelings but also on grounds of strictest scientific insight, that all law is the law of a specific *Volk*. It is a truth of cognitive theory that only someone who participates in the law-creating community [*rechtschöpferische Gemeinschaft*] in a way corresponding to one's own being and determined by one's kind [*artbestimmt*], and only someone who existentially belongs to that community, is capable of seeing facts correctly, hearing statements correctly, and evaluating impressions of men and things correctly. Man stands within the reality of this belonging to *Volk* and race on the level of the deepest, most unconscious movement of the feelings, but also on that of the most tiny fibers of the brain.[34]

This argument might be considered a form of Nazi universalism oriented around a debased version of the German Idealist "folk-soul." The argument stands in contrast with the basic thrust of Schmitt's public invective from the same period, which suggests an *anti-universalism* defining various kinds and races as essentially unequal. What now seems to be suggested is that *one* specific race needs to be eliminated, since its rigid maintenance of a literal interpretation of its alien law represents a danger to the German soul. Although the name of this enemy is not spelled out at any point in the text, it would have been more than clear to contemporaries who is *really* being aimed at in the Nazi struggle against a muddying and weakening of its concepts by "an assimilation [*Assimilierung*] to alien categories."[35]

As in numerous other passages, Schmitt's obsessive hatred of the Jews is here accompanied by a careful, systematic avoidance of any direct mention of them—in other words, he engages, in a way, in a process of literal elimination.[36] As in his writing from the Weimar period, polemics are not absent, directed for instance against Georg Jellinek's *General Theory of State (Allgemeine Staatslehre)* and against Hans Kelsen.[37] In a thoroughly usual form of antisemitic discourse, Schmitt leaves it to his readers to add the missing words by steadily following his train of thought. He thus can avoid contaminating his texts with the name of the *enemy*. The texts appear theoretically serious. And in this circumspect form their author might, perhaps, be protected in the event of sudden political change.

In the course of his book *State, Movement, Volk*, Schmitt further sharpens the concepts of *Gleichartigkeit* and *Artgleichheit* by equating them with the concept of race:

> *Artgleichheit* of the German *Volk*, unified in itself, is the most indispensable premise and foundation for the concept of political leadership of the German *Volk* [*sic*]. When at the National Socialist German Conference of Jurists, the thought of race was repeatedly placed at the center . . . in the powerful closing speech of the Führer, this was no theoretically devised postulate. Without the principle of *Artgleichheit*, the National Socialist state could not exist and its legal life would not be conceivable; together with all its institutions, it would be handed over to its—sometimes superciliously critical, sometimes submissively assimilating—liberal or Marxist enemies.[38]

Hence the "principle of *Artgleichheit*" is not a "theoretical postulate." On the one hand in postulating such a "principle" Schmitt is hiding the fact that the Nazis actually had great difficulties developing a coherent theoretical position regarding the basic idea of race; on the other hand he is transforming an apparent weakness into a political strength. A way of thinking that rejects all abstraction does not need to explain itself, since every explanation rests on a certain process of abstraction. The state thus retains the discretion of defining *Artgleichheit* anew from case to case—in order to achieve the goal of a political unity based on homogeneity.[39]

The Lords of *Lex* Subjugate the *Rex*

In May 1934 Schmitt published a long article in *Deutsches Recht* titled "National Socialist Legal Thinking" ("Nationalsozialistisches Rechtsdenken"). In this article, whose underlying euphoria is represented in the declaration "we are on the side of coming things!" he in fact discussed

the—for him explosive—connection between what he viewed as
"Jewish" and "German" legal thinking. As far as I am aware, this was
the first occasion that he considered such a connection in a direct rather
than encoded form. Even in his essay of 25 January 1934 in the same
journal, reflecting on "One Year of the National Socialist Constitutional
State" ("Ein Jahr nationalsozialistischer Verfassungsstaat"), Schmitt still
did not utter the word "Jew."[40] The backdrop against which he came
to speak of Judaism was his frequently stressed opposition between an
ascendant thinking based on "concrete order," itself emerging from
Nazi concepts of "blood and land," and the "bankrupt *idées générales*"
that determined the entire nineteenth century:

> For an entire century, European humanity produced such *idées
> générales*, such general concepts [*generelle Allgemeinbegriffe*], as a sche-
> matic "spirit" [*Geist*]. Even jurisprudence, which by no means leads
> an isolated existence in the life of peoples and ages [*Völker und
> Zeiten*] aligned itself with this total movement and tried zealously
> to erect a ghostly world of general concepts upon concrete reality.
>
> All countries and people [*Länder und Völker*] seek to return to
> their own land [*Boden*], to their own blood [*Blut*], and to the natural
> forms of order that emerge from blood and land, and to free them-
> selves from the artificial superstructure of *idées générales*. Our Na-
> tional Socialist striving for German law and German jurispru-
> dence stands at the forefront of this great process of renewal,
> taking in the entire world.[41]

The "normativistic method" is here the juridical expression of the abstract *idées générales* against which Schmitt is battling. This method, he
indicates, would detach general norms and rules from the "concrete situation" and "concrete order," thus absolutizing law.[42] Now what is especially important in regards to the problem of Schmitt's antisemitism
is that in this article, he directly holds the "influx" of the Jewish *Volk*
on alien territory *(das Einströmen des jüdischen Gastvolkes)* decisively responsible for the normativistic method's expansion in Germany.[43] For
Schmitt, one reason that precisely the Jews are to blame for this development's acceleration is "the peculiarity of the Jewish people [*die Ei-
genart des jüdischen Volkes*], who for thousands of years have lived not as a
state on a piece of land [*auf einem Boden*], but solely in the law and norm,
hence which in the true sense of the word is 'existentially normativistic.'" Another reason is the historical situation of the Jews as a "guest
people":

> In the second place it is self-evident that a stranger, a guest, an alien
> [*Metöke*], views the law of the people hosting him normativistically
> and only from the angle of legal certainty. For after all, he does not
> belong to the reality of the people within which he lives. . . . He
> wishes to have the train schedule in order to know when and where
> he can get on and leave the train. As a result he replaces law under-
> stood as *Recht* with law [*das Gesetz*] in the sense of a previously de-
> termined, quantifiable norm.[44]

In this respect, it is notable that in *On the Three Types of Juristic Thought
(Über die drei Arten des rechtswissenschaftlichen Denkens)*, Schmitt contrasts
the law as a "train schedule" *(das Gesetz)* with the true law *(das Recht)* of
the nomos: "The law as ruler, the nomos basileus, cannot be any sort of
arbitrary, merely positive norm, rule, or legal determination; the nomos
meant to bear a true king [*sic*] must contain within it certain highest,
immutable, but concrete qualities of order. One would not say that a
merely functional mode or a train schedule is 'king.'"[45]

Schmitt's repeated reproach that Jews had no relationship to land
or soil was so widespread in the Weimar Republic that even the *Jüdische
Lexikon* article on "landed property" (1927) ends defensively with a list
of Talmudic passages "refuting" the "reproach" that in Judaism "land is
only valuable as capital."[46] In this regard, the notion is certainly credible
that Diaspora Judaism leans toward a highly specific approach to the
problem of absent political territory. And what from a universalistic perspective might be seen as a categorical advantage might in turn be seen
as a categorical deficit from a *völkisch* perspective. Schmitt approached
the phenomenon of Jewish statelessness by appropriating it into an essentialist definition of Jewish thinking: a form of essentialism not only
found among antisemites but also among many philosemites and some
Jews. Its attractiveness rests in part on an inherent radical reductiveness,
the promise of ready solutions to complicated historical problems.

In the postwar period, Schmitt would expand on the connections
between land and law and between historical and legal evolution.[47] But
a shift from a polemical presentation of his reproaches against the Jewish people to something like a systematic presentation is already evident
in *On the Three Types of Juristic Thought*. Appearing in the monograph series of the Academy for German Law, edited by Hans Frank, the book
is based on lectures that Schmitt delivered in Berlin on 21 February
1934 at the Kaiser Wilhelm Society for the Sciences, and again on 10
March 1934 at a meeting of the "Reich Council of Junior Barristers"

(Reichsfachgruppenrat der Referendare [*Jungjuristen*]) in the League of National Socialist German Jurists.[48] As the book's title indicates, Schmitt here moves the difference between three types of law to the center of his own reflections. These types are normativism, decisionism, and "concrete order"-based thinking.[49] His intent is to show that both the German *Volk* and "other European nations" have discovered forms and expressions of "self-protection against normativistic positivism."[50] In contrast to his essay "National Socialist Legal Thinking," Schmitt here once again avoids explicitly mentioning the Jews, being content with the following hint: "There are peoples that exist without land, without state, without church, but only in the law [*Gesetz*]. For them normativistic thinking appears the only rational legal thinking, and every other kind of thought [*Denkart*] incomprehensible, mystic, fantastic, or ridiculous."[51]

It was important to Schmitt that this text be taken seriously as a piece of *scholarship*. He thus laid special weight on it not appearing in the *political* series he edited, *Der deutsche Staat der Gegenwart*, but instead in the series published by the Academy for German Law.[52] In this way, Schmitt transferred historical and anthropological notions and prejudices into jurisprudence. His book does not in fact focus on the simple "difference between sorts of juridical thinking."[53] Rather, it discusses "purely normativistic" or "*Gesetz*-based" thinking in terms of its "political-polemical intent": a usual argumentative procedure for Schmitt.[54] What emerges is his discovery of an abolition of the concrete "king or leader [*Führer*] arrangement [*Ordnung*]" through the "rule of *Gesetz*," as championed by Hans Kelsen "in the period between 1919 and 1932 with particular 'purity' [a reference to Kelsen's important "pure theory of law"]." This reasoning culminates in the sentence "The Lords of *Lex* Subjugate the *Rex*" *(Die Herren der Lex unterwerfen den Rex)*.[55] In another book also published in 1934, *State Structure and the Collapse of the Second Reich (Staatsgefüge und Zusammenbruch des zweiten Reiches)*, Schmitt depicts the "victory of the citizen over the soldier" through a constitutional state in which "*Lex* and not *Rex*," hence "a norm and not a leader," was the "determining factor."[56]

It becomes clear that the reproach of normativism is in fact double in nature. The above citation, which can only be understood as an allusion to a Jewish people existing only within *das Gesetz* and lacking "land," contains a twist that is typical for Schmitt's way of arguing. At first he simply seems to confirm that the "different peoples and races" *(Völker und Rassen)* are "aligned with different types of thinking [*Denktypen*]."[57]

But as suggested, Schmitt then ascribes normativistic thinking to the Jews. It is, he suggests, the only legal thinking that seems rational to them, since they "exist without land, without state, without church, but only in the *Gesetz*." In this way Schmitt follows old popular traditions and theological notions defining the wandering, Ahasuerus-like existence of the "landless" law-bound Jewish people as a confirmation of Christian faith.[58] But Schmitt never rests with mere description—his discourse is always polemic. Stylizing his opponents into political enemies, he insinuates that they think and argue just like he does. He thus does not merely fight normativistic positivism as a method. Rather, he suggests that it is striving for a "reign of *Gesetz*," in opposition to a "reign of human beings" and in a struggle to subjugate the *Rex*, or Führer.[59] Schmitt's thinking, method, and especially his polemic are consistently staged as self-protection. His aggression announces itself as a defensive measure directed against the treacherous powers of *Gesetz*-based faith, hiding beneath the mask of normativism.

In his battle against the "lords of *Lex*" Schmitt was drawing on texts from the Weimar period. At that time, he had already raised objections to the state being ruled through the law's sovereignty rather than through a concrete political sovereign. This is one of the basic themes in *Political Theology* of 1922, along with his battle against (Kelsen's) normativism. He had the book published again in 1934, without the earlier edition's confrontation with Kaufmann but retaining the attack on normativism. In his *Value of the State (Wert des Staates)* of 1914, Schmitt speaks out clearly and bellicosely against normativistic positivism—against the prevailing liberal idea of law, and the constitutional state's legalistic tendency to consider itself a "servant" of the law.[60] To be sure, in this early text he maintains the decisionistic approach he later will declare out of date. Nevertheless, it seems that the basic shift in Schmitt's political orientation was a more serious development than any substantive changes (changes pointed to in the foreword to the new edition of *Political Theology*). In at least the most important works stemming from the opening phase of the Weimar Republic, Schmitt appears first of all as the republic's critic; in 1934 he is mainly interested in affirmatively endowing the new regime with its overriding meaning. He now declares "a word like 'National Socialism'" to be "necessary."[61] In *Political Theology* he still waxes enthusiastic about the creative energy of the "exception" (or of states of legal emergency): "in the exception, the energy of real life breaks through the crust of a mechanics frozen by repetition."[62] In contrast, he now embraces the new order:

For the jurisprudential distinction of forms of legal thought [*juristische Denkarten*], it is of much greater and deeper importance that the distinction is expressed in the postulated and fundamental ideas of a total order [*Gesamtordnung*], in the ideas of what can be viewed as a *normal situation*, of who is a *normal* man, and of what, within legal life and legal thinking, constitute the concrete figures, meant to be presumed as *typical*, of that life meant to be judged as just.[63]

At the same time, inside a framework lacking real coherence, we do find some elements in Schmitt's early work giving a certain continuity to his move from the exception to the rule. We thus already find the beginnings of Schmitt's notion of "concrete order" in *Constitutional Theory (Verfassungslehre)* of 1928. The book contains both a critique of the constitutional state as a "*Gesetz*-state" *(Gesetzesstaat)*[64] and the opposing idea of the nomos. Schmitt viewed the main problem of the bourgeois state's constitution as lying in its concept of law. He understood that concept, like the concept of the constitution itself, as having three parts: formal, material, and political.[65] In line with his argument in *Political Theology* of 1922, *Constitutional Theory* defines the main error of bourgeois constitutional states as lying in a consistent suppression of a concept of political law. Schmitt indicates that under the influence of Laband, Jellinek, and Kelsen, such states subsume everything under formal and material law, reflected in their principle of rule not by a concrete, existing sovereign but by a "sovereignty of the law."[66] Schmitt juxtaposes this concept of law, which he understands as false, with the nomos concept (mentioned here for the first time, and then in only one passage), viewed as a higher instance: "What is lacking is precisely the nomos, and the misuse lies in the failure to recognize what has to remain as a minimum from the old rational concept of a true law—in the failure to recognize the general character of a legal norm."[67]

In its emphasis on the concept of a nomos, Schmitt's talk at the German Conference of Jurists offers a clear indication of the way his legal ideas are developing. As indicated in this venue, he declares that following the Führer's will is "likewise a nomos." From this he concludes that Adolf Hitler's will "is presently the nomos of the German *Volk*." "One can only speak," he explains, "of a real nomos as a real king . . . when nomos signifies, precisely, a total concept of law, taking in a concrete order and community. . . . Just as the nomos is *king*, the *king* is nomos, and here we already again find ourselves in concrete decisions and institutions instead of in abstract norms and general rules."[68] From now on the nomos concept would be a vital element in Schmitt's project for a thinking based on "concrete order." But in his talk as elsewhere, the concept is highly nebulous. In order to clarify a meaning that is never spelled out, always only hinted at, it is helpful to look at earlier debates about the nomos informing Schmitt's own ideas.

Carl Schmitt and the Political Theology of German Protestantism

In the crisis years at the end of the Weimar Republic and in the first years of the Nazi state, Carl Schmitt had narrow ties with important spokesmen for the political theology of German Protestantism.[69] While largely neglected, this relationship is extremely important for understanding Schmitt's attitude toward the Jews and Judaism. The relationship was of a multifaceted nature. On the one hand, in both their theory and terminology Schmitt and the Protestant political theologians influenced each other. On the other hand, they had direct contact, and this had concrete political effects. The contact had to be mostly hidden, since as a Catholic professor of public law Schmitt could not easily meddle in questions of Protestant Church policy: these questions were highly sensitive, and in the Third Reich's opening phase they were highly controversial. The importance of this relation's practical aspects lies above all in what they reveal about the common interests at play —and about the resulting proximity of Schmitt's ideas to those present in Protestant political theology.

Schmitt's intense engagement with Protestant nomos theory deserves a special look. In the course of the Weimar Republic, the rise of virulently racist *völkisch* ideas placed increasing pressure on German Protestantism.[70] At the same time, Protestant theology was becoming open to radically antisemitic ideas. For both these reasons, nationalist, *völkisch* antisemitism became worthy of *theological* discussion. In other words, this antisemitism gained an appearance of dignity through its specific political-theological vocabulary. As a key node in the Protestant debate about the position of Germany's Jews in face of church, state, and *Volk*, Weimar's political-theological nomos clarifies an important aspect of Schmitt' own thinking before and after the decisive years 1932–33.[71]

The Origins of the "Volksnomos"

Schmitt introduced the concept of "political theology" to Weimar Republic legal theory in a book of the same name published in 1922. As

early as 1924, the author Hugo Ball (co-founder of Dada) tried in
Hochland, the most important German-language Catholic cultural journal, to treat all Schmitt's extant writing in terms of that concept. Schmitt
himself would come to highly favor this approach.[72] In the foreword to
his second edition of *Political Theology* (dated November 1933), he notes
that "among the Protestant theologians, especially Heinrich Forsthoff
and Friedrich Gogarten have shown that without the concept of secularization an understanding of the last century of our history is entirely
impossible."[73] Schmitt was thus writing in the knowledge of contemporary controversies within Protestant political theology; and he was aware
of the different contexts in which the concept had been and continued
to be discussed.

The rendezvous between Schmitt and the concept had been encouraged by some commentaries appearing in Young Conservative journals
appearing a few years earlier. In 1931 Schmitt's student Ernst Forsthoff
(son of the German Christian activist Heinrich Forsthoff), writing in *Der
Ring* under the pseudonym Georg Holthausen, announced an alliance
between Protestant political theology and its counterpart in public law.
Forsthoff used a review of Alfred de Quervain's book *Die theologischen
Voraussetzungen der Politik (The Theological Premises of Politics)* as grounds
for the following pronouncement: "Both positively and critically, de
Quervain here encounters that political science with a Catholic disposition [*katholischer Artung*] (Carl Schmitt, Heinz Brauweiler), an encounter
that bodes well for the future."[74] And in 1932 Wilhelm Stapel pointed
to Schmitt's doctrine as "decisive in an essential way" for the political
theology represented by himself, de Quervain, Friedrich Gogarten,
Hans Blüher, and (the Catholic) Karl Eschweiler. [75]

But what sort of "political theology" did these mainly Protestant
theologians have in mind, and what was their attitude toward National
Socialism? Some of them, in particular the so-called German Christians, considered a total synthesis of Nazism and Christianity to be
possible and even desirable.[76] Hitler had himself removed the main obstacles between 1924 and 1928. In those years he distanced himself from
people he had long admired—Dietrich Eckart, Artur Dinter, and the
circle around Erich Ludendorff—who represented the wing of the
völkisch movement that made a religion out of Teutonism and was radically hostile to Christianity. [77]

In the period that followed, a German Protestant political theology
oriented toward *völkisch* thinking became increasingly popular. After the

Nazis took power in January 1933, the new rulers used this movement to promote Nazi policies within the church. Most notably, the extensive and quickly executed biologizing of theological and political metaphors in German law and society could rely on this theology.[78] In order to understand its nature, we need to stand back from certain ideas that are mainly linked to Schmitt. For example, political theology is *not* a history of ideas defining all the basic elements of political science as having theological origins, in this way identifying a structural relationship between theological and legal terms.[79] Likewise, it does not simply present an eschatological worldview opposed to the modern secularization process—although the construction of an "anti-secular front" was one of the most important political goals of Protestant political theology.[80] Rather, it was a movement that saw itself as modern and made the question of defining a "political ethic" into *the* central question of church policy and theological understanding.[81] At the same time it defined *political decision* as the most important criterion within theology.[82]

It is the case that every type of theology can in a sense be understood as political. But in the course of the Great War and during the Weimar Republic, a steadily growing group of mainly Protestant theologians discovered a new ethical center of gravity for a form of theology leaving hated liberalism behind. This center was the "fate" *(Schicksal)* of the *Volk* or "nation": a development closely tied to the talk of a "German God" and widespread religious nationalism emerging with the war.[83] Wilhelm Stapel, Friedrich Gogarten, Emanuel Hirsch, and Paul Althaus were the group's most important figures.[84] Correspondingly, in place of the old formula of throne—incarnation of order within the society and state— and altar, these theologians offered the more contemporary formula of God and *Volk*.[85] Here, *Volk* was understood, in Stapel's words, not as "an idea of human beings" but as an "idea of God."[86] In this way, the *Volk*-concept was systematically sacralized. Along with the more or less synonymous concept of "nation," it was seen not as the result of a historical development or political decision but of divine will. (The concept was thus openly informed by the Old and New Testament theme of the "chosen people."[87]) The shift in the basis of the legitimacy of rule from divine favor to popular sovereignty—a shift announced, of course, by the French Revolution—was in this case given a new and specifically Christian meaning. The question of the nature of just rule was meant to be theologically formulated; it was posed programmatically under the rubric of a Christian "theology of nationalism."[88] Thought of as a cultural, religious, and in part biological unity, the German *Volk* was thus set against the individualistic, contractual idea of the secular bourgeois nation, itself condemned as "western" or "French."[89]

In prompting a general spread of *völkisch* ideologies, the German defeat in 1918 also strengthened the roots of Protestant political theology. This affected the position of the Jews in German society: the concentration on a pseudoreligiously conceived "fate of the *Volk*," instead of the fate of the individual or of the secular democratic state, led to a massive intensification of Protestant debates about the "Jewish question."[90] From the perspective of the political theologians, the status of assimilated Jews within the salvational history of the German *Volk* seemed especially doubtful. With the sacralization of the national idea, these theologians could now draw closer to positions with which they had previously competed. In attacking the Jews as a counter-*Volk* or counter-race, proponents of *völkisch* antisemitism had rejected the missionary element in Christianity. But in the eyes of the Protestant political theologians as well as these antisemites, a conversion made a Jew into a "Jewish-Christian," certainly not into a "German." And for followers of both movements, conversion carried the inherent danger of rendering the Jews *invisible* elements in a *Volk*-mixture. This possibility catalyzed a massive defensive reaction.

Under the influence of political theology, German Protestantism itself drew increasingly close to *völkisch* ideology, sharing with it an absolutization and exaltation of the German *Volk*. Based on political theology, the "Religious Movement of German Christians" advocated Nazi positions in an increasingly open manner. Now notorious, the guidelines they issued on 26 May 1932 included the following clause: "We stand on the grounds of positive Christianity. We profess an affirmative belief in Christ appropriate to one's kind [*artgemäss*], as befitting the German Luther-spirit and heroic piety."[91] To a certain degree, from the new political-theological perspective *völkisch* antisemitism had to be approved, since it manifestly had the same goal: the fateful-heroic salvation of the German *Volk*. Political theology placed the church in a new position vis-à-vis this antisemitism, through a basic concern with upholding a God-given order it identified with the *Volk*. Suddenly, the Protestant church found itself indebted to the antisemites, hence obliged to channel their "rowdy" attitude in a more proper, legal direction.[92]

With this development, the problem of the so-called non-Aryan Christians took on a crucial role in discussions of theology and church law. True, the Jews could still convert to Christianity; to a degree the mission of completely converting the Jews was maintained. But this did not make the Jews part of the German *Volk*. For his part, Stapel had the idea of placing converted Jews in a kind of quarantine, in order that the conversion would only take full effect with their grandchildren:

> Whoever wishes to convert must take his rejection of the community so seriously that he desires both [the conversion and the rejection] not only for himself, and not for himself *as well*, but rather for his entire race [*Geschlecht*], hence for his descendents. He must take the martyrdom [*das Martyrium*] upon his person of relinquishing one community without having the right to enter the other community. The same with his offspring. Acceptance into the desired other community is only realized with the third generation. For the interval [*Karenzzeit*] placed between the generations furnishes a certain assurance that the conversion has not been undertaken in one's own interest but out of inner necessity.[93]

With his programmatic statement regarding "what we expect from National Socialism," Stapel spoke for a large number of Protestant political theologians. His turn away from the concept of a speedy missionizing of the Jews, his embrace of the concept of weighty obstacles placed in the path of the move from the "law of one community" to the "law of the other community," represented a shift in basic purpose. Missionizing the Jews in fact no longer occupied the foreground but rather protected the German *Volk* from Jewish influence.[94]

The "Total State" and Church Politics in 1933

Introduced into legal theory by Schmitt in 1922, the concept of political theology was mainly taken up at the time in connection with the German Christian movement; this movement considered a complete synthesis of Nazism and Christianity to be both conceivable and desirable. The existence of a *Volksnomos* was a central tenet of German Christian theology, which was rooted in a set of vulgarly romantic and idealistic ideas.[95] Wilhelm Stapel was a pioneer of this theology, his writings reflecting a certain reading of Herder, Arndt, de Lagarde, and above all Fichte. His political-theological doctrine was mainly directed against Judaism and assimilated Jewry. But his antisemitic energy was also aimed at Eastern European Jewry, *Ostjudentum*, which in his eyes destroyed "the symbiosis of Germans and Jews" through its "penetrating vitality."[96] Stapel thus agreed with Nazi ideologues on an important point. After 1933 he tried to practically realize his political-theological ideas by supporting a unified Protestant church that would accept the antisemitic "Aryan paragraphs," in subservience to the "Führer-principle."[97] Since Stapel did not wish to join the Nazi party, his practical political possibilities remained limited to his activities as a publicist; his close connections with Schmitt—himself increasingly more influential after 1933—changed nothing in this respect. Nevertheless, in 1933 Stapel's doctrine of the *Volksnomos* was one of the most-discussed theological schemas in Germany.[98] For this reason it had considerable impact on the later development of Nazi policies regarding the church.

In contrast, the close friendship between Schmitt and the German Christian activist and Rhineland bishop Heinrich Oberheid (1895–1977) had direct political consequences. Oberheid had been an intimate friend of Schmitt since the jurist's time in Bonn, probably since 1926.[99] In 1933 and 1934, he used Schmitt's political contacts and friendships in order to promote his radical plans for the church.[100] The friendship between Schmitt and Oberheid would survive World War II, Schmitt's admirers considering Oberheid their school's "mediator" and "ceremonial master."[101]

The example of Oberheid points to the mutual influence between Schmitt and Protestant political theology. A soldier in the Great War, Oberheid had pursued a highly varied career in the Weimar Republic. After the war, rather than continuing his earlier study of Evangelical theology and philosophy, he quickly wrote a dissertation in the field of state economics, then working as director of the Stinnes coal-trading and shipping concern.[102] His early political leanings are revealed in his membership between 1920 and 1922 in the radically antisemitic Deutsch-völkischer Schutz- und Trutzbund.[103] After the French march into the Ruhr area on 11 January 1922 Stinnes commissioned Oberheid to help organize German economic resistance. This led to his spending some days in prison, justly suspected by the French of economic sabotage. In 1925, following the death of Hugo Stinnes a year earlier, Oberheid left the Stinnes firm; in 1926 he again took up his theological studies in Bonn, his goal being a second doctorate. His friendship with both Carl Schmitt and Erik Peterson stemmed from this period.

As his biographer Faulenbach indicates, Oberheid's "path to the church" involved a "turn to National Socialism."[104] He joined the Nazi party in 1928 and the Sturmabteilung (SA) in 1929, then decided to become a clergyman. In February 1933 he was ordained for the clergy.[105] By the summer of 1933, having just been appointed pastor of a small congregation in the town of Ansbach, he stood at the head of the

Rhineland's German Christian movement.[106] His professional experience, German Christian convictions, and political connections now facilitated a speedy promotion to Rhineland bishop and "theological advisor" in the office of Reich Bishop Ludwig Müller.[107] Around this time, a recommendation from Carl Schmitt gave him access to Reich Justice Commissar Hans Frank, who named him advisor on questions of church law at the newly founded Academy for German Law. In this way, he was able to furnish his political plans for the church with an official party imprimatur.[108] But when it came to these plans, the connection Schmitt arranged to Prussian finance minister Johannes Popitz was even more important.[109] Schmitt thus had a decisive role in the advancement of Oberheid's career as an extreme representative of German Christian ideas—a role allowing his precipitous emergence as a key figure (together with August Jäger) in Nazi church politics.[110]

In his new position, Oberheid tried to apply Schmitt's idea of the "total state" to a reading of constitutional law harmonizing with his pro-Nazi church policies; he did so in close collaboration with his church colleague Heinrich Forsthoff.[111] Hence in the first years of Nazi rule Schmitt's ideas—those of a "Catholic" jurist—had as great an importance for Protestant church policy as did his political connections. The dazzling idea of the "total state" was here paramount. It could be used to push the Protestant church toward the Nazi state, against the expressed will of the Confessional Church and many church members.[112] The German Christians' "total state" was meant to be a Nazi state tolerating no independent church and supervising the church's activities. Oberheid defined the liberal idea of religious freedom as a *contradictio in adjecto*.[113]

Schmitt had already used the term "total state" a few years before Hitler became chancellor.[114] He first used the term in a critical sense: as a comment on bourgeois society's increasing tendency to make social and economic matters a concern of the state.[115] The term would now be promoted as a political slogan with a very different meaning. In 1932 it was already being used as a battle-slogan in circles surrounding Schmitt and his students. Its first use by Schmitt in this new sense was in a talk he delivered before the Langnamen Society in Düsseldorf shortly after he had warned against the "slogan" of the "total state" being "pinned" upon him.[116] Schmitt here drew a distinction between a liberal total state stamped by "weakness" and an antithetical, "strength"-stamped total state that could tell friend from foe. (He was here appropriating a distinction that had been proposed by Waldemar Gurian.) But only the term's latter sense was taken up in its increasingly wide reception.[117]

With Hitler's takeover of power, the concept of a state that was strong "in the sense of quality"[118] attracted increasing interest. At the center of the discussion of the "total state" by Schmitt and his students in 1933 was the "essence" *(Wesen)* of the Nazi state: after the Enabling Act of 24 March 1933, could Germany still be basically understood as a bourgeois constitutional state? Or should it now be understood as fully ruled by the law of the "total state"?[119] This debate was also of great importance for the Evangelical Church, which was facing the question of whether the Weimar Republic's laws should still be considered valid. If they were actually invalid in the framework of the "total state," then the legal separation of church and state, as stipulated in Article 137 of the republic's constitution, itself no longer existed.[120] In addition, if the Enabling Act were not merely a temporary emergency law but actually a "provisional constitutional law," then all previous constitutional laws were in fact null and void.[121] Even with such an interpretation of the Enabling Act, very different paths naturally could be taken by the Evangelical Church. For broad circles in the church, the traditionally narrow ties between German Lutheranism and the state suggested that *Führertum* and *Artgleichheit* should be made the basis for a new ecclesiastical order.[122] Schmitt's political contacts and concept of the "total state," the latter gaining widespread appeal through the work of his friends and students, played a leading role in the development of a co-opted Nazi Evangelical Church.

The Nomos of Wilhelm Stapel and Albrecht Erich Günther

In fulfilling both its theological and practical political needs, Protestant political theology relied on Schmitt. For his part, the jurist Schmitt made use of the conceptual arsenal of Protestant political theology. In particular, he used the nomos concept, which he juxtaposed ever-more directly with a bourgeois concept of law he viewed as "Jewish"-influenced. The mutual ties at work are a key to understanding both the political theology of Schmitt's constitutional theory and his attitude toward "the Jews." It is thus striking that for a long time this mutual influence was largely neglected in work on both Schmitt and the German church in the Nazi period.[123] Put pointedly, the semantic field that Schmitt laid out through his nomos concept can only be grasped by taking account of this radical theological current.[124] Since Schmitt developed this seminal concept of Protestant political theology into a core aspect of his constitutional theory, it is helpful to explore the idea's political semantics.[125]

It is important to note for a start that the Protestant political theologians fused the concept of the nomos so tightly with that of the *Volk* that we can speak of a "theology of the *Volk*-nomos." Albrecht Erich Günther thus declared that the nomos functioned "for the concrete polis" in the same way as did the "*Volkheit* for the concrete *Volk*."[126] In the course of the Weimar period, a *theological orientation,* complementing an intense concern with the *Volk,* emerged at the center of the world of ideas inhabited by Young Conservative ideologues. In 1930 this development was intensified through classical philologist Hans Bogner's polemical introduction of the nomos concept.[127] For Bogner, "nomos" signified "the order of life ordained by the gods" in the Greek polis. He saw the nomos as "corroded" *(zersetzt)* by the Sophistic enlighteners. Spirit was still biologically bound up in the nomos, which was manifest as the unity of laws and origin and simultaneously as a divine commandment whose strict observance was an unbreakable duty. Bogner thus defined the nomos as a biologically determined, sanctified order inside a political entity.[128]

Wilhelm Stapel and Albrecht Erich Günther were friends of Schmitt and coeditors of *Deutsches Volkstum.* Adapting Bogner's approach to the nomos, they gave it a central function in Protestant political theology. For both authors, the nomos represented the "life spirit of political unity itself, formed by that spirit over a long span of time." For both, following Bogner, it amounted to a divine law meant to determine the life of every human being and every people.[129] It is worth noting that Günther was willing to go rather far afield, to "Africa," in his application of the nomos concept.[130] But more significantly in this context, in Bogner's wake both Günther and Stapel steadily aimed it at those they viewed as undermining the divine law. Stapel could thus present his attack on Judaism and the Jews as a purely defensive struggle, one meant to save the German *Volksnomos* from its most dire enemy. The same strategy would be taken up by Schmitt.

It is no coincidence that Stapel used the nomos concept for the first time in relation to Judaism—more precisely, in the context of the question "is the racial question an obstacle to Christianity?"[131] Informing this question was Stapel's concern that Nazi racism, centered as it was around what he himself viewed as a fundamental "opposition between Germans and Jews," might pose an obstacle to Christianity on the road to Nazism.[132] Arguing against Hans Günther's racial theories, Stapel first asserted that the Nazi movement was not bound to any specific scientific racial theory.[133] (In this respect it is notable that in the same period he did not hesitate, in reflections over a "practical solution to the

Jewish question," to define the "physical appearance" of "the Jew" as
posing a problem for "the disposition of the Jews toward being German
[*Deutschtum*].") "The doctrine of the special value of the Nordic race,"
Stapel indicated, was not officially binding on the party; it was merely a
"predilection" *(Liebhaberei)* of certain circles. In this way he underplayed
the problem posed by racial antisemitism for a Christian theology that
had not yet entirely abandoned its universalistic missionary ideas: He
came to the lapidary conclusion that "racial questions and Christianity
are not in contact." But at the same time, *antisemitism*, he stressed, was
indeed official party doctrine, while also being legitimated by Christianity. Stapel introduced the nomos concept in this context: "We find
Christianity's great confrontation with Judaism as a religious national
community [*religiöse Volksgemeinde*] with its special 'nomos' in the New
Testament itself."[134]

Namely, the New Testament itself recognized the inferiority of the
Jewish nomos, which Paul considered "valid for the Jews themselves, but
only as a first step towards belief."[135] Every "genuine people" *(echte Volk)*
including the Jews had its nomos, determining the "hierarchy of values
in a national community [*Volksgemeinschaft*]."[136] As Wolfgang Tilgner has
shown, the effort to practically realize the idea of the *Volksnomos* meant
elevating the biological structure of the historical *Volk* to a mandatory
national-religious doctrine.[137] The antisemitic thrust of this "pseudo-
religious development"[138] is more or less innate. Stapel popularized
what he termed his "theology of nationalism" in numerous publications, embedding it in his doctrine of the *Volksnomos.*

This doctrine involved an effort to solve the central problem of what
Waldemar Gurian described as the "new nationalism," referring to the
"conservative revolutionaries" and above all the Nazis: following defeat
in the Great War, how was Germany to find an authority creating and
standing for political unity?[139] Together with Günther, Stapel attempted
to ground this unity in an eschatologically conceived "German
nomos."[140] For both figures, this nomos unfolded in sharp opposition to
the "nomos of the Jews"; in a sharp distortion of reality, Judaism was
here identified with the Torah, the Old Testament, and sometimes the
Ten Commandments alone. Importantly, the identification itself had
deep historical roots, their source apparently being an incorrect Greek
translation of *torah* (Hebrew "teaching") as "nomos" and a subsequent
incorrect Latin translation of "nomos" as *lex*. This was one basis for the
traditional prejudicial Christian definition of Judaism as a legalistic religion,[141] as well as for the centuries-long failure of Christian theologians

to acknowledge the Talmud, not the Torah, as the main basis of Jewish law.[142] For its part, Stapel's nomos-theory involved a disparagement of the Old Testament, which he understood as a *"Sachsenspiegel for the Jews"* — the reference here being to the most important medieval compilation of Saxon custom-based law. As such, it was in his view not binding for a "German Christianity" *(deutsches Christentum)*.[143]

Stapel thus sharpened a critical stance toward the Old Testament that is part of the Lutheran tradition and that has sometimes intensified into complete rejection. Even an author such as Adolf von Harnack, seen as a liberal Protestant, opposed the book of the Old Covenant to that of the New Covenant and the Gospels, denying the Old Testament's canonic authority in the process: "For that which is Christian cannot be perceived in it."[144] Many years after Harnack, against the backdrop of the mass murder of the European Jews, Ernst Jünger and Carl Schmitt appear to have shared a fear of, precisely, a "Jewish morality" stemming from the Old Testament and now become "virulent": "There is only a choice between the Old and New Testaments: every attack upon the New is to the benefit of the Old. This is one of the reasons for the enormous spread of Jewish morals, putting aside the fact that this morality has now become free and virulent through the extermination of the Jews to whom it was tied."[145]

Paul already defined the difference between Judaism and Christianity in terms of the law: "For Christ is the end of the law and brings righteousness to every one who has faith" (Rom. 10:4).[146] Stapel placed the "nomoi" present in the "conscience" of those nations called to Christianity on an equal footing with the nomos of the Jews.[147] He rejected the possibility of a universally binding Christian moral law, hence of a nomos with a claim to validity beyond a specific national framework: something he saw applying particularly to the Ten Commandments. For this reason Karl Barth considered Stapel's theses to be a "complete betrayal of the Gospels." Jesus himself, Barth indicated, had never renounced the observation of Jewish laws. Consequently, the nomos concept emerged as a focal point in the unfolding *Kirchenkampf,* the conflict within German Protestantism between German Christians and other Christians not wishing to collaborate with the regime.[148]

A basic principle following from the *Volksnomos* doctrine is the impossibility of Jews and Christians — and of "Jews" and "Germans" — being subject to a single law, or part of a single political structure. For this reason, Stapel looked positively on Herzl's Zionist vision.[149] At the same time, he viewed the very existence of an emancipated German Jewry as a provocation. The civil rights that Articles 136 and 137 of the Weimar constitution guaranteed all German citizens, whatever their confession, were antithetical to the idea of homogeneity cherished by the Protestant political theologians. As Stapel put it, they were antithetical to the common interest of "Germans and Jews in their real communities—let us call them *Deutschtum* and *Judentum*—remaining untangled [*unverwirrt*]."[150] For the homogeneity guaranteeing the political unity of the German *Volk* was meant to stand under a Christian law tinged with political theology. Anchored in a God-given *Volksnomos*, that law could not and was not meant to be applied to the Jews.

The theology of the *Volksnomos* had clear political implications for the legal situation of Germany's Jews. In a special issue of the *Europäische Revue* devoted to the "Jewish question," Albrecht Erich Günther formulated his approach to the question in the framework of this theology.[151] By the time of the article's appearance, Günther had become a close friend of Schmitt, and his remarks reflected Schmitt's strong influence.[152] His opening premise was that the "aversion [*Abneigung*] toward recognizing the Jews as fellow Germans [*Volksgenossen*]" was "almost universal," this aversion being understood as the "sign of a metaphysical enmity":

> Carl Schmitt has shown that the essence of the political is the distinction between friend and enemy. For this reason everything political is oriented toward the emergency [*Ernstfall*], namely toward existential extinction through violence [*Vernichtung durch Gewalt*]. The political draws its characteristically penetrating tension from the possibility of this emergency. . . . To the extent the German *Volk* is disinclined [*abgeneigt*] to recognize the Jews as fellow Germans, it is expressing the conviction that the Jews do not share our distinction between friend and enemy. This is not meant to express the suspicion that the Jews evade their civic duty, a suspicion that could be considered refuted de facto, but rather that our struggle is not and cannot be their struggle in the same sense. This conviction is not only grounded in the insight that for Jewry [*das Judentum*] as an international community every war amounts to a catastrophe. Rather, in the most extreme emergency it is here palpable that Jewry lives from another vital law [*Lebensgesetz*] than our *Volk*. Every *Volk* has its own nomos, a law of growth that is characteristically its own, achieving its expression in its life forms and in its valuations.[153]

This reasoning led Günther to define "exemption of the Jews from military service" as a necessity, hence to argue for annulling the most important facet of German Jewry's emancipation in the nineteenth century. His purpose, he indicated, was creating "a new order" for the Jews as part of a project to "put a new stamp on the political nature [*Staatlichkeit*] of the Germans."[154] The argument for "exemption" and the conviction that Jews could not share the German friend-enemy distinction were aimed at acknowledging a "split between legal participation in civil society and denial of membership in the *Volk* [*Volksgenossenschaft*]."[155] Günther makes use of a particularly revealing quasi-egalitarian rhetoric to express his vision of Jewish fate in the framework of a new Germany. The framework is that of a "well-constructed state" in which a "noble sense of rule" *(vornehme Herrschaftsgesinnung)* prevails, and which "is capable, to the extent it is up to us, of granting the Jews temporal justice — until the day on which Israel's destiny [*Verhängnis*] ends and the blindfold is removed from the synagogue's eyes (2 Cor. 3:13–16)."[156] In this passage, the political implications of the nomos doctrine become fully apparent. The decision in favor of a *völkisch* nomos and against a bourgeois-constitutional concept of law makes any political integration of Germany's Jews structurally impossible.

The Nomos of Carl Schmitt

In what manner did Schmitt use the idea of the nomos in his discussion of constitutional law and the state?[157] This question is linked to the question of the concept's general role in German constitutional theory after its transfer from Greek philosophy to the Weimar Republic's political-theological discourse. Bound as it was to a specific *Volk*, the concept was clearly very well suited for Schmitt's polemic against Hans Kelsen's "pure theory of law," with its claims to universal validity. More broadly, it was very well suited for Schmitt's struggle against the basic universal principles of the liberal constitutional state. His confrontation with these principles needs to be scrutinized against the backdrop of the secularization thesis he presented in *Political Theology:* "all pregnant concepts of modern political theory are secularized theological concepts."[158] Following Schmitt, then, the bourgeois constitutional state's notion of law—the basis of political liberalism—gains its potency through its origins in secularized theology. Looking back in 1950, Schmitt observed that the German word for "law," *das Gesetz*, was an especially difficult word since present-day German was (in contrast to French, the juridical language par excellence[159]) "to a large extent theologians' language."[160] The word was "deeply entangled" in the theological opposition between "(Jewish) law and (Christian) grace, (Jewish) law and (Christian) gospel."[161] Luther had elevated this "theological opposition" to the constitutive horizon of Christian theology. To do so, he had drawn on Paul's distinction between the law on the one hand, and Christ, grace, and spirit, on the other hand, on Augustine's distinction between spirit and letter, and on medieval scholastic discussions of the Old and New Covenants.[162] Following Stapel, Schmitt defined the idea of a constitutional state as rooted in what he understood as the Jewish law of the Old Testament. At the same time, the nomos of Protestant political theology furnished Schmitt with the possibility of founding a new "law" with no ties to the bourgeois-constitutional order.

Although *The Nomos of the Earth (Der Nomos der Erde)* was first published in 1950, parts of it represent material from the Nazi period. Schmitt devotes one section of the book to the connections between law and nomos,[163] thus giving clearer contours to his notion of a thinking based on "concrete-order."[164] The book offers important clues regarding the genesis of the historical-political semantics of the nomos concept. Nevertheless, due to its late appearance, it needs to be used with great caution in trying to understand the concept's function for Schmitt during the Nazi period. In English, the book's full title is *The Nomos of the Earth in the International Law of Jus Publicum Europaeum* [European Public Law]. As the title indicated, in 1950 Schmitt was no longer openly interested in a "nomos of the German *Volk*"[165] meant to replace an idea of law that was *artfremd*. Now he was interested, it seemed, in the presence of the idea of a "nomos of the earth" in European international law.[166]

Ironically, Schmitt pointed for the first time to the political-theological and *völkisch* origins of his nomos concept in a remark meant to distance itself from those origins. "I have a great deal of respect," he wrote, "for the efforts of Wilhelm Stapel and Hans Bogner, which have endowed the 'nomos' with the significance of a 'vital law.' But I am troubled both by the word 'life,' degenerated [*entartet* (!)] as it is into a biological realm, and the word 'law,' which must be avoided here under all circumstances."[167] In actuality, the nomos concept Schmitt placed at the center of his "concrete order"-based thinking in *On the Three Types of Juristic Thought* can be understood only in relation to his own, radically biologizing political thought: a biologizing already apparent in his earlier use of the notion of *Artgleichheit*.

In the face of Schmitt's retrospective self-denial, it is useful to return to that text's most striking passage:

> The different peoples and races are aligned with different types of thinking, and spiritual—and with it political—rule over a people can be tied to the dominance of a specific type of thinking. There are peoples that exist without land, without state, without church, but only in the *Gesetz*. For them normativistic thinking appears the only rational legal thinking, and every other kind of thought incomprehensible, mystic, fantastic, or ridiculous.[168]

Against this "rule or *Gesetz*-based thinking [*Regeln- oder Gesetzesdenken*] (normativism)"—again, a transparent reference to Judaism—Schmitt sets "Germanic thinking," with its focus on "concrete order."[169] For any serious historian, his effort, supported by some of his former students, to retroactively remove his thinking from its *völkisch*, Nazi context and defend it as an approach stamped by Catholicism is simply misleading. To fully understand why this is so, we need to further consider the reasons for Schmitt's rejection of any translation of "nomos" as "law."

Schmitt already uses the nomos concept in his *Constitutional Theory (Verfassungslehre)* of 1928. In doing so, he is taking over Heinrich Triepel's critique of the Reichstag's legislators for failing to subordinate *Gesetz* to *Recht*,[170] in order to deepen and render concrete his own criticism of the "reign of *Gesetz*" in the bourgeois constitutional state. "Law is not holy as *Gesetz*; law is only holy as *Recht*," he argues.[171] He then defines *Gesetz* as subservient to *Recht*, juxtaposing the "helpless formalism" of a positive understanding of law with a "truly understood concept" with "certain qualities."[172] In this context, Schmitt's designation of the nomos as "precisely what is lacking" to create the concept of a "true law" (*echtes Gesetz*) deserves special attention. Although at this point he does not completely avoid the nomos concept, he also does not develop the distinction that will emerge in *The Nomos of the Earth* between nomos and *Gesetz*; but the Triepel citation itself points to the sacral and theological nature of his idea of law. In both the *Nomos of the Earth* and supplementary texts (for which he used the unusual term *Corollarien*), Schmitt reflects on the original usage of the term "nomos," in order to justify a standpoint he defines as both antipositivist and antinaturalist.[173] He here views the term as signifying *more* than merely "true" or "authentic" law, *echtes Gesetz*. He views it as above all denoting—as in the Greek—appropriation, the taking of land, and then dividing and pasturing. These concepts evoke a unity of space and order, locus and law as *Recht*. They harmonize with Schmitt's desire to negate the abstract understanding of law as *Gesetz*. With help of the three foundational categories of the nomos—taking, dividing, pasturing—Schmitt hopes to mediate between the polarities of existence and obligation, right and power, state and economy.

It is striking how Schmitt's circling around the etymological meaning of the nomos in *On the Three Types of Juristic Thought* is complemented with a turn back to Pindar as the concept's supposed source. He thus defines the Greek poet as destined to stand for a sacralized, non-normative and non-Jewish type of law. More precisely, he supports his argument with a particular interpretation of the nomos basileus, an interpretation he claims is being offered by the poet Friedrich Hölderlin in a cryptic passage from the poet's commentary on his own translation of Pindar. Schmitt cites the passage as follows:

> The *nomos*, the law [*das Gesetz*], is here the same as discipline [*die Zucht*, with its simultaneous connotation of "rearing" and "training"], in that it is the form within which man encounters himself and the god [*der Gott*], the church and the law of the state [*Staatsgesetz*] and precepts [*Satzungen*] inherited from past ages, which, more strictly than art, hold on to the living connections in which a people [*ein Volk*] has met and meets itself over time."[174]

The citation is of Hölderlin's gloss on the following lines from his Pindar translation: "The law, / the King of everyone, mortal and / immortal; it steers just / so with force / The most just law with the highest of all hands."[175] On the basis of the citation, Schmitt argues that Hölderlin is here himself describing a narrow connection between nomos and ruler—Schmitt even speaks of an identical *Gestalt*.

Schmitt refers to Hölderlin's remarks as "eternally correct." However, it would appear that Hölderlin never offered them in such a form. At least in the edition of Hölderlin's collected works published by Norbert von Hellingrath in 1928—an edition that was already considered authoritative on account of its high philological standards at the time Schmitt's *On the Three Types of Juristic Thought* was published—the passage in question reads as follows:

> But strict mediation is the law [*das Gesez*]. But for this reason it forcibly steers the most just law with the highest of all hands. Discipline [*die Zucht*], to the extent it is the form in which man encounters himself and the god, the church and state law and inherited precepts (the holiness of God and for men the possibility of a recognition, and explanation), these forcibly steer the most just law with the highest of all hands, they hold on more strictly than art

to the living connections in which a people has met and meets itself over time. "King" here signifies the superlative that is only the sign for the highest ground of cognition, not for the highest power.

Both in the identification of "the law" as "strict mediation" and the definition of "[this law,] the king" with "the superlative that is only the sign for the highest ground of cognition," the passage in the Hellingrath edition differs drastically from the version Schmitt offers. The differences underscore all the more sharply Schmitt's determination to *use* Hölderlin in support of his claim for an original connection between nomos and king—between the will of the Führer, Adolf Hitler, and the "nomos of the German *Volk*." At the same time, it is clear that Schmitt is here trying to align his concept of the nomos with a specific, ideological approach to Hölderlin. This approach, emerging from a nearly identical reading of Nietzsche, was highly popular in Germany in the interwar period. It involved the poet's apotheosis as spiritual savior of the Germans: as a central figure in a pan-German allegory constituting both a response to and apology for the German catastrophe in the Great War.[176] But as the source of the nomos throughout Schmitt's oeuvre, Protestant political theology, not Hölderlin, here actually informs Schmitt's self-stylization in terms of an artificial tradition.

In all his elaborations on the nomos concept, Schmitt voiced his opposition to the mistaken translation of the Greek word "nomos" with the Latin word "lex"—in other words with law as *Gesetz,* bound up for Schmitt with Jewish-normative rootlessness.[177] Schmitt maintained that the translation error could be traced back to the Jewish Hellenistic philosopher Philo of Alexandria, who equated nomos and *Gesetz* in connection with the Old Testament.

Rejecting the apologetics of much of the work on Schmitt, with its division of his career and writing into distinct phases, we need to acknowledge the lasting quality of his anti-Jewish discourse. This discourse is manifest in his early assertion of a "Jewish" mistranslation of the nomos concept; it is likewise manifest in the concept's propagation by Schmitt as the fulcrum of his "concrete order"–based thinking—as the starting point for a "new idea . . . of what a jurist is."[178] In his postwar writings, he defines the fundamental connection between order and space, law and locus as rejected by *one people alone:* a people without its own land, existing among alien peoples as a "guest nation." And once again, we find the assertion that the Pentateuch served as an "abstract law" for the Jews in their Diaspora situation. He now adds that "rootless" law made its way in this manner into the Christian tradition.[179]

Nuremberg—"The Constitution of Freedom"

Schmitt only infrequently referred directly to Jews and Judaism. Nevertheless, he placed great emphasis on furnishing Jews with *names* clearly marking them as Jews. In reality, the "name problem" was bound up with a question of basic importance for the feasibility of Nazi antisemitic policies: that of the administrative-bureaucratic definition of Jews.[180] Who was to be considered a member of this group? Like many other antisemites, Schmitt believed that "Jewish names" were among the most important markers of otherwise "invisible" assimilated Jews. Correspondingly, names were a repeated theme of Nazi laws and edicts. The Prussian justice ministry concerned itself with the problem for the first time on 3 April 1933: "Applications for change of name on the part of Jews: in Prussia such applications are to be forwarded to the Justice Ministry for confirmation, in order to prevent the origins from being masked." On 22 April a decree was issued with the following contents: "Forbidden to use Jewish names for spelling when conveying telegrams by telephone."[181]

Legally mandating the names "Sarah" and "Israel" for all German Jews was the most notorious reflection of the Nazi antisemitic obsession with names. A clear distinction of Jews from non-Jews became an urgent matter as soon as passing and enforcing anti-Jewish laws was on the agenda. In the 1890s the antisemitic members of the German Reichstag had failed to submit a single anti-Jewish law because they could not agree on how to define a Jew.[182] As the antisemites had always presumed they could formulate a definition among themselves, this represented no problem on a party level. In their party program of 24 February 1920 the Nazis already spelled out their enemies: "Only *Volkgenossen* can become citizens. Only those with German blood, regardless of confession, are *Volksgenossen*. For this reason no Jew can become a *Volksgenosse*."[183] But the underlying problem remained. When facing the task of formulating the "Law on the Restoration of the Civil Service" (meant to exclude Jews from such service) that would be passed on 7 April 1933, the Nazi interior ministry had to try to solve the problem. The ministry was headed by Wilhelm Frick together with State Secretary Wilhelm Stuckart, who was responsible for legislation and basic law.[184] The initial strategy they came up with involved an avoidance of the terms "Jew" and

"Judaism," referring instead to officials of "non-Aryan origin" being forcibly retired.[185] A "Decree on the Execution of the Law on the Restoration of the Civil Service" of 11 April 1933 then specified that "non-Aryan origin" applied to persons that had "non Aryan, especially Jewish parents. It is sufficient that at least one Jewish parent or grandparent is non-Aryan. It is thus to be presumed particularly when at least one parent or grandparent *belonged to the Jewish religion.*"[186] In this manner, in contrast to the usual assumption of historians, the Nazi interior ministry offered no "racially" grounded criteria for defining the terms "Jew" and "Aryan." Since racist fantasies could not be empirically proven, the central criterion had to remain religious affiliation.

Following Hitler's orders, the "Reich Flag Law," the "Reich Citizenship Law," and finally the notorious "Law for the Protection of German Blood and German Honor" were passed at the "Reich Party Conference of Freedom" held in Nuremberg on 15 September 1935. This latter law marked the first time the explicit focus was not on "non-Aryans" but on "Jews." Marriage "between Jews and citizens with German blood or related blood-kind [*artverwandtes Blut*]" was directly forbidden.[187] In addition, the law forbade "Jews" "to employ female citizens of German or related blood-kind under 45 years old in their households" or "raise the flag of Reich and nation."[188] Nevertheless, the law lacked any stipulation of who was a "Jew"; long discussions of this issue then took place between the Nazi party and the interior ministry, with final acceptance of a suggestion of ministerial council Lösener, laid out in a "Decree Regarding the Reich Citizenship Law" of 14 November 1935 (§5,1): "Whoever has stemmed from at least three grandparents who are fully Jewish [*volljüdisch*] by race is Jewish." But this decree itself did not explain how to define belonging to the Jewish "race," and the explanation would not be supplied elsewhere. The decree settled for the explanation that "grandparents are always [*ohne weiteres*] to be considered fully Jewish when they belonged to the Jewish religious community" (§2,2).[189]

Raul Hilberg is thus correct in indicating that in actuality these laws and decrees were only termed "racial laws" for propagandistic purposes.[190] They contain no "racially" grounded criteria, but rather rely on religion. In order for, say, an applicant to the SS to demonstrate purely "Aryan" origins, he had to present his own birth and baptismal certificates as well as those of his parents and grandparents. Since before 1875 births were registered only by the churches in Germany, the German churches had administrative duties in the initial steps of the Nazi extermination process.[191] For realization of the various phases of the Nazi anti-Jewish campaign—definition, dispossession, expulsion, ghettoization, deportation, extermination—it was thus in the end unimportant whether or not the antisemitic *Weltanschauung* was legally supported by racial or religious criteria.[192] The only important thing was the bureaucracy having specifications that could be set in practice.

Immediately after the "Reich Party Conference of Freedom," Schmitt wrote a commentary in the *Deutsche Juristen-Zeitung* greeting the three new laws, which he described as "the constitution of freedom, the core of our present-day German law."[193] These were not simply "important laws alongside others," he indicated. Rather, they represented the source of "what will be named morality and public order, decency and proper manners."[194] Against "Germany's enemies and parasites" (1133), against the "typical camouflage-forms of alien rule" (1133), the "demon of degeneration [*Entartung*]" (1135), and "alien spiritual rule" (1134), for the first time in many centuries the concepts at work in the constitution were "once more German" (1134). With "German blood and German honor" rendered central juridical terms after the laws of 15 September, the German people was now truly "*deutsches Volk*," in the legal sense (1135). In another, longer article also focusing mainly on the Nuremberg Laws, first delivered at a 28 November 1935 meeting of the International Law Association in Berlin and then published in the *Zeitschrift der Akademie für Deutsches Recht*, Schmitt stressed the "essentially *defensive* character of our racial legislation." He then observed that "the fundamental *völkisch*-defensive character of not only these laws but the entire National Socialist worldview here emerges in convincing fashion. All further complications and nuances are taken care of effortlessly by recognizing this, since the National Socialist legislator has himself decided the greatest and most difficult portion of this entire set of problems."[195]

It is interesting that at one point in his commentary on the Nuremberg Laws, Schmitt hazarded a distinction between Jewish and German liberalism. He formulated the distinction in terms of an effort to protect "German jurists" from their Jewish counterparts: "We do not wish to disparage our liberal forefathers. They were Germans and belong to us. Penetrating the errors of their liberal views, the German substance is also discernable in their case, and the voice of German blood is often audible. What German jurist could not presently distinguish a Lorenz von Stein from a Stahl-Jolson, a Rudolf Gneist from a Lasker, a Rudolf Sohm from a Friedberg?"[196] It is by now a truism that the Nazi laws embraced so warmly by Schmitt contained radically antiliberal and antisemitic elements replacing basic civil rights with criteria defined as "racial": "Only the citizen [*Staatsbürger*] of German or related blood-kind is a citizen of the Reich [*Reichsbürger*]. . . . The citizen of the Reich is the sole bearer of complete political rights according to the law."[197] Such formulations were aimed first and foremost at the Jews. For both Schmitt and the Nazis, the linkage between Judaism and liberalism was as self-evident as it was inevitable. Nevertheless, the linkage posed a clear-cut problem for Schmitt: If it was so self-evident and inevitable, why had so many non-Jewish jurists offered liberal arguments? How could one aim at "Jewish" jurists without placing "Aryan" jurists at equal risk? The problem could be confronted on very different levels, Schmitt's response being both simple and illuminating: "Our liberal fathers and grandfathers" were not to be made responsible for liberal thinking, as they were simply "entangled in the conceptual net of non-German systems."[198] Still, the flat distinction expressed here, involving a completely contentless "German substance" or, even more irrationally, "voice of German blood,"[199] fell far short of a detailed explanation of the relationship between liberal and Jewish thinking. Schmitt only exhaustively considered the distinction, as well as the relationship, in 1936—at that point going as far as to devote an entire, elaborate academic conference to the general theme.

4

"Judaism in Legal Studies"

Schmitt's active antisemitic engagement had its highpoint in his organization and chairmanship of a conference organized by the Reichsgruppe Hochschullehrer des Nationalsozialistischen Rechtswahrerver-
bund (Reich Group of University Teachers in the National Socialist
Association of Legal Guardians) on "Judaism in Legal Studies," meeting
in Berlin on 3 and 4 October 1936.[1] According to the front matter of the
conference proceedings, "far more than a hundred university teachers
of law and economics from all *Gauen* of the Reich" participated.[2] The
proceedings inform us that taking part in the conference were a "Reich-
group-ruler," and that State Council Carl Schmitt greeted representatives of the German Legal Front, the Reich Office of the National
Socialist Party, the ministerial office of Reich Minister Dr. Frank, the
Academy for German Law, and various other Nazi organizations including the German Christians and members of the Institute for the
Study of the Jewish Question.[3] *Gauleiter* Julius Streicher was "prevented
from coming" and could only telegraph his "greetings and best wishes"
for the success of the conference; Schmitt's mentor Hans Frank could
himself not attend, his address being read by Lower-Court Counsel
Dr. Gubrod.[4] We know that these absences were the result of an intense
power struggle between the SD and Schmitt—a struggle that would
take a turn in Schmitt's favor during the conference itself.[5] There was
another absence: one of Schmitt's close friends, the Rhineland Bishop
and German Christian activist Heinrich Oberheid. On a postcard he
mailed to Schmitt's wife, he indicated that he had "so very much looked
forward" to attending the "Jew conference" *(Judentagung)*.[6]

The other talks delivered at the conference were as follows: "Judaism
in Economic Theory" by Reich Lecturer Dr. Rath (Göttingen); "Judaism
in Constitutional Law" by Prof. Dr. Tatarin-Tarnheyden (Rostock);

"Judaism in Administrative Law" by Prof. Dr. Maunz (Freiburg); "Judaism in Competition Law" by Dr. Rilk, attorney (Berlin); "Judaism in Civil Law" by Lecturer Dr. Bartholmeyczik (Breslau); "Judaism in Trade Law" by Prof. Dr. Würdinger (Breslau); "Positivism, Free-Law Theory, New Theory of Legal Sources" by Prof. Dr. Jung (Marburg); "Judaism in Penal Law" by Prof. Dr. Klee (Berlin); "Judaism in Criminal Psychology" by Dr. Mikorey (Munich); "Judaism and Criminality" by Dr. v. Leers (Berlin);[7] "The Influence of Jewish Theorists on German Theory of International Law" by Lecturer Dr. Gürke (Munich); and "Judaism in International Civil Law" by Prof. Dr. Müller (Freiburg).[8] When it comes to the level of the talks, their titles speak for themselves. The fact that all these scholars, some of them with prominent university chairs, were ready to support such a conference underscores the extent to which Schmitt's antisemitic engagement harmonized with that of his colleagues.

In Schmitt's formulation, the goal of the conference was to mark a decisive beginning in the scholarly "struggle," "as difficult as it is necessary," "against the claims to dominance of the Jewish essence [*jüdisches Wesen*] and Jewish spirit [*jüdischer Geist*]."[9] Along with Hofmann and Göppinger, Koenen has discussed the conference at greatest length; he argues that another, hidden goal, that of "setting Christian anti-Jewish motifs against racial antisemitism," lay behind the formulation.[10] But for reasons already detailed above, the argument, framed by Koenen's broad interpretation of Schmitt in terms of "Reich theology," seems very dubious; the notion of a sharp distinction between two forms of anti-Jewish ideology is historically ill founded. There is in any case no compelling evidence of Schmitt speaking up at the conference in favor of a specifically Christian form of anti-Judaism, however we define it. What emerges far more clearly in both his talks is an expression of his own form of "reflective" racial antisemitism.[11]

In his opening remarks for the conference, Schmitt offered a religiously couched "phrase of the Führer" as a guiding principle: "In defending myself against the Jew, I am fighting for the work of the Lord." He ended his final remarks with the same citation.[12] For Koenen, this double gesture is what reveals Schmitt's effort to push the "anti-Judaistic motif into the foreground" — "anti-Judaistic" here signaling "Christian" rather than racist prejudices. Horst Göppinger offers a more plausible assessment of the conference's function: "The Nazis in power were manifestly intent on winning precisely the university teachers as champions of Nazi racial theories, in order to give the impression that the persecution of the Jews was no outbreak of the primitive, but rather a defense against the destructive effects of Judaism in legal theory, a cry of help by the violated German spirit [*Geist*] against the 'Jewish anti-spirit' [*Ungeist*]."[13] But the Hitler-citation itself speaks against Koenen's reading in that it demonstrates the Nazi readiness to mix Christian themes with racism for the sake of the "Führer-state."[14]

Hans Frank used similar formulas; Frank certainly counted among the Nazi movement's "old warriors" and can hardly be aligned with an "anti-Judaistic," which is to say Christian, perspective. In his function as Reich Jurists' Leader *(Reichsjuristenführer)*, Frank thus greeted the Führer at the Leipzig Conference of Jurists held in autumn 1933 with these words: "German Jurists, we swear allegiance and obedience with all our might in this divine struggle for right, the eternal right of the German *Volk*. . . ."[15] Here as well, the difficulty the Nazis had in severing their "racial" antisemitism from its Christian roots is evident. This was the case in both its "pure" and politically instrumentalized forms.

The two other guiding phrases selected by Schmitt for the conference stemmed, respectively, from Frank and party-hero Theodor von der Pfordten (killed on 9 November 1923 in the course of the Hitler-putsch[16]). Both phrases warn the "German *Volk*" of the "Jewish danger" and of a "flood of un-German efforts" to undermine the "state structure"—to penetrate "our scholarship [*Wissenschaft*] with deadly poison." Neither phrase invites identification of a specific "anti-Judaistic" tradition standing apart and opposed to "racial" antisemitism. The remaining contents of Schmitt's opening address themselves offer no support to Koenen's thesis. We here find a programmatic observation that "a merely emotionally grounded antisemitism and the general rejection of some particularly obtrusive and unpleasant Jewish manifestations is insufficient; cognitively grounded certainty [*erkenntnismässig begründete Sicherheit*] is needed." Such "cognitively grounded certainty," Schmitt indicates, "was already achieved in Vienna before the war by a lonesome, poor young German, at a time when official scholarship was still deeply in thrall to the Jewish spirit and almost all of us were doubtlessly still trapped in a blindness conveyed by all the concepts and institutions of bourgeois education [*bürgerliche Bildung*] of the time." Once again, the position being expressed here cannot reasonably be defined as "Christian-anti-Judaistic." That would be grounded in correct faith, not in science or "cognitive certainty."[17] The nature of the science Schmitt is in fact recommending is made clear in his direct reference to the young Hitler's well-known evocation of an "antisemitism of reason."[18]

One of Schmitt's main concerns was showing how it was possible that "typical Jewish thoughts are considered as the only scientific ones, while all other opinion is considered unscientific and ridiculous." For only those who became aware of "this intellectual power [*geistiger Macht*] of Judaism," its "great depth" and "full scope" could appreciate the greatness of the Nazi victory "for the German spirit [*deutscher Geist*] and German legal theory."[19] What is here quite transparent is Schmitt's satisfaction, mediated by a downright infantile resentment, at his victory over his Jewish professional competitors. He now seeks to legitimate this satisfaction in some sort of scientific form. An important motif in his address is *liberation* from Jewish falsifications: a motif that Claus-Ekkehard Bärsch has defined as a basic element of the Nazi worldview, together with a desire for salvation, in his study of Goebbels, *Erlösung und Vernichtung*. Schmitt's variation on the motif brings us back to the question of how the "Jewish" can be recognized, that is, to his call for a "cognitively grounded" antisemitic "certainty."

Schmitt's polemic fails to clarify what he means by "the Jewish." The polemic generates insoluble problems, which he tries to evade through awkward tautologies: "When we speak here of Jews and Judaism, what we have in mind here is the Jews and nothing else," and so forth. Curiously, he seems to recognize that the definition of the Jews as *artfremd* is not necessarily negative: "If we here render the concept of strangeness into a general concept comprising those both related by and strange by kind [*Artverwandte und Artfremde*], then specifically Jewish influence can no longer be scientifically recognized. Then the influence that, e.g. Italian music had on our great musicians Händel, Bach, and Mozart appears on the same level with the Jewish infection emanating from Marx or Heine."[20]

In this context, Schmitt's special interest in Richard Wagner's notorious essay "Judaism in Music" is noteworthy.[21] This essay is one of the building blocks of modern political-racial antisemitism.[22] In the volume of the composer's writings found in the Schmitt archive,[23] all but pages 66–85—those pages containing the essay—remain uncut. Especially in light of Schmitt's remarks on "German" music, it seems entirely plausible that he meant to refer to the essay in naming his conference "Judaism in Legal Studies." In light of the broader apologetic significance of the "anti-Judaism" thesis, it is important to emphasize one thing in particular: Schmitt's opening remarks reveal no effort to separate himself from the sort of virulent racial antisemitism that Wagner helped pioneer.[24]

An additional compelling argument against such interpretations is the extreme improbability that Schmitt invited radical racial theorists like Falk Ruttke and *Gauführer* Hermann Schroer to his conference in order to distance his views from theirs. Koenen's reading can only rest on the fact that the SD found Schmitt's antisemitism unconvincing; but this is something easily explained by the realities of Nazi power politics.[25] Schmitt does, however, seem to have identified a basic problem various racial theories continue to have: that with the distinction between different human "races," no hierarchy has yet been established among them. In itself, racism is not yet antisemitism; indeed, it is not the real source of antisemitic convictions. At the most, it can legitimate antisemitic sentiments that are already present. In order to underscore the uniqueness of the "Jewish question," Schmitt does not wish to see it "masked by general concepts," "rendered harmless or falsified." Since he also does not wish to hazard a definition, he remains entirely "concrete": "We are speaking of the Jews and naming them by their name."[26] In a final remark Schmitt added to this concluding pronouncement, he stylized himself, as he would do repeatedly from that point into the postwar period, into a victim of those he was slandering: "I know from firsthand experience what insults and slander one must endure if one takes on this struggle [*Kampf*] [against the Jews]. I also know the hatred with which Jewish emigrants and their allies try to destroy the scholarly honor and good name of every person who escapes their claim to intellectual dominance [*geistiger Herrschaftsanspruch*]" (17).

In any case, through his "concreteness" Schmitt abandoned any possibility of arriving at scientific insight, for this always involves a certain level of abstraction. Schmitt was aware of the problem—which, however, allowed him a highly flexible standpoint on the level of internal Nazi power struggles. In a "preliminary remark" in the conference-proceedings he expressly indicates that the material there should "not for instance determine future research" (6). Hence exactly when it comes to central questions such as defining who was Jewish, a certain caution on Schmitt's part needs to be understood partly in relation to the conference's political backdrop.

Still, in some "closing words" he offered at the end of the proceedings, Schmitt tried to review theoretical and practical results in light of "immediately pending tasks" (28). The first practical task, he indicated, was the "necessary task of bibliography," "for it is self-evidently requisite to determine as exactly [*exakt*] as possible who is and who is not a Jew" (29). Schmitt here stepped into a realm well beyond abstract speculation on the Jewish spirit's influence on "German men" *(deutsche Menschen)* (28). His intent was a concrete one, to create the bureaucratic conditions for expelling Jews from all realms of legal studies. His first priority was a precise identification of all Jewish authors. With help of this "exact catalogue," he envisioned a second step: "cleansing of the libraries," in order "[to preserve] our students from confusion." For Schmitt, the confusion lay in the fact "that on the one hand we refer to the necessary struggle against the Jewish spirit, while on the other hand at the end of 1936 a normal law-seminar library looks as if the larger portion of legal literature were produced by Jews" (29).

Schmitt's proposed "library cleansing" was connected with another measure he called for in his "closing words": from now on it was "downright irresponsible" to cite "a Jewish author as chief witness or indeed as any kind of authority": "For us a Jewish author has no authority, even 'purely scholarly' authority" (29–30). With the expression he placed in quotation marks, "purely scholarly" *(rein wissenschaftlich),* Schmitt was continuing his attack on Kelsen's "pure theory of law"—Kelsen had been one of two living Jewish jurists (the other being Friedrich Julius Stahl) whom Schmitt attacked directly by name at the conference, as "the Jew Kelsen." He offered the following explanation: "A simple naming of the word 'Jewish' will already produce a healing exorcism." Through practice of this "exorcism" on "Stahl-Jolson" and "the Jew Kelsen," Schmitt wished to demonstrate the sincerity of his precept regarding "Jewish authors."[27] For he viewed the general thrust of the conference as amounting to the fact that "today in the Jewish question there are no longer any peripheral matters. Everything is interconnected most closely and inwardly as soon as a true struggle over *Weltanschauung* begins."[28]

But in order to effectively carry out his exorcism, Schmitt once again had to clarify questions of definition. Like his colleagues in the ministries responsible for anti-Jewish measures, in his own realm he was involved with "clarifying many individual questions." He was thus involved with the question of "half Jews, of those closely related to Jews, etc."[29] Schmitt tried to play down these questions as "marginal and interpolated" *(Grenz- und Zwischenfragen).* But it was clear to him that in Nazi practice precisely the opposite was the case. The "Catalogue of Jewish Authors" announced at his hate-filled antisemitic conference[30] had to be withdrawn from circulation shortly after its publication, it seems because it was riddled with errors. Schmitt would have recognized this withdrawal as being more than a minor matter.[31] From our perspective as opposed to Schmitt's, the withdrawal underscores the failure of Schmitt's effort to separate "Jewish" from "German" legal theory, and, on a more banal level, Jewish from German authors.

Schmitt's concluding comments offered some ideas regarding the direction he thought a definition of "Jewish" thinking should take. His concept of "*Gesetz*-based thinking" here took central stage: "Running through all the presentations has been a recognition of how strongly Jewish *Gesetz*-based thinking achieved domination in all realms of legal life [*Rechtsleben*] and how slightly this *Gesetz*-based thinking can be connected, even relatively, to the feeling for *Recht* and *Gesetz* of German individuals."[32] Schmitt proceeded to indicate that the Jewish *Gesetz* had emerged

> as salvation from a state of chaos. *The remarkable polarity of Jewish chaos and Jewish legality [Gesetzlichkeit], of anarchistic nihilism and positivistic normativism, of crudely sensualistic materialism and the most abstract moralism,* now stands so clearly and plastically before our eyes that we can count on it as a decisive scientific basis, emerging as the decisive insight of our conference and also pertinent for research on the race-soul [*Rassenseelenkunde*], for further work in legal theory.[33]

The concept of the *Rassenseele* had been introduced to "science" by Gustave Le Bon.[34] Schmitt believed that such "insight" had salvaged the "honor as a science" of legal studies in face of "the other achievements" pointed to by "Dr. Falk Ruttke." This was a reference to Ruttke's anthropological racial theory.[35]

Schmitt was so committed to his antisemitic beliefs that within their framework he could tolerate no exceptions. Naturally there have been Jewish positivists and anarchists, materialists, moralists, and so forth; certain focal points of Jewish scientific and scholarly accomplishment are also evident. These focal points can be understood in social-historical and cultural-historical terms. For example, the discrimination experienced by German-Jewish researchers meant frequent placement in important interstitial zones of their various disciplines. Within these zones, they could work toward significant advancement in knowledge.[36] But this does not imply a specifically Jewish essence or way of thinking. The broad spectrum of Jewish scholarly achievement would seem to suggest the contrary. But Schmitt could not accept this. Instead he inverted the weakness of the antisemitic argument, rendering the disparate reality into the very *criterion of the Jewish,* the "remarkable polarity" into a marker of specifically Jewish thinking.[37]

Schmitt operated in a similar way with the historical-political dimension of his problem. In this respect, he did not differ essentially from other antisemitic authors. On the one hand, he correctly identified the widespread liberal-positive perspective of bourgeois German-speaking Jewry. On the other hand, there have always been liberal, socialist, Marxist, and conservative Jews, and this refutes his assertion that Jews always acted in the framework of "general Jewish behavior," "on the basis of specific racial dispositions."[38] Schmitt dissolved the obvious contradiction between historical reality and antisemitic *Weltanschauung* by means of a conspiracy theory: the "demonically recondite change of masks" *(Maskenwechsel von dämonischer Hintergründigkeit)*[39] emerged as a key concept in his assessment of Jewish history. He did not try to explain the range of responses of Germany's Jews in the important years 1815, 1830, 1848, 1871, 1890, 1918, and 1933 in historical categories or in relation to a given situation. Rather, he demonized the responses. Schmitt's malicious assertion of a Jewish "change of masks" evoked the Antichrist; he defended the image in Social Darwinist terms. The "great adaptability of the Jew," he indicated, had been "elevated into the monstrous [*ins Ungeheure*]" through "his several thousand-year history, on the basis of specific racial dispositions; and the virtuosity of mimicry [*die Virtuosität der Mimikry*] has been promoted through long practice."[40] At the start and end of his conference, he framed the "great adaptability," mimicry," and "demonically recondite change of masks" of the Jews with Hitler's reference to the "Jewish dialectic": a heading found in *Mein Kampf.*[41]

Schmitt's concluding question regarding "Judaism in Jurisprudence" was also formulated in this context:

> How could thousands of decent and upright *Volksgenossen* succumb to the Jewish spirit in such a manner over many decades? From where the susceptibility of many men of German blood, and from where the weakness and benightedness of German kind [*die Schwäche und Verfinsterung deutscher Art*] in that historical moment, the lack of resistance to Judaism? . . . The Jew does not concern us for his own sake. What we seek and what we are struggling for is our unfalsified own kind [*unser(e) unverfälschte eigene Art*], the intact purity of our German *Volk.*[42]

Possibly Schmitt does not state the function he accords the Jews in politics and constitutional law more clearly in any other passage of his work.

The Jews are here defined as helping to constitute one's own "unfalsified" purity. But they do not only represent a *Volk* that is hostile in certain historical moments, such as the French or English. Rather, they represent an autonomous *Geist*, a "spirit." Outwardly, the French, English, Russians are political enemies in certain phases of German history. But they are never capable of a spiritual enmity that inwardly exploits the "weakness" of German "kind" in such a manner, thus exposing that weakness. The Jews are not the alien other; rather, they are one's own, intimate Other.

PART 2

UNIVERSALISM: EMANCIPATION AND COUNTERREVOLUTION

5

The French Revolution and the Catholic Reaction

From Carl Schmitt's perspective, with the November Revolution of 1918, the declaration of the first German republic by Philipp Scheidemann, and the establishment of the Weimar constitution, the ideas of the French Revolution had again gained currency. From that revolution, Schmitt derived a concept of "national homogeneity." He defined this homogeneity as a "precondition" for a "national democracy" he supported, in contrast to the liberal-constitutional democracy he opposed. He saw himself as a wholehearted theorist of democracy, interpreting Weimar's parliamentary constitution as an effort to form a belated connection with the French constitutional tradition. But neither proponents nor opponents of the new republican form of government actually oriented themselves around the French model.[1] Starting with the defeat of the "Weimar coalition" in the Reichstag elections of 6 June 1920 the number of proponents had steadily risen; the number of opponents steadily declined. In his radical critique of the Weimar Republic's "situation" within the history of European ideas[2]—a critique he had presented most mildly in the fourth chapter of his *Political Theology*—Schmitt drew heavily on arguments formulated by nineteenth-century Catholic thinkers. These thinkers had already struggled against the "ideas of 1789," in other words against the Enlightenment and the revolution, understood as intertwining phenomena.[3] Schmitt was here proposing a very dubious analogy between the Weimar situation and that of post-1789 France. He viewed the French Revolution as the decisive event of the modern age, that age conceived in a legal-political sense and not sociologically or economically. His confrontation with the revolution's results is especially apparent in important texts he wrote in the Weimar Republic's early years, texts that established his scholarly reputation: *On*

Dictatorship (1921) was concerned with the French Revolutionary origins of the specifically modern concept of the sovereign dictatorship;[4] *Political Romanticism* (1919) defined the French Revolution as the "determining point" of modern history.[5] For this reason, Germany's political parties could be grouped according to their approaches to the "ideas of 1789." At the same time, while citing the ideas of Adam Müller he took up a sharp critique of romanticism that had already been leveled at the French Romantics by Pierre Lasserre and Charles Maurras in the framework of the right-wing, nationalist Action Française. Lasserre's *Le Romantisme Français* is an outspoken attack on what he sees as the decadence of modern French culture. That culture emerged, he indicates, from nineteenth-century romanticism and an individualism bearing Rousseau's stamp.[6]

Lasserre's book, much of which could be read before publication in his *Revue de l'action française,* influenced Maurras (as well as T. S. Eliot[7]) in expressing enmity toward a Romanticism purportedly under Jewish influence. Schmitt's embrace of a critique originally directed at French Romanticism allowed him to place himself in an apparently radical counterposition to German political romanticism. But this was, in fact, a slight of hand. For Schmitt's decisionism, in contrast to his own assertion of its purely "occasionalistic" nature, itself drew deeply from the wells of German Romanticism.[8] Like a great many other modern authors, he wished to assert the presence of an otherwise ungroundable, or entirely arbitrary, ephemeral insight inside the "suddenness" of an event: a "moment" *(Augenblick)* within which a reality that was negative could now be positively reinterpreted.[9] As with some (but certainly not all) of these other authors, Schmitt's decisionism can only be understood against the backdrop of a fundamental hostility to the emancipatory principles of the Enlightenment. Schmitt did not directly take up the *antisemitic* tenor of Maurras and Lasserre in this context. But he did repeat the projection of a grotesquely distorted image of the enemy— something already observed by his contemporaries. For instance, the scholar of Romance literature Viktor Klemperer observed that "Schmitt cannot have enough in his hostility toward Romanticism; he sees it as 'a contradictory and mendacious product,'" the romantics being characterized by "'lack of consequence and moral helplessness against every new impression.'" Klemperer's conclusion: "Who has told him that Romantic passivity in daily life results from egoism and not from inner necessity? Only his political embitterment has told him this."[10] Schmitt shared this embitterment not only with Maurras and the distinguished novelist Maurice Barrès but with a pair of earlier nineteenth-century authors, both ideologues of the French counterrevolution: Vicomte de Bonald, author of a *Théorie du pouvoir politique et religieux* (1796), and Comte Joseph de Maistre, whose texts included *Essai sur le principe générateur des constitutions politique* (1808) as well as *Du Pape* (1819). In addition, he could draw on the "embittered" writings of the Marqués de Valdegamas: Juan Donoso Cortés, Spanish publicist and diplomat (1809–53), the author of numerous attacks on liberalism and socialism, and defenses of the monarchic principle. Schmitt oriented his thinking around such figures. He made their enemies his own.[11]

The political emancipation of French Jewry resulted from the logic of the ideas of 1789. Correspondingly, the attack on the Enlightenment and revolution by the above-mentioned thinkers was marked by an emphatic hostility to that emancipation. This hostility was conveyed through a blending of traditional anti-Jewish motifs with a modern anti-universalism that had emerged as a reaction to the Enlightenment's demands.[12] Such anti-universalism is encapsulated in a proclamation of Bonald directed at the revolutionary declaration of universal citizenship: "the universe has no citizens."[13] De Maistre sharpens this perspective in his polemic against the Universal Declaration of the Rights of Man: "In my lifetime I have seen Frenchmen, Italians, Russians, etc. . . . But I declare that in my lifetime I have never seen a human being; he must have been present without my knowledge."[14] According to this logic, the famous demand of Count de Clermont-Tonnerre after his switch to the Third Estate must have sounded like nonsense to the counterrevolutionary thinkers: "Everything for the Jews as citizens; nothing for them as a nation!"[15]

6

The Counterrevolution in the Weimar Republic

The Grand Inquisitor

Basic elements of Schmitt's anti-Jewish thinking thus have their source in nineteenth-century France. More precisely, they have their source in the Catholic counterrevolution's critique of emancipation—a critique that eventually would be expanded on by Edouard Drumont, the anti-semitic Charles Maurras, and the Action Française.[1] In France, the struggle against emancipation and assimilation signified more than a continuation of Catholic anti-Jewish traditions, since it had gravitated toward a realm of political conflict. In his *Lettres à un gentilhomme russe sur l'inquisition* (Moscow, 1815), de Maistre tried to justify the Spanish Inquisition to enlightened and liberal philosophers such as Montesquieu and Voltaire. Beyond that, he presented the Inquisition as a model: like all "ecclesiastical organizations," he indicated, it was "in its nature good, gentle, and supportive."[2] Against Voltaire, he stressed that the "Holy Office" was not an instrument of the church but of the state.[3] He praised the institution for those and the following reasons: "At the end of the fifteenth century Jewry had rooted itself so deeply in Spain that it had almost entirely choked the national plant. Through their wealth, influence, and ties with the most noble families of the monarchy, those inclined toward Judaism were most fruitful; it was in actuality one nation within another. . . . The Jews were almost lords and masters of Spain."[4]

For de Maistre, then, the Inquisition persecuted the Jews on political rather than theological grounds. The "state within a state" theme through which he presented his argument had been used against the French Jews since the end of the eighteenth century. In the course of the following century, it would also be used against Huguenots, Jesuits, and Freemasons.[5]

In 1922, hence toward the start of the Weimar Republic, Carl Schmitt subtly recalled the Spanish Inquisition through a reference to Donoso Cortés, for him embodying the "self-aware grandeur of a spiritual descendant of grand inquisitors."[6] Only a few years later, he would view Donoso Cortés as one of the great diagnosticians of the nineteenth century: a man who recognized how "the proletariat joins up with Polish and Jewish rioters and ambitious intellectuals."[7] In 1923 he also evoked the Inquisition for readers of both *The Intellectual-Historical Situation of Present-Day Parliamentarianism (Die geistsgeschichtliche Lage des heutigen Parlamentarismus)* and, more strongly, *Roman Catholicism and Political Form.* In the latter book, the first paragraph already refers to Dostoyevsky's depiction of the Grand Inquisitor in *The Brothers Karamazov.*[8]

The French Revolution is tied to the Spanish Inquisition in that the institution was abolished by Napoleon in 1808, during Spain's struggle against French occupation.[9] Furthermore, in its last phase the Inquisition saw to the forced renunciation of the French Revolutionary events in Spain and its colonies.[10] For the Catholic counterrevolutionaries, the Inquisition was thus very much alive as a sort of antipode to the ideas of 1789. In its anti-emancipatory ideals, the Catholic institution thus had a great deal more meaning than that attached to its span of time and place. In fact, it represented a broad sociopolitical problem. In Yosef Yerushalmi's formulation, striking "phenomenological affinities" are apparent between processes of assimilation and accompanying antisemitism on the Iberian peninsula between the fifteenth and eighteenth centuries, on the one hand, and in nineteenth- and twentieth-century Germany, on the other hand.[11]

The Spanish Inquisition was a legal procedure introduced by the Catholic Church for the investigation *(inquisitio)* of heresy. As is very well known, the procedure was carried out with the help of torture.[12] In the Inquisition's first two decades, up to 99 percent of its victims were of Jewish descent,[13] the procedure being aimed at the Marranos, Jews who had been Christianized (mainly forcibly) but still practiced their faith and customs in secret. The so-called Old Christians made many efforts to keep the Marranos out of public life. Some public institutions set exclusionary guidelines, and "blood-purity statutes" *(estatutos de limpieza de sangre)* were passed that led to a qualitatively new relationship between Jews and Christians.[14] Since the nature of these statutes conflicted with

Christian doctrine, Ignatius of Loyola declined to accept them; but the order of Jesuits that he founded would come to adhere strictly to blood-purity doctrine.[15] It was concern over heresy among the *Conversos* that caused Queen Isabella of Castille to appeal to Rome in 1478 for establishment of a special investigative body.[16]

The proceedings were initiated by a Grand Inquisitor named by King Ferdinand of Aragon, then confirmed and authorized by Pope Alexander VI (the Catalan Rodrigo Borgia). The first Grand Inquisitor was the Dominican Thomas Torquemada, who took up his duties in 1483. Although the Spanish royalty would exercise great influence over the new institution, and would use it to further its own political interests, the Grand Inquisitor always received his jurisdiction from the pope.[17] Through this close connection between worldly and spiritual powers, the Inquisition produced and battled against its theological enemies; but in practice it was a tool of the state, the pope not even having the capacity to intervene in designation of the inquisitor.[18] Using the charged term *political theology* is thus here appropriate: the term designates a political instrumentalization of theological forms that is, at the same time, a theologizing of political theory and practice. In Spain, this political theology was primarily aimed, as indicated, against converted Jews. It thus constituted the most important historical link between traditional Christian persecution of Jews—*not* aimed at converts—and modern antisemitism.

When Schmitt took up the theme of the Grand Inquisitor in his Weimar Republic writings, he did so in a different context than the Spanish Inquisition. At that time in Germany, the figure of the Grand Inquisitor was almost always tied to the character in Dostoyevsky's novel. The figure had played an important role in de Maistre's apology for the inquisition, *Lettres à un gentilhomme russe sur l'inquisition,* which had been published in Moscow in 1815. But apparently, his presence in *The Brothers Karamazov* more directly reflected Dostoyevsky's reading of Charles Robert Maturin's great Gothic novel *Melmoth the Wanderer* (Edinburgh, 1820). Within the German reception of Dostoyevsky, the Grand Inquisitor became a political metaphor, circulating in various settings. We here need to take special note of the importance Dostoyevsky had in Germany around the time of the Great War: he was considered as important a figure as Nietzsche; Heidegger even thought him more important.[19] The first Russian edition of Dostoyevsky's novel was published in St. Petersburg in 1881; a German translation appeared in Leipzig (with Grunow) as soon as 1884, followed by an entire series of others: Leipzig (Schulze) in 1901; Leipzig (Insel) in 1919; Minden (Bruns) in 1922; Leipzig (Hesse and Becker) in 1923; Leipzig (Reclam) in 1924; and Berlin (Knauer) in 1925. A remark Schmitt made in 1923 appears to have reflected this reception history: "In the singular case of a Russian Orthodox figure, Dostoyevsky, anti-Roman horror [*Entsetzen*] rises once again, [this time] to the secular greatness of his depiction of the Grand Inquisitor."[20] But what at first seems merely a reference to a figure Schmitt wishes to banish turns out to have other motives. The inquisitor surrounds his authority with an aura of the truly Christian: he knows that his order-generating power can only be exercised upon a strictly faithful populace, this faith being grounded in a corresponding theology. At the same time, the inquisitor's own faith does not prevent him from burning hundreds of heretics in a single day, "for the greater glory of God." He is certain that people need faith, dogmas, and the institution of the church in order to ease the pain felt from being unable to bear the freedom promised them by Jesus. In this manner, the Grand Inquisitor's view of humanity is stamped with such extreme pessimism that he always favors a form of rule based on more fear and violence to one based on less fear and violence. The legitimacy claim of such an order is, in the end, of a radically utilitarian nature.

It would thus appear that Jacob Taubes's description of Schmitt as "an incarnation of the Dostoyevskian 'Grand Inquisitor'" was quite on target.[21] Schmitt, in any case, seems to have placed himself in this tradition when praising Donoso Cortés along the same lines as his earlier remark on Dostoyevsky: for confronting "atheistic anarchism" with the "natural wickedness of human beings," and doing so with the self-conscious greatness of a spiritual descendent of Grand Inquisitors.[22] Schmitt regarded the idea that human beings are by nature *dangerous* as the anthropological fundament of both his *Political Theology* and the later *Concept of the Political.*[23] In his summary of what he termed the "actual significance of counter-revolutionary political philosophy," the Grand Inquisitor's distinguishing feature was the "consequence" with which he made decisions and his acute sense of the "moment of final struggle" *(Augenblick des letzten Kampfes),* in other words, of "radical evil." To be sure, Schmitt did not explain what comprised this evil.[24] After World War II, he tried to characterize Dostoyevsky's famous figure as follows:

> To render harmless Christ's impact on the social-political realm; to de-anarchize Christianity while still leaving it with a certain legitimizing effect and in any case not to renounce it. A clever tactician renounces nothing unless it is totally useless. We can thus ask

ourselves: to whom is the Grand Inquisitor closer, the Roman church or Thomas Hobbes's sovereign? Reformation and Counter-Reformation revealed themselves as related in direction. Name me your enemy, and I will tell you who you are. Hobbes and the Roman church: the enemy is our own question as form [*Gestalt*].[25]

In the 1920s Schmitt did much to help the Grand Inquisitor reconquer the place in political history he had lost as a result of the French Revolution. It is difficult to decide on the basis of his texts whether he was here on the side of Hobbes or the Roman church—unless we declare one of his various positions to be the "authentic" one and make exaggerated claims of coherence on that basis.[26] In our context, Schmitt's interest in inquisitional authority, as represented by the Catholic counterrevolutionaries de Bonald, de Maistre, and Donoso Cortés, is simply an example of the background against which he developed his vaguely interrelated "Four Chapters on the Doctrine of Sovereignty" (the subtitle of *Political Theology*). His location of the source of sovereignty in a pure act of decision that was centered around a state of emergency is superbly encapsulated in the Grand Inquisitor's role as embodiment of decision-making power: in other words, of the state.

Schmitt, like Dostoyevsky, did not directly describe his Grand Inquisitor as struggling against the Jews. Nevertheless, it seems difficult—and would certainly have been so for Schmitt—to reflect on the Spanish Inquisition and not think of its obsession with "hidden Jews" and its innumerable Jewish victims. The Inquisition's true core has been addressed with resounding silence by those commenting on Schmitt's use of the theme. In view of this silence, the political context of his inquisitional propensity, hence the latent antisemitic content of his thinking circa 1933, needs to be stressed. The image of the Grand Inquisitor that had developed in the framework of a broad reception of Dostoyevsky belongs to the political iconography of the Weimar Republic. In order to understand the iconological subtext of Schmitt's own ideas, we need to now consider its emergence against the backdrop of a particular widespread Weimar-Republic motif.

Weimar as "Republic of the Jews"

The collapse of the German Kaiserreich plunged both Protestantism and Catholicism into a crisis. For Protestantism the crisis was more significant, since in the Protestant-stamped Kaiserreich, Catholicism already defined itself by necessity as distant from the state. Both Christian confessions were national, monarchic, and true to the Kaiser; the declaration of a republic and flight of the Kaiser was thus a shock to both.[27] For Schmitt, a constitutional theorist working in a Catholic milieu, the problem was encapsulated by the new Weimar constitution,[28] which transformed a state that still had some anchoring in religion into one that was neutral in respect to both religion and *Weltanschauung*.[29] In postrestoration France, the separation of church from state had been formally confirmed in 1905, in the wake of the Dreyfus Affair. In Germany the process would only be undertaken in the Weimar period, Jews now being allowed to hold public office—at least formally—for the first time. This development ran into widespread resistance, reaching its apogee in the murder of Walther Rathenau, one of the most famous Jewish representatives of the new republic. Around this time, the following sentence appeared in the program of the German National People's Party: "We stand emphatically against the dominance of Jewry in government and public life, emerging evermore banefully [*immer verhängnisvoller*] since the revolution."[30]

It would be misleading to suggest that the German Jews had general difficulty identifying with the Kaiserreich. In the Great War one could readily observe the opposite; both Jews and non-Jews tended to favor the ideas of 1914 over those of 1789. Nevertheless, it is obvious that the Weimar Republic's parliamentarianism and pluralism was far more suited to the objectives of Germany's Jews as a religious minority. For this reason, many Jews now identified politically with republicanism—an identification with grave consequences for both the Jews and the Weimar Republic. The French Republic's victory had refuted integralist reproaches of not being able to defend the nation against its external enemies. In France, the charge of stirring disunity leveled at the Jews thus hardly carried conviction, despite efforts by the political right to conjure up a dire threat from a Bolshevism on the ascent after 1917.[31] The French state had been able to show that the situation was very different, despite accusations leveled against it of constituting a *République juive*.

It was otherwise in Weimar. Since 1920 at the latest, the republic was broadly despised, seen as the inheritor of a lost war. The Weimar constitution was attacked by publicists, politicians, and academics as the product of Jewish–Western interference,[32] and broad swathes of the German population considering the Jews responsible for both military defeat and the monarchy's demise. The "stab in the back" legend offered an interpretation of the war's outcome annulling the real meaning of the defeat.

This interpretation made those guiding the new parliamentary republic responsible for a misery that seemed unbearable.[33]

Even today, many political theorists consider Schmitt's settling of accounts with Germany's new parliamentary order, especially in *The Intellectual-Historical Situation of Present-Day Parliamentarianism,* to be one of the most lucid critiques of this democratic system. In contrast, the sustained effort of his great opponent Hans Kelsen to defend that system is now virtually unknown.[34] In any event, there was no clear social-historical imperative behind Schmitt's rejection of parliamentary democracy. Where the revolutionary developments were mainly greeted negatively within German Protestantism, Catholic opinion was in fact split. The sort of anti-Catholic *Kulturkampf* that had been possible in the Protestant-dominated Kaiserreich could hardly be feared in the Weimar Republic, with its far-reaching religious neutrality. Indeed, the advent of the Center Party meant that politically German Catholicism was now engaged with the state to an unprecedented degree; and culturally, a Catholic renewal was underway that could reasonably be compared to the "Jewish Renaissance" unfolding in the same period. (The two developments shared the same chronological pattern: emergence already in the pre–Great War period; increased momentum after the defeat.) Clearly, the new ties to the state furnished many advantages. This notwithstanding, the idea of forming a government with precisely the left-liberal German Democratic and Social Democratic parties could not have corresponded to general Catholic desires. It would actually be incorrect to flatly define Schmitt's antiparliamentary stance as unrepresentative of Weimar Republic Catholicism, in other words, to declare Schmitt an outsider. His position did represent the sharpest contradiction to the domestic and foreign-affairs policies of the Center Party, which most Catholics supported.[35] In its opinions regarding the new republic, political Catholicism in fact remained of mixed minds, represented in all governments but never wholeheartedly confirming parliamentarianism as the state's order.[36] In this context it is important to note Pope Pius X's condemnation of modernism in his so-called *Encyclica Pascendi* and *Encyclica Lamentabili* of 1907, and his introduction in 1910 of a compulsory Oath of Antimodernism for all clerics beginning their duties. In this way, Schmitt found himself in harmony with a deep-seated Catholic view of Weimar as incarnating rejected symptoms of modernity: liberalism, socialism, and communism, all symptoms attached, in turn, to the assimilated Jews.[37]

7

Catholic Atheism

The deep-seated tensions and general difficulties at work in the opening phase of the Weimar Republic, its sullen rejection by a large proportion of the German bourgeoisie as a "republic of Jews," furnished the context for Schmitt's recourse to de Bonald, de Maistre, and Donoso Cortés. For Schmitt, the German Revolution of 1918, with its "bloody decisive battle," amounted to a fundamental redefinition of legitimacy, one analogous to the French Revolution.[1] Over the course of the Weimar Republic, he repeatedly discussed Catholic counterrevolutionary political theory. Toward the republic's end, in a review of the second edition of *The Concept of the Political,* his student Günther Krauss pinned down the motivation for this interest succinctly, and with much more accuracy than many recent interpretations: "In truly political Catholicism (Bonald; Maistre; Cortés; E. Drumont, author of *La France juive;* Bernanos) the liberal ideology has been overcome."[2] Krauss here observed two things often overlooked in the work on Schmitt. On the one hand, he extended the line of French counterrevolutionary tradition cited by Schmitt into the present of the Third Republic. On the other hand, with the reference to Drumont's book *La France juive,* he was pointing directly to what had come to be the symbol of "the liberal ideology" that needed to be "overcome"—the Jews. In Germany, Drumont had already become well known in the nineteenth century through his foreword to August Rohling's hate pamphlet "Der Talmudjude" (1871; 6th ed. 1890).[3] In this way Krauss extended the field of struggle upon which Schmitt wished to overcome liberalism. It was the identical field taken aim at by Julien Benda in his famous *Trahison des clercs.*[4]

Schmitt masked this facet of his intellectual genealogy for various reasons. In a general way it was less problematical for him to refer to the classical thinkers of the Catholic counterrevolution than to the radical authors of the Action Française, with their partially journalistic writings.

Clearly, the most salient factor was the highly tenuous relationship between that movement's members, especially Charles Maurras, and the Catholic church. In 1926 Pius XI condemned the movement, ostensibly on grounds of its atheism but in actuality to counter the alignment of political Catholicism with antidemocratic currents.[5] He forbade any Catholics to join it, and two years later its members were excommunicated. (In 1939 Pius XII would lift the membership ban imposed by his predecessor.)

Schmitt's structural proximity to the Action Française was recognized by another of his students, Waldemar Gurian. The connection became clear to Gurian in the course of intensive research into precisely the historical line extending from the Catholic counterrevolution to the antisemitic ideas of the Action Française.[6] Born to Jewish parents in St. Petersburg in 1902, Gurian was given a Catholic baptism at the age of twelve, after moving with his mother to Berlin.[7] In 1923 he rounded off studies in Cologne, Breslau, Munich, and Berlin with a doctoral thesis under Max Scheler on the German youth movement.[8] In the Weimar Republic period, Gurian's interests centered on the possibility of moving beyond the liberal political tradition initiated with the French Revolution. Here he drew heavily on the French Catholic authors Léon Bloy (*Le salut par les juifs*, 1892) and Georges Bernanos (*La Grande Peur des Bien-Pensants: Édouard Drumont*, 1931), whose writing he discussed in numerous essays. In the 1920s these authors were also very important for Schmitt.[9]

Perhaps Gurian's most important work was his study of the social and political ideas unfolding within French Catholicism between the French Revolution and the Great War;[10] in this work's foreword he points to the personal context of its origins: "Herr Professor Hermann Platz sparked my interest in France. Herr Professor Carl Schmitt prompted my concern with Lamennais. . . . Many conversations with the Bonn constitutional theorist between 1924 and 1926 strongly helped clarify the author's viewpoint." Gurian had participated in Schmitt's Bonn seminars and maintained an extensive correspondence with him.[11] By the last years of the Weimar Republic, the communication between the two men already displayed some tension.[12] Nevertheless, Schmitt's pursuit of a Nazi career was a clear disappointment to Gurian, who observed it from Swiss exile. This disappointment was most clearly expressed in the essay "Decision and Order" ("Entscheidung und Ordnung"), appearing under the pseudonym "Paul Müller (Cologne)."[13]

The *German Letters* Gurian coauthored with Otto Michael Knap was a two-volume collection of often scathing reports on events in Nazi

Germany, written from Swiss exile. In these volumes, Gurian examined Schmitt's role as "crown jurist of National Socialism," the jurist emerging as an embodiment of cynical *Gleichschaltung*—the carefully planned elimination of political opponents.[14] In various writings from this period, Gurian repeatedly drew attention to contradictions in Schmitt's Nazi career. His observations went beyond moral critique to offer an interesting overview of Schmitt's work between 1914 and 1934, with both clear gaps and deep continuities becoming apparent. One of his summarizing remarks underscores the nature of his own relation with Schmitt:

> But despite Carl Schmitt's astonishing capacity to adapt . . . he cannot be dismissed as a more or less skilled opportunist. . . . For his case reveals a typical development; his questions are not questions presenting the mood of an isolated individual but real questions driven by the crisis that unfolded in the nineteenth century as something self-evident for prevailing legal and social assumptions. . . . For this reason his inclination to join a movement apparently constituting the antithesis of the illusory order he has seen through, despite all the personal weaknesses and vanities the movement has revealed, is not merely personal happenstance but a tragic occurrence.[15]

In his writing from Switzerland, Gurian drew attention to Schmitt's former ties to various Jews; these remarks proved useful to Schmitt's enemies in the Nazi security services (the SD).[16] Even so, Gurian's role, and that of the emigrant press in general, in the internal Nazi party power struggles costing Schmitt his official positions at the end of 1936 should not be exaggerated. At the most his observations could offer additional material to, for instance, researchers working for the SD. This notwithstanding, the remarks about Gurian circulating in Schmittian circles after 1945 were often marked by a special vehemence. For example, in a letter to Edgar Salin, who had been the political economist in the famous circle surrounding the poet Stefan George, Schmitt's longstanding friend Heinrich Oberheid referred to Gurian as "a dark figure from that period."[17] But already in the Weimar years, Gurian was treated with great distance as a "Jewish convert" in the Bonn circle of Schmitt's friends and students. This is reflected in a letter from Paul Adams to Erik Peterson, who had become, for a time, a close friend of Schmitt's, having gotten to know him in 1924 after moving to the University of Bonn, where Schmitt had been a professor since 1921:[18] "The Jewish converts are indeed a serious and mostly melancholy business.

Don't trust Gurian too much. He's no friend of yours, as indeed he is no friend of any human being [*keines Menschen Freund*]."[19]

We can compare Adams' assessment with Hannah Arendt's recollection of Gurian as "a man of many friends and a friend to all of them, men and women, priests and laymen, people in many countries and from practically all walks of life. Friendship was what made him at home in this world and he felt at home wherever his friends were, regardless of country, language, or social background." Remarks such as those of Adams do invite the question of Gurian's own attitude toward the "Jewish question" and antisemitism, an element entrenched in both his personal circle and among the French authors he worked on. He grappled directly with antisemitism as an independent theme only after becoming exiled from Germany.[20] But he did discuss it as an element in the Bolshevist movement in his book on the topic of 1931. It is thus striking that antisemitism is only marginally mentioned and not discussed in his book on Maurras and the Action Française published that same year. Hannah Arendt and Gurian's biographer Heinz Hürten both try to explain this in terms of antisemitism only becoming a central political theme after 1933. But in light of the situation of the Jews in the Weimar Republic's final phase, the same period in which Gurian devoted a book to the precursors of a prominent French antisemitic constellation, the explanation does not seem very convincing.

It seems that Gurian did not *recognize* a linkage between Charles Maurras' antisemitism and his political thinking. He did see, however, that Schmitt's position moved beyond the framework of Catholic faith and that it had close affinities with the position of Maurras. In a letter to Erik Peterson written in 1926 he put it as follows: "How similar Maurras is to Schmitt; Maurras is simply more honest; he does not outwardly claim to be Cathol.! He's a pagan, the church a pillar of order! The same fear of theologians as external authority, the same caprice, the same mix of meticulousness, industry, and bohemianism, the same approach to other people, the same impression of him; uncanny!"[21] As Barbara Nichtweiss has suggested, it seems very likely that Gurian's description of Maurras's doctrine was oriented toward his image of Schmitt.[22] It is in any case striking that in 1933, when Schmitt shifted from his role as "diagnostician of illnesses of society and our times" to that of "therapist,"[23] what emerged was the very aspect of his thinking that Gurian overlooked, remarkably, in his study of Maurras: virulent antisemitism. In *Decision and Order* Gurian indicated that Schmitt was constantly searching for a "highest instance of decision" that could pave the way for an end to his "despair at an anarchy identified behind all its facades."[24] At the same time, he suggested, Schmitt was aware that pure decision would be inadequate without an authentically legitimating basis. For this reason, after his "conversion to National Socialism," he wished to locate a "substantive order" *(inhaltliche substantielle Ordnung)* within the Nazi movement.[25] But this substance no longer rested on Catholic doctrine. Rather, it rested on a common struggle against the "Jewish spirit."

Among the Weimar Republic's pronouncedly Catholic authors, Ernst Michel, Carl Neudörfer (both connected to the *Rhein-Mainzische Volkszeitung*), Heinrich Getzeny, and the social scientist Gustav Gundlach had spoken out against Carl Schmitt in various Catholic journals. Above all, they attacked his one-sided legal understanding of the church,[26] the same reservations expressed by Gurian (regarding Maurras) here playing a basic role. In 1927 Getzeny observed in his *Schildgenossen* that Schmitt's *Roman Catholicism and Political Form* revealed a tendency to make the church's outer, representative forms of legal organization an end in themselves and that this tendency was pernicious.[27] The most extreme consequence of such an overvaluation of order-generating church powers and institutions would be a Catholicism summarized in the well-known expression "I am Catholic but I am atheist."[28] This reference to the writings of Maurras, which were condemned by the church in 1926, would have been very clear to contemporary readers.[29] It thus seems clear that a range of authors observing Schmitt shared Gurian's diagnosis. An authoritarian political thinker was presenting himself here as the author of a specifically Catholic constitutional theory.

Schmitt's Struggle against Universalistic Law

The last of the "Four Chapters on the Doctrine of Sovereignty" Schmitt published in 1922 under the title *Political Theology* is devoted to the counterrevolution's political theory. Here as well, the figure of the Grand Inquisitor casts its shadow on Schmitt's thinking. That figure's authoritarian decisions, aimed from a Catholic perspective at protecting church and state from the Jews, now emerges as the model for an idea of sovereignty basically centered on an absolute "monopoly over decisions."[30] Through such a monopoly, the "fanatical Grand Inquisitor"[31] sets his stamp on a specific form of sovereignty whose authority is expressed in "not needing to have right in order to produce it."[32] The "intensity of the decision"[33] originates in a certainty of preparing for the "bloody decisive battle," or else of already being in the heart of the battle.[34] The "blood" imagery here ties the Spanish Inquisition's concept of "purity of blood" with both the French Revolution and the trauma of the Great War.[35]

At the center of Schmitt's reflections on the "problem of sovereignty as a problem of legal form and of decision"—the title of chapter 2 of *Political Theology*—stands Thomas Hobbes's laconic dictum that "authority, not the truth, makes law."[36] The dictum had already been important for de Maistre, who saw it as offering an adequate counter, in the form of a metaphysical concept of sovereignty, to the catastrophe of 1789: the negation of the king's sovereign rights. Sharpening Hobbes's own viewpoint while still presuming a harmony between the general good and the ruler's will, de Maistre derived sovereignty from an *authoritarian decision*. In the process he rejected any form of legitimacy grounded in reason, discussion, or indeed popular will: "In the last analysis there will always be a power that can commit evil with impunity, hence which from this perspective is despotic in the full force of the word." Provoked by the Enlightenment's excessively optimistic view of humanity, de Maistre painted an extremely dark picture of sovereignty, one presenting humanity as a contemptible nothing. This nothing had its last and final priest in *the executioner*, emerging as the fundament of human society, both its "bond and terror," through his rule over the final sacrificial altar.[37]

Around a century later, taking up de Maistre's theme, Schmitt set Hobbes's dictum against Locke's dictum that "The Law gives authority."[38] This was the context for Schmitt's initial use of the concept of decisionism, which would later come to be considered a basic feature of his own work. "The classical representative (if I can use this phrase) of the decisionistic type," Schmitt declared, "is Hobbes."[39] That philosopher was here being enlisted in support of Schmitt's decision against "the rule of *Gesetz*" and in favor of authority. For in the end, Schmitt explained, law, *das Gesetz*, did not clarify "to whom it has given authority."[40] But in the early 1920s, Schmitt already went beyond Hobbes in his struggle with the bourgeois constitutional state and parliamentary democracy. In his *Intellectual-Historical Situation of Present-Day Parliamentarianism*, he defined the struggle as grounded in "irrationalistic theories of the direct application of violence." Looking back in 1940, he saw this text—now published in the essay collection *Positions and Concepts (Positionen und Begriffe)* under the title "The Political Theory of the Myth" ("Die politische Theorie des Mythus")—as the starting point for his "battle with Weimar-Geneva-Versailles."[41] Hobbes's "decisionism" had led Schmitt to a pragmatic separation of validity or authority from truth in confronting the *Gesetz*. He considered the separation a "paradox," since he did not want to abandon the idea of an absolute truth as the basis for legitimizing power.[42] It is actually difficult to grasp the logic through which Schmitt tried to resolve the paradox. What is apparent is that he tried to resolve it with the methods of the Catholic counterrevolution: through a battle both against the *Gesetz* and for pure "decision." In place of law came a command that was now the new law.

Schmitt evaded the question of the legitimacy of laws by having it vanish into the question of their enforceability. For the "reality of the life of the law," the only thing that mattered was "who decides" (95; 34). The "intellectual-historical [*geistesgeschichtlich*] situation" alone here furnished an answer: decisions were to be made by those ready—like de Maistre—to undertake a "reduction of the state to the moment of decision" (83; 66), in order to enter the "bloody decisive battle" following the French Revolution (75; 59). This battle was to be carried out between atheistic socialism—a "true opponent" for whom Schmitt often revealed a certain sympathy, while harboring only contempt for liberalism—and Catholicism, as the only two competitors possessing the power of decision in 1922.

Schmitt's insistent decisionism emerged from his struggle against any universal law and especially against the idea of law as something imposed by parliament that had developed as a result of 1789: "The general applicability of the law results from the law (in opposition to the will or command of a single person) being only reason [*ratio*], not will [*cupiditas*]. . . . In many modifications, but always with the distinguishing mark of the 'universal,' this concept of law becomes the basis of constitutional thought."[43] The decision, the personal command, was Schmitt's response to the generally valid law, which is essentially depersonalized. With de Maistre's concept of infallibility, the decision could now be endowed with a needed special strength.

In taking up this concept, Schmitt revealed an important shift of perspective.[44] Resulting from the revolution, the separation of state and church had been legally established in France for the first time on 21 February 1795. As a response to this formal separation, de Maistre tried to transfer a modern Hobbesian concept of sovereignty into the papal context: to locate political ideas in a theological space. Papal infallibility, he insisted, had to become the foundational idea of postrestoration European society. In formulating his argument he drew on a classical approach to sovereignty introduced by Jean Bodin,[45] in this manner exerting a strong impact on both the development of the doctrine of papal infallibility and nineteenth-century Catholic political theory.[46] For his part, Schmitt tried in *Roman Catholicism and Political Form* (1923) to extol papal infallibility as a model for the political sovereignty *of the state*. He thus argued in precisely a reverse manner: he *theologized the political*, offering a modern definition of sovereignty via an apparent detour of papal infallibility. It thus seems clear that Schmitt's interest in the counterrevolutionary thinkers was not related solely to the sovereignty-problem. Rather, what interested him was the radicalism with which they questioned the foundations and results of the French Revolution. This radicalism culminated in both Schmitt's decisionism and what he referred to as his own "doctrine of the absolute sinfulness and depravity of human nature." Schmitt's doctrine even went beyond the Tridentinian dogma of original sin, emerging as limitless contempt for liberalism's "systematic and metaphysical compromise."[47]

But what form of law did Schmitt desire? How are we to understand his relentless hatred of law grounded in a constitution? These questions need to be answered against the backdrop of his split relationship with the French Revolution. In line with Ilse Staff, we can summarize the basic ideas surrounding the revolution as (1) the idea of the nation as sovereign state authority; (2) representation through a parliament working in society's interests; (3) separation of powers; and (4) human rights and civil rights, the guarantee of a sphere of individual freedom.[48] Schmitt fully accepted the idea of the nation and the irreversible shift of legitimacy from God's grace to popular sovereignty—from monarchy to democracy. He saw Donoso Cortés's achievement as involving a recognition of this process.[49] But in carrying on the cause of the Catholic counterrevolutionaries, he was battling the idea of a parliament-created rule of law. Put otherwise, he was opposing what he understood as a principle of exclusively formal equality resulting from the proclamation of human and civil rights. In short, he was attacking the final form of state legitimacy, which has become legality, within the modern world.[50]

Not a Hobbesian principle of authority, but rather the question of *representing* authority informed Schmitt's strongest argument against a legalistic constitutional state—a state he saw as lacking representation. Where de Maistre had focused on papal infallibility, papal representation here occupied the core of Schmitt's reflections. Declaring that "with the spread of economic thinking understanding for any kind of representation" had vanished,[51] he stressed the specific contribution of

Catholicism and the Catholic church to modern political form. Schmitt's representational concept was not meant to be merely a "technical device mainly used by democracy."[52] In his *Constitutional Theory* of 1928, he explained that it was "no normative process . . . but something existential. Representation means making an invisible Being [*unsichtbares Sein*] visible and bringing it to mind through a publicly present Being."[53] Schmitt distinguished various sorts of "Being" in arguing that "in representation a higher kind of being [*Art des Seins*] becomes manifest concretely."[54]

To realize this "higher," ontological "kind of being," Schmitt saw his "idea of representation" as ruled by a "conception of personal authority." The conception was itself stamped by the model of papal authority.[55] For Schmitt, this idea of form developed historically through a distancing of Christianity from "Jewish monotheism" and its "absolute transcendence." As an outcome of this process, both the church and papacy created institutions oriented around a mediation between transcendence and immanence.[56] Hence as Schmitt saw things, representation only emerged through an overcoming of a Jewish law that was abstract in its focus on divine transcendence. From this perspective, Jewish law emerges as a yoke laid on the Jews. It is a *legal* form incapable of generating any *political* form on account of its normative nature and absence of concrete personal authority. This idea corresponds, of course, to Schmitt's approach to parliamentary law as an "impersonal law" marking a victory of the Jews.[57]

Despite Schmitt's advocacy of a political theology, his critique of the parliamentary concept of law—his belief that the concept contained a "Jewish" essence—cannot be reduced to Roman Catholic theology given a political turn. Rather, Schmitt should be understood as carrying an *atheistic* political-theological tradition to an extreme. With roots in de Bonald and de Maistre, the tradition was expressed most radically in the atheistic "Catholicism" of Maurras and the Action Française. In its relation to Catholicism, the conservatism of the two earlier French thinkers is located in a remarkable intermediate zone. On the one hand, they both understood themselves as Catholics. On the other hand, their philosophical justification of Christianity consists of a *positivistic functionalization* that can just as easily be read as a kind of agnosticism. What Robert Spaemann says about de Bonald can just as easily be said about de Maistre: "Bonald was a Catholic. We have prayers from him that testify to the sincerity of his faith. He doubtless would have been willing to die for God. But philosophically he could have only fixed the sense of this death for God from the idea of preserving society, and to this extent he occupies the precise border between Christianity and positivism."[58]

There is, in fact, ample evidence that de Maistre was not concerned with the revelatory contents of Christian doctrine. His focus was not on confronting centuries-old theological debates such as those carried out in the church councils he condemned to nonimportance. Rather, he was concerned solely with the Catholic church's powers to establish order and legitimacy. Both for de Maistre and de Bonald, these powers were a *vehicle* for restoring a monarchic legitimacy shattered by the revolution. As Spaemann indicates, this restoration was understood as the basis for preserving society itself.[59] The anti-Enlightenment linkage of church and state was in harmony with the postulate of a unity between church and society. The general function of religion was here derived from the imperative of allowing a monarchic social order.[60]

This imperative formed the heart of de Maistre's central concept of papal infallibility. According to the "general laws of every social alliance," he maintained in his foreword to the second edition of *Du Pape* (1819), "the words sovereignty and infallibility are two natural synonyms."[61] With the powers of final decision demanded for the state sovereign being transferred to the pope, hence with a pragmatic separation of truth and validity in this dogmatic realm as well, we can here speak of a *radical detheologization* of the Roman Catholic church. At the same time, the confrontation with those possessing different beliefs—those doubting or even entirely denying the new papal infallibility—was to be carried out with utmost severity. The "unbelief" of both Jews and Protestants had suddenly taken on political relevance. Once belief in infallibility was made the sole basis for the unity of throne and altar, then "unbelief" could be interpreted as a state-threatening act.

As indicated, this detheologized Catholic political theology had its most eloquent and virulent expression in the work of Maurras. The radically antisemitic literature stemming from the Action Française and published in the course of the Dreyfus Affair has been discussed extensively.[62] In its basic tenor, this literature was somewhat more elaborate than Edouard Drumont's hate-filled and venomous tractate *La France juive* (1886), one of the nineteenth century's greatest bestsellers. In his book, Drumont condemned the Jews as the true source of modern disorder, and their invisibility as the true source of all its wickedness ("the most powerful disturbing factor [*der mächtigste Störfaktor*] that the earth has ever produced").[63] At the same time, in line with his title he condemned modern France itself as a *république juive,* steered by a Jewish cabal: by conspirators guilty of both ritual murder and deicide.

Maurras transformed Drumont's antisemitism into a clear political doctrine by linking it to the radical nationalism of Maurice Barrès. As an author who had himself departed from the ideas of 1789, Barrès was championed by his admirers as the founder of a new, unadulterated or *integral* nationalism.[64] It is well known that the slanderous accusation of treason leveled at Dreyfus served as a platform for the integralist vision. The campaign against this French Jewish officer was here equated with the "integral" nation's struggle for the monarchy and against the corrupt republic with its "rights of man." Within the revolutionary tradition, these rights had always been intertwined with an idealized concept of "fatherland," or *la patrie*. Consequently, in the course of the Dreyfus Affair such rights, as the basis of Jewish emancipation, occupied the center of political discussion. The Dreyfusards thus founded a "League for the Defense of the Rights of Man"; opposed to it was the "League of the French Fatherland," in which Maurras participated in an important way.[65]

The arguments of Maurras were based on those of de Maistre, de Bonald, Drumont, and Barrès, on the one hand; on various texts of Renan and Taine's synthesis of culture, geography, and climate, on the other. For the Action Française, his texts offered an elaborate counter-revolutionary doctrine that Ernst Nolte defined in the early 1960s as a paradigm of fascist thinking.[66] This approach was later developed controversially by Zeev Sternhell, who has focused on nineteenth-century France as the main source for twentieth-century fascism.[67] For Nolte, Nazism represented a synthesis of Italian fascism and the Action Française; but Nolte did not try to establish any direct connection between these spatially and temporally separate political streams.[68] More recent French research has itself stressed the differences between Nazism's biologistic aristocratism and Maurras' approach to the constitution; the latter is seen as aimed at decentralization and establishing structure through both institutions and the estates. The same research has pointed to disparities in historical understanding between the two ideological systems. Hitler compensated for his radically negative stance, his obsessive stress on the powerlessness and particularism of German history, with a unificatory myth. But for Maurras, a positive recourse to France's prerevolutionary conservative-monarchic traditions was possible. The details of this juxtaposition have tended to contradict Nolte's theory,[69] suggesting that it is inadequate as an etiological paradigm for Nazism. But the theory at least maintains its value for illuminating an important dimension of Schmitt's thinking—a dimension broadly neglected in the literature on Schmitt.[70]

Let us now more closely consider the way Maurras characterized his enemies.[71] These can be divided into two groups. The first group was composed of political concepts, taking in liberalism, democracy, socialism, communism, and anarchism. Within these concepts, Maurras recognized and battled against the basic principles of individualism and revolution. The second group was composed of people he viewed as not belonging to the "integral nation": Jews, Protestants, Freemasons, and *métèques* ("naturalized" foreigners).[72] Maurras rejected all these people on the basis of a Catholic agnosticism more clear-cut in nature than that of either de Bonald or de Maistre. For unlike his predecessors, de Maistre was *actually* not a believer.

In his own instrumentalizing of the church as a order-creating power, Maurras made the Jews into his principal enemy, symbols of the "stranger," thus as with Drumont of the perverse and the wicked.[73] Hence Maurras once himself conceded that everything would be unsustainably difficult without the help of antisemitism, which simplified everything and made many things possible. "If one were not an antisemite by virtue of patriotic will," he indicated, "one would become an antisemite through a simple sense of opportunity."[74] Indeed, the decisive reproach he leveled at Protestantism is what he considered its "Jewish" nature. In the end, Germany and England also counted among his enemies, with Germany condemned as a center of Jewry and German-Jewish finance. Through these enemies, Maurras constructed an "outside" operating on different levels. The aim was here to form an "inside" or sense of "we" needing protection from a group of abstract "outside"-stemming threats: dissatisfaction, criticism, and ambivalent feelings.

In remarkable fashion, Schmitt's choice of the Jews as his primary, obsessive enemy reveals the same phenomenological dynamic, as well as the same historical matrix, that is at work in Maurras' writings. Here, it is helpful to return briefly to Dostoyevsky's Grand Inquisitor. For the novelist's description of this figure—in a masterful work centered on a special form of political theology—offers a good model for better understanding Schmitt's inquisitorial leanings. Schmitt's effort to transfer the papal idea of representation to a political level was aimed at using a Christian form in a realm *beyond* Christianity. Perhaps he personally believed, like Dostoyevsky's character, in the existence of Christ; but his primary interest was in submitting to the "political" laws concerning the separation of friends from enemies, in order to make his own decisions accordingly. Schmitt was never concerned with theology; to the contrary, following Albericus Gentilis he proclaimed *silete theologi in munere alieno* (let theologians mind their own business). He was very much concerned with political questions: the legitimacy of power and the basis of law in a secularized world.[75]

In Schmitt's writing we even find an echoing of the inquisitorial obsession with unmasking Jews as pseudo-Christians through torture. In his work, the unmasking process is repeated again and again, since his enemies always appear in masks. They are always swindlers, at their worst representing universal ideas: "Whoever says humanity wants to deceive" *(Wer Menschheit sagt, will betrügen!)*.[76] The swindling accusation appears frequently, and in commented passages. References to the power of what is secret and to the *arcanum* of those who hold power appear just as frequently.[77] These themes have steered nearly all antisemitic thinking.[78] They have done so perhaps most effectively and notoriously in the *Protocols of the Elders of Zion*, contrived in France during the Dreyfus Affair with the help of the Russian secret services in order to tie Dreyfus to a Jewish conspiracy.[79] The esteem this falsification was held in by the Nazis is revealed in their own desire to set up a similar conspirative organization: the SS, seen as the fulcrum of an Aryan death-struggle against the Jews.[80] With the will to power being viewed by Nazism as the *law* of the world, for Hitler this struggle contained history's final meaning.[81] Within this struggle, the Jews were imagined, phantasmagorically, as those who held power—hence as in a sense the model whose imitation promised victory. In his own way, Schmitt offers tribute to this idea in praising the following words of Bruno Bauer as great words of wisdom: "Only he can conquer who knows his prey better than himself."[82]

Increasingly widespread in the course of the nineteenth century, the myth of a world Jewish conspiracy and a fear of secret, invisible forces sparked a desire for a strong counterforce. Its power, it was hoped, would be derived from a *metaphysics of pure will*. A similar idea was at work in the various forms of hyperbolic decisionism running through the Weimar Republic's right-wing political spectrum. Secret conspirators and conspiracies had already been blamed for the French Revolution and accompanying terror by contemporaries to the events. At least to a strong extent, this can be explained by the fact that the Enlightenment ideas leading up to the French Revolution had often been disseminated from esoterically organized circles. Reinhart Koselleck has encapsulated this chronological development with his now standard term "critique and crisis."[83]

Repeatedly, the direct impact of the *Lumières* on the revolution has generated euphoric fantasies of history as a seamless and steerable process. The expectations nurtured on various sides regarding the emancipation and assimilation of Europe's Jews, processes themselves exceeding the experiential horizon of those who observed them, were strongly informed by such fantasies. The counterpart to this belief in the formative nature of history is an equally fantastic belief in the power of secretive conspiracies. In this sense, we can hardly understand radical antisemitism, which in the end always claims to be responding to a large and dangerous conspiracy, without taking account of the consequences of 1789. This is the case despite the conspiracy fantasies having far deeper, theological roots.[84]

The main affect tied to the Nazi mirroring of what they understood as the world Jewish conspiracy was not mainly fear. Rather, it was a complex made up of fear, admiration, and a powerful dose of envy. This seems to represent something very close to the envy Freud describes in *Moses and Monotheism* as sparked by the foundational myth of the Jewish people.[85] In the case of the Nazis, this emotion was closely connected with the Jews' imaginary role as God-chosen rulers over the law: a role signifying both a wound and challenge. Jewish law was *abstract* law, meant to be replaced by concrete law of a "racial" nature, since there was no possibility of *two* chosen peoples. Schmitt himself did not articulate specifically biologistic legal visions. But he undertook an analogous struggle against "abstract" Jewish law, which he saw as destined for eradication by a new German law that for the most part remained obscure.[86]

This similarity becomes all the more clear with a look at what distinguishes "abstract" Jewish law from Nazism's "concrete" racial law. The latter was ostensibly derived from the vocabulary of the natural sciences. But the tie actually amounted to an ideological assertion, despite being believed in by numerous Nazis. Nazi law did not, in fact, derive from biology. With the *Führerprinzip* standing at the very heart of Nazi ideology, Hitler not only protected that law, as Schmitt asserted in one of his more notorious essays,[87] but also—mostly by way of the *Führerbefehl*, i.e., direct command—created it as well. In contrast, in one of its most popularly known ideal-typical forms Jewish law is framed by its ultimate legislator being located in an entirely other, eternally unreachable sphere.[88] For Christian antisemites, the abstraction resulting from this form of law—which actually has certain modern elements—operates as a provocation: it is God's murderers who are following such a law, which functions without any representation. Only those who have committed deicide follow a law that is abstract and without a Führer.

In Schmitt's writings, a blending of prejudice against the liberal legal state with openly antisemitic conspiracy theory is evident only after the Nazi takeover. The following citation from this period, published in the *Deutschland-Institut* journal of German-occupied France, underscores the direction in which Schmitt had now headed:

> A Frenchman possessing the most genuine freedom of the spirit, at the same time a conscious pragmatist, Georges Sorel, could in the end only have his position regarding the Dreyfus case defined, without consideration of justice or injustice, by the fact that procedural errors occurred to the disadvantage of the accused; he only turned filled with disgust from the entire *Affaire* when he saw that what was at stake was not ideals of procedural justice but the struggle of secret powers to maintain their interests [*der Interessen-kampf geheimer Mächte*].[89]

In the same article, Schmitt discussed Germany's approach to the Dreyfus Affair:

> The French *Volk* has always preserved its interest in procedural politics [*prozessförmige Politik*], grounded in that heroic age of the legists. A Dreyfus Affair, in which everything moves around legal proceedings, could not have happened with any other *Volk*. That an inner split of an entire *Volk*, resembling a civil war, could center on the question of whether a military court has justly or unjustly condemned a Captain Dreyfus, is entirely unprecedented in this form. When in the postwar period some efforts were made, mainly organized by Jews, to stage something similar in Germany and make the so-called cases of Fechenbach, Bullerjahn, and others into German Dreyfus Affairs, then nothing else became apparent than the truly wretched disparity, indeed the complete absence of any relationship, between the Jewish spirit and the German *Volk*.[90]

Schmitt maintained this position after the Holocaust: "Let the *J'accuse*-types play their role on the world-stage. I find the prosecutorial even more uncanny than the inquisitorial."[91]

PART 3

PARTICULARISM:
THE JEWS AND
THE CHRISTIAN STATE

Schmitt's work amounts to far more than constitutional theory in the spirit of Catholic resentment. Two motives inform his struggle against revolutionary universalism: on the one hand, exploring a special relationship—its nature will be discussed below—with the secularization process; on the other hand, and connected with this, linking all of his enemies with "particularistic" goals. Such motives emerge most clearly in Schmitt's confrontation with Hans Kelsen. In his Weimar Republic polemic with Kelsen, many elements were at play that had roots in the controversy about Jewish emancipation breaking out in the German *Vormärz* (the period of politic turmoil extending from 1815 to the March 1848 revolution). This historical context has been broadly neglected in the scholarship on Schmitt, although there has been a great deal of emphasis on his closeness to and admiration for Bruno Bauer, arguably the period's most important anti-emancipatory theorist. Schmitt's critique of Kelsen's "pure theory of law" was not merely theoretical. It was part of a historical tradition encapsulated in the conflict over secularization and emancipation: a conflict brought to a head in the accusation of "particularism" Schmitt leveled at the Jews.

8

Political Theology as a Festschrift
for Max Weber

In 1923 Carl Schmitt published an article on the "Sociology of the Concept of Sovereignty and Political Theology" in a festschrift for Max Weber.[1] Schmitt's book *Political Theology*, published the year before, consists of this article together with another section on the Catholic counterrevolution's philosophy of state. As signaled by the festschrift in which it appeared, the article is directly connected to what Schmitt termed the "prodigious sociological material" contained in Weber's writing.[2] Weber's influence on Schmitt is evident in many ways. However, especially between 1933 and 1945 he masked the influence, for the Prussian State Councillor did not wish to be located in the vicinity of an exemplary liberal figure.[3] Wolfgang J. Mommsen was the first to underscore the Weberian stratum of Schmitt's famous first sentence, gnomic and scarcely translatable, of *Political Theology:* "Sovereign is he who decides on the state of exception" *(Souverän ist, wer über den Ausnahmezustand entscheidet).*[4] Weber's essay "The Three Types of Legitimate Rule" contains the following passage: "The *real* structure of rule is determined according to how one answers the question: what *would* happen if a statutorily indispensable compromise (e.g., about the budget) were *not* to take place. A King of England ruling without a budget would risk his throne (today); a Prussian king would not."[5] Starting with the classical Prussian constitutional conflict over budgetary law (1862–66), both Weber and Schmitt defined the sovereign in relation to the question of who had the right to decide in the event that, in exceptional circumstances, no legal precedent existed. Schmitt radicalized this problem of constitutional law to address the general decision-making authority of every sovereign ruler. He treated this authority under the rubric of "political theology" — essentially a form of "conceptual sociology."[6] In this respect as well,

107

he followed Weber, who did not approach modern legal ideas from a socioeconomic but from a religio-sociological perspective.[7] In other words, Weber saw not economic factors but religious convictions and theological terminology as mainly responsible for the development of these ideas. For his part, Schmitt tied his "doctrine of sovereignty" to his above-cited dictum that "all pregnant concepts of modern political theory are secularized theological concepts."

In the course of the nineteenth and early twentieth centuries, the concept of secularization expanded considerably;[8] in this light, it is important to more closely consider the context in which it was used by Schmitt. Notably, Weber's own use of the concept itself played a major role in Schmitt's writing on the sociology of religion.[9] In discussing secularization, Weber steadily focused on the development of the specific features of Occidental rationalism. His rigorously "value free" reconstruction of the Western rationalizing process, his methodically analytic disenchantment, were of an essentially liberal nature. They drastically differed in tone and tenor from Schmitt's consciously polemical political argumentation: from a confrontation with modern rationality and secularization grounded in a Catholic "fundamental position" (Mehring).

Weber came up with his formula of "the disenchantment of the world" in the course of his analysis of ancient Judaism—an analysis that is problematically stamped by its Protestant premises.[10] Famously, in his *Protestant Ethic* (1904–5), Weber described economic rationalism, engendered by ascetic Protestantism, as the outcome of this disenchantment process. Already in his early cultural criticism, Schmitt problematized this outcome,[11] arguing that economic rationalism was "rational" in its means, not ends: "In modern economies a form of production rationalized to the extreme corresponds to a completely irrational consumption. A wonderful rational mechanism is at the service of one or another demand, always with the same seriousness and the same precision, whether the demand has to do with silk blouses or poisonous gas or something else."[12] Both in his *Political Theology* and his *Roman Catholicism and Political Form* Schmitt expressed considerable skepticism toward an approach to life he termed "economic" or "technical" or "mechanical-scientific," with little distinction. Just as was the case with Oswald Spengler or, in a more exalted realm, Martin Heidegger, Schmitt here revealed a type of thinking widespread in Germany: a thinking that focused on the dark side of modernism.[13] To be sure, this darkness had already been recognized by Weber, albeit with an entirely different orientation and sense of purpose.

In *Roman Catholicism and Political Form*, Schmitt confronted the rationalism of modern capitalism and the Occident, as analyzed by Weber, with a "Catholic" rationalism and a "Catholic" counterthesis possessing a juridical stamp.[14] Both this book and Weber's *Protestant Ethic* had been preceded by Werner Sombart's 1911 argument, in a book titled *The Jews and Economic Life (Die Juden und das Wirtschaftsleben)*, that "Jewish rationalism" was the source of the "capitalist spirit."[15] The resulting controversy between Sombart and Weber had led to intense focus by Weber on ancient Judaism. The dispute that emerged between the two regarding the role of the Jews in modern capitalism's evolution was *not* centered on the dubious "facts" and sources that Sombart had mustered for his book. For Weber in the end approached the Jews and Judaism in a similar framework to Sombart's, quite often simply overlooking, for instance, the basic difference between ancient Judaism and its Talmudic and modern counterparts.

Weber thus did not challenge either Sombart's approach to "Jewish rationalism" and its relation to the Jewish religion or his anti-Jewish, essentialist description of the "Jewish spirit."[16] Rather, the preliminary remarks to Weber's essays on the sociology of religion seem to suggest that when it came to the Jews he himself accepted a connection between "certain types of rationalization" and "inherited qualities."[17] The only pronounced difference was in each author's assessment of the historical influence of an essential "Jewish rationalism" on modern capitalism. Weber tried to explain the existence of this specifically Jewish rationalism through his concept of a "pariah people." He did see similarities between Judaism and the ascetic Protestant movements; but the "pariah people" concept itself makes clear that the differences had much more weight for him than the things in common. Weber did not accept Sombart's assertion that Puritanism was the *same* as Judaism:[18] the fact that in the pre-emancipatory period Jews never organized themselves in a modern market-economy framework spoke against this.[19] Although, importantly, he accepted aspects of ancient Judaism such as Hebrew prophecy as constitutive for the Occident's development, he felt that other conditions not stemming from Judaism had to be present for the development to take place.[20]

The dispute between Weber and Sombart led to a broader debate with many participants. Nevertheless, Schmitt's attitude toward the Jews cannot be explained adequately in relation to the debate.[21] Rather, the link with both figures was a method that gave secularization a basic role. The location of religion at the center of the interpretive model was more important here than the function of a specific religion (for Weber, Protestantism; for Sombart, Judaism; for Schmitt, Roman Catholicism). But at the same time, Schmitt's writing reveals a perspective basically different from Weber's. For Weber, one of the most important facets of modern capitalism, and one of the most important outcomes of secularization, was the "rational structure" of law; he wished to explore that law's various origins. (Hence the question he asked at the start of his essays: From where does the modern state get its law?[22]) Schmitt's thinking moves in the opposite direction. In his work, political theology signified both diagnosis and program.

Schmitt's initial task, as he saw it, was identifying the "structure-identity" *(Struktur-Identität)* of the concepts at work in theological and juridical arguments and insights.[23] He did not object, in the "shadow of Max Weber" (Norbert Bolz), to secularization in principle, and he was not trying to defend an already-defeated reactionary position.[24] He simply saw the Catholic Church, understood as a *complexio oppositorum*, a uniting of all opposites, as a positive model for a political form. He saw canon law as a model for "pregnant" conceptualization. Schmitt's central premise was the theological origin of all "pregnant" concepts of modern constitutional doctrine. He even rejected any concepts *not* understood as originating in Christian theology, or that had been formed in deliberate opposition to originally theological concepts. His main concern was thus the conflict between secularized theological ideas or different ideas of political theology. In this manner he moved far beyond Weber's diagnostic approach. As we have seen, he moved into the vicinity of the Protestant political theologians—especially Heinrich Forsthoff and Friedrich Gogarten. Gogarten himself viewed secularization as a "necessary and legitimate consequence of Christian faith." At the same time, he saw secularism as a "degeneration of secularization" *(Entartung der Säkularisierung)*.[25] Schmitt's viewpoint hovers similarly between two poles. On the one hand he greets secularization as a positive development, for instance when religious neutralization creates a state sovereignty capable of ending civil war. On the other hand, secularization emerges as the chief abstract enemy of his own thinking.

Schmitt described Hans Kelsen's "pure theory of law" as the "systematic" endpoint and apogee of a rejected development within secularization.[26] Kelsen's doctrine will be closely considered later. For now, we can observe that in his work he went further than anyone previously in severing jurisprudence from historical, sociological, and theological

considerations: an approach he took great pains to legitimize theoretically.[27] Schmitt, of course, practiced anything but "pure" jurisprudence. As Leo Strauss observed, he wished to offer a "fundamental
critique" of a prevailing "cultural concept" stamped by both Protestantism and Judaism, and of that concept's "liberal" separation into autonomous spheres (law, ethic, art, theology, and so forth). In this manner,
Schmitt's struggle can be understood as a struggle with "Jewish" neo-
Kantianism.[28] Schmitt's antiliberalism was naturally mirrored in his
legal method: a method we need to examine now in relation to his critique of certain results of secularization.

This relation can only be adequately understood against its historical backdrop, that is, in terms of the nineteenth-century origins of
many of Schmitt's ideas. We have already seen how Schmitt took up a
critique of Jewish emancipation tied to the Catholic counterrevolutionary tradition, and how he radicalized his own doctrine in the direction
of an atheistic-utilitarian Catholicism. Inversely, Schmitt's secularized
constitutional ideas point to another crystallization point of his intellectual genealogy, the discussion of Jewish emancipation that unfolded
in Germany in the first half of the nineteenth century. The debate
between Karl Marx and Bruno Bauer on the emancipation of the Jews
in the "Christian state" occupied center stage in this discussion. Eighty
years after the debate, Bauer's ideas concerning the "Jewish question,"
at times sharpened and transferred to a legal level, found a new home in
Schmitt's political theology. The objections raised by Schmitt to Kelsen
might, in fact, be read as a revival of the controversy between Bauer
and Marx. Here again, at the heart of the controversy stood the question of the complete separation of the political from the theological (or
juridical from the political) spheres.

As Marx observed, the question of Jewish emancipation sparked
the more general question of "freeing" the state from both "Judaism"
and any religion whatsoever. While knowledge of modern connotations
of "secularization" was of course absent, the debate provoked by Bauer
circled around questions identical to those concerning Schmitt in the
1920s. How had those secular concepts considered important in the
modern constitutional state emerged? What significance was to be accorded the Christian theology from which they presumably stemmed?
How could Jews emancipate themselves, if this not only meant political
equality but integration into bourgeois society? And how could they do
so if the secularized concepts stemming from Judaism involved a sense
of the modern state entirely different from the Christian sense?

Posed by Bauer, such questions reveal the idiosyncrasies of a Protestant ex-theologian strongly stamped by readings of Hegel. Bauer's reflections on the position of the Jews in the bourgeois constitutional state
and his fear of particularistic ideas led to the embrace of a radically
anti-emancipatory and anti-Jewish viewpoint. These reflections thus expressed a variant of the antisemitic Protestant-atheist views that would
complement Schmitt's Catholic atheism. The intellectual streams that
Schmitt combined here were not *arbitrary* in nature. Rather, his ideas
were part of a broad tradition. They emerged from a long-standing discussion of the social and legal status of the Jews in the modern
nineteenth- and twentieth-century state.

9

Jewish Emancipation or a "Christian State"

The Conservative Reaction to Jewish Emancipation

Borrowed from the controversial "Catholic emancipation" in England, the catchphrase *Judenemanzipation* was first used in 1828 by the liberal Leipzig philosopher Wilhelm Traugott Krug in his book titled *On the Relation between Different Religious Parties to the State and on the Emancipation of the Jews (Über das Verhältnis verschiedener Religionsparteien zum Staate und über die Emanzipation der Juden).*[1] The phrase then made its way into Germany's political debate over the "Jewish question."[2] With *Judenemanzipation*, Krug meant complete Jewish equality of rights and duties, especially the right of Jews to serve as German officials.[3] From an Enlightenment perspective, the emancipation of the Jews was not different from that of other socially and politically marginalized groups. Krug considered the "Jewish question" as basically the same as the "Catholic question": emancipation was the rational outcome of religious freedom and freedom of conscience, to be accomplished without any effect on the political foundations of the state.[4] For this reason, the "Edict of 11 March 1812 Concerning the Civic Conditions of the Jews in the Prussian State" could expressly declare those Jews to be Prussian *citizens*. With the edict, Jews were no longer legally different than other subjects of the Prussian state, although stipulated exceptions and, most importantly, a lack of decision regarding official employment meant that the Jewish situation was by no means secure. The right to citizenship would remain the central demand of the supporters of Jewish legal emancipation throughout Germany.[5] In 1815 the Congress of Vienna confirmed the need for such emancipation. But there would be more setbacks than progress over the coming decades, a reflection of the restoration period's illiberal climate. Jews and non-Jews agreed that the process required a certain degree of social and cultural assimilation, eventually leading to integration into bourgeois society.[6] This strengthened a sense that political emancipation had to be preceded by educational laws aimed at assimilation.[7]

With Friedrich Wilhelm IV's accession to the Prussian throne in 1840, the debate over the position of the Jews took a decisively sharp turn. Influenced by conservative-romantic themes, Friedrich Wilhelm IV viewed the political constitution as closely tied to religion, so that any political integration of the Jews into the Christian state seemed impossible to him.[8] The new king and his consultative "camarilla"[9] thus confronted the supporters of emancipation with the need to preserve a "Christian state."[10] In a first step, an official privileging of Christianity would remove the possibility of Jews becoming officials. Then in a decree issued in December 1841, the king abandoned all the previous decades' efforts at Jewish assimilation. The Jews were to form their own political "corporation," located outside the state; since their ties to the state would only be indirect, mediated by individual members of the Jewish "corporation," individual Jews were no longer to have rights as citizens, but only those rights granted as "corporation" members.

With this attack on the core idea of the edict of 1812, the powers of renewed religiosity, both Catholic and Protestant, hoped to keep the new state free from the "rationalistic intellectual state"—the *rationalistischer Verstandesstaat*—and the influence of Judaism. A concrete realization of these plans would have meant, self-evidently, the abolition of Jewish emancipation in Prussia; the plans were thus fiercely contested by the Jews.[11]

The most famous single effort to counter the growing anti-assimilatory tendency was a polemical text, published in 1842, by the first German Jewish judge, Gabriel Riesser: *Concerns and Hopes Regarding the Future Status of the Jews in Prussia (Besorgnisse und Hoffnungen für die künftige Stellung der Juden in Preussen)*.[12] More generally, the political consequences of the idea of a "Christian State" were in such extreme conflict with prevalent regulations that establishing a timely new order in line with the king's wishes was simply impossible. In any event, for state officials a corporative system represented the opposite of a modern, rationally organized government.[13] In the end the reaction of the Jews, together with the objections of state administrations and individual *Landtag* delegates, was enough to block the gravest consequences of the royal order.[14] And with the outbreak of the 1848 revolution, Prussia's anti-emancipatory forces were placed on the defensive for several decades.[15]

Despite this development, it is fair to say that after taking on an increasingly conservative tenor under Friedrich Wilhelm IV, political theory in Prussia was marked by ever-more theologizing throughout the first half of the nineteenth century.[16] The nebulous idea of a "Christian state" stood at the center of that process, which Carl Schmitt addressed as follows: "When theorists of the restoration accuse their opponents of atheism, a theological concept has become a political one."[17] The theologizing tendency is all the more evident when we take account of the previous movement in the opposite direction, a reflection of the French Revolution's impact. This movement was concretized most dramatically in the Prussian secularization edict of November 1810, transforming all clerical possessions into "state property." The edict's practical effect was to divest Prussia's Catholic Church of its entire worldly domain.

In a treatise written in 1847 emerging from parliamentary debates about Jewish political equality that had taken place that same year, the conservative legal philosopher Friedrich Julius Stahl (a convert to Christianity of Jewish origin) discussed the "Christian state,"[18] extolling it in a manner relevant to our context. "It is the entire infinite wealth of Christianity," he declared, referring to Christian cultural accomplishments and the influence of Christian ideas of social and political form, "that must also reveal itself in the state of a Christian people."[19] In deriving the need for a "Christian state" from the "Christian" character of its *Volk* and the latter's contribution to the emergence of this state form, Stahl reflected the impossibility of defining what, precisely, was to be understood by "Christian." He meant a state composed of Christians, but its designation as a "Christian state" said nothing about its concrete shape. What is clear is that within an understanding of the state centered on a homogeneous *Staatsvolk*, the position of non-Christians, be they deists or Jews, becomes precarious. And indeed, the only concrete conclusion Stahl could draw from his idea of a "Christian state" was the exclusion of Jews from higher state offices.[20]

The critique of Jewish emancipation on the part of conservative thinkers in the *Vormärz* period was rooted in their adherence to the idea of a "Christian state." If the ethical categories of Christian moral theology were to form the state's chief point of reference, the state thus not being grounded in an immanent autonomous morality à la Hegel but rather in Christianity, then the demands of emancipation would in a sense form a natural opposition to such a conception of the state.[21] A corporatively constituted Christian monarchy radically conflicted with the idea of legal equality for the Jews. In essence, the Prussian conservatives were faced with a single alternative: Jewish emancipation *or* a Christian state.

The Radical Reaction to Jewish Emancipation

The conservative idea of a unity of throne and altar, state and church, allowed no place for the political emancipation of the Jews. At the same time, despite their own insistence on separating these two spheres, there was also a "Jewish question" for the Young Hegelian thinkers who developed and promulgated radical ideas between 1835 and 1845.[22] For in its critique of the Prussian state, the dialectic conceptual movement embraced by the Young Hegelians wished to reach emancipation by way of a *negated* (historically transcended) Christian revelatory religion, itself reached through a negation of Judaism.[23] On the level of political theory, this historical model posed special problems for Jewish emancipation. How, for instance, were the Jews to take two simultaneous steps on the dialectic ladder? In the case of the Jews, dialectic philosophy of history sets up a barrier to the universalistic goal of Jewish emancipation. The barrier was in fact especially directed at the supposed particularism of Judaism and the Jews.

Bruno Bauer's Critique of Judaism and Jewish Emancipation

The Young Hegelian philosopher and publicist Bruno Bauer (1809–82) is mainly remembered through the critique leveled against him by his student Karl Marx.[24] Between 1839 and 1843, Bauer participated in the Young Hegelians' radical activities. As the author of many books criticizing religion, he made such a mark in this period that the Prussian police confiscated and destroyed some of his works before their publication. These, however, still managed to circulate in circles around Arnold Ruge, Karl Marx, Friedrich Engels, and Max Stirner. But after the Prussian state's suppressive measures finally led to a collapse of Young Hegelianism, Bauer did not join any of the liberal or socialist movements. Bauer considered his dismissal from his theology post in Bonn to be an event with world-historical significance. The weak (in his opinion) general response to the dismissal had destroyed his faith in the power of the oppressed masses, leading to a withdrawal from all practical political engagement and a sense that his mission was of a theoretical nature.[25] Following 1848, the formerly radical atheist emerged as a conservative politician and collaborator on conservative newspapers. As the guiding spirit behind the twenty-three-volume *Staats- und Gesellschafts-Lexikon* (Berlin: Heinicke, 1858–67) edited by the social conservative Hermann Wagener (1815–89), he wrote many articles for the lexicon, including some concerned with the "Jewish question."[26] Bauer was among the most important pioneers of modern political antisemitism. He synthesized secularized theological prejudices with "modern" racial ideas at a strikingly early time: already in 1863 he contemptuously referred in Wagener's lexicon to "the Jew" as the "white negro" *(der weisse Neger).*[27]

Bauer's texts from the *Vormärz* period mirrored the Protestant theologian's transition to atheistic Young Hegelianism: a process of radical "de-Christianization" that would become the chief focus of his thinking.[28] For Bauer himself, the connection between his atheistic position and Christian starting point was self-evident. What is crucial here is that the same emergence of modern political ideas from Christian theology that Schmitt explored in 1922 under the title *Political Theology* had paradigmatic status for Bauer. His critique of contemporary liberal and conservative ideas constantly emphasized their theological origin. From his perspective freedom, human rights, emancipation, the core ideas of bourgeois liberalism, were merely *abstract,* hence empty formulas, as long as they could not be understood as products of a "critique of Christianity."[29] Applied to Jewish emancipation, the following problem developed from this critique: how could the concepts translated from Christian theology into modern political theory be applied to the Jews? This question was the backdrop for Bauer's rejection of political emancipation of the Jews. Bauer approached authors who in theological circles were considered the most provocative antagonists of the Christian faith in a framework defining all decisive contemporary-liberal ideas as secularized Christian-theological ideas. Sparking much controversy, his text on the "Jewish question" poses the question of whether the political concepts emerging from the Christian secularization process, along with the political demands that accompanied it, could be transferred to the situation of the Jews.

For Bauer, the "Jewish question" only represented a part of the more general question "on whose solution the age is working." Namely, both the Christian state and the Jews had to abandon their essence in order to achieve *freedom* (3). The emancipation of the Jews was thus defined as one aspect of a movement for "freedom, rights of mankind, emancipation, and amends for a thousand-year injustice" (1). Bauer's Hegelian description of freedom's premises had an eschatological undercurrent: "Without having passed through the fire of critique, nothing [*Nichts*] will be able to enter the new world that has come close by" (2). Realizing this critique was the goal of Bauer's book on the "Jewish question."

To this end, Bauer took up a traditional Protestant theme. He understood the chief difference between Judaism and Christianity as lying in Judaism's absolute transcendence and the liberating immanence offered by Christianity through Christ, God become human. In Christianity, he observed, the human being himself—most immediately in the figure of Jesus—was placed on the plain of the divine. For that reason the religion could be understood as the highest form of human emancipation. In Judaism human beings were freed from nature only in order to preserve an absolute transcendence in God, hence an absolute nonfreedom; in Christianity this final separation was itself overcome.[30] But, Bauer's argument continued, even if Christianity had ascended to the highest form of religious consciousness, it could not attain the very last stage of *human* consciousness. This was possible only through a complete overcoming of all religion. Only Christianity stood more *closely* than Judaism to this final step to atheism; it had not yet taken that step. Bauer's texts were marked by a persistent tension: where the present was still dominated by various religions, true human emancipation had been announced in the thought of the radical atheistic pioneers of the world spirit.[31] Bauer expounded at greatest length—around nine hundred pages—on the theological backdrop of his critique of the Jewish religion in his unfinished *Critique of the History of Revelation: The Religion of the Old Testament Described in the Historical Development of Its Principles.*[32] As suggested in its subtitle, the work revealed the tie between Bauer's Hegelian concept of history and his theological concepts more clearly than did his later, openly atheistic texts. In the prologue to the second volume, Bauer used a theological terminology to condemn Jewish law and the Jewish idea of history. The Jews refusal to proceed beyond the "standpoint of the law" was, he indicated, a "sin," since this "early definiteness [*Bestimmtheit*] of religious self-consciousness" had been demoted to a curse and injustice through Christian revelation.[33] The "sin" of the Jewish position, understood as particularistic as a result of being stamped by Jewish law, thus involved a refusal to participate in the development of self-consciousness—hence to fit into Bauer's Young Hegelian idea of progress.

Bauer's Critique of Jewish Law and Jewish History

Friedrich Wilhelm IV's plans to establish a corporative legal structure for Germany's Jews form the historical background both for Bauer's book on the "Jewish Question," published in 1842, and for his essay

"The Ability of Today's Jews and Christians to Become Free," published in 1843.[34] Both texts, with their attacks on Jewish law and history, found widespread resonance among Jews (including Abraham Geiger, Samuel Hirsch, and Gustav Phillippson) and non-Jews. Taking up his earlier theological arguments, Bauer's critique is once more based on traditional anti-Jewish themes. But it also prepares the basis for his attack on calls for Jewish emancipation.

Bauer's approach to Jewish history is based on his approach to Jewish law, which repeats a reproach of the young Hegel in focusing on its alleged "positivity." Hegel had charged the Jewish people with "slavish" conduct, concluding from this that the Jews only possessed a positive, "laid down" *(gesetzt)* form of law *(Gesetz)*. As a "passive nation," it could itself not produce its own laws: "The liberator of his people [that is, Moses] was also its lawgiver;—[that] could mean nothing other than: he who freed that people from its yoke imposed another one on it. A passive nation that gave itself laws would be a contradiction."[35] For Hegel, then, positivity was a sign of the servile Jewish consciousness, incapable of standing up to Moses the lawgiver. The philosopher juxtaposed such positivistic fidelity to the law, which he saw as having penetrated Christianity through Judaism, with the teachings of Jesus, who "set [*entgegensetzen*] the human being against the positivity of the Jews, virtuous qualities [*Tugenden*] against laws [*Gesetzen*] and their duties, and within the former annulled [*aufheben*] the immorality of the positive human being."[36] Notably, the extent to which Bruno Bauer's own views are based directly on Hegel rather than general Christian prejudice seems unclear. What is clear is that he carried forward the Hegelian linkage of Jewish positivity and an inferior morality. For Bauer, "positive" *Gesetz*—Jewish religious law—had left the Jews outside general history. Above all, it had left them outside general human interests and the public sphere, stuck in a sphere centered on "private advantage."[37]

As Bauer saw things, Jewish legal positivism was embodied in the "ceremonial laws."[38] In this point as well, he was echoing Hegel, who had described these laws as a sign of the absent freedom and the servility of the Jewish spirit. Since, Hegel indicated, within the Jewish religion everything stood under the power of the ceremonial laws, the freedom necessary for the development of morality was absent, only "continual domination" present.[39] For Bauer, since the highest duty within Jewish law was a consequent performance of ceremonies, such law was robbed of any possibility of historical development: "The Jews speak correctly of the law as fence: the law fenced them off from history's influence, fenced them off all the more in that from the beginning precisely their law ordered separation from the gentiles."[40] Such untested, unaltered positive-ceremonial law, upheld by the Jews, consequently maintained them *as* Jews. Their continued existence was thus not only outside of, but indeed posed *against*, the movement of history.[41]

Bauer's disapprobation was aimed not only at Jewish positive law in general but also, specifically, at the Talmud. He equated the Talmud with a "Mosaicism that became boundless" *(bodenlos gewordner Mosaismus)*.[42] He criticized Jewish law in a similar way to Spinoza in his *Tractatus Theologico-Politicus*, where the validity of the law is defined as dependent on the existence of a Jewish "realm"—rendered by Bauer into a "state."[43] Bauer was well aware of his debt to Spinoza, who he stressed was "no longer a Jew when he created his system": a reflection of his sense that the Jews could contribute nothing to the "formation [*Bildung*] of Europe."[44] For Bauer, the Talmud had merely developed the laws of the Old Testament in a changed situation. For this reason he defined Jewish law as "chimerical": "Mosaicism transferred to the air is the only appropriate Mosaicism" (26). He perceived such a "transfer" "higher into the airy region of the chimerical world" as immoral, in that roots no longer anchored in the real world could not intertwine with humanity's moral interests (27–28). In comparison to surrounding peoples, who were starting to gain their authentically grounded consciousness in history, the Jewish population was still determined by the "landlessness"— *Bodenlosigkeit*—of its existence. Bauer saw this landlessness as directly connected with the specific "consciousness" of the Jews, whose conservation of the prejudice of "chosenness" had become an "abstract category" (28).

Following his break with Protestant theology and the Christian religion, Bauer carried on his anti-Jewish theological attack: on Jewish law as abstract, hence estranged from the world, with particular stress on the opposition between that abstraction and what was "concrete." In this context, he tied the abstraction concretely to the "landless" social circumstances of Diaspora Judaism—the *special quality* of that Judaism was its *abstraction*.[45] He likewise repeated his traditionally grounded reproach that the Jews had set themselves against the "wheel of history." But their lack of a desire to change, their turn against progress, the "first law of history," did not mean that they were mere passively patient sufferers.[46] Rather, they in fact had a thoroughly active world-historical role, albeit one played out beyond both "the interest of the [other] peoples" and, in particular, "corporative interests and those of the estates" *(Standes- und Corporationsinteressen).*[47] Bauer linked this special Jewish position to what he considered the Jews' lack of scientific and artistic productivity, which he viewed as rooted in their Oriental nature.[48] In this regard, he was once more taking up an argument of his teacher Hegel, who in the *Lectures on the Philosophy of History* (1822–32) had distanced Christianity from Judaism by tying the latter to the world of China and India. Hence already for Hegel, where Christianity belonged to the Western world, entering onto the scene after the Greeks and Romans, Jewish religious history was situated on the edge of an Oriental world described in distinctly inferior terms.[49]

What is, for Bauer, the special quality of the "Orientalism" of the Jews, and what is the meaning of his reproach to that effect? Bauer viewed the Orient as the locus of "inherently stationary peoples" *(stationäre Volkswesen),* because those living there had not yet recognized freedom and reason as their essence, instead seeing their highest duty as the "enactment of ceremonies lacking reason and grounding."[50] For both an individual and a nation, such limitations on freedom meant an impossibility of following any universally fixed laws. Consequently, with history being equivalent to a development of *general* human freedom, "the Oriental" *had* no history.[51] In their "Orientalism," the Jews thus found themselves in the unique situation of being one of the nations inscribed in history without possessing their own history—an idea that would reemerge later, with a positive twist, in the work of the Jewish Hegelian and philosopher of history Franz Rosenzweig.[52] For Bauer, then, the location of the Jews outside of the history of nations was responsible for the development of particular Jewish characteristics. And these characteristics stood in the way of Jewish emancipation.

Bauer's Critique of Jewish Emancipation: Human Rights and Civil Rights

Bauer placed the capability of the Jews to emancipate themselves in question by playing off their special historical role against them. From his perspective, the Jews stood out by not being concerned with general humanity, with the other, but only with themselves. They stood out by possessing no universalistic but exclusively particularistic interests. As Jews had to separate themselves from others, in Bauer's view, in order to preserve their characteristic qualities, he saw the question raised of whether "the Jew as such, i.e., the Jew who himself admits that he is forced by his true nature [*Wesen*] to live in eternal separation from others, is capable of being granted general human rights."[53]

Bauer's objections to the basic demand of those pressing for Jewish emancipation, the granting of general *human rights* to the Jews, have a double basis: first, his characterization of the Jews; second, his description of the Christian state. This state, he indicated was not in the position to preserve its Christian essence while integrating the Jews as equal citizens. Political emancipation and human rights would not affect the Jews *as Jews*, but as human beings. Consequently the Jews would first have to abandon their specific otherness, thus no longer being distinguished as Jews from non-Jews, in order to become human beings in Bauer's sense. Since their religion "obligated" them to "eternal separation," they were in their essential nature Jewish, not human. Importantly, Bauer considered the same to be true of Christians: "Jews and Christians can only consider themselves and treat each other as human beings when they abandon their special natures, which separate them and obligate them to 'eternal separation,' and acknowledge the general nature of human beings [*das allgemeine Wesen des Menschen*], considering it their true nature."[54] Just as importantly, however, Christianity had a decisive advantage over Judaism in this respect, as the very concept of a general human nature could emerge only within Christianity—albeit, Bauer conceded, only in religious form.[55] For as suggested, Bauer discovered in Christianity a position resulting from a negation of Jewish particularism, the Christian religion thus being further on the road to true universalism. Only Christianity could combat Christianity, since it contained "the concept of human nature *as its own enemy.*"[56]

The "concept of human nature" formed the axis of Bauer's argumentation, itself meant to emancipate humanity from Christianity and lead it to atheism. Bauer saw human rights solely as a product of Christian secularization history. They were not eternal, which is to say given rights, but principles gained through "self-formation," *Bildung,* in other words through Christianity's struggle with itself. As the Jews had not taken part in the struggle, they had no right to the rights.[57] In this manner, human rights presumed a concept of "general Christian love" that Christianity had developed through an annulment of Judaism.[58] But in line with Bauer's underlying logic, he stressed that Christians could themselves not attain human rights as long as they did not abandon their Christianity. Correspondingly, a "Christian state" under Friedrich Wilhelm IV could not grant the Jews such rights since it did not dispose over them: "What is not owned by either of two sides cannot be given to or received from the other."[59] But even here, we find a surfacing of the idea expressed more clearly in "The Ability of Today's Jews and Christians to Become Free": "The Jew faces more difficulties if he wants to raise himself to freedom."[60]

Bauer argued analogously in the question of citizenship. It was not only that the Jews could receive no general rights as long as the "Christian state" did not have them. Beyond that, equal rights for Jews and Christians were impossible on ground of religious difference alone: the state was *based* on this difference. As Bauer put it, the Jews did not believe "Jesus to be the Messiah." They were thus incapable of entering into an "honest relation" with Christians, for whom that belief was "the only true cord of all unity."[61] These objections could, it seems, be reduced on the one hand to Hobbes's maxim of minimal allegiance, "Jesus is the Christ"; and on the other hand to a simple postulate of the homogeneity of the state. But beyond such objections, "the Jew" could in any event never be a citizen for Bauer. As long as he was a Jew, his "Jewish and limited nature," containing no *general* concepts, would always triumph over his human and political obligations.[62]

The reality of a social and historical Jewish community is disturbing for all *systematic* philosophies of history. The survival of the Jewish people does not seem to have a rational explanation in any of them.[63] To find an explanation Bauer, like many others, had recourse to traditional interpretive models. His description of the "rigidity of the Jewish national consciousness" scarcely hides its origins in the Christian myth of the Jewish role in the history of salvation. From one traditional Christian perspective, the existence of the Jews after the appearance of Jesus represents a provocation. Bauer was able to translate theological anti-Jewish resentment into a secular language—into a realm of modern political concepts. Through this translation, his critique removed the possibility of a theological solution to the "Jewish problem," something most often involving Jewish conversion. The critique's significance lies in that fact. An uncompromisingly radical demand for the Jews to have "freedom" and "equality" only as "human beings," never as Jews, leaves no place for politically realizable compromises. Bauer's conception centered first of all on refuting the liberal idea that political emancipation could be realized independently of religious affiliation.

With this goal in mind, he took aim at the notion that within the constitutional order, everyday co-existence between Christians and Jews would develop naturally. Rather, he cited French Jewry to exemplify the enduring nature of the differences and the persistence of inequality so long as Jews did not fully renounce their Judaism and Christians their Christianity.[64] Bauer pointed to the decision by the supposedly religiously neutral French state to make Christian holidays official, to the disadvantage of the Jews. This, he argued, underscored the "hypocrisy" of the *juste-milieu* in speaking of complete Jewish emancipation: such secularization was exclusively Christian, not Jewish, in form. For Bauer, this marked the borders of the liberal project. Neither the bourgeois revolution of 1789 nor that of 1848, he stressed, had realized the ultimate goal of those advocating Jewish emancipation. But within Bauer's eschatological speculation, no place was available for necessary compromises: "History . . . will not be taken for a fool."[65]

"The Jewish Question": Bruno Bauer and Karl Marx

The publication in February 1844 of Karl Marx's now famous polemic essay "On the Jewish Question" in the *Deutsch-Französische Jahrbücher* marked the start of an open conflict between himself and Bauer, two previously closely allied radicals. The essay prompted Bauer to criticize Marx, even before Max Stirner did so, in a series of articles in the *Allgemeine Literaturzeitung*.[66] The essay attests to the influence of Bauer's ideas, which Marx would later deny.[67] The influence involved Marx's model of political estrangement and his idea of the relationship between religion and the state, on the one hand, and his description of Judaism, on the other hand. The description kept to the "facts" Marx was furnished by Bauer.[68] Marx had spared little interest for contemporary Jewry; his ignorance regarding the demands of this oppressed social group has often been discussed.[69] There is one statement deviating from his basic "hostility to the Jews" (Edmund Silberner), in a letter to Arnold Ruge:

> The head of the local Israelites just came to me regarding a petition for the Jews in the Landtag and I intend to do it. While the Jewish faith is repellent to me, I think Bauer's view is too abstract. The important thing is to punch as many holes in the Christian state as possible and to smuggle in what is rational, as much as possible. We need to at least try this—and the bitterness grows with each petition rejected under protest.[70]

It is striking how much authority in this question Bauer still had for Marx in 1843. Beyond this, the letter indicates that Marx, exactly like Bauer, wished to do more than simply offer a contribution to the debate on Jewish political emancipation in bourgeois society. For both "metaphysical revolutionaries" the Jews were more than a symbol of the wicked world against which they wished to rise up.[71]

Bauer's ideas regarding the "Jewish question," amounting as they did to a nearly insurmountable barrier to emancipation, represented a challenge to the Young Hegelians, among whom were some Jews.[72] Marx clearly wished to break with his former teacher;[73] after a period of neglect his essay had an extraordinary impact. In the essay's first part, Marx defends the political emancipation of the Jews against objections based on the sociology of religion. In the second part, he attempts to "break with the question's theological conception" and to link socio-economic perspectives with the "Jewish question" in a radical manner.[74] In this enterprise, he plays with the double meaning of the word *Judentum* (Jewry) that emerged from the medieval equation of *iudaeus* and *mercator*, Jewry and trade.[75] "Self-interest," "haggling," and "money" are the features that Marx ascribed to "real" Jewry.[76] The metaphor of *Judentum* thus became a crystallization point for all the negative qualities Marx associated with bourgeois society—the basis for an ongoing discussion of Marx's "Jewish self-hatred" or "antisemitism." On the surface this would appear to be a terminological issue, being tied to one's definition of "antisemitism" or "self hatred." If by the former term one means, in line with Edmund Silberner, "hostility to the Jews," then Marx was certainly an antisemite.[77] But what mattered far more at the time was whether Marx was for or against Jewish emancipation. That as a radical atheist he would reject the Jewish religion as such was self-evident. Still, interpreting the position he takes in his essay is difficult since his approach to "the Jews" is not clearly separate from his argument against religious Judaism, or *Judentum*. One is left with a split impression.

The distinction between "political" and general "human" emancipation is at the center of Marx's discussion.[78] He suggests that Bauer has engaged in an "uncritical confusion" of these two emancipatory steps, in that manner formulating preconditions for the political emancipation of the Jews in no way grounded in their "nature" *(Wesen)* (270). In the first part of his essay, Marx thus freshly considers political emancipation. Where for Bauer Jewish emancipation is determined by both the Jews and the Christian state, for Marx it is simply a special example of the state's political emancipation from religion. Marx defines Jewish emancipation as essentially based on the "emancipation of the state from Jewry [*Judentum*]"; in this way, he indicates, it is a precondition for the state in its modern, "realized" form, that is, the state freed from religion in general (278). He sees the "Christian state" as first needing to emancipate itself from "Christianity" in order to become a political state. But having thus become atheistic, the state faces a society that might well still be religious. Consequently, in the atheistic state human beings remain in condition of servitude; they are only atheistic because of the state: "Just as Christ is the intercessor upon which man imposes the burden of all his divinity, all his religious fixedness, the state is the intercessor to which man attributes all his non-divinity, all his human perplexity" (273).

In his response to Bauer, Marx says nothing in favor of Bauer's idea that atheistic political form depends on its Christian antithesis. Still, the diction of the above citation appears to completely support that idea. Likewise, to assume that Marx's demand for the state's emancipation from religion is simply an effort to mitigate Jewish emancipation would be mistaken. To the contrary, Marx sees with great clarity that the privatization of religion in no way softened religious differences and tensions. For Marx as for Bauer, the conflicts Bauer exemplified in the relation of the French state to the Jews persist. This is the reason for Marx distinguishing between political emancipation from religion and *human* emancipation—political emancipation can solve only part of the problem. But since Marx is also in favor of this first emancipatory step, he introduces a possibility of compromise into the debate, something Bauer would have never accepted. Marx raises the unjustified objection that Bauer has failed to distinguish between the existing Christian state and the future "free" state: a misreading decisive for the course of Marx's argument.[79] Bauer's reluctance to accept Jewish political and human emancipation, he indicates, stems from his derivation of the basic concepts and forms of political thinking from Christian theology. Bauer knows no "political" emancipation because for him, the political has never lost its dependence on a secularization of the theological.

In contrast to Bauer's construction, for Marx the state can indeed emancipate itself politically from religion even if a "great majority" of its citizens remained religious. Since in the Hegelian sense the state has "annulled" religion by declaring religious differences to be unpolitical, the various religions no longer represent a political problem for the state. In introducing the following passage from paragraph 270 of Hegel's *Philosophy of Law*, Marx inverts the relationship once again: "The state only gained and brings to existence the generality of its thought, the principle of its form, through the *particular* churches." Marx comments, "to be sure!" and observes that "the state constitutes as a generality only so, *through* the particular elements."[80] Hence not only is there no contradiction between the modern atheistic state and the existence of religions, but the former presupposes the latter.

In this passage Marx makes use of Hegel's authority in order to neutralize Bauer's objections to Jewish emancipation. In the same paragraph 270, Hegel offers an extensive comment on granting the Jews civil rights; his argument is here more far-reaching than his remarks on the relation of state and religion that will be taken over by Marx. Hegel speaks of the "clamor" raised against emancipation. He defends the concept not only in the abstract, principled sense of Marx but concretely— the Jews are "to be considered part of a foreign people"; equal rights will neutralize both ethnic differences and differences grounded in religion. And he points to exclusion of the Jews as contradicting the role of the modern state as an objective institutional power.[81]

Marx places Hegel's reflections on the political separation of religion and state in a wider context, reducing the conflict between adherence to a particular religion on the one hand and citizenship on the other hand to a worldly split between political state and bourgeois society. In his view, the contradiction he perceives between religious and political man is the same contradiction of the bourgeois with the citizen or, in his formulation, that "between the member of bourgeois society and his political lion's skin."[82] For Marx the political emancipation of the Jews cannot represent a separate problem since with the political emancipation of the state religion is banished from public to private law (276).

But this does not render religion problem-free. Rather, now transformed into "bourgeois society's spirit," it continues to make its mark in the "sphere of egoism," of the "war of all against all" (276). It is, however, no longer society's moment of homogeneity but the "expression of the separation of the human being from his community [*Gemeinwesen*], from himself and other human beings" (277). Marx then offers the following key insight: "The dissolution of the human being into the Jew and citizen, the Protestant and citizen, the religious man and citizen, is no lie against citizenship, no evasion of political emancipation, but is political emancipation itself, the political way to emancipate oneself from religion" (277).

Since for Marx the modern state expresses its generality and its principles by taking a nonpolitical stance regarding religion, he sees the Christian state as an expression of a Christian *denial* of the state. It is thus no modern state, since it approaches religion politically and politics in terms of religion (278). His article on the "Jewish question" is not grounded in a critique of Judaism, as is Bauer's text on the same theme, but in a critique of the Christian state. Marx's "Jewish question" is thus first and foremost a question of the Christian state, of the emancipation of the "Christian state" from Christianity. At considerable length, Marx shows how the "authentic" form of human and civil rights in North America and France does not conflict with the Jewish religious community but, above all, with the "Christian state" (283–91). The first part of his essay is couched in terms closely resembling a liberal defense of those rights (a tendency even more clear in the chapters of *The Holy Family* for which he was responsible, that work involving a further confrontation with Bauer[83]). To repudiate Bauer's arguments against granting the Jews religious freedom, he shows that in declaring such freedom to be irreconcilable with the principles of Judaism, Bauer has argued past the political concept of religious freedom. This concept does not amount to the liberation of men from religion but the liberation of the state from religion. Individual citizens, Marx argues, are not *freed* from their religion but receive *religious freedom*.[84] In the same way, they are not robbed of their property or earnings but receive freedom to own property and practice a trade.[85] Hence for Marx, himself of Jewish origin but baptized at the age of six, as long as the state has not emancipated itself from religion the "Jewish question" is a religious question: "The Jew finds himself in religious opposition to the state that acknowledges Christianity as its basis."[86] As suggested, Bauer sees the opposition as much deeper and as insurmountable: "The Jew as such" is a Jew by his "nature," *Wesen*, and not a "human being," *Mensch*; in the same manner the Christian is not a "human being" by nature but rather a Christian. For Bauer, the Jew, as long as he is a Jew, remains the "other"; he cannot enjoy the same rights as a Christian.[87]

In the second part of "On the Jewish Question," Marx does his best to surpass Bauer's anti-Judaism. Wolfgang Essbach has explained Marx's extreme statements in terms of the "Young Hegelians' laws of group discussion," driving Marx to out-trump Bauer through recourse to an antisemitic motif.[88] But social-psychological factors also seem at work here, prompting Marx to speak about "the Jews" in a language completely covering up his rabbinic family origins.[89] Marx first summarizes Bauer's position in "The Capability of Today's Jews and Christians to Become Free." Bauer, he indicates, has transformed the question of Jewish emancipation into a religious question by repeating in Enlightenment form the theological question of who has better chances to attain bliss: "which of the two is more capable of emancipation?"[90] Marx here addresses the core of Bauer's argument. But he then takes over Bauer's argumentative strategy regarding the question of the continued, concrete existence of a Judaism putatively surpassed historically by Christianity. Bauer assumes the existence of a theological substance to the Jewish religion, postulating this as the cause of the survival of the Jews as an ethnic community. Marx breaks with a theological conception of the "Jewish question" and inverts the question: what social elements needed to be overcome in order to "annul"—*aufheben*, in the Hegelian sense—Judaism? In this context Judaism is not defined by the Jewish religion but by "real, worldly Jews." Where in his criticism of religion Bauer designates Judaism as a law-based religion hostile to progress, Marx shifts the critique to an economic plane. But he himself articulates intense anti-Jewish resentment. This is especially clear in one notorious passage, referred to above: "What is the worldly basis of Jewry? Practical need, *self-interest*. What is the worldly cult of the Jews? *Haggling*. What is his worldly god? *Money*."[91]

"The Jew" here takes over the role Marx later assigns the bourgeoisie.[92] Although the critique of Jewry precedes that of the bourgeoisie, Marx's thinking is here already oriented toward the structures of political economy. The later dialectic of bourgeoisie and proletariat finds its equivalent in the relation between *Judentum* and *Christentum*, emancipation from "haggling and Judaism, i.e. from practical, real Jewry" being the "self-emancipation of the age."[93] In this way, Marx defines Jewish emancipation as emancipation of humanity from Jewry (294). For until that point, what will continue to hold true is that "the Jews have emancipated themselves to the extent that the Christians have become Jews" (294). Jewry, then, has taken over "practical rule" of the "Christian world" (295): a distortion that, whatever else may have been tied to Marx's speculation, corresponds closely to the paranoid worldview of various antisemites. But Marx takes an additional symbolic step. Since Jewry, "as the practical-Jewish spirit," has emancipated itself by way of Christian society, it has found its highest development within that society (295). Modern, bourgeois society is thus continuously producing Jews (296). Jewry understood in this way, as practical "egoism," can only realize itself in bourgeois society, which has "born" the political, atheistic state "out of itself" (296). Within that society the "secularized [*verweltlicht*] God of the Jews" has, for Marx, become a "world-God" *(Weltgott)*. Christianity has again "dissolved itself into Jewry" (296–97).

Within Marx's vision, only social emancipation of the Jews allows society's emancipation from Jewry (299). Adhering to Marx's model, if one asks whether Christians or Jews face more difficulties in being emancipated, then it appears that Christianity needs one step more than Jewry: it has to transform itself into "practical Jewry" in order to be humanly emancipated. For Marx, Jewry is thus closer to the nineteenth century's economic spirit than Christianity. This is one idea that Carl Schmitt would perhaps have shared with Marx.

10

Protestant Atheism

In the 1930s, Schmitt's explicit and increasingly aggressive antisemitism did not only feed on his Catholic or "atheistic-Catholic" sources. The anti-emancipatory reflections of "Protestant" atheists and Young Hegelians represented an additional pole of his anti-Judaism. Schmitt's debates over constitutional theory in the Weimar Republic, particularly those with Hans Kelsen, can already be read as a continuation of the debates about Jewish emancipation between Bauer and Marx.

In formulating his basic premise that "all pregnant concepts of modern political theory are secularized theological concepts," Schmitt always meant *Christian* theological concepts. But apparently on the basis of either Marx or Disraeli, he did pose the question of the influence of secularized concepts from Jewish theology and religion on modern constitutional doctrine. Bruno Bauer had already expressed doubts regarding the relevance of secularized Christian concepts for secularizing Jewry. This was the truly radical aspect of Bauer's attack on Jewish emancipation and, as we have seen, one of the grounds for his dispute with Marx. The attack in any case had more than a merely diagnostic framework. Schmitt, for one, saw in it a "deep feeling of having been betrayed. [Bauer] thus discovered falsifications everywhere, especially in the Gospel according to St. John. The Jew thus becomes a primal symbol [*Ursymbol*] of falsification and betrayal."[1]

Secularization, emancipation, and particularistic betrayal formed the backdrop to Schmitt's critique of Hans Kelsen. Kelsen's concept of state was here an axial point. In polemicizing against the idea of "pure" legal theory advocated by Kelsen, Schmitt made particular use of Bauer's attack on what he saw as the abstract, positive nature of Jewish law. In his post-1933 writings, Schmitt also took up Bauer's critique of the alleged "landlessness" of positive Jewish law, trying now to offer a response to this "landlessness." To this end he developed the nomos idea already formulated in his *Constitutional Theory* in 1928. In his Weimar Republic writings, Schmitt offered no alternative to the legal concept he was criticizing. He simply attacked Kelsen's effort to separate the spheres of politics, religion, and law, here following Bauer's vehement attack on Marx's standpoint.

In the Weimar Republic period, then, the conflict between Bauer and Marx was mirrored in the confrontation between Kelsen's "pure theory of law" and Schmitt's political theology. Both thinkers were primarily concerned with the question of how properly to evaluate the fact that, in Kelsen's words, "doctrine of state" stood in "very striking harmony with divine doctrine, with theology."[2] Similarly to Marx, Kelsen understood religion as "social ideology," which he subjected to a radical critique supported by Kant, Feuerbach, and Freud. From this standpoint, he attacked "all the older and newer theories of state," which had aligned themselves in "startling parallel to theological theories."[3]

In *Political Theology*, Schmitt cited Kelsen's accomplishment in pointing "with his own accent" since 1920 "to the methodological relation between theology and jurisprudence."[4] But Schmitt made this relation into the *basis* of his program for a "pregnant" political theology. The program, was aimed at a secular political science whose acuity, precision, and economy would be an expression of its theological origins. In 1970, Schmitt returned to his doctrine of sovereignty, observing that "my text *Political Theology* of 1922 . . . is concerned with . . . a problem of theory and conceptual history: the structure-identity of the concepts at work in theological and juridical argumentation and perceptions."[5] He here appears to have been referring to a special kind of conceptual history that involves a structural relationship between theology and law. Ernst-Wolfgang Böckenförde has referred to this schema as a *juridical* political theology, in distinction to its *institutional* and *appellative* counterparts.[6] Schmitt's doctrine was political theology in a strong and particular sense. It not only concerned itself diagnostically with analogies between theology and jurisprudence, but, beyond this, placed *itself* in a positive relation to the result of this Christian secularization process.

Schmitt's thinking circled around a number of concepts owing their "pregnancy" to a secularization of Christian forms. The concepts at play in the time of the Weimar Republic included *state, sovereignty, dictatorship, law (Gesetz), state of emergency,* and *decision.* Kelsen's argumentation moved in the opposite direction. He postulated a legal doctrine "purified of all political ideologies and all elements from the natural sciences."[7] He was concerned particularly with overcoming theological tenets embedded in humanistic studies and the social sciences, and—based on Freud—on dissolving hypostasized notions of God and state into their individual-psychological elements.[8] But unlike Marx, he did not wish to eliminate the state altogether.

Five years after the end of World War II, in his book on Donoso Cortés, Schmitt offered his longest and most positive assessment of Bauer. It includes the following statement: "No one could execute theological-philosophical critique and guide it to its end like Bruno Bauer: that critique understood in its full sense and in all the fatality tied to the words *critique* and *crisis* over the last two centuries of German intellectual history."[9] His other comments on both Bauer and Marx likewise mainly stem from the decades following the war's outbreak. They are often found in letters, books, and notes located in the Schmitt archives;[10] the most important are contained in Schmitt's extensive correspondence with Hans Körniken.[11] At the end of April 1939, Schmitt also tried to persuade Ernst Jünger that "the by far most significant remarks [*das weitaus Bedeutendste*] on Jewry are by Bruno Bauer, *On the Jewish Question*, 1843, then in some chapters of his critique of the gospels in the vanished volume IV (1852) and in the essay 'Jewry in Foreign Lands' ['Das Judentum in der Fremde,' 1863]."[12] (A month earlier Jünger had already told Schmitt that he was turning to Bauer as a result of his prompting.[13]) It is clear from the material in the archives that Schmitt owned many of Bauer's texts. Before the age of copying machines, he in fact had many of them elaborately photo-duplicated. He knew almost all the texts concerned with the "Jewish question"; his comments reveal an intense study of them.

In Schmitt's published works, there are few direct references to Bauer, one exception being his reference in the preliminary remarks to his book on dictatorship.[14] At the same time, despite the fact that Schmitt's self-reflections need to be approached with great caution, they nevertheless underscore the extent and direction of his interest in Bauer. In February 1946 he wrote a *depositum* intended for his friend, the historian of religion and Jesuit father Erich Przywara (1889–1967), himself the author of many texts on the "Jewish question."[15] With the aid of three selected authors, Schmitt here tried to show how his thought was tied to "German history of the past centuries":

> In first position Bruno Bauer, the most illuminating figure in the long process of the self-dissolution of German Protestantism and

Idealism, author of some astonishing highly Christian attacks on Christianity, starting with his critique of D. F. Strauss's *Life of Jesus* that had just appeared (1835) and continuing through the scattered writing of his old age about Philo, Bismarck, Disraeli, and "Christ and the Caesars" (1877), author above all of the *Jewish Question* of 1843, which is certainly as important as Karl Marx's world-famous answer from the same year, author as well of *Judaism in Foreign Lands* (1863) and the text, frequently rediscovered for some years now, *Russia and German Being* [*Germanentum*] (1853). . . . In a book by[16] Karl Löwith, *From Hegel to Nietzsche*, the intellectual-historical path that Bruno Bauer signifies is well noted. But Löwith conceals [*verschweigt*] Bruno Bauer's texts on Jews [*Judenschriften*], and with them a specific German-Protestant orientation, so that that book *From Hegel to Nietzsche* still wears the blindfold one finds on medieval statues of the synagogue. I treated the context in several talks, 1943 and 1944. . . .

Couched as an antisemitic jab, the gap Schmitt points to in Löwith is interesting. The gap seems to resemble Gurian's neglect of Maurras' antisemitism. Schmitt's emphasis in this passage on Bauer as the "author of the *Jewish Question*" suggests the presence there of motifs Schmitt found of interest for his struggle against Kelsen's "pure theory of law."[17] Schmitt's modern and future-oriented way of thinking did not harmonize well with fantasies of an estate-ordered Christian monarchy, as cultivated by the conservative opponents of Jewish emancipation. (As indicated, he specifically praised Donoso Cortés's break with such fantasies.) What bound him with the Young Hegelian Bruno Bauer was the question of the origin and impact of modern political-legal concepts. As with Weber, his central interest here was in the secularization process.

It is by now a commonplace that secularization has had an enormous effect on the norms and values of the Jews.[18] The reverse influence of self-emancipating European Judaism on the secularization process of the "Christian state" perhaps was defined most provocatively in the above-cited dictum from Marx's *Jewish Question:* "The Jews have emancipated themselves to the extent that the Christians have become Jews."[19] In his postwar *Glossarium*, Schmitt wrote as follows: "Just as Karl Marx says that the emancipation of the J. took place in such a way that the Christians became Jews, assimilees [*Assimilanten*] of Kurt Hiller's stamp have conceived not only emancipation but also assimilation in the same way. In the end the whole village is meant to *mauscheln* [i.e., talk Yiddish jargon]."[20] In another diary entry he combines a famous pronouncement attributed to Marx with words from Disraeli's *Tancred*, "Christianity is Judaism for the multitude, but still it is Judaism":[21] "From there the *infandum scelus* [nefarious deed] is to be measured that lies in the two sentences: (1) Religion is opium for the masses and (2) Christianity is Judaism [*Judenthum*] for the masses. Both these sentences stem from the time before 1848; their echo needed almost a century."[22]

11

"Pure Legal Theory" as Secularized Theology of the Enemy

Jesus or Barabbas?

The eighteenth chapter of the Gospel according to John describes Jesus's arrest, his presentation before the Roman governor Pilate, and his subsequent interrogation.[1] In response to the ironic question, "So you are the king of the Jews?" Jesus is here reported to have answered, "My task is to bear witness to the truth. For this I was born; for this I came into the world, and all those who are not deaf to truth listen to my voice."[2] Pilate then responds: "What is truth?" before going before the Jews and saying, "For my part I find no case against him."[3] For this reason, he explains, he is ready to release Jesus in the framework of the amnesty accorded a single man each Pesach: "Would you like me to release the king of the Jews?"[4] The Jews are now reported to answer "Not him; we want Barabbas!"[5]

For centuries, this New Testament passage was one of the most important sources of Christian anti-Judaism. Encapsulating many basic problems, the passage became an issue in the Weimar Republic's constitutional theory; Hans Kelsen placed it at the center of his radically antimetaphysical theory of democracy. In any event, a general re-theologizing of German constitutional theory accompanied its crisis in the 1920s. This crisis primarily affected legal positivism. That approach to law was represented in Germany mainly by Gerhard Anschütz and Richard Thoma, to large extent from a defensive position.[6]

The New Testament passage's implications for the legal positivists even surfaced in West Germany a few decades after the war's end. Fritz Bauer, the most important German state prosecutor dealing with Nazi war criminals, had apparently been interested in the passage over the course of his career. In 1965 in an article titled "The Trial of Jesus," he posed the familiar question, "if it was a false verdict, who is guilty?"[7] During his childhood in Stuttgart, Bauer had been subjected to antisemitic taunts involving the old charge of deicide.[8] The purpose of his article was ambitious: not only to offer what he viewed as a just account of the trial but, beyond that, to make the latter fruitful for a West German understanding of basic rights stamped by natural law. In this respect his interpretation differed sharply from Kelsen's, which will be examined closely below. But the two authors were linked by a preoccupation with this "theological" account in the framework of secular legal theory.

In a manner that was both open and concealed, Carl Schmitt offered readers of *Political Theology* a parenthetical journal and page reference[9] steering them to his archenemy Kelsen's discussion of the New Testament passage in his essay "On the Nature and Value of Democracy" ("Vom Wesen und Wert der Demokratie").[10] For Schmitt, this article was Kelsen's "avowal of democracy." Such an "avowal" was, however, merely the expression of the "political relativism" evident in a "scientificity [*Wissenschaftlichkeit*] freed of miracles and dogma and grounded in human reason and critical doubt."[11] Turning to Kelsen's essay, we can see easily enough why Schmitt begins his attack here. The text indeed amounts to a spectacular apology for Kelsen's programmatically relativistic, democratic worldview, presented on the basis of the account of Jesus's trial offered in John 18. Kelsen describes that New Testament chapter as a "tragic symbol of relativism—and of democracy."[12] Not only Schmitt considered the description provocative: in a review of the text's expanded version, Otto Koellreutter, Schmitt's later rival in the Nazi power-struggle over the "new legal theory,"[13] would write that "light doubt may be felt whether this depiction from the Gospel according to John is in place as a conclusion to Kelsen's deductions."[14] Clearly the objections at play in this remark were not only theoretical; critics would allow their nontheoretical objections to shine through with a greater or lesser degree of elegance.

At the center of Kelsen's argument is one, particular assertion: that Pilate, the Roman governor, did not know what Jesus, "in the Roman's eyes simply a poor fool," meant when he said, "My task is to bear witness to the truth. For this I was born; for this I came into the world, and all those who are not deaf to truth listen to my voice."[15] Pilate, Kelsen indicates, could only rely on earthly truths, and could thus only draw on human insight as a guiding principle for realizing social goals. Likewise, he could only justify a force that was indispensable to that end by acting with the approval of at least the majority of those for whose well-being the power-order had been established. Pilate, this "man from an old, tired, and hence now skeptical culture," thus appealed to the Jews and arranged a referendum. The "popular referendum" was decided against Jesus, the people deciding that the "thief" Barabbas be spared.[16]

It is important to note that Kelsen is here inverting the usual description of the Romans as a "young" people—in contrast to the Jews. This passage is informed by the jurist's sense that the ability of the Roman state to maintain positive law with "stoic tranquility" was more than coincidence. For Kelsen, Roman "resignation is the fruit of an old culture that already had all phases of philosophical speculation and political struggle behind it, and that already retained a certain fatigue at any excess of pessimism or optimism."[17] In any event, Kelsen's discussion of the chapter in John is in many respects startling, implicitly raising the question of why he closes his book on the nature and value of democracy with precisely this material. The extent to which Kelsen appears to ignore this particular gospel's anti-Judaism is in any case remarkable. A number of passages in John suggest unmistakably that Pilate does not wish to condemn Jesus. Kelsen cites Pilate's formulation, "I find no case against him." In John 19, it is made even more clear that Pilate condemns Jesus against his will, in order to avoid the wrath of the Jews: "From that moment Pilate tried hard to release him, but the Jews kept shouting, 'If you let this man go, you are no friend to Caesar. . . . We have no king but Caesar.'"[18] This last sentence has always been treated in Christian theological literature as evidence that the Jewish people renounced its messianic claim, and hence itself.[19] It is clear that the Gospel according to John implies a certain sympathy on Pilate's part for Jesus; in this way it comes closer to a charge of Jewish deicide than the other gospels.[20]

At the same time, the connection Kelsen proposed between Pilate's supposed democratic-relativistic worldview and Jesus's crucifixion is artificial. The Gospel according to John does not speak of a "popular referendum"; nor is Pilate impelled to question the people because he "does not know what truth is."[21] In fact, the contrary seems to be the case. Kelsen transforms a conflict between the Jews and Jesus into a conflict between Jesus and Pilate, who emerges, intimidated by the Jews, as a model of democratic sensibility. Kelsen's reshaping of the lapidary account in John—which he considered one of the greatest passages in "world literature"[22]—is thus highly forced.[23] Rather than Jewish disbelief, his own opposition between the absolute truth of Jesus and the relative truth of Pilate is at the core of his reading.

In this way the "tragedy" at work in Kelsen's symbol for relativism and democracy has a double meaning. On the one hand, it addresses the inability of political relativism to arrive at absolutely correct decisions, since its nature is to possess only relative truth. But the last section of Kelsen's text suggests another, much more far-reaching meaning. Kelsen comments that political believers can only take his example and turn it against democracy if they are as certain of their "political truth" as was "the son of God."[24] This comment can only be understood as ironic, since Kelsen always presumes the inaccessibility of absolute truth to human cognition. If, however, such absolute certainty were ever realized, a situation would result that Kelsen describes with the help of John 18. Its tragedy would lie in the democratic-relativistic order possibly or even preferably killing such a divine human being. The democratic model, in short, would always have to opt *for* deicide, because of its political rather than religious constitution, its incapacity for integrating absolute truths. Kelsen supports this reading in a parallel passage linked to Plato's *Politics*, citing Socrates' response to the question of what the ideal state would do with a genius: "We would honor him as a man worthy of adoration, wonderful and lovable; but after we brought to his attention that such a man did not and was not allowed to live in our state, we would lead him over the border, salving his head with oil and adorning it with a wreath."[25]

In his first passage, Kelsen defines the tragedy of democracy as lying in its sometimes leading to false decisions. In his second passage, he makes clear that democracy cannot allow itself "absolute truth." Kelsen thus describes relativism as the worldview at the heart of democratic thinking. For democracy, he indicates, is based on the principle that the opposite opinion from what currently prevails had to be considered possibly right.[26] Here, a proximity to Mill's argument in *On Liberty* is striking: transfers of power characteristic of democracy can only take place when momentarily prevailing opinion recognizes that the opposition's ideas are not absolutely false.

Jesus or Christ?

In the fourth chapter of his *Political Theology*, Carl Schmitt again took up Kelsen's "symbol of relativism." He did so in a manner displaying an interesting juncture of different reference points, evoking the Catholic counterrevolutionary Donoso Cortés in order to turn that symbol against liberalism:[27]

> For Cortés . . . liberalism with its inconsequences and compromises only lives in the short interim in which it is possible to answer the question "Christ or Barabbas?" with a motion of continuance or the establishment of an investigative commission. Such an approach is not arbitrary, rather being grounded in liberal metaphysics. The bourgeoisie is the class of freedom of speech and press; it does not achieve these freedoms through one or another random psychological or economic circumstance. . . . That the idea of liberal rights to freedom stemmed from the North American states was known for a long time. When more recently Georg Jellinek demonstrates the North American origin of these freedoms, this is a thesis that would have hardly surprised the Catholic philosophers of state (as little in fact as Karl Marx, author of the essay on the Jewish question).[28]

Schmitt does not delve here into the parallels constructed by Kelsen, his juxtaposition of the opposition between Jesus and Pilate with that between absolute and relative truth, and between autocratic and democratic forms of state. Kelsen's democratically defined Pilate receives no mention. The question Schmitt formulates, "Christ or Barabbas?" is merely rhetorical, already containing the essential point, namely that Jesus is *Christ*. There can be no doubt that for Schmitt the passage Kelsen discusses was not merely an extract from "world literature"; such a designation would have evoked all the hostility toward "cultivated" Protestant-Jewish culture he had maintained since his student days. Rather, his question was posed from a Christian religious perspective. In this respect, it is notable that in the 1963 new edition of the *Concept of the Political*, Schmitt describes the question of whether the sentence "Jesus is the Christ" is interchangeable as a "systematic basic problem" in Hobbes's political doctrine; as usual with theological questions, Schmitt does not make his own opinion clear.[29]

Schmitt had developed his sharp critique of liberalism's "eternal conversation" in *Political Romanticism*, as part of his effort to define the structure of the romantic spirit, hence to diagnose "modernity."[30] In his later critique of that "conversation,"[31] liberalism's indecisive "investigative commissions," he was following his Grand-Inquisitorial hero Donoso Cortés, who viewed the "principle of discussion,"[32] the parliamentary idea of a "government by discussion,"[33] as a monumental, nearly religious error: "For infallibility cannot emerge from discussion."[34] Like Donoso Cortés, Schmitt saw his opponents' arguments as amounting to the "theology of the opponent." More precisely, he saw these arguments as reflecting the *secularized* theology of his enemies.[35] His "resolutely intellectual-historical examination" was exclusively intent on isolating the "metaphysical kernel" of their ideas.[36] But what was the essence of this "metaphysical kernel," the secularized theology he sees as hiding itself behind liberal conceptual structures? To answer this question, we need to recognize the fusion of Schmitt's attack upon the "universalistic" Jewish spirit, an attack aligned with Joseph de Maistre and Juan Donoso Cortés, with his allied attack upon Jewish *particularism,* aligned with Bruno Bauer.

It is no coincidence that in the above passage Schmitt mentions Marx's "On the Jewish Question," an essay, we will recall, that made political emancipation of the Jews into a touchstone of liberal bourgeois emancipation in general. The reference is in that part of *Political Theology* where Schmitt attacks Kelsen's theory of democracy.[37] There can be no doubt that Schmitt knew that in Germany the concept of the *Staatsbürger,* the bourgeois citizen of the civil state, first appeared in the emancipation edict of 1812.[38] Its implied separation of religion and politics stood, as he later will explain, in direct connection with the desire of the Jews for political emancipation. In this manner, within Schmitt's polemic the liberal worldview is historically tied to self-emancipating Jewry.[39] Schmitt's question "Christ or Barabbas" refers as much to Jewish *decide* as to the "metaphysical kernel" of the liberal worldview. For Schmitt, the scandal of this worldview was that it responded to the question with its "eternal conversation." In any event, the far greater scandal of relativistic democracy-theory, brought to its highpoint by Kelsen in his continuation of the work of the Jewish authors Marx and Jellinek, consisted in its articulating a specific decision: one *against* Christ. For Schmitt, then, behind the liberal conversation stood a decision against the absolute truth of Christian revelation.[40] And he perceived the decision as encapsulated in the work of the assimilated Jew Hans Kelsen. Apparently, Kelsen had this theological motive in mind when, writing retrospectively from exile in Geneva in 1934, he spoke of the "nonscientific" grounding for the "unparalleled passion and opposition bordering on hatred" in face of the "pure theory of law."[41]

"Pure Theory of Law": Beyond State and God

In his *Political Theology* Schmitt refers to Kelsen's book *The Sociological and Juridical Concepts of State.*[42] Schmitt maintains that "a large number of to be sure diffuse analogies" between theological and juridical method are at work in the book: analogies allowing "deeper intellectual-historical insight into the inner heterogeneity of [Kelsen's] starting point in cognitive theory and his . . . democratic results, amounting to a worldview."[43]

Kelsen's legal theory was meant to be "purified of all political ideologies and all elements from the natural sciences, aware of its own particular nature because of being aware of the laws defining its object."[44] His "cognitive theory" can thus be understood as a further development of nineteenth-century positivist and neo-Kantian jurisprudence.[45] His project, founding a science of law beyond politics and theology, was tied to a penetrating criticism of both those realms. In pointing to structural analogies between jurisprudence and theology, he wished to apply arguments emerging from radical critiques of religion to core concepts of legal theory. The removal from legal theory of just those elements Schmitt placed at its center was thus an expression of Kelsen's systematic thinking.

Alongside Kant, Locke, and Marx, whom Schmitt directly or indirectly describes as Kelsen's predecessors, Sigmund Freud had an important influence on Kelsen's treatment of religion and theology. Freud was a personal friend of Kelsen, who discussed Freud's ideas about law and religion—as presented in *Totem and Taboo* (the second edition of 1920), "Group Psychology and the Analysis of the Ego" (1921), and *Civilization and Its Discontents* (1930)—in many texts. Kelsen directly took over Freud's interpretation of the psychological relation between the ideology of state and the ideology of God, an interpretation that itself owed much to Robertson Smith's *Religion of the Semites*.[46] Considering Freud's description in *Totem and Taboo* of the sacrificial meal's role in forming kinship networks, Kelsen thus observes that the original merger of "many individuals into a [social] unit" was expressed in the substance of the (totemic) sacrificial animal devoured by the unit's members.[47] From this he concludes that the social unit had "a religious character from the start." It could only emerge, he indicates, thanks to the tie to the godhead made possible through the sacrificial meal.[48] Hence for Kelsen, religion, understood as a society's social ideology, is "originally identical with that social ideology which one [would] designate in the most extended sense as state [ideology]."[49] In this way Kelsen widened the structural analogy between political doctrine and theology that Schmitt already formulated. But crucially, he did so in only one direction. Namely, the concepts developed in the framework of political theory can be applied to theology. The concept of sovereignty, in particular, has in his words "excellent" uses "for the goals of divine doctrine," since in the end the concept simply expresses an absolutization of its object (182).

Kelsen's approach to the concept of sovereignty is a good example of his basic intent. In jurisprudence, he argues, the theological absolutization of God is continued as an absolutization of the state in the sovereign, the state's sovereignty corresponding to God's omnipotence. Kelsen's critique of this concept stands in the context of a much broader critique of all the concepts at work in political science. His central concern is dissolving their substantive contents into functions. A pure legal theory of the state is a "doctrine of state without a state" (192). Correspondingly, the concept of the sovereign is meant to be understood functionally—not substantively, and neither as a myth nor a person. Indeed, in Kelsen's modern political science, sovereignty lacks any function; hence as Schmitt accurately observed, the concept has no role in Kelsen's theory. Rather, it is relegated to the old "theology of state" with its systemic dualism of God and world, state and law (253).

Kelsen's critique of sovereignty begins with a critique of this systemic dualism. As he sees it, this was a constitutive element of Jewish-Christian theology, which opposed the system of nature with a system of God, with the "hypostasis" of a single God being established behind a unified nature.[50] The essence of theology was thus determined by an irreconcilable gulf between divine and natural systems. The miracles of a "supra-natural" God fulfilled what was impossible for human beings in the realm of nature. According to Kelsen, a single system emerging in place of this "double truth" would amount to natural science and, as long as theology is understood simply as a system of religious norms, to ethics.

Kelsen argues that if a science of positive law or a sociology of statesmanship is to emerge from the old political science, the systemic dualism of state and law needs to be treated in an analogous manner. A supralegal idea of state thus needs to be understood as, in essence, the expression of certain political presumptions not recognized in the legal order; political or religious desires in conflict with the legal order are accommodated through the construction of a "meta-legal" state system (252). The state's transcendence of law thus corresponds to divine transcendence of nature: the basic characteristic of state sovereignty is nothing other than an assertion of the state as an absolute (222). In both theology and jurisprudence this absolute entity appeared as an absolute substance, a real person. Kelsen wishes to eliminate this substance from both the political and juridical spheres (224).

Until this point, Kelsen's "pure theory of law" could be understood as a critique of all monotheistic religions. But as soon as he turns to the relationship of God to nature and the state to law, the critique is unmistakably of Christianity and its doctrine of God's appearance in human form (226–30). Kelsen first turns to the problem of God's transcendence of the world—a transcendence aimed primarily against pantheistic religious systems—leading to God suddenly facing an independent world. This was, however, irreconcilable with God's attributes, a solution thus being called for. A supranatural God consequently transformed himself into the world, that is, into a human being. God's essence split itself into God the father and God the son. For Kelsen, the same problem is present in jurisprudence. The metalegal state could not be accompanied by a completely independent legal order without its having to abandon its self-definition as sovereign omnipotent source of power. Legal theory solved this problem by presuming a "self-obligation" by the state: "The metalegal state becomes law by submitting to itself and thus limiting itself" (230). Kelsen indicates that Schmitt's definition of sovereignty offers an even more theological solution, the sovereign state stepping into the legal sphere at the emergency moment. For Schmitt, then, according to Kelsen, the sovereign mediates as "God-Man" between the "God-state" and the worldly legal order.[51]

Reflecting the strong influence of Kant, for Kelsen any statement about God lies beyond human validation. Similarly with his definition of the metalegal state: it can only be conceived as a political or religious "ideology." It exists solely for those believing in it, that is, for political believers.[52] For all other individuals, the state order and legal order have to be conceived as identical.[53] Sovereignty thus emerges as an "essential feature of both state and law" (87) But for Kelsen, this feature does not involve any decision about a "legal miracle"; rather, it involves the existence of a positive legal order independent of any pre-given ethics or religious dogma (87). Kelsen here breaks radically with the idea of a "parallelism of logical structure" between doctrine of state and theology (222). His theory does not mirror God's transcendence of nature in the classical manner, juxtaposing law with a sovereign, omnipotent state. Rather, he defines law, state, and the sovereign as identical. The state thus loses the "uniqueness" it enjoyed as a consequence of its sovereignty (223). As we have seen, the systemic unity of law and state in Kelsen's "pure theory of law" also means an absence of any need for a mediating "substance" or person.

In a talk delivered in 1911 at Vienna's Soziologische Gesellschaft, Kelsen already examined the "borders between juridical and sociological method" in relation to Kant and Georg Simmel. He defined these borders in terms of the methodological opposition between "being" *(Sein)* and "obligation" *(Sollen)*.[54] Kelsen's further careful shaping of jurisprudence into a normativistic discipline, that is, one concerned exclusively with the "world of duty," led to ever new delimitations of his "pure theory of law." Most impressively, it led to his theory's distinction from doctrines of natural law.[55] With the exclusion of politics and theology, all concepts meant to mediate between different spheres incorporated into law become superfluous. The postulate of "systemic unity," adhering strictly to the epistemology Kant presents in the *Critique of Pure Reason,* does not admit the validity of two simultaneously operating ordering systems.[56] Kelsen does not exclude the possibility of the existence of different systems. He simply wishes to maintain a strict space between them.

In a clear cut manner, Kelsen's "pure theory of law" demotes concepts Schmitt made use of in formulating a political theology stemming from Bauer. The question that emerges is whether Kelsen tied this difference to one of religious conviction, as did Schmitt. To answer this question, it is important to again note Kelsen's debt to Kant in trying to construct a legal theory free of all metaphysics. Kelsen concedes that "a good deal of metaphysical transcendence" is at work both in Kant's *Critique of Pure Reason,* that is, in the "thing in itself," and, above all, in the philosopher's practical philosophy (in *Critique of Practical Reason* and *Metaphysics of Morals*). For this reason, he indicates, Kant could not unambiguously embrace the relativism that is the unavoidable consequence of a true overcoming of metaphysics. But why was it impossible for Kant's "philosophical genius" to achieve what he, Kelsen, is aiming at, extending the transcendental theory of cognition to the realm of law? Overcoming metaphysics, Kelsen suggests, was impossible for a "personality still rooted in Christianity," which could not allow the necessary relativistic worldview.[57] In a certain way, Kelsen's viewpoint here harmonizes with Schmitt's—with the difference that for Kelsen, what Schmitt defines as the essence of Christianity's greatness is, precisely, Christianity's essential deficit.

Before submitting his academic qualifying thesis, the agnostic Kelsen had himself converted to Protestantism, a step later interpreted as a practical concession in an Austrian Catholic environment.[58] Be this as it may, he was thoroughly aware of the problems posed by the demands of positivism: by an abandonment of an absolute grounding for the legal order, an abandonment of any religion or other social ideology. For the "need for an absolute founding" for a given social order is a powerful one. Positivism, Kelsen suggests, has needed to assert itself against metaphysical ideologies and legal arguments grounded in natural law, in an "eternal, never resolvable struggle of spirits." In 1928 Kelsen diagnosed a new natural-law movement that accompanied a "rebirth of religious feeling." He observed that an antimetaphysical, scientific-critical worldview, with its ideal of objectivity, could thrive only in epochs marked by social stability. To be sure, it was possible for Kelsen to *conceive* a legal theory free of politics and theology on the basis of a transcendental-logical "basic norm"—an (otherwise not specified) "minimum" of positive law.[59] But the struggle against the renaissance of metaphysics, revealing itself paradigmatically in Schmitt's political theology, remained undecided in the "intellectual-historical situation" of the Weimar Republic.[60] Kelsen was in any case well aware of the danger posed by Schmitt's politico-religious ideas for his relativistic legal theory.[61]

Sovereignty and the "Legal Miracle": The State of Emergency

With the appearance of Schmitt's *Guardian of the Constitution (Der Hüter der Verfassung)* in 1931 and Kelsen's response that same year, *Who Is To Be the Guardian of the Constitution? (Wer soll der Hüter der Verfassung sein?)*, the confrontation between Carl Schmitt and Hans Kelsen reached its apogee.[62] At the conflict's center was the question of whether the judicial system or the president of the Reich offered the most effective protection for the Weimar constitution. Presuming a constitution that represented the nation's political unity, Schmitt decided for the president of the Reich.[63] For his part, Kelsen understood the constitution as the "upper level" of a positive legal order. And he understood this order as legitimized by a "basic norm" to be presumed a priori. He thus viewed the independent Constitutional Court as the more appropriate body for controlling constitutional violations by either a legislative or executive organ.[64] The sharp difference between Schmitt and Kelsen that emerged here can be clarified against the backdrop of their opposing approach to the concept of sovereignty.

On the front page of the first edition of Schmitt's *Political Theology*, Schmitt indicates that the book was written at the same time as his essay

"The Political Idea of Catholicism"—a text that would appear under the title *Roman Catholicism and Political Form*. In this text, Schmitt argues that the doctrine of the Trinity supplemented "Jewish monotheism and its absolute transcendence" with "elements of God's immanence."[65] This distinction forms a subtext to Schmitt's confrontation with Kelsen's ideas. He contrasts Kelsen's abstraction and secularism with a concrete political science derived from Christian theology. For Schmitt, God's absolute transcendence of the world is mirrored by Kelsen on a secular level in an absolute separation of various spheres. In Kelsen's theory, he suggests, there is no place for the mediation between God and world achieved by Christianity; the rejection of Christ is thus followed by a denial of sovereignty. Schmitt here transfers the difference he identifies between Judaism and Christianity to his doctrine of sovereignty. He "translates" an a priori idea stemming from theology, the presumption of a super-natural divine order independent of natural laws, to the framework of political science.[66] Where, he argues, God's freedom from natural laws is manifest in miracles, the essence of the sovereign is manifest in his freedom to decide on states of emergency. This is the source of the already-cited opening sentence of *Political Theology:* "Sovereign is he who decides on the state of exception." When Schmitt declares that Kelsen "could do nothing systemically" with the state of emergency, the difference between their approaches becomes very clear:[67] as Schmitt sees things, the forgetting of the significance of the exceptional moment that began with the Enlightenment takes on a "systematic" structure in Kelsen's writing.[68]

In actuality, Kelsen by no means "forgets" the presence of "belief in miracles." Rather, he devotes some important pages to the phenomenon in his "critical examination of the relation of state and law."[69] Unsurprisingly, he views the discussion of states of emergency, "legal miracles," as a problematic assimilation of Catholic dogma into legal thinking. From Kelsen's perspective, whenever no explanation for a natural law has been apparent, Catholic dogma has had recourse to miracles. He considers the same construction to be at work in the equivalent political theory: "when things will simply no longer do, in other words when certain political interests—to be sure differing interests depending on the prevalent standpoint—call for it, then one may appeal to the metalegal system."[70] Kelsen thus understands the legal miracle as a political strategy for breaking through the normative legal system.

Since Schmitt defines sovereignty in relation to the state of emergency, the possibility arises that with an avoidance of such episodes through an appropriate constitution or correct political measures, an extralegal legal reference point will become unnecessary. The sovereign in Schmitt's sense will then vanish. To counter this objection, Schmitt first insists that asking whether the state of emergency can be eliminated is no juridical question but depends on "philosophical, especially historical-philosophical or metaphysical convictions."[71] But, Schmitt insists, normal, nonemergency situations were less interesting than emergency situations. Schmitt is thus not interested in avoiding the latter. To the contrary, he directly inserts his own "metaphysical" conviction as a methodological argument: normality proves nothing, the exception everything; not only does the exception confirm the rule but the rule only exists thanks to the exception. For, Schmitt argues, "in the exception, the power of real life breaks through the crust of a mechanics frozen in repetition" (15). Only the exception allows a pathos pointing beyond the liberal world against which Schmitt is struggling. It alone conceives "the general with energetic passion": a closing citation of Kierkegaard, who was reflecting not on politics but on the nature of ethical faith, and whom Schmitt simply refers to as an anonymous "protestant theologian" in order to underscore the theological origins of his own political idea (15). Schmitt's definition of sovereignty is thus composed of borderline concepts. According to his metaphysical convictions, a meaningful definition of the exception has to be formulated not in relation to the "normal case" but to the "marginal case," the "outermost sphere" (9).

When Schmitt writes that there is a "juridically logical reason" for deriving sovereignty from the idea of the exception, he is transferring his legal irrationalism to the realm of legal logic.[72] As the veiled Kierkegaard reference reveals, the resulting "fundamentalist theory of constitutionalism,"[73] while laying claim to being a diagnosis of secularization in general, is nevertheless heavily in debt to Christian metaphysics. As Schmitt indicates, on Roman Catholicism's theological plain "many mediations" with "Jewish monotheism" are conceivable—for example, both the Old and New Testaments have their validity. But it appears that such mediations no longer have a place on the plane of Schmitt's political theology.[74] He formulates his stance in the words of Cardinal Newman: "No medium . . . between Catholicity and atheism."[75] To the contrary, the conflict between these forces is even sharpened, since the "era" (*Zeit*) following the bourgeois revolutions of 1789 and 1848 demands "decision."[76]

Alongside the idea of the state of emergency, that of "decision" is central to Schmitt's definition of sovereignty. Here, the connection between Schmitt's decisionism and his "personalism" is extremely important. The latter prevents an abstractly valid ordering principle or "basic norm" (Kelsen) replacing concrete state sovereignty. Schmitt sees himself as engaged in a struggle against all efforts to establish "law" as the antithesis of *commission,* the personal order. He would have been able to sharpen his argument even further with Hobbes's definition of decision in his *Leviathan* (chap. 26, "Of Civil Laws"): "And first it is manifest that law in general is not counsel, but command." In Schmitt's view, then, only the law's linkage to the command, indeed only an actual identity between them, makes the urgency of the question of decision palpable. Or, in Schmitt's words, "The reality of legal life depends on who decides. That is the unavoidable *quis interpretabitur?* and the everlasting *Quis judicabit?*" [77] For—and this is the point of Schmitt's argumentation— the rule of law is actually a *masquerade.*

Behind all law stands a decision concerning what the law is and the nature of the legal person the decision applies to. For Schmitt, the masquerade lies in juridical thinking being "overpowered" by scientific thinking and thus depersonalized, transformed into pure abstraction. Scientific thinking wishes to explain all miracles in terms of natural laws and finally ban anything extralegal from nature. Brought into the juridical realm, this way of thinking has led, for Schmitt, to a negation of the decisive tie to an extralegal authority.[78] Schmitt names Hugo Preuss, father of the Weimar constitution, as the most important representative and accelerator of such "degeneration" *(Entartung)*.[79] Preuss, he indicates, "rejects the concept of sovereignty as a residue of the authoritarian state." He has gotten by "without sovereignty" in a similar way to Kelsen.[80] In addition, Schmitt rejects the arguments of Dutch political scientist Hugo Krabbe,[81] directed against Paul Laband's idea of constitutional law. As has been shown elsewhere, Schmitt's critique of Krabbe shows that although stylizing himself into an opponent of Laband's system, in a number of decisive questions he inherited that system, while both Kelsen and Krabbe broke with it.[82]

In his *Political Theology,* Schmitt attacks Kelsen's project of a "pure political science" *(reine Staatslehre),*[83] meant, like the "pure theory of law," to be free of all metaphysics. Schmitt names the project "monistic metaphysics" and "mathematical mythology," as well as "methodological conjuration and conceptual honing" *(methodologische Beschwörung und Begriffsschärfung)*.[84] Schmitt's own thinking is so radically "political-theological" that he cannot imagine a theory defined as occupying a space free of theology and politics as anything other than a theology of the "antitheological" and anti-Christian.[85] His most intense suspicions are, in any event, aimed at Kelsen's rigorous suppression of the notion of sovereignty,[86] which he defines as a liberal negation of the state in favor of law.[87] Schmitt views Kelsen as negating or evading the problem of decision as well. Importantly, this is a major inaccuracy on Schmitt's part in that the clear step-based model Kelsen offers in his *Pure Theory of Law* directly addresses the question of decision-making competence.[88] All told, the emotional content of Schmitt's polemic is only partially focused on Kelsen's liberalism. Rather, what steadily emerges is a suspicion that behind his opponent's liberal mask lurks a decision in favor of a *hostile theology.*

This suspicion becomes more clear with a look at how Schmitt defines sovereignty in the framework of his sociology of legal concepts. He first distinguishes his method from that of the sociology of knowledge, which he sees as aimed more strongly at the background of those producing the knowledge. As an example of this rejected form of sociology, Schmitt observes that "One might consider Kelsen's jurisprudence to be the ideology of the juridical bureaucrat who works through changing political circumstances; who tries, under the most disparate forms of rule, with relativistic superiority over the political power at hand, to process the positive rules and regulations that are thrown his way." In contrast, his own conceptual sociology is meant to reveal an epoch's political form in structural analogy to its "metaphysical image" *(metaphysisches Bild).*[89]

Schmitt, however, does not analyze a given epoch in terms of its own metaphysics. What counts for him is its jurisprudence and power structure.[90] The basis for his approach involves both finding "the last, radically systematic structure" of juridical concepts—their purposive driving to a "metaphysical" and "theological" edge—and comparing them with an epoch's conceptually captured "social structure."[91] He defines the "sociology of the sovereignty concept" as follows: ascertaining an identity between an epoch's metaphysical image and the structure of the political organization shedding "immediate" light on the epoch (59). Schmitt does not explain how this "immediate" illumination of power structures is meant to take place. He identifies an ever-growing loss of transcendence beginning in the seventeenth century; this loss, he asserts, produced an immanence-stamped idea of sovereignty starting in the mid-nineteenth century. He views Kelsen's doctrine, postulating an identity between state and legal order and allowing no space transcending law, as marking an endpoint to this development (63). Schmitt's dictum "Sovereign is he who decides on the state of exception" was directed against this perceived development in political science: through the analogy between juridical and theological forms of conceptualization, he hoped to block the progress of relativistic theories of law and democracy. As will be shown in part 4, Schmitt blamed the progress of relativism on the assimilated Jews.

It is not always easy to understand against whom Schmitt is actually aiming. At one point he polemicizes against liberalism, for instance against Kelsen; at another time against atheistic socialism; and yet again against Bakunin: the anarchist as the true antitheologian, the dictator of an antidictatorship, against whom he battles with the help of Catholic counterrevolutionary political theory. The actual significance of the Catholic political thinkers for Schmitt lies in "the consequence with which they decide." But his own decisionism is markedly indecisive. On the one hand, he is concerned with simple decision for its own sake. On the other hand, he refers to "exacting moral decision" as the core of the political idea (83). His only example of an instance displaying both aspects of this equation is the Catholic Church with its dogma of infallibility. Schmitt thus cites de Maistre to the effect that "the two words infallibility and sovereignty are *'parfaitement synonymes'*" (71). The *complexio oppositorum* with which Schmitt designates the essence and form of the church can also bridge this theoretical opposition.[92] The church's sovereign, the pope, can be understood as the sovereign of sovereigns.[93]

In 1922 Schmitt juxtaposes Proudhon as a "mortal enemy" and "demon" with Donoso Cortés's Catholic thinking. In 1929 in an article titled "The Unknown Donoso Cortés," he corrects this assessment, now naming Marx the actual leader and "heresiarch of atheistic socialism."[94] While a great part of Schmitt's argumentation is concerned with Kelsen's ideas, Marx emerges as the chief nineteenth-century opponent of his political theology, and, in his role as "clerk become an economic expert," as an exemplum of that century's basic direction.[95] Schmitt views Marx as the most powerfully influential Jewish pioneer of the separation of realms Kelsen has brought to its endpoint. Marx, he suggests, wished to transform the Christian state into an economic enterprise, Kelsen to see it entirely dissolve into law. And indeed, Kelsen did not accept the difference between law and state, since he considered "every state a legally based state."[96]

In Schmitt's attack on Kelsen's legal theory, the latter is presented as the transmission of secularized Jewish forms into the political doctrine of the modern Christian-secular state. In his polemic against both legal positivism and the "pure theory of law," Schmitt suggests that Kelsen's liberalism is a cover for the secularized *theology* of the enemy. Since in his text on the "Jewish question" Bauer attacked the influence of secularized concepts stemming from Judaism, he can be considered Schmitt's predecessor.

Following the Nazi advent to power Schmitt once again saw fit to defend his struggle against the "Jewish" influence on German political science and the course of German history. Again and again, he stressed that the nineteenth century's liberal tradition was, in reality, only masked Judaism:

> At the height of the Prussian constitutional conflict, a Jewish delegate, Dr. Eduard Simson—1848/1849 president of the Frankfurt national assembly preparing a constitution and leader of the deputation tendering the Kaiser's crown—. . . the Jew Simson called out to Prussian Minister President Bismarck on 10 February 1866, under "long-lasting applause" of the house in the Prussian Landtag, as follows: "You are engaged in a struggle with the spiritual and moral forces of our present age; sooner or later you will succumb to these forces." At that time the German liberals, who applauded these recondite [*hintergründig*] words with unwitting enthusiasm, had bound eyes and ears. The struggle of those "spiritual and moral forces" thus proceeded, for them invisible and inaudible at once, until Germany's defeat in 1918 appeared completed. Today, following the renewal of the power of the German *Volk* [*deutsche Volkskraft*] through Adolf Hitler, the same struggle reveals itself to the same degree that it achieves world-political dimensions.[97]

The approach to secularization Schmitt suggested in his *Political Theology* of 1922 could be read as a refinement of Weber's argument regarding Protestantism. As these words reveal, what now emerged was a brutal battle call. In paranoid fashion, it traced all problems of the nineteenth-century German state back to the destructive influence of emancipated Jewry.

PART 4

ACCELERATION: KATECHON AND ANTICHRIST

The two previous parts of this book examined Carl Schmitt's worldview, in which a double accusation of particularism and universalism directed at the Jews played a central role. One particular conspiracy theory was here foregrounded: that through a proclamation of universal ideas, the Jews hope to realize their particular interests. To cite once again: "Whoever says humanity wants to deceive." The positive law of the parliamentary state became a crystallization point for Schmitt's conspirative ideas blossoming in a juridical realm, becoming concrete in the here and now. The following pages consider a third anti-Jewish accusation leveled by Schmitt: *acceleration*. Although seemingly disparate, together these accusations amount to the crux of Schmitt's perspective on the Jews.

The idea of acceleration and the role assigned the Jews in the acceleration of history are best understood against the backdrop of Christian concepts of time. These concepts center around St. Paul's notion of time as a *fixed quantity*.[1] This is an eschatological principle encapsulated in the New Testament Greek term for the "restraining power" or "agent of delay," the Katechon. Informing the term's emergence are a pair of key interrelated problems within Catholicism: how can the institutions of state and church be justified, and how can they sustain the ambivalence with which they must be approached on theological grounds?

Schmitt discovered the Katechon in the early 1940s. He then placed it at the center of his historical-philosophical speculation. But on a structural level, the motif of negatively charged acceleration was already present in the earlier writing, along with the idea of rendering mythical and theological figures and concepts fruitful for political science. Above all the mythic sea monster Leviathan took on tremendous significance in his thoughts about the state. For this reason, we need to review some aspects of Schmitt's political mythology, before turning to the role held within it by the Jews. The mythology's backdrop is Schmitt's confrontation with those he deemed enemies of the political. We will see that before it was specified in mythic-theological terms, Schmitt's acceleration-metaphor was already contained in the argumentative structure of his *Concept of the Political*.

12

The Jews in the Christian History
of Salvation

Leviathan and Behemoth as Jewish "Battle Myths"

The sea monster Leviathan is referred to in the book of Job, chapters
40–41. Later it emerged as the main title of Thomas Hobbes's most famous work,[1] where it symbolized state power so absolute that all personal freedom has been sacrificed to it.[2] Inside and outside Nazi Germany, Hobbes's political thinking and the Leviathan-symbol so closely
tied to it sparked a broad debate. This was meant to supply orientation
regarding the nature of the new type of German state.[3] Especially in
circles around Schmitt, the debate was tied to the question of the nature
of the "total state."[4] A symbolic linkage of the myths of both Leviathan
and Behemoth with the actual situation of the Nazi state was perhaps
expressed most clearly by Schmitt's former student Franz Neumann:
"Since we believe National Socialism is—or [is] tending to become—a
nonstate, a chaos, a rule of lawlessness and anarchy, which has 'swal-
lowed' the rights and dignity of man, and is out to transform the world
into a chaos by the supremacy of gigantic land masses, we find it apt to
call the National Socialist system *The Behemoth.*"[5]

Because of the work's thicket of ambiguities, a reading of Schmitt's
Leviathan presents many interpretive problems. The demand for strict
biographical ordering that is often made in regard to Schmitt poses
additional difficulties, since precisely in regards to the period of that
book's writing (1937–38), Schmitt's attitude toward the Third Reich is
hotly disputed. The book unquestionably appeared after Schmitt's
greatest influence on the Nazi state was over. But to place it on the side
of Ernst Jünger's *Marmorklippen* (1938), as reflecting "an inward journey"
(Maschke's term) is possible only when its contents are distorted by

carefully falsified citations. This is the procedure adopted with good grounds by Schmitt himself in his self exculpation, *Ex Captivitate Salus* (1945–47). In 1938 Schmitt wrote as follows:

> But if the public authority [*Macht*] only wishes to be public as long as state and creed force inner belief into the private realm, then the soul of a people [*Volk*] sets out on the 'mysterious [*geheimnisvoll*] path' that leads inward. Then the counterforce of stillness and silence grows stronger. In the moment when a distinction between inside and outside is recognized, the superiority of the inner to the outer and with it of the private to the public is in essence already decided.[6]

In the winter of 1945–46, he offered a drastically distorted version of his earlier statement: "In the summer of 1938, a book appeared in Germany in which it is said: 'If in a particular country only a public organized by the state power is considered valid, then the soul of a people set out on the mysterious path that leads inward; then the counterforce of stillness and silence grows stronger.'"[7] In 1938 he held the "restless spirit of the Jews" responsible for the unfolding of reservations against inner belief. The Jews had, he indicated, pursued this process "with the steadfast instinctive sense that such an undermining and hollowing out of state power best serves to paralyze an alien people and emancipate their own Jewish people." In 1945 Schmitt suddenly made himself responsible for the process.[8]

Schmitt's *Leviathan* does not directly speak of the German *Volk* "to whom leadership is due."[9] At the same time, the work does *not* represent a first critical reflection on the now apparently entrenched Nazi state. Within that state, Schmitt's role as the regime's intellectual interpreter was no longer unreservedly approved. Despite the development, various passages (e.g., Schmitt's reference to the "Judeo-Christian destruction of natural unity"[10]) suggest a continued embrace of Nazi positions. In the following three years, his basic political leanings would be reinforced through a turn to Nazi "greater territory" *(Grossraum)* theory.[11] Nevertheless, the *Leviathan* text is marked by many ambiguities, first of all involving his attitude toward Hobbes; these have rendered any simple interpretation impossible. Where later Schmitt would describe Jean Bodin and Thomas Hobbes as two of his "friends,"[12] in *Leviathan* whether or not this is the case is in fact completely unclear. In particular, Hobbes, the incomparable political mentor, is strongly criticized as the origin of and collaborator in the process of state disintegration. Schmitt's book is meant to trace on a historical and mythic level. To be sure, he points to "Jewish" authors, from Spinoza to Mendelssohn to Marx, as bearing primary responsibility for the state's destruction and as having destroyed it in a conspirative manner. But this does not signify any diminution of Hobbes's own role in the disintegrative process.[13]

Schmitt begins his study of Hobbes's political theory with an analysis of the mythic symbolism of Leviathan. The text is marked by shifts from the symbolic to the theoretical level, without a clear separation of these spheres ever being apparent. To the contrary: the true sense of Schmitt's theoretical analysis emerges only in his symbolic interpretation. Hobbes, he indicates, created a "positively intended" political myth to counteract the "Jewish fracturing" of "original political unity." This myth was aimed at a restoration of the "original unity of life" *(Lebenseinheit)*.[14] Schmitt remarks that Hobbes's symbolic confrontation with Judaism presents itself as a "struggle against all kinds of indirect force [*Gewalt*]." He argues that whoever recognizes the confrontation as Hobbes's "fruitful accomplishment will understand his theory of the state."[15] Schmitt thus offers not only a description of a political symbol's ultimate failure but also, as his book's subtitle itself suggests, a reconstruction of the *meaning* of the symbol, hence an introduction to Thomas Hobbes's actual theory of state.

Political mythology had central importance for Schmitt's political philosophy. In the Weimar Republic period, the rediscovery of myth as a determining factor in human and societal behavior drew the strong interest of many German scholars.[16] But where for example Ernst Cassirer and Aby Warburg saw the fascination with mythology above all as the sign of a threat to liberal values, Schmitt succumbed to the fascination. As early as 1923 he located a "theory of myth" behind the success of Marxism and Fascism and viewed this "theory" as superior to the "relative rationalism of parliamentary thinking."[17] The "political theory of myth" would also figure at the beginning of the collection *Positions and Concepts*, intended to document his struggle with Weimar (parliamentarianism), Geneva (the League of Nations), and Versailles (the peace treaty). Schmitt's analysis of the Leviathan myth is located within the tense field he outlines in this collection, its range extending from the "myth" (1923) to the "Reich" (1939). In the interpretive conflict over Hobbes's idea of Leviathan, Schmitt wished to show how the power of political myths and symbols could puncture an abstract theoretical framework. A victorious counterinterpretation of a myth can even discredit the theory tied to it, as Hobbes's writing itself experienced ("Leviathan's name casts a long shadow; it has struck the work of Thomas

Hobbes"[18]). For, Schmitt suggests, in contrast to widespread opinion Hobbes did not aspire to establish a "golem's dominion," Rather, he presumed a relation involving protection and obedience that imposed duties on both the sovereign and individual citizens.[19] Hobbes presents Leviathan not as an "enemy" but as "God, who brings security and peace."[20]

According to Schmitt, a "conventional Jewish interpretation" has been chiefly responsible for the failure of Hobbes's symbol. Described by Schmitt on a number of occasions, this "Jewish interpretation" is of special interest in our context because Schmitt understood it as a specific expression of the "completely abnormal expression and attitude of the Jewish people in face of all other peoples."[21] In his 1937 study "The State as a Mechanism in Hobbes and Descartes," he points to the writing of Jean Bodin as an example of the dissolutive influence of the "Jewish interpretation."[22] In Schmitt's view, a knowledge of Kabbalistic writing led Bodin to play his part in shaping the image of Leviathan as a Moloch, a "Golem crushing everything." For, he indicates, according to the Kabbala Leviathan is an enormous animal with which the "Jewish God" plays daily for an hour. But at the start of the Messiah's chiliastic reign, the monster will be slaughtered, its flesh distributed to and devoured by the blessed residents of the millennial kingdom.[23] (Here, Schmitt is referring to an idea found in some Jewish apocalyptic literature.) It remains unclear which specific Kabbalistic texts, if any, Schmitt has in mind. A legend of God playing with Leviathan three hours daily is found in Rabbinic literature;[24] and in one Talmudic tractate (Baba Bathra 74 b), Rabbi Jochanan indicates that at some point God will "prepare a meal for the pious from the flesh of Leviathan." But any reference here to a tie between the state or heathen peoples and Leviathan is absent. With Schmitt citing not the Talmud but unnamed Kabbalistic texts, the strong possibility emerges that he is referring to Kabbalistic knowledge metaphorically, as a way of describing what he imagines to be the secret, esoteric knowledge of the Jews. The many more extensive passages in *Leviathan* devoted to this supposed Jewish battle-myth themselves cite no Kabbalistic sources. In this light it is very likely that a basic source for Schmitt's gloss on "Jewish" literature was a notorious early eighteenth-century antisemitic tome he refers to once in a note, Andreas Eisenmenger's *Jewry Uncovered (Entdecktes Judentum)*.[25]

For Schmitt, the "Jewish" account of world history, discussed in both *Leviathan* and *Land and Sea (Land und Meer,* 1942), involves a steady struggle between the heathen peoples. He describes the account as symbolically expressed in a mythic wrestling of Leviathan, the sea powers, with Behemoth, the land powers. The Jews here stand by and watch the earth's peoples engage in mutual slaughter, in order to celebrate the "thousand-year feast" of Leviathan after the mutual destruction of the two battling powers.[26] Since, Schmitt explains, this struggle is "lawful" and "kosher" for the Jews, they see themselves as eventually eating the flesh of the slaughtered peoples and living from it.[27] In *Land and Sea*, Schmitt states that "the Kabbalist" most often cited in regards to the historical interpretation of the feast of Leviathan is Isaac Abravanel. (In fact Abravanel was no Kabbalist but a prolific fifteenth-century rabbinic commentator and statesman from one of the most wealthy and distinguished of all Spanish Jewish families.[28]) In the text's revised version—not, to be sure, described as such, in line with Schmitt's usual practice—of 1981, Schmitt adds a reference to an account of the feast in "a famous poem" by Heinrich Heine.[29] The poem being referred to is in fact "Disputazion" from the "Hebräische Melodien" (1853), itself the third part of Heine's *Romanzero*. Heine's sharp and richly ironic description of a disputation between a (vehemently anti-Jewish) monk and a bon vivant rabbi actually contains a detailed description of the feast of Leviathan.[30] Heine could here rely on a number of Jewish sources, the most probable being a hymn found in Jewish prayer books for Shavuoth (the feast of weeks).[31] Although both Heine and the traditional Shavuoth hymn contain elements found in Schmitt's reading, they are nevertheless far-removed from the "battle mythology" he described. The horrendous historical-political allegory of "peoples" is entirely lacking.

The question remains of whether Schmitt's myth can be found in the work of Isaac Abravanel. In "The Sea against the Land" ("Das Meer gegen das Land"), an essay written at the same time as *Land and Sea*,[32] Schmitt writes as follows: "Medieval Jewish Kabbalists—among them the world-wise Abravanel—supplemented these descriptions in an important way by noting that the two great animals kill each other, the Jews, however, observing the battle and eating the flesh of the killed animals." Schmitt does not note where Abravanel commented on this myth—namely, in his commentary on Genesis—and the rabbi is not cited in any of the important reference works that treat the Leviathan myth.[33] Abravanel's remarks themselves refer to the above-cited Talmudic tractate Batra 72 b; a political interpretation of the myth on his part is not evident in his Genesis commentary. It is thus striking that Schmitt chose this particular author when writing on the Jewish interpretation of biblical Leviathan.

Heinrich Meier has noted that Schmitt laid stress on Abravanel's wealth and power while remaining silent regarding his flight from the Spanish Inquisition and the numerous expulsions marking his life.[34] Toward the end of *Land and Sea*, Abravanel is mentioned once again, now in the context of a parallel drawn between the royal treasurer of Portugal and Castille—an intimate of Isabella—and the leading politician during Victoria's reign: "Disraeli," states Schmitt, "was a nineteenth-century Abravanel." Both figures, he observes, were close to the most powerful women of their age, and both offered literary contributions on the relationship between Judaism and Christianity.[35] Schmitt's remarks about Disraeli in *Land and Sea* are particularly in debt to a book by Bruno Bauer, *Disraeli's Romantic Imperialism and Bismark's Social Imperialism*, which Schmitt already cites in 1921.[36] He begins to grapple with the Leviathan myth in 1937—as it happened, the year of Abravanel's five-hundredth birthday, prompting many publications regarding the Sephardic commentator.[37] Schmitt was at least familiar with the article by Leo Strauss, although in light of various commemorations by German Jewish communities and a memorial exhibition at Berlin's Jewish Museum,[38] he may well have read other texts as well. In 1934 Valeriu Marcu's *Expulsion of the Jews from Spain (Die Vertreibung der Juden aus Spanien)* was published in Amsterdam. The work contained an impressive account of Abravanel's struggle with the Holy Office and against its anti-Jewish proceedings.[39] Abravanel had displayed great openness to Christian exegesis and had in turn been discussed at length by numerous seventeenth- and eighteenth-century Christian scholars.[40] The symbolic resonance of Schmitt's negative transformation of this Jewish commentator is entirely clear. Schmitt's purpose, in fact, was to "unmask" the noble Spanish Jewish pioneer of religious tolerance as a bloodthirsty "Kabbalist."

In his *Leviathan*, Schmitt goes a step further. He now projects the "Jewish battle myths" onto the real influence of the Jews upon the history of the Christian peoples. This transferring of the mythic narrative to a historical realm has furnished his exposition with continued relevance, reflected in very different reactions to his description of the myth. For example, in 1982 the editor of the second edition of Schmitt's book referred to "antisemitic remarks that for their time were very tame indeed,"[41] while in contrast Paul Bookbinder confirmed in 1991 that "the vicious and vituperative character" of Schmitt's prose might have stemmed from a Julius Streicher or Joseph Goebbels.[42] A look at responses by readers offered after the book's first appearance and now preserved in the Schmitt archives would seem to support Bookbinder's assessment. A great many such readers viewed precisely the Jews' slaughter of and dining on Leviathan as the thematic heart of Schmitt's discussion. His lurid depiction of the Jews was either welcomed or condemned.[43]

In a short but eloquent postcard dated 13 July 1938, Schmitt's former friend Erik Peterson indicated that "the remarks about the Jews' dining on Leviathan seem mistaken [*irrig*] to me. Precisely the question of kosher meat makes no sense for the Leviathan & Leviathan = kosher pagan meat seems unproven to me. . . . The polemic against the *potestas indirecta* only makes sense when one has renounced being a Christian & decided for paganism. With best regards, your E.P."[44] With his last remark, Peterson was once more making clear what he had suggested in his treatise of 1935 titled *Monotheism as a Political Problem (Der Monotheismus als politisches Problem):* that from his perspective Carl Schmitt's political theology had no support in Trinitarian Christianity.[45] His concerns of that time were reinforced by the anti-ecclesiastical tendency manifest in Schmitt's *Leviathan*, which he correctly saw as an attack on the church as an indirect power. The reproaches Schmitt leveled at the Jews were also implicitly leveled at any church that did not acknowledge a creed dictated by the state or that withdrew entirely from the political sphere. This being the case, we can understand *Leviathan* as a declaration of war against followers of the Confessional Church and as a confirmation of the aspirations of both Catholic and Protestant political theology.[46]

Openly antisemitic organizations also showed interest in Schmitt's arguments. The Institute for Racial Studies, National Biology, and Rural Sociology thanked Schmitt for receipt of the book; an institute member indicated that he had found it "instructive in various ways."[47] Colleagues of Schmitt considered the book's portrait of the Jews to be the outcome of serious scholarship. Hence in a thank-you letter to Schmitt the jurist Gottfried Neesse (1911–87) wrote as follows:

> The role of the Jews in scholarship, in any case in constitutional studies, has until now mainly only been uncovered with the help of general maxims. You [on the other hand] furnish clearly outlined, distinct examples of a sort never before recognized or at least discussed. Any one who himself writes knows the amount of research involved in achieving such results. Heil Hitler.[48]

Against the backdrop of the widely accepted antisemitic theme of the "state within a state,"[49] many academics found enlightenment in

Schmitt's idea that every Jew had "played his part in castrating a vigorous Leviathan," in other words, in eroding the state the monster symbolized.[50] For these readers, Schmitt had offered serious scholarly confirmation of their own position. Schmitt's effort to transfer mythology
onto constitutional history was significant, because such a transferring
process had led to the radically anti-Jewish reading of history that his
book itself articulated.

Schmitt's foreword to *Leviathan* sets the thematic tone of the book as
a whole. The foreword is concerned with the intrusion of the "Jewish
spirit" into constitutional history. It thus takes up the theme of the 1936
Jew-hating conference that Schmitt had sponsored. He begins his account with the following methodological remark: "I have tried to do justice to the theme with scientific objectivity . . . without cheap dissections
that only lead to explanation of a subject having no object."[51] But a
belief that mythic symbols, images, and phantasms "break through the
framework of any merely conceptual theory or construction," thus becoming historically potent, would seem to contradict a schematic distinction between objective concreteness and abstract (Jewish) dissection.

A schematic table leads the reader from the Leviathan-symbol's
"Old Testament origins" to its failed interpretation by Hobbes, which
does not "stand up to a counterinterpretation."[52] In Schmitt's opinion,
only Hobbes's mythological blunder made it possible for Spinoza, the
"first liberal Jew," to effectuate a "decisive turn in the fate of Leviathan"
over a few short years: a process involving a "small, switching movement
of thinking that emerged from Jewish existence."[53] In the following
pages, Schmitt repeatedly turns back to John 18, which both he and
Hans Kelsen focused on several years earlier. This is a reflection of a renewed preoccupation with the trial of Jesus, as documented in his correspondence with Erik Peterson.[54] At a central point in his text he addresses the same question by Pilate that Hans Kelsen put forward to the
"believing" political theologians several years earlier: "What is truth?"[55]
This question, argues Schmitt, can be understood as an expression of
"superior tolerance," or as "weary skepticism," or again as an "agnosticism remaining 'open' toward all sides." But it can also be read as a special kind of "technical perfection of a machine of state" exercising neutrality for the sake of rationalizing administrative technique (67; 44).

Through his severing of validity—"authority"—from truth on
the level of action, Hobbes occupied a singular position in the spectrum that Schmitt constructed (68; 45). Schmitt's confrontation with
the "neutralization of every truth" (65; 43) can be interpreted as a

problematization of his own position. For Hobbes's positivizing of law, directed against religiously grounded civil warfare, was something Schmitt doubtless approved of. He would have done so despite its forming the "decisive first step" in the process of secularization and acceleration—a process Schmitt himself points to in *Leviathan* as attacked in his talk "The Age of Neutralizations and Depolitizations" ("Das Zeitalter der Neutralisierungen und Entpolitisierungen," 1929/1932).[56] In *The Turn to a Discriminatory Concept of War (Die Wendung zum diskriminierenden Kriegsbegriff)*, a book that appeared at the same time as *Leviathan*, Schmitt maintains Hobbes's position, applying the dictum "authority, not the truth, makes law" in the context of international law.[57] Conflict between states is not to be decided by principles of higher morality or truth, which involve discriminating against one of the warring parties; rather, a nondiscriminatory concept of war is desirable. Schmitt's main concern here is replacing an international proscription of war with its "cultivation" *(Hegung)*.[58]

In Schmitt's view, the application of Hobbes's dictum to the domestic sphere leads to a problematic situation. Namely, the evasion of the question posed by Pilate, "What is truth?" through a "response" by Hobbes meant to prevent civil war says nothing about the truth-content of the sovereign's answer. And as Schmitt notes, this neutrality in regards to the truth renders doubtful the unity of religion and politics symbolized by Leviathan.[59] As Schmitt sees things, the "fault point" reveals itself in the problem of belief in miracles, with Hobbes here making an "ineradicable, individualistic" proviso (84; 57). Although he leaves the power of deciding what will be designated a "miracle" within the state to the sovereign authority, he grants individuals their own inward, "private" judgment (85; 57f.). In doing so he sets the stage for disastrous distinctions between private and public reason, faith, and creed—distinctions that will be developed over the following centuries in the direction of the liberal rational and constitutional state.

Hobbes's furnishing of Leviathan with only limited existence appears to have reflected a Christian-eschatological sense of the temporal limitation of everything immanent, including the state. But for Schmitt, the "mortal god" Leviathan already carries his "death germ" in the form of ideas of freedom of thought and belief absorbed into the political system (86; 57). The origins of the modern, "neutral" state, he maintains, lie here, and not in the "religiosity of Protestant sectarians"—an obvious swipe at Weber (86; 56). From a historical perspective, it is striking how much stress Schmitt lays on the Jews as the agency for the misguided development he sees starting with Hobbes. In exploiting the "hardly visible fault point" of Hobbes's *Leviathan*, the Jews were able to *accelerate* the disastrous movement conveyed by a specific political symbolism (86; 57). Spinoza was the first to "invert" the relationship created by Hobbes between outer and inner, public and private, into its opposite.[60] Through an emphasis on the merely external meaning of the religion of state, the Jewish philosopher "removed the soul of Leviathan from within."[61]

Schmitt indicates that he has taken the motif of "soul removal" from the "demonic" approach to Leviathan of Jean Bodin. He ties the motif to the persona of Spinoza himself. Spinoza's inversion of the relationship between public peace, based on laws imposed by a sovereign state power, on the one hand, and individual freedom of thought, on the other hand, emerged, he explains, from the philosopher's Jewish "existence." It emerged as well from Spinoza's marginal position vis-à-vis the ruling state religion, a marginality tied to that "existence" (89; 58). Through his demonizing metaphorics, Schmitt here thrusts his belief that Spinoza's philosophy and understanding of state stand in direct connection with the Jewish philosopher's social-historical position into an irrational sphere. At this point the German jurist's explication of the "Jewish-Kabbalistic" commentary on Leviathan flows into his theoretical reflections. The "law" *(Gesetz)* of the nineteenth-century bourgeois constitutional state is reduced to a "technical means" for taming the mythic monster. Schmitt sees this process as encapsulated in the English expression "to put a hook into the nose of the Leviathan" (99; 65). And the expression is itself expressed graphically in a medieval image reproduced on the jacket of his book's first edition.

According to Schmitt, in the eighteenth century Moses Mendelssohn followed Spinoza as a pioneer with "unerring" instincts for the separation of "internal and external, morality and law, inner sensibility and outer behavior." Mendelssohn's goal, he insists, was an "undermining and hollowing out of state power" and a "paralyzing of the alien" *Volk* for the sake of an "emancipation of one's own Jewish *Volk*" (92; 60). In the nineteenth century, "the view of a Jewish philosopher, Friedrich Stahl-Jolson," carried the separation forward (106; 69). Then the "young Rothschilds, Karl Marx, Börne, Heine, Meyerbeer, and many others" formed a broad front that succeeded in "ideologically confusing and spiritually paralyzing the German state" (108; 70). Schmitt's critique of Friedrich Stahl and Stahl's idea of constitutional monarchy is especially harsh. As an antithesis of parliamentary monarchy, this idea he indicates, was responsible for the "Prussian military state [*Soldatenstaat*] having to collapse in October 1918 under the tolerance-test of a world war" (109; 70). As the *Leviathan* proceeds, Schmitt carries his virulent "stab in the back" fantasy forward: Stahl followed the "general line" *(Gesamtlinie)* of his *Volk,* operating in terms of the "double being of a mask existence" *(Doppelwesen einer Maskenexistenz);* he did his work as a "Jewish thinker" by "carrying forward the broad historical line leading from Spinoza through Moses Mendelssohn into the century of 'constitutionalism.'" This is the context for Schmitt offering the crude image cited above: "in order to remain in the picture," Stahl "played his part in castrating a vigorous Leviathan."

The Katechon in 2 Thessalonians

Thanks to the authority of St. Paul, the pseudo-epigraphic book of the New Testament (known as the second letter of Paul to the Thessalonians) strongly influenced the development of church and empire. The book's apocalyptic section (2:1–12) rendered it into one of the most influential texts in the Christian Bible—part of the basic canon, along with Daniel 7–12, Revelation 13–17, and Matthew 24, upon which the extensive Christian eschatological literature and equally extensive anti-Christological literature is based. [62] The description of the appearance, deeds, and downfall of the Antichrist became the basis for various efforts to explain and legitimate secular history as an expression of Christian salvation. The description can thus be understood as a response to the problem of the delay in Christ's second coming. Profane political questions were drawn into this interpretive horizon.[63] The characterization of the Antichrist in 2 Thessalonians 2:9–10 served as a model for interpreting various political figures: "The coming of the wicked one is the work of Satan; it will be attended by all the powerful signs and miracles that falsehood can devise, all the deception that sinfulness can impose on those doomed to destruction, because they did not open their minds to love of the truth and so find salvation."[64] Starting with Pope Gregory IX and Emperor Friedrich II, popes and emperors thus designated each other as "Antichrist"; this was the source of the figure's role in political polemics.[65]

For Schmitt, bourgeois belief in the "age of security" was an Antichrist-prompted delusion; he feared the Antichrist "because he knows how to imitate Christ, making himself so similar to Him that he tricks everyone out of his soul."[66] Deception and masks have traditionally been considered the Antichrist's most prominent features—his

mendacious signs have made it impossible for the nonbeliever to distinguish Christ from Antichrist.[67] Through its enigmatic language, the
"minor apocalypse" in 2 Thessalonians 2:1–12 made it possible for Christian interpreters of history to speculate richly on both the Antichrist's activities and his presumed identity. The epistle also offered an explanation
of the delayed Second Coming, the key passage in this respect being
2 Thessalonians 2:6–7: "You know, too, about the restraining power
which ensures that he will be revealed only at his appointed time, for
already the secret forces of wickedness are at work, secret only for the
present until the restraining hand is removed from the scene."[68] Within
a certain reading of this passage, the Antichrist's arrival has been held
back by the delaying or restraining agent, the Katechon, so that a certain amount of time lies ahead before Parousia, the Second Coming;[69]
likewise, as long as the Katechon exercises his powers, this event cannot
be expected.

But 2 Thessalonians offers no enlightenment regarding the identity
of Katechon and Antichrist. Even the sex of the "restraining power" or
"restraining hand" is uncertain: one time it is masculine, the other time
neuter.[70] The epistle's author seems to have used a baffling diction to in-
crease the number of possible interpretations. What does seem clear is
that, in contrast to cyclical historical schemas, Christian historical theology, like the Jewish ideas on which it is founded, tends to approach the
phenomenon of time as a sort of appointed period.[71] Delaying and ac-
celerating forces *accommodate* the period within which profane history
unfolds.[72] For the period's chronological length is not determined in
advance, although there have been repeated efforts to predict the ap-
proaching end. How long profane history will last remains uncertain,
since according to this conception it will last only as long as the Katechon can counteract the forces of acceleration, thus putting off the end.
Against this temporal backdrop, Schmitt's special instrumentalization of
theological notions through his own mode of temporality takes on a
sharper contour.

The Jews: Delaying or Accelerating Agents?

Among the various interpretations of the Katechon-passage in 2 Thes-
salonians, identification of the Katechon as the Roman Empire and
Holy Roman Empire took hold in an especially widespread manner.
The identification became a near dogma.[73] In his old treatise on the

Antichrist, Bousset indicates that the Antichrist concept itself only "influenced history and had a historical mission" through the Katechon's definition as the Roman Empire.[74] Schmitt's own view of the Katechon as that force restraining the forces of acceleration owes much to this political reading. In his context, acceleration means the movement, alteration, neutralization, depolitization, and desubstantialization of any prevailing order. Early on, he discovered the accelerator of this movement in the figure of an eschatological antagonist, an Antichrist. Although his speculation on the Katechon only took written form in the years between his *Leviathan* book (1938) and *Land and Sea* (1942), he already describes fear of the Antichrist's deep deception as a distinct symptom of the age in *Theodor Däubler's "Northern Light"* of 1916. Here he speaks of the "uneasy feeling of being eternally betrayed and finally the doubt whether Christ and Antichrist can even be distinguished."[75]

In various formations, the figure of the Antichrist is present throughout Schmitt's work. In contrast, it is difficult to pin down when, precisely, he first encountered the idea of the Katechon. Schmitt uses the idea only at a late stage, when it is stylized into a key to the Christian image of history in general. But his acquaintance with the idea probably stemmed from his friendship with the then Protestant theologian Erik Peterson (Peterson would convert to Catholicism in the closing years of the Weimar Republic). The use of a New Testament Greek term itself suggests Protestant influence, since in the nineteenth and first part of the twentieth century Catholicism adhered to the Vulgate's Latin.[76] Peterson's preoccupation with the Katechon had already begun before the 1920s. The striking apocalypticism of his diary entry of 7 July 1918 conveys an approach standing in basic contrast to the later approach of Schmitt: "May the Katechon . . . suspend its delaying activities. Let the last act play!"[77] Schmitt would later suggest that Peterson viewed the Katechon as symbolizing the Jews' disbelief, delaying Christ's Parousia.[78] Such an interpretation of 2 Thessalonians 2:6f. is in any case hard to theologically locate. That figure does not directly delay Christ's return but rather it delays "the secret forces of wickedness," understood as the Antichrist. Although at least since the twelfth century, in mystery plays the Antichrist was presented as a Jew from the tribe of Dan, an identification of the Katechon with the Jews is *not* found in the theological literature.[79] To be sure, identification of the Katechon as the Antichrist itself raises a problem, since the Antichrist is in fact not operating against Christ but against the Katechon. For his part, Schmitt sees

Peterson as pointing to the Jews as delaying both Christ and Antichrist. But despite what Schmitt suggests, Peterson actually never linked the passage from 2 Thessalonians with the Jews in any way.

Schmitt's own linkage of the struggle between Katechon and Antichrist—between delayers and accelerators—has no theological foundations. It is thus remarkable how self-evident he presents the linkage as being. Although his interpretation may not actually reveal anything about Peterson's theological argumentation, it does reveal the obsessive, negative centrality the Jews have in Schmitt's reading of salvational history. On the one hand, for Schmitt, Peterson the apocalypticist sees the Jews as delayers of a desired end through their insistence on a false faith. On the other hand, for Schmitt the counterrevolutionary the Jews are allies of the Antichrist and historical accelerators who can be held back only by the Katechon's restraining powers. In other words, from fully contradictory perspectives Schmitt always places the Jews on the rejected side. However, he does not simply equate them with a direct antagonist. Rather, they merely serve as agents of a process. They are commissars, not representatives, to use his own terminology.[80] They cannot spark the process, only speed it up or carry it on.

The Katechon: A Response to Slaughtered Leviathan?

Actualized by Schmitt for his own historical purposes, the figure of the Katechon is itself located in a rich patristic and medieval literature on the Antichrist. Just as there is no unified picture of the Antichrist in the New Testament, the eschatological Katechon, developing together with the Antichrist, only took on concrete shape in the post-New Testament period. The New Testament contains a number of eschatological antagonists of Christ whose deeds unfold in various ways. In the "synoptic apocalypse" (Mark 13), the Revelation of John, 1 and 2 John, and 2 Thessalonians, there are "Antichrists" and figures who might be aligned with them, who vary greatly in both their nature and salvational function. The identity of the myths grounding the Katechon-Antichrist conception thus emerges as a problem. The originally diffuse Christian ideas of anti-Christian powers stem from various, chronologically disparate eschatological antagonists and mythic figures of horror.[81] There are influences from the book of Daniel, as well as echoes of the mysterious figures Gog and Magog, the serpent from the story of Adam and Eve, the mythic sea creatures Raha and Leviathan, and the land creature Behemoth.[82]

From the perspective of political mythology it is thus no coincidence that Schmitt's reflections on the Katechon emerged from his earlier concern with the "political fate" of his *Leviathan* book.[83] This occurred in 1942 in *Land and Sea,* that book's title already evoking *Leviathan.* The Katechon is introduced in the third chapter of these "world-historical reflections" — *Land and Sea*'s subtitle, probably meant to evoke Jakob Burckhardt. The chapter begins with a return to Leviathan and the sea monster's "Jewish" enemies. As this juxtaposition indicates, Schmitt developed the Katechon concept at a time when he was confronting the *political* myth of Leviathan. His launching of the Katechon figure can be understood as a result of the failure of the Leviathan symbol, a failure described in his book. Schmitt wished to avoid repeating what he viewed as Hobbes's error. For this reason he searched for a New Testament image not already subject to what he perceived as an influential Jewish counterinterpretation. At the same time, his choice of image made clear that the model of the modern state symbolized by Leviathan had ceased to exist in historical reality. Later, one of his most prominent students would put it bluntly: "The state is dead."[84]

In 1930 Schmitt indicated that the political concept of *deferral* embodied in the Katechon had to be understood in relation to the "concrete foreign and domestic political antagonism" of its time of origin.[85] In fact, in Schmitt's discussion of the Katechon his theologically couched language makes it easy to forget that for him "every political concept is a polemical concept."[86] The identity of those against whom the concept is theoretically and practically aimed is thus as important its literal contents and literary sources.

Schmitt's *Leviathan* describes the decline of a mythological and historical image. In his last chapter he states that "Here the history we have identified of the mythic image Hobbes created has its end."[87] As understood by Schmitt, Hobbes's mythological and historical diagnoses complete and complement each other in support of Schmitt's underlying argument: that the "inherited Jewish interpretation" of Hobbes's book will finally destroy the state (even when this is a "total state").[88] Schmitt here anticipates an idea he will expand on in the essay "The State as a Concrete Concept Bound to an Historical Epoch" ("Staat als ein konkreter, an eine geschichtliche Epoche gebundener Begriff," 1941): the epoch of states had come to an end.[89] At the same time, in "The Sea against the Land" he indicates that Leviathan, symbol of the element of the sea (England) facing that of the land (France, Germany, etc.) will soon be a "historical episode in the great history of peoples.

And we will recount the saga of the world empire of Leviathan to our grandchildren."

The question emerges of a possible historical and mythological replacement for the rule of Leviathan. Schmitt does not offer an answer in either *Leviathan* or *The Turn to a Discriminatory Concept of War* (as indicated, both 1938), an absence that he would later note.[90] The two books simply offer descriptions of a declining old order and the political myth connected to it. At the highpoint of Nazi power before World War II, Schmitt tried to close the gap: "The new ordering concept of a new international law is our concept of the Reich, emerging from a *Volk*-oriented [*volkhaft*] organization of the greater territory [*Grossraum*] born by the *Volk*."[91] This sentence is found in both *Organization of Greater Territory in International Law* (1939) and the last essay in *Positions and Concepts* (1940), "The Concept of the Reich in International Law" ("Der Reichs-begriff im Völkerrecht").[92] The sentence can be considered Schmitt's initial response to what he perceived as his destruction of the Leviathan myth.

The "Reich"-idea was an important element in the political-theological vocabulary of radical Weimar Republic nationalists (Moeller van den Bruck's book *Das Dritte Reich* is one of many examples). The idea had particular resonance among Nazis.[93] The special quality of Schmitt's use of it is tied to its place in a particular long-standing salvational tradition: a tradition grounding the Reich in the Katechon, or else understanding the Reich as equivalent to the Katechon. As Schmitt puts it in his *Nomos of the Earth*: "'Reich' signifies the historical power capable of delaying the appearance of the Antichrist and the end of the present eon."[94] The concept of the delayer, the Katechon, had not gained any importance in the framework of modern political discourse; its use by Schmitt was thus significant. Schmitt uses the concept less frequently than that of the Reich and introduces it rather haphazardly. Nevertheless, the Reich is only a specific historical form of the Katechon, which remains salvationally effective after the Reich's destruction. From this perspective, the Katechon, a purely New Testament eschatological figure, responded in a deeper way than could the Reich to the "destruction" of the Leviathan myth, with its Old Testament backdrop.

As indicated, the response was offered in 1942 in the third chapter of *Land and Sea*. Schmitt here details the "Kabbalistic" reading of the Leviathan myth and its world-historical significance: "The Jews have interpreted the battle between land and sea in their own fashion."[95] After the thousand-year feast of the Jews, Schmitt observes, little was left of the sea monster (17). But the Roman Empire, as well, had been defeated by

Vandals, Saracens, Vikings, and Normans; what remained was the Byzantine Empire, which, to be sure, had no expansive plans. It had been "pushed entirely into defense," after serving "many centuries long" as a "true 'delayer,' a 'Katechon,'" against Islam (19).

Schmitt's Katechon concept was developed out of the Leviathan context and embedded in a historical image colored by Christian doctrine. ("I do not believe that another historical image than the Katechon is at all possible for an originally Christian form of belief," he would write later, apparently referring to an agnostic standpoint "originally" emerging from Christian faith [29].) The concept's defensive character reflected a shift in the Third Reich's military-historical situation. In the winter of 1941–42, following many successes, the Wehrmacht experienced its first major setbacks, the worst of them being the failure of the German assault on Moscow. On December 8, 1941, Hitler instructed the entire German army on the eastern front to shift from offense to defense; the failure of the strategic concept behind the Russian campaign was becoming increasingly clear. Against the backdrop of this highly concrete foreign situation, Schmitt's shift from the expansive ideas of Reich and "greater territory" to the defensive idea of the Katechon becomes coherent. Wolfgang Abendroth has indicated that already at an early point, Schmitt had lost any illusions about the Wehrmacht's situation. Ideas that were basically conservative and preservative seemed an appropriate response.[96] Through his conceptual shift, the Third Reich could be stylized into a "delayer" stymieing the Allies, the "accelerators"—although these were, he concedes, sometimes "accelerators against their own will."[97]

In line with Schmitt's own stress on "concrete obstacles in foreign policy" in his 1930 book on Hugo Preuss, not only external or foreign but also equally "concrete" domestic events help clarify the development of his Katechon concept. As antagonist of the Antichrist, the Katechon delays the end of history, thus gaining time. In 1942 Schmitt called on "historians and philosophers of history " to investigate the different types and figures of "world-historical delayers and postponers." He offered a rather odd list of examples: the systematic philosopher Hegel, the Hapsburg emperor Franz Joseph, the Czech president Masaryk, the Polish marshal Pilsudski.[98] Schmitt would only expound on such "delayers" at greater length after the war, for instance in his review of Karl Löwith's book *Meaning in History* (1949).[99] In *The Nomos of the Earth* (1950), most of which was written during the war, a subchapter is devoted to "the Christian Empire as Delayer of the Antichrist (KatEchon)."[100] Schmitt here underscores the entry of the legend of the

Antichrist into social and political history, its acquiring an autonomous historical mission.[101] It seems remarkable that he does not contrast the series of delayers with a series of accelerators.

By 1942 the murder of the Jews in the extermination camps was well underway. Schmitt's antisemitic statements in the conference he had organized on "Judaism and Legal Studies" had not yet lost their resonance. Perhaps in that year it would have been clear to most readers which inner enemy Schmitt had in mind when speaking of the Antichrist. In any case the idea of the Antichrist as a Jew was a longstanding theological topos.[102] For Schmitt, the connection between the Jews (especially those who were assimilated) and a certain form of "acceleration" was constantly present.

To clarify this connection, we need to first look more closely at the main sources of Schmitt's idea of "delay." This means consulting Schmitt's correspondence, as few indications of that sort are available in his published texts. The Schmitt archives contain many letters from 1942 referring to the Katechon. For example, the famous constitutional historian Otto Brunner expressed himself as follows: "Honorable *Herr Staatsrat!* . . . Without a doubt your concept of the Katechon strikes the core of the problem."[103] And Hans Körniken, with whom Schmitt corresponded on both this theme and Bruno Bauer, offered an interpretation closely aligned to Schmitt's own ideas:

> Much still weighs on my heart regarding the Katechon. Deciding who a Katechon is depends on finding a constructive guiding line for historical development. The decision is easier for the past than for the present. Whoever has created a great synthesis, an impressive clustering of opposites, and led them to victory, slows down the tempo of history and becomes a "delayer." When Hegel's synthesis [and] with it the Young Hegelian revolution falls apart, the development collapses . . . ![104]

But even this rather detailed comment contains no reference to concrete sources. In contrast, a letter of 4 June 1942, from Schmitt to Professor Martin Dibelius, Heidelberg *Ordinarius* for New Testament theology and a man who came into conflict with the Nazis, contains some important hints:

> Highly honored *Herr* colleague! With your friendly mailing of
> the proofs of your academy lecture "Rome and the Christians
> in the First Century" you have done me an extraordinarily great
> service.[105] I thank you sincerely. In an essay in the well-known

weekly *Das Reich* of April 19 of this year I had mentioned the Katechon; indeed this emerged from a long preoccupation with the theological problem. Your position thus has special interest for me. I will mention that the text of the Protestant minister Adolf Zahn (*On the Concept of Esteem*, Amsterdam 1899, foreword) convinced me. With thanks once again and heartfelt greetings.[106]

The importance for Schmitt of the writing of both the court preacher Adolph Zahn (not to be confused with the theologian Theodor Zahn) and Martin Dibelius has been widely overlooked by the Schmitt scholars.[107] The foreword by Zahn that Schmitt mentions seems to have been especially important since it is the only more recent text he directly links to his own research.[108] That Schmitt only mentions it in one letter does not speak against this reading, because leaving his readers unclear about the background of his knowledge was a basic part of his rhetorical strategy.

Still, Schmitt's reference is not easy to interpret. For in all essential points Zahn's exegesis of 2 Thessalonians 2:6f. seems to contradict Schmitt's own reading. It in fact fully adheres to the Calvinist understanding of the Katechon as the preached Gospel.[109] Schmitt understood his Katechon as a political concept, juxtaposing it directly with Protestant neutralization. In contrast, the Calvinist approach "depoliticizes the idea of the Katechon."[110] What aspect of Zahn's text would, then, have actually "convinced" Schmitt? Zahn presumes that when speaking of the Katechon, Paul was "thinking of himself or better of power, which he bears."[111] But in a "wandering through Scriptures," he searches for each in a series of powers having "Katechonic" effect. He thus observes that "The Jews have the somewhat self-satisfied but still not untrue idea that their own Abraham preserved the entire world as it was" (vi). Zahn views each separate Katechon as responsible for repressing the Antichrist, who is always "present" (ix). His text concludes with an attack on Rome as the "last swindle in world history" (xii).

Schmitt certainly had no sympathy to spare for the latter idea. Rather, the idea he took over from Zahn was that one has to proceed through world history according to each reigning Katechon. For Schmitt, the equivalence between Katechon and Reich is less important than the fact that, as Zahn writes, a power always has to be in place to restrain the Antichrist. For this reason, Schmitt considers Hegel, the Protestant, to be a "Katechon." Berthold's argument that Schmitt's notion of Catholic "intensification" *(Verschärfung)* was a response to Protestant interpretations of the Katechon thus seems questionable. Schmitt uses both Protestant and Catholic sources to the extent they can support his "political-theological" constructions. He draws on a Protestant source for the sake of constructing a world history of delayers and preservers. Here as elsewhere, Schmitt is concerned with the political, not the theological. His thesis of acceleration is most closely connected with his concept of the political and is not explainable simply against his Catholic background.

13

Depolitization

Günter Meuter's 1994 study *Der Katechon* shows how extensively the Katechon concept is already present in Schmitt's early writing.[1] Similarly to the case with the nomos concept, before 1933 both the Katechon and the theme of delay appear mainly in negative and polemical contrast to their supposed opposite. Schmitt's attack on what he defines as the bourgeois constitutional state's purely normative idea of law forms the backdrop to his interest in the nomos. The attack shows parallels to his treatment of the Katechon. That concept directly emerges only after a long-term confrontation with various elements of acceleration: secularization and neutralization of the political; the formalization and desubstantialization of constitutional doctrine. The process of acceleration that Schmitt opposes plays itself out in highly different forms. In Schmitt's writings before World War II, the image of the Katechon is directed at a range of developments that can be summarized under the rubric of "modernity."

Schmitt most clearly lays out his basic philosophical-historical schema in the speech he delivered in 1929, "The Age of Neutralizations and Depolitization." The speech's title refers to a historical process Schmitt diagnoses as having unfolded in Europe over the past four hundred years. During this period, he indicates, the European spirit has developed in four great "secular steps": "from the theological to the metaphysical, from there to the humanitarian-moral, and finally to the economic."[2] Schmitt describes this process as both secularization and depolitization, but also as a far-reaching normativation and desubstantialization. (In place of normativation, one might more accurately speak of formalization. But since for Schmitt the concept of form has a specific, positive content,[3] while the concept of normativity is always negatively loaded, the terminological shift might be confusing.) Schmitt defines depolitization as a steering of each central politicized realm of

175

human thought to a new nonpoliticized realm. No one would sacrifice his life for this new realm; it is not determined by struggles potentially leading to war. With the political understood as the "degree of intensity of a tie or separation, an association or dissociation," this shift of locus involves an effort to diminish "intensity."[4] A basic concern running through history is locating such a "neutral" realm.[5] Schmitt considered the most momentous step in this direction to be the seventeenth-century transition from "Christian theology" to a "system of 'natural' scientificity."[6] With the depolitization and privatization of religion, the direction was set determining all developments "to the present day."[7]

Every additional depoliticizing step is thus an additional step of secularization. One might read Schmitt's *Concept of the Political* as a project meant to block this movement toward a theologically neutral referential realm.[8] But such a reading mistakenly presumes that Schmitt viewed the church as in essence more than a successful ordering model. To reiterate: Schmitt's central concern is neither the Catholic Church nor Christian theology, but rather the realm of the *political*. His struggle of principle is not against secularization in general but against the depolitization and desubstantialization he understands as tied to it. This is the core of Schmitt's genuine radicalism. He sees a *depolitization of the political* as the final step of the process he opposes. Such a step amounts to a disappearance of the intensity forming the basis of any human life that is something other than banal play.[9] Noteworthy here is Ernst-Wolfgang Boeckenförde's observation that Schmitt's concept of the political is "neither bellicistic nor pacifistic . . . but aimed at sacrifice."[10] Within Schmitt's depoliticized society, there are no longer any substantial *victims,* any bloody sacrifice of life; sacrifice is, he explains, fully "out of reach" of and "incapable of being grounded" in liberal individualism.[11] With the liberal political system thus being incapable of forming a true political unit,[12] Schmitt disputes the very feasibility of its existence.

In Schmitt's analysis, the friend-enemy distinction and the status of the political as a form of extreme intensity have been neutralized by an increasingly accelerative movement. This is a movement from substance to pure form, the concrete to the abstract, the public to the private, the particular to the universal. Although the movement is irreversible, through reversion to an "integral knowledge" it can be arrested (95). Schmitt does not explain what such knowledge comprises. We simply learn that it works against "the secret law" (94) of enemies with accelerative powers. It is consequently important to consider Schmitt's "enemy" more closely.

Up through the 1932 edition of the *Concept of the Political*, the nature and identity of Schmitt's "enemy" remained highly ambiguous. Schmitt was aware of this lack of clarity and would address it in the foreword to the book's new edition of 1963. He has, Schmitt indicates, not yet clearly enough distinguished "conventional, real, and absolute enemies" from one another (17). In another text treating General Salan's situation in the Algerian war of independence between 1958 and 1961, he emphasizes that the concept of the enemy contains an *inherent* confusion: "The enemy is our own question as form. When our own form is unequivocally defined, what is the source of the enemy's double nature?"[13] For what reason does one's "own brother" suddenly surface at one's "back" as the most dangerous of enemies, after the absolute enemy has apparently already been discovered?[14] Even for the decisionistically grounded thinker, spotting the enemy is nearly impossible. The important thing is thus always seeing to it that the range of "temporal costumes" does not obscure the actual core question of the "real enemy."[15]

"The actual political distinction is the distinction between friend and enemy," Schmitt declares in 1933 at the beginning of the third edition of *The Concept of the Political*.[16] Formulated in the book's earlier editions as well, this is "the specifically political distinction to which political actions and motives can be traced."[17] At the same time Schmitt postulates that all political terms and concepts have a "polemic meaning" and are bound to a "concrete situation."[18] What, then, was the polemical content of his apparently neutral or "symmetrical" definition of the political?[19] To answer this, we need to distinguish between two forms of enemy at work in Schmitt's theoretical construction. With his *Concept of the Political*, Schmitt is turning not against his political enemies but against those he considers *enemies of the political*.

The Political Enemy as the Stranger *and* Other

Schmitt begins his definition of the political—not of politics—with an "uncovering" of specific political categories. These are the "last distinctions" back to which political action can be traced.[20] In his friend-enemy distinction, Schmitt does not explain what he means by "friend." He explains that the enemy is not necessarily morally wicked, aesthetically ugly, or economically in competition: "He is simply the other, the alien [*der Fremde*], and his essence is defined by the fact that in an especially intensive sense he is existentially something other and alien. . . ."[21] In the 1933 edition of *The Concept of the Political*, the concept of the "other" is transformed into the concept of "another kind" *(Andersgear-tete)*, in harmony with the prevailing *völkisch* vocabulary.[22] The "other" and "being of another kind" now emerges at the political decision's core, as a potential danger to one's own existence. In all the book's editions, Schmitt defines his idea of the enemy through the "other" and the "alien." He explains neither what the difference between the "other" and the "alien" is nor what the difference means for his construction of the enemy.

The concept of the alien opens a verbal field taking in the "Staatsfremder"—the stranger within the state. The concept of the other does not necessarily imply such a location. Consequently, Schmitt's sense of the enemy included the "enemy" not outside but inside the state. In Germany, the "alien"-"other" distinction had its imagined parallel in a distinction between foreigners and Jews. Bruno Bauer had already very consciously defined the Jews as "others," not as "foreigners"; Jewish legal equality would mean that from a constitutional perspective they were no longer "foreigners." Modern antisemitism was thus directed in the first place against the Jews as "others," not foreigners. Dan Diner has placed great emphasis on this often obscured difference: "The Jew does not stand for the foreigner, the unknown, but for the other: the other as the constitutive counterpoint of one's own self. Within Occidental consciousness, that other is concentrated into a secularized hostility toward Jews that is hardly perceived as such due to its various displacements."[23] Such displacements can frequently be sensed in Schmitt's work; unearthing them in the pre-1933 writing is in any case difficult. If my objections to the prevalent opportunism-theory are well grounded, then Schmitt's aggressive antisemitic polemic in the years after Hitler's rise to power exposed a position that had previously remained concealed. Within this alternative interpretive framework, the polemic would need to be understood in connection with the Nazi politics supported by Schmitt: a politics revealing its antimodernist face in the annulment of Jewish emancipation.[24]

From Schmitt's perspective, the Nazi effort to replace secularization with a "political religion"[25] might have amounted to a delaying and indeed reactionary movement conforming more or less seamlessly to his own thinking. But it is more likely that he welcomed Nazism's radicalization of the friend-enemy distinction, which finally disposed of the liberal Weimar "system." Despite what his Katechon concept might suggest, Schmitt was not simply a reactionary, but an "intensifier." He was determined to exacerbate oppositions, when this guaranteed the pathos and "seriousness of life." Not only in this respect, Schmitt was a true "accelerator"—not a delayer.

The "purely scientific" *(wissenschaftlich)* definition of the concept of the other in the third edition of *The Concept of the Political* supports this interpretation. For through such definition, the other gains the most hostile possible characteristics within Schmitt's thinking. Perhaps nothing can more fully reproduce a late nineteenth-century Catholic incarnation of the Jewish enemy than the idea that a group of persons is conspiring to use universal, dissolutive ideas in order to actually realize their particular political interests. The other is imagined in the "Jew," for whom Schmitt's slogan of the enemy comprising his "own question as form" applies to a special degree.

The same Hegelian dialectic informing this slogan is at the basis of Schmitt's *Concept of the Political,* as he indirectly suggests. He finds in Hegel's writings a definition of the enemy "usually avoided by modern philosophers" and with which he strongly agrees:

> The moral [*Das Sittliche*] must itself look at its own animation [*Lebendigkeit*] in its difference, and do so in a way that the nature [*Wesen*] of this facing living entity is posited [*gesetzt*] as something alien [*Fremdes*] and to be negated. . . . Such a difference is the enemy. . . . For the moral, this enemy can only be the nation's [*des Volkes*] enemy, and can itself only be a nation. . . . War is not war of families against families but nation against nations, and in this way hate is itself undifferentiated [*indifferentiiert*] and free of all personality.[26]

Schmitt's reception of Hegel's idea that between these enemies "hate is itself undifferentiated and free of all personality" is important for understanding both his definition of the political and the later texts on international law, which propose a "nondiscriminatory" concept of the enemy. From this passage, Schmitt also extracts the idea that only a nation, a *Volk,* can be a potential enemy. The enemy, he writes, is constantly a public and no sort of private enemy: *hostis* and not *inimicus.* Since, he observes, the German language does not distinguish between private and public enemies, many "falsifications" *(Fälschungen)* are possible here. Hence the frequently cited injunction to "love thy enemies"—*diligite inimicos vestros* (Matt. 5:44; Luke 6:27)—ought not be transferred from private to *political* enemies. Schmitt stresses this point in all three editions of his book.[27] The injunction, he explains, does not indicate that one should love and support the enemies of one's *Volk.*[28] In this manner, Schmitt directly inverts the injunction's apparent meaning, so that it now reads as follows: Whoever loves the political enemy is in conflict with the Gospels.[29] Implicit in this inversion is Schmitt's claim not only to be in harmony with the basic thrust of Christian theology but, beyond that, to be continuing Christianity's "thousand-year struggle" on behalf of Europe.[30]

The inner logic of another of Schmitt's books, *Political Theology*, points to his concept of the enemy as itself one of his own secularized theological concepts. The formal symmetry of the friend-enemy distinction is thus problematic. Through both the claim to theological grounding and the choice of metaphors, Schmitt's ostensibly nondiscriminatory and radically neutral idea of the enemy is in fact *asymmetric*. A rich range of resentments inform the idea. The resentments hardly mask their own roots in nineteenth- and early-twentieth-century antimodernist Catholicism, and in the same period's body of antisemitic belief.

The Jews as Enemies of the Political

The Fraud of Universalism

"The concept of the state presumes the concept of the political": Schmitt begins his explication of the political with this assertion.[31] If politics precedes the state, every attack on the concept of the political is directly aimed at the state. As a result, for Schmitt corrosion of the political is tied to an "extirpation [*Ausrottung*] of the state" (75) and the "order of human things" it guarantees (95). On the basis of this interaction, Schmitt is here again contributing to the conflict over the state, although now on the plain of the political. But in reality, Schmitt already decided against the state and for the political sphere in 1932, in his second edition of his *Concept of the Political*. He did so through an endowment of that sphere with a quasi-ontological status beyond the state.

Schmitt discovers the genuine antithesis to the concept of the political in the "unpolitical purity" Hans Kelsen advocates in his legal theory (21). He devotes astonishingly vehement rhetorical energy to that "purity." In his view, Kelsen's "pure theory of law" is not only a "pretention" *(Prätention)* (21), but indeed an "intellectual snare" (62). Schmitt's specific reproaches are an outcome of the political-theological system in which he himself is trapped. The reproaches illuminate his position: whoever negates the theological is an "antitheologian"; whoever rejects the political friend-enemy distinction is "in truth" engaging in politics in an "especially intensive" way. In the end, no position is admissible allowing for anything else but Schmitt's "snare." Whoever stakes a claim to working for a world without war, "a world without the distinction between friend and enemy and consequently a world without politics," is committing "manifest fraud" (35). In harmony with Schmitt's principle that "whoever says humanity wants to deceive," he is intent here on exposing humanitarian, universalist concepts as a mere cover for the pursuit of particular, political and theological interests. It is thus no surprise that he reduces the entire approach of the British-Jewish theorist of pluralism Harold Josef Laski to the "monistic-universal" concept of "humanity." Likewise, it is no surprise that he declares Max Scheler to be a "preconizer" *(Präkonisator)* of easy technical comfort, promising a utopian "sphere of peace" without confessional, national, or social strife.[32] (The accusation is in any event one-sided, considering Scheler's book *The Genius of War and the German War [Der Genius des Kriegs und der Deutsche Krieg]* of 1915.)

It is indisputable that the instrumentalization of various ideas and theories is a standard technique of political battle. We need only recall observations of the Cambridge School regarding political theory as political action in historical context, for instance Wittgenstein's motto "words are deeds" and James Tully's confirmation that "the pen is a mighty sword."[33] Such observations apply very well to German scholars of constitutional law in the Wilhelminian and Weimar Republic periods. Schmitt was in this respect no exception—he considered his intellectual labor as "war with a massive reality and presence."[34] But Schmitt defines the political instrumentalization of universal concepts as *systematic* fraud or deception. This is the basis for his unflinching repetitions. The enemy of the political is thus no usual political enemy but a fraudster with a specific *vokabularium* following a "secret law."[35]

Schmitt's "true enemies," the systematic fraudsters, are theorists who "consciously or unconsciously" presume a human being who is "good by nature," advocate eternal peace, and desire progress and an end to all enmities.[36] In *The Concept of the Political* the "theology of the opponent"[37] is represented first and foremost by the positions of a series of prominent assimilated Jews. In the second edition of 1932, Hugo Preuss, Walther Rathenau, Karl Marx, and Franz Oppenheimer join Kelsen, Laski, and Scheler as objects of attack. In the third edition of 1933, Schmitt initiates a "dialog of absent parties" (Heinrich Meier's phrase) with the young Leo Strauss.[38]

As indicated, Schmitt's "secular confrontation" was born forward by Catholic-stamped resentment and an image of the enemy rationalized in Protestant terms.[39] Structurally, there can be little doubt that assimilated Jewry was at the heart of this confrontation. Schmitt's notes written between 1947 and 1951 make this clear, even if caution is called for when using this source, which sometimes reveals a self-justifying intent. The *Glossarium* entry of 25 September 1947 spells things out clearly: "Precisely the assimilated Jew is the true enemy." For this reason, Schmitt indicates, it is "pointless to prove the *Protocols of the Elders of Zion* to be false," since "Jews always remain Jews. While the Communist can improve himself and change. That has nothing to do with northern race etc."[40] Some days earlier, Schmitt offers the following observation, in relation to the "concept of the Jews" in Hamann, Bauer, Kierkegaard, and Nietzsche: "Unchaining of the virulence of a concept through detheologization."[41]

Although the "truest" of Schmitt's enemies was always Kelsen, it is still useful to consider two other enemies as well. First, Schmitt views the "Berlin-Frankfurt sociologist Franz Oppenheimer"[42] as representing the liberal demand for the state's "extirpation." In 1912 Oppenheimer had published a book titled *Der Staat* in the sociological series Die Gesellschaft, edited by Martin Buber. There is no reference in this book to an "extirpation of the state." What one does find is the announcement of a victory "all along the line" of economics over "political means." This development is outlined at the book's end, which also offers, by way of a metaphor of the Passion, an evaluation of Christianity's goal marking the exact opposite of Schmitt's political-theological evaluation: "That is humanity's path of suffering and salvation, its Golgotha and wakening to the realm of eternity: from war to peace, from the hostile splintering of the hordes to the peaceful unity of humanity [*Menschheit*], from animality to humanity [*Humanität*], from the state based on plunder to a free citizenry."[43]

As Karl Löwith already noted in 1935, Schmitt's attack on Oppenheimer is even sharper in the third (1933) edition of *The Concept of the Political*. The economic sphere Oppenheimer favors is now caricatured as the "world of fraud," since "exchange and deception [*Tauschen und Täuschen*] are often closely aligned." Hence precisely when it remains "unpolitical," an economically based form of rule would "appear to be a frightful deception." Schmitt's spiteful remarks recall his constant attacks on the "non German" Walther Rathenau, who himself saw not politics but the economy as representing fate. "Usurers [*Wucherer*] and blackmailers" would "unfortunately" also have recourse to the economically fundamental motto "treaties are to be honored [*pacta sunt servanda*]."[44]

Second, the work of the political scientist Harold J. Laski is discussed in the fourth section of each edition of *The Concept of the Political*.[45] In the first edition of 1927, Schmitt describes Laski's theory of state as the most important in recent decades.[46] He locates its value "in a phenomenologically correct description of the present-day state's existence [*heutiger Staatlichkeit*]."[47] But these enthusiastic words stand in sharp contrast to Schmitt's later assault on the theory, which has prompted Nikolaus Sombart to suggest that in the second edition of *The Concept of the Political*, Laski takes over the "place of Jewish whipping-boy" that Kelsen occupies in *Political Theology*.[48] The assault demonstrates Schmitt's functionalizing of assimilated Jews as agents of acceleration and a depoliticizing of the political.

Schmitt wishes to understand the political realm in terms of a sovereign decision of a "political unit" over the "authoritative [*massgebend*] case"[49] As a result of his reading of Laski, in 1930 he begins to render his concept of the political more precise by defining it in terms of the "degree of intensity of a unit."[50] The stark contrast with Laski's pluralistic state theory thus becomes evident. For Laski disputes the very existence of a sovereign political unit as understood in the classical sense.[51] (This was initially a reaction to what he considered the British state's claims to omnipotence in the Great War.) Schmitt thus defines Laski's pluralism as a theory of the "dissolution or refutation" of the state, or any analogous political unit, a theory lacking any relation to the political. With the *political* human order dissolved into a multiplicity of social units, that order, comments Schmitt, would no longer be in a position to make decisions in a "case of emergency." Likewise, it would no longer be in position to engage in political conflict or warfare against another state.[52]

For Schmitt, Laski's theory overlooks the idea of the political at the proper center of any theory of state. "All of its sharpness [*Scharfsinn*]" — Schmitt mainly uses that term against Jewish opponents[53] — is directed against the state by means of a "liberal individualism." In the process, the state decays into a *society* alongside and between many other societies.[54] Pluralism, Schmitt argues, places *political* unity alongside other social ties such as religious society, nation, union, and family. The political is thus no longer treated as an independent and authoritative criterion. In the edition of 1933, he names the resulting "complete identity [*Wesensgleichheit*] of all human groupings" a "basic dogma" of pluralistic theory of state, which he attributes with its own "political theology." Aside from one footnote,[55] there is no further mention of Laski in this edition. The connection between the reference to "political theology" and Laski's work can thus be established only through a reconstruction by way of the earlier editions.[56] In contrast, more stress is laid on Gierke's organicist state-theory.

Schmitt offers the *Kulturkampf* as a historical example more closely describing the pluralistic approach. The example was already Laski's, a fact passed over in silence in the third edition of *The Concept of the Political*. Schmitt stresses that although Bismarck's lack of success against the Catholic Church and socialists revealed the limits of state "omnipotence," it did not limit his sovereign capacity to wage a war.[57] With his example of the *Kulturkampf*, Laski touched on a sensitive point. For a central experience running through German Catholic culture was successful resistance in that crisis. This resistance was perceived not only as religiously determined but also as political and cultural opposition to "state omnipotence," subsequently as politically potent.[58] Schmitt thus intends to show that his concept of the political, consistently emerging from the idea of the exceptional case or state of emergency, is not damaged by the events of the *Kulturkampf* and Bismarck's battle against the socialists.

In the third edition of Schmitt's book, the jurist lays special emphasis on what he views as the purpose of "pluralist" support for equal treatment of churches and unions. The purpose, he explains, is bringing the two forces together in opposition to the state.[59] This is the context for the single footnote devoted to Laski: "In fact the church only serves the Social Democrat pluralist Laski as a theoretical booster for the Social Democratic unions and his liberal individualism."[60] In other words, Laski, the assimilated Jew, is merely using the example of the *Kulturkampf* to hide his own interests, or at least give them a theoretical cloak. Six years later Schmitt will simply refer at this point in his book to "the Jew Laski, mainly cited in relation to English pluralism." According to Schmitt, in their underlying effort to dissolve the state and with the "slaughter" of "mighty Leviathan," the pluralistic theorists are bent on playing off the Roman Catholic Church against the state. In 1930, he already reproaches Laski for "conjuring up the shadow of the most militant church father (Athanasius) for his socialism of the Second International."[61]

The Denial of Original Sin

In *The Concept of the Political* Schmitt underscores what he has already suggested in *Political Theology* and other earlier works: that there is a methodical connection between theological and political premises. But now the connection does not involve an astonishing analogy between the miracle and state of emergency. Rather, it involves the "theological dogmas of sinfulness."[62] For such dogmas are the "necessarily conceptual premises" for theology *and* political theory. Along with the distinction between friend and enemy, the theologically "basic dogma of the sinfulness of the world and men" is what has led to their classification into groups, rendering an undifferentiated idea of humanity impossible. According to Schmitt, all his "true enemies," although otherwise having various opinions, deny the reality of original sin and thus cannot understand the background to his concept of the political. "Denial of original sin" is the basic theological premise for denial of the political, necessarily leading to universalistic and "unpolitical" thinking.[63] This, Schmitt emphasizes, is the true "theology of the opponent." It is a "theology" hiding behind the deceitful, camouflaging language of purity.[64] Making use of what he considers the Antichrist's slogans, "peace, security, and harmony of all with all," Schmitt caricatures his "unpolitical" opponents. He leaves it to the reader to see through their game and sense his insight into that game.[65]

The Schmitt archives contain an essay by the jurist's friend and interlocutor Albrecht Erich Günther, "Der Ludus de Antichristo, ein christlicher Mythos vom Reich und dem deutschen Herrscheramte," published in *Glaube und Volk* in 1932.[66] The "Ludus de Antichristo" is a twelfth-century liturgical drama of unknown authorship. Günther cites (122) the conclusion from the drama as follows: "After the fall of those blinded by delusion *peace and security* covers the world." In an article published two years later, Ernst Forsthoff maintains that developments within the constitutional state that are prompted by a striving for "security" have probably been influenced by a "specifically" "Jewish sense of law." Forsthoff himself ties these thoughts to the Antichrist:

> It might be rewarding to pursue ideas regarding security, especially legal security, from their Jewish beginnings into the Middle Ages (play of the Antichrist) until the present. Such an investigation would probably cast new light on a development of the constitutional state that was sustained in a very basic way by the striving for calculability and security.[67]

Schmitt's own contribution to this intellectual genealogy is to define "human paradise" as the most mendacious promise offered by the anti-Christian neutralizers.[68] He sees the critique of the Christian idea of original sin as itself stemming from the accelerative forces against which he is struggling. In fact, the Fall and expulsion from paradise form both the *Christian* political-theological core of Schmitt's concept of the political and the basis of his secular political theory. His one-sided belief, shared with Schopenhauer, that the Fall and original sin represent, in the philosopher's words, Christianity's "center and heart,"[69] was also maintained by the political theologians to whom Schmitt was so close. For Wilhelm Stapel, "Paul did not derive original sin from his Judaism, for he was persecuted by the Jews precisely on account of his doctrine of sin and salvation." Likewise, the theologian indicates, "nothing is more alien than 'original sin' to 'present-day Jewry.'" What he terms its "un-Jewish" nature thus marks the demarcating line from the Jewish religion.[70]

Importantly, we need to understand Schmitt's belief in original sin in a secular framework, where it formed the basis for Schmitt's particular idea of the enemy. Schmitt wished to render his concept of the political plausible by placing it in the context of both original sin and a dogmatic interpretation of the first three chapters of Genesis.[71] The dogma of original sin was narrowly tied to the Christian religion's fourth century incorporation into the Roman state. That process involved something like a theologization of political concepts, with earlier ideas of political rule transferred to a theological realm and theological concepts being endowed with political meaning.[72] With Constantine's conversion in 313, the previously suppressed movement of Christian faith gained the possibility of sharing Rome's imperial power. Once subject to brutal persecution, the Christian bishops now became both favored subjects and patrons of that power.[73] Such proximity was mirrored in the age's Christian theology, marked by a radical change in the approach to state power. This was most apparent in a fundamentally altered theological anthropology that sought legitimation in a new form of biblical exegesis. The story of Adam, Eve, and the serpent stood at the center of this exegesis, which—to follow the basic contours of Elaine Pagels' account— had separated itself drastically from the Jewish interpretive tradition.

Until that point, most Jewish and Christian interpreters had approached the story as a demonstration of moral freedom of decision and human responsibility (xxiii). Now sinfulness instead took center stage. The sin of Adam was viewed as having led to a loss of unblemished morality and an acquisition of tainted sexuality. It was also viewed as the source of an incapacity for political freedom (xxvi).

Moving against the traditional Jewish and Christian conception, Augustine himself focused on the extreme sinfulness of human nature.

"Original sin," he indicated, had made human beings ill, wracked with suffering, and not to be saved (99). Augustine's most important opponents, the Pelagians, maintained that such sin, *peccatum originale*, only consisted of imitating Adam's bad example. In confronting Pelagius and his followers, Augustine radicalized and systematized his notion of sinfulness.[74] Through the Fall, Adam had lost both "original righteousness" *(iustitia originalis)* and the "aid of grace" *(adiutorium gratiae)* thanks to which he could have persevered with goodness. Through divine imposition of punishment, human nature had been transformed.[75] On 1 May 418, with the approbation of Roman bishop Zosimus, an African provincial synod dogmatized the basic Augustinian idea. To be sure, it did so without integrating Augustine's idea of the complete incapacity of human beings to stay on the path of good.[76]

According to Augustine, Adam's sin had rendered all of humanity into a *massa damnationis*.[77] His interpretation of the Fall offered grounds for both contemporaries and later Christians to approach human beings as unsuited for autonomy. The interpretation thus legitimized rule from afar and above in the realms of both church and state.[78] Even in its Augustinian context, this interpretation of the story of Adam and Eve fulfilled an essentially political function. In 410, Alarich conquered Rome and Augustine faced pagan reproaches. By interpreting the Fall as he did, he hoped to show that Christians and Christianity bore no blame for the catastrophe, that Christianity was a doctrine supporting, not destroying, the state.[79]

Augustine's doctrine of original sin was aimed at opponents both inside and outside the church. In the former domain, his radical doctrine of sin led to the church's strengthening. Since all those living after Adam's fall bore the *tradux peccati* or original sin within them, each person was dependent on the church's grace. In this manner, until the Council of Trent (1545–63) and beyond to the Vatican Council (1869–70), the Augustinian viewpoint was tied dogmatically to the requirement of baptism. Correspondingly, the decree on original sin issued by the Council of Trent on 17 June 1546 stipulated that whoever "denies that newborn children are to be baptized immediately after birth . . . is excommunicated.[80] Correspondingly, it was only within the church that human beings could be torn from their sinful state.[81] In this manner, an enormous potential for ecclesiastical power emerged from the doctrine of original sin. At the same time, Augustine's policies were well suited for demonstrating that Christian theology was not to be viewed as a basis for rejecting worldly rule per se. Rather, it was obliged to support such rule, since the story of Adam and Eve taught that people were not in a position to rule themselves.[82]

With his dogma of original sin, Augustine thus furnished the Christian religion with an instrument for political thinking and acting.[83] Now Schmitt clearly relativizes the idea of the absolute corruption of human nature, as found, for instance, in the works of de Maistre and Donoso Cortés. Nevertheless, he declares that dogma to be a premise for *any* political theory. At the same time he aims the dogma at anyone arguing outside a Christian framework.[84] On the one hand, he writes that it is possible "to test the anthropology manifest in all theories of state and political ideas, before classifying them according to whether, consciously or unconsciously, they presume a human being who is 'wicked by nature' or 'good by nature'" (59). But on the other hand, he makes amply clear which side of this division he considers valid political theory. A theologian would stop being a theologian if he no longer considered human beings to be sinful and in need of salvation, no longer distinguished the elect from those who are not so. Likewise, political ideas and conceptual processes cannot "take an anthropological 'optimism' as their starting point" (63–64). Since in the end the sphere of the political is determined, for Schmitt, by the "real possibility of an enemy," in doing away with the possibility of an enemy a positive anthropology would also do away with any specifically political purposiveness (64). Through his concept of the political, Schmitt wishes to oppose precisely such a development.

In 1928 Rabbi Max Dienemann observed that "Judaism and Christianity part in a basic way in regards to the doctrine of original sin." As a rule, he indicated, the rabbinic commentators reject the notion of sin as a fatefully inherited quantity. Rather, they see it as something that can be positively denied through individual actions and decisions.[85] Since according to Jewish tradition God expresses his will in the Torah, the Jewish concept of sinfulness is rooted in this premise, not in a particular idea of human nature.[86] The Jewish interpretation of the first three books of Genesis is thus at a basic remove from the Augustinian tradition. It tends to read the story of Adam and Eve in terms of God's gift to Adam—not to a king or ruler—of rule over the earth, Adam here serving as representative of "humanity."[87] Noteworthy in this context is the finding of the theologian Julius Gross, in a meticulous study based on Jewish and early Christian sources, that "the dogma of original sin" lacks any historical basis. For Gross, Augustine thus emerges as the dogma's creator.[88]

Although Carl Schmitt was no scholar of ancient Judaism and early Christianity, he seems to have sensed the absence of a pessimistic theological anthropology in the ancient and medieval corpus upon which Judaism is based. And he seems to have perceived that fact's connection to, in his words, the "denial of original sin" by "numerous sects, heretics, romantics, and anarchists."[89] His speculation on both the origins of pregnant political concepts and the original-sin dogma at least implicitly suggests, without directly spelling out, that the dogma's absence from Judaism has had fatal consequences for the political theory conceived by assimilated Jews. That the suggestion involves a rationalizing of deepseated resentment is already evident in Schmitt's incorporation of Helmuth Plessner's political theory, as presented in his *Power and Human Nature (Macht und menschliche Natur)* in 1931, into the second edition of *The Concept of the Political* in 1932.[90] In 1933, following the Nazi advent to power and Plessner's flight from Germany, Schmitt eliminated all references to the philosophical anthropologist from the book's third edition.

14

Desubstantialization

The motif of desubstantialization can best be described in the context of a particular historical process: the far-reaching use of Article 48 of the Weimar constitution by the Brüning cabinet in 1931. The bitter controversy between Schmitt and Hans Kelsen was played out in this context. Schmitt's distorted way of describing Kelsen's work, and, to cite Horst Dreier's careful formulation, his "not always scientifically grounded reservations" regarding Kelsen, were repeatedly taken over by Schmitt's students. This skewed approach to Kelsen has historical implications going far beyond questions of state theory.[1]

In the debate over the "guardians of the constitution," Kelsen criticizes Schmitt's definition of the president of the Reich as a neutral power, hence as a duly appointed constitutional guardian. He designates this argument as the "oldest stage set" from the "constitutional theatre's junk room." "Dusty props," he suggests, reveal Schmitt's proximity to a compromised ideology, one that even stylized the monarch into a neutral force.[2] Kelsen here locates Schmitt in the tradition of Laband's and Jellinek's constitutional theory. This is the framework for his charge that Schmitt is fusing scholarship with politics in order to expand presidential and cabinet power at the cost of an ostensibly pluralistic state-dissolving parliament. At the same time Kelsen underscores that Schmitt has entirely neglected the Austrian model for a constitutional court, a model which Kelsen helped draft. By doing so, he suggests, Schmitt has committed precisely the error with which he, Kelsen, has been charged by Schmitt: engaging in "objectless abstractions" (1879f.). At the same time, Kelsen issues an emphatic warning concerning Schmitt's unclear concept of the "total state," a concept using a "fiction of collective interest [*Gesamtinteresse*]" to mask the real situation of the various interests that are in play (1897).

We do not need to review the individual points in Kelsen's extremely detailed, sometimes biting critique of a book he refers to as revealing "no paucity of logical surprises."[3] Peter Caldwell has described the most important contrast emerging here between Kelsen and Schmitt: "In his call to exclude 'politics' from judicial decisions and to place the 'political decision' in the hands of the real 'substance' of the state Schmitt's book attempted . . . to isolate precisely the 'representative' of that substantial will that, as he had asserted in his *Constitutional Theory*, lay at the basis of the constitutional system. Schmitt's search for a real substance in the world represented the point where Kelsen's and Schmitt's theories diverge. The notion of a pure substance was completely alien to Kelsen's skeptical and critical theory."[4] Hence the concept of *substance* represents a decisive starting point for reflections on the conflict between Schmitt and Kelsen. The question of desubstantialization and formalization defines the conflict, unfolding in the framework of problems of state, sovereignty, law, and the meaning of democracy. Already evident in their early writings, the gulf between each theorist's position is perhaps most easily traced in Schmitt's constant battle against "pure" abstract law, from *Law and Judgment* (*Gesetz und Urteil*, 1912) to *Political Theology* (1922) and onward to *The Nomos of the Earth* (1950). His polemic against Kelsen as a "zealot of blind normativism" fits perfectly into the broader picture.[5]

The background of Kelsen's effort to formalize the law, and his resistance to any effort to substantialize constitutional rule—for instance through a monarch or president as embodiments of the people's political unity—was presumably the historical situation of multinational Austro-Hungary. This political entity was better preserved through purely formalized rule than through the construction of a specific general interest. Although the theme has not been researched at any length, it appears that Austrian constitutional theory showed a markedly stronger tendency toward formalism than was the case in the German Kaiserreich.

Kelsen does not explain his skepticism regarding substantialism in view of its historical background alone. At the same time, at the end of an essay titled "God and State," he grounds it in "modern science [*Wissenschaft*]," which he describes as striving "to dissolve all substance into function." For this reason, he explains, "the reduction of the extralegal concept of state to the concept of law is the indispensable precondition for the development of authentic legal studies [*Rechtswissenschaft*], as a science of positive law purified of all natural law."[6] And in his essay

"The Concept of State and Psychoanalysis," he observes that "as a substantial concept like 'strength' or 'soul,' as a personificative fiction, the concept of state enters into a parallel with the concept of God." For Kelsen, the self-evident answer to this problem is to sunder legal theory from the concept of state.

Drawing on Freud's *Totem and Taboo*, Kelsen places reliance on "substance" on the plane of "primitive totemic" thinking. Within such thinking, he indicates, the tribe's social unity is realized through the shared consumption of a sacrificial offering.[7] For his part, Schmitt defines the essence of all political unity as grounded in a capacity to offer sacrifice.[8] Since for liberal individualism the claims of sacrifice can "in no way be achieved or grounded," he sees the political as ceasing to exist in liberalism's putatively sacrifice-free society.[9]

The central concept Schmitt used in the Nazi period to oppose what he considered the purely normative Jewish concept of law was the concept of the nomos. Following 1933, the concept thus emerged as the core of his "concrete order"-based thinking, revealing his opposition to Kelsen in that context. In the confrontation's pre-1933 form, Schmitt's main concern was convicting Kelsen of deceit on the basis of lack of substance in his thinking. It is striking that both Schmitt and Kelsen gained their sense of the role substance played in law while grappling with questions of theology and religion. Kelsen became concerned with theological questions in the 1920s because, as he indicates in his *General Theory of State*, "the critical illumination of theology" reflected back on theory of state, "whose problems only entirely reveal themselves in this light."[10] Hence the analogy between the "theory of the state's self-obligation and the dogma of God become flesh" was meant to demonstrate the metaphysical character of prevailing constitutional theory and prepare the ground for a modern, scientific jurisprudence.[11] At the same time, in the books *On the Nature and Value of Democracy* (1920/1929) and *State Form and Weltanschauung (Staatsform und Weltanschauung*, 1933) Kelsen developed the radically relativistic perspective at work in his theory of democracy: a perspective formulated in view of possible objections from "political believers," and as a critique of the idea of a divine human being.[12]

Kelsen had already tried in 1911 to cast light on the doctrine of state self-obligation and had already done so through an analogy with the Christian theological problem of God become man. Within Jellinek's doctrine of state self-obligation, law was viewed as the state's "creation." As a substantive entity, the state here had precedence over law. At this doctrine's core was the idea that after the state had created law, it subsumed itself to its own creation. Kelsen demonstrated the legal dogmatism and untenable logic of the doctrine, thus striking at the heart of Laband's and Jellinek's constitutional theory.[13] He did this through the use of the same argument with which he tried in the 1930s to refute Schmitt's thesis of the president of the Reich as guardian of the constitution.

The reproaches Schmitt leveled at Kelsen and about which Kelsen would complain—along with engagement in "objectless abstractions," the use of both "fantasy-full metaphors" and "goose-leg logic" *(Gänsebeinlogik)*[14]—were grounded in a radically different sense of the role meant to be played by substantial concepts in constitutional theory. It is remarkable that both theorists formulated their positions regarding such concepts in relation to religion; more precisely, they did so in relation to Christianity and its core tenet of Jesus as Christ. In this respect, we have seen that in asserting that the "pregnancy," potency, or substantiality of constitutional theory was tied to its theological origins, Schmitt took over the array of prejudices assembled by Protestant and Catholic theology over the course of many centuries.

In 1933 Schmitt confronted the secular concept of law maintained by the constitutional parliamentary state with a new "substance." In *Entscheidung und Ordnung*, his student Gurian indicates that Schmitt was always searching for a "highest instance of decision" that could end his "despair at the anarchy he discovered behind all facades." At the same time, Gurian suggests, Schmitt was well aware that a pure act of decision without an authentic legitimatizing basis would be insufficient. For this reason, following his "conversion to National Socialism," he claimed to recognize a "substantial order" within that movement, beyond its pure decisionary competence.[15] The substance upon which this order was meant to rest was self-evidently not grounded in Catholic doctrine but, rather, in a common struggle against the "spirit of Judaism." Consequently the "substance" for which Schmitt claimed to stand was only defined negatively. It was part of the same complex as his struggle against "Jewish" decomposition through depolitization and desubstantialization. In this regard Schmitt's approach was not different in any basic way from that of Kelsen's other Nazi critics. In the article on Kelsen in the 1939 edition of *Meyers Lexikon*, this approach is clearly stated. Kelsen, the article's author indicates, is a

> radical representative of "pure theory of law," the typical expression of the Jewish destructive spirit, as manifest in the postwar

period in the realm of law and political science. In the complete emptying out of any substantive reality [*Wirklichkeitsgehalt*] from his general formal concepts, K. denies any legal or state substance. His community-destroying concepts [*gemeinschaftszerstörende Auffassungen*] stand, as political nihilism, in sharpest contrast to the National Socialist viewpoint.[16]

PART 5

SELF-STYLIZATIONS

Adam and Eve had two sons, Cain and Abel. Thus begins the history of humanity. Thus appears the father of all things [=Heraclitus's famous description of war]. This is the dialectic tension maintaining the movement of world history, and world history is not yet at an end.

Carl Schmitt, Ex Captivitate Salus (1947)

The enemy is our own question as form. This means in concreto: only my brother can call me into question and only my brother can be my enemy. Adam and Eve had two sons: Cain and Abel.

Carl Schmitt, Glossarium (entry 13 February 1949)

The average German looks for the causes of the last war not in the deeds of the Nazi regime but in the events that led to the expulsion of Adam and Eve from paradise.

Hannah Arendt, "Besuch in Deutschland" (1950)

15

The Flight into Religion

In Germany following World War II, both Nazi criminals and simple fellow travelers used a range of strategies to deny or relativize their responsibility for their deeds. Carl Schmitt was open about the purpose of his personal efforts: "For myself and my *Volk*, I seek a not-guilty verdict for the crime."[1] A general tendency of the period was self-absolution through the isolation of a group of "true criminals." The group was defined in a increasingly narrow manner until it consisted of Hitler, Himmler, and Goebbels, or at the most, of the twenty-two chief defendants at Nuremberg. This handful of "Hitler people," as Schmitt named them, were thus made responsible for Nazism's many millions of victims.[2] In West Germany, the path to a legal exoneration of horrific crimes was often laid out as follows: the killing-squad leaders who had born direct responsibility in Poland or Russia would claim that they were forced to follow orders, while their former direct superiors in the Central Office for Reich Security would claim to have known nothing of what their subordinates in the east had been doing. This line of argument also generated a welcome sense that the German *Volk* had itself been a victim of Nazism and was to be treated as such. Correspondingly, concrete questions of responsibility and any real sociolegal confrontation with the recent past were evaded. The main tools used in this process were polemics directed at a largely imaginary "collective guilt" thesis promoted by the victors, and a shift of attention to the most general possible historical-philosophical, theological, and anthropological problems.[3] Such a widespread strategy of denial was supported in a decisive way by the incapacity or unwillingness of much of West Germany's postwar political and judicial establishment to punish all but those who, as the consensus had it, were the "true criminals."[4]

Already for the Allied occupiers, when it came to creating the greatest possible break with the past, the problem existed of which institutions and which cultural inheritance were to be reactivated, which not.[5] The Protestant and Catholic churches were broadly seen as among the most important instruments for democratization.[6] Both churches viewed themselves as moral agents, grounding that claim in a previous *resistance* to Nazism's anti-Christian dimension. In view of the strong degree of cooperation by both Protestant and Catholic church officials with the Nazis, accompanied, in general, by the highest possible degree of indifference to the persecution and mass murder of the Jews, the extent to which the Allied occupiers embraced this perspective is in fact astonishing.[7] As things turned out, both churches managed to present the anti-Nazi resistance of individual Christians as their own basic policy.

The churches, especially the Catholic Church and "political Catholicism," in fact had had an increasingly powerful opponent in the Nazi Party's security service, the SD, which had attacked Christianity as one the movement's ideological adversaries.[8] The Nazi ideologue Alfred Rosenberg had likewise been a prominent enemy of the Catholic Church — one who could not realize his goals in his confrontation with it.[9] After 1945 a particular historical construct, the *Kirchenkampf,* offered both churches a flourishing groundwork for retrospective self-stylization into core elements of "the other Germany." Correspondingly, Christianity offered individuals who could not or did not wish to announce themselves as former opponents (democratic, socialist, communist) of Nazism a possible shelter: Christian faith now demonstrated one's own distance from the Nazis. This was itself ample motivation for a flight into religion.[10]

A view of Nazis as crude and anti-intellectual, a view held especially by their opponents, offered another distancing possibility to intellectuals who had worked for the Nazi state. The image of the violent SA man or camp guard was not easily reconciled with that presented by bourgeois individuals such as the economist Otto Ohlendorf (head of SS killing squad D in the Crimea), the SS jurists Reinhard Höhn (one of the individuals who helped Reinhard Heydrich establish the SD), Werner Best (Heydrich's deputy and head of Department 1 in the Reich Security Main Office), and Carl Schmitt. In his 1949 dissertation on the "conservative revolution in Germany," Armin Mohler, who himself had fruitlessly tried to enter the Waffen-SS as a Swiss citizen, came up with the key term for distinguishing such intellectuals from the "real" Nazis: the "conservative revolution."[11] The term was appropriately diffuse. Within its fictional perspective, the "conservative revolutionaries" had been part of "another Germany," albeit one coming from the right. In the course of an effort to rescue the concept of a "conservative revolution," Rolf Peter Sieferle has acknowledged the term's "originally apologetic basis": "to protect a majority of positions and authors belonging to the extreme right from the reproach of being merely forerunners, or allies of Nazism.[12] In his "nonapologetic" defense of the concept, Sieferle chooses to focus on figures such as Ernst Jünger, Werner Sombart, and Freyer, not on those members of the inner circle of Nazi leaders who cherished the same ideals and values and helped plan the extermination of European Jewry; he thus evades the essential question of what, if anything, separated those individuals ideologically from their less dirtied counterparts. In this context, Mohler speaks of Nazism's "Trotskyites,"[13] proposing an analogy with the non-Stalinist extreme left and, so it would seem, its fate under Stalin.

Carl Schmitt's postwar self-stylizations and self-reflections need to be considered against this backdrop. For Schmitt engaged in a retreat into *both* Christianity and the "conservative revolution." It is important to here keep in mind that by and large, no clear line can be drawn between Schmitt's self-stylization and his reflection. The extent to which Schmitt believed in his own poses is difficult to determine. What we can understand is the difference between his political strategy, that is, his efforts at personal and political self-justification, and his ideological motives: the contents of his ideas.

Schmitt's Situation after the End of the Nazi State

"Who are you? *Tu quis es?* That question opens an abyss. At the end of June 1945 I plunged into its depths when Eduard Spranger, the famous philosopher and educator, waited for my response to a questionnaire." This "abysmal" question regarding Schmitt's Nazi past stands at the beginning of *Ex Captivitate Salus,* subtitled "Experiences of the Age," one of Schmitt's first postwar publications. It also stands at the beginning of Schmitt's postwar self-stylization.[14] More precisely, the book opens as follows: "In memoriam Dr. Wilhelm Ahlmann, d. 7 December 1944. *Caecus deo propius.*" This dedication ("The blind man is closer to God") is to the blind *Ministerialrat* Wilhelm Ahlmann (b. 1895), who took his life to evade arrest following the failed attempt to kill Hitler on 20 July 1944. Through the dedication, Schmitt was attempting to locate himself in the circle of the conservative German resistance.[15] But, despite Günter Maschke's suggestion to the contrary, there are no indications of any active or passive opposition on Schmitt's part to the Nazi cause.[16] Naturally, his enthusiasm for the regime would have waned somewhat once it was clear that the war was lost. Reading between the lines, one may well detect such reservations. But transforming such sentiments into "resistance," or indeed "opposition," is at best wishful thinking.

For Schmitt, the period after Germany's defeat was ushered in by the famous Allied questionnaire, which he refused to answer. The period would be marked by a number of incarcerations.[17] On 30 April 1945 Soviet troops arrested Schmitt at home in Berlin-Schlachtensee. They released him after several hours of interrogation, perhaps, as Schmitt later speculated, because of intervention by the Soviet Occupation Zone's Commissar of Culture, the writer Johannes R. Becher.[18] In the course of that year, American soldiers searched Schmitt's residence and confiscated his books, according to Piet Tommissen at the urging of the political scientist Karl Loewenstein.[19] The books would be returned to Schmitt in 1963.[20] In September 1945 there was a renewed arrest, this time accompanied by imprisonment, since the Americans had now classified Schmitt as a security threat.[21] In October 1946 he was released on the basis of some positive character-references.[22] One of these was from Cornelia Popitz, the daughter of the Prussian minister of finance, Johannes Popitz, executed by the Nazis on 2 February 1945. Schmitt had known him since 1930; in 1958 he would dedicate his *Essays in Constitutional Law (Verfassungsrechtliche Aufsätze)*, writings covering the 1924–54 period, to Popitz's memory. In doing so, he was again suggesting proximity to the resistance.

Schmitt never agreed to undergo denazification. In his case the chances for a positive outcome to the procedure were slim. He himself described the refusal as resulting from a personal verdict on the procedure: "Why don't you let yourself be denazified? First: because I do not like being imposed on and second, because resistance through collaboration is a Nazi method but not my taste." In March 1947 Schmitt was again arrested by American soldiers, then brought to prison in Nuremberg as a witness and potential defendant.[23] He was interrogated by the jurists Ossip K. Flechtheim and Robert M. W. Kempner; Kempner would serve later as deputy chief prosecutor at the Nuremberg trials. Having returned to Germany from exile, both men knew Schmitt from the 1920s. Both were especially interested in Schmitt's relation to the Nazi rulers as well as his theory of "greater territory." Kempner brought up the antisemitic remarks Schmitt had made in the latter context. Astonishingly, the two interrogators passed over the far more incriminating "Judaism in Legal Studies" conference he had organized in 1936.

Schmitt's entry in the *Glossarium* for 17 August 1949, concerning his "new masters," is as follows:

> Until the present, for five years, I have never spoken with an American, but only with German Jews, with Herr Löwenstein, Herr Flechtheim and such like, who were not at all new to me but whom I knew well for a long time already. A singular lord of the world, this poor Yankee, new-fashioned with his primeval Jews. . . . always with only German or Austrian Jews.[24]

Otherwise than has been generally asserted in the literature on Schmitt, the jurist distanced himself neither from the antisemitic views expressed in his work on international law nor from similar views evident in his previous writings. To the contrary, he defended his antisemitic pronouncements during his interrogation in 1947 by Kempner, a defense that opened as follows:

> KEMPNER: How did you stand regarding the Jewish question, both in general and how it was treated in the Third Reich?
>
> SCHMITT: For a huge misfortune [*ein grosses Unglück*], and indeed from the start onwards.
>
> KEMPNER: Did you consider the influence of your Jewish colleagues who taught international law to be a misfortune?
>
> SCHMITT: Besides Erich Kaufmann no Jewish law professors were there. He was a militarist and bellicist. The phrase "The social ideal is the preventive war" comes from *Die clausula rebus sic stantibus und die 'Grundlage des Völkerrechts.'* . . .
>
> KEMPNER: Wouldn't you say that a certain difference exists between a Jewish-influenced international law and constitutional law and the sort you taught and propagated?
>
> SCHMITT: The approach of my Jewish colleagues was not unified enough for that.
>
> KEMPNER: You never wrote anything going in that direction?
>
> SCHMITT: No.
>
> KEMPNER: You never wrote anything?
>
> SCHMITT: I only once wrote that in territorial theory [*Gebietstheorie*] the Jewish theorists had no sense for this territorial theory.

Following this interchange, Kempner asked Schmitt to explain the "Goebbels style" of the following passage from the fourth edition of *Greater Territory [Grossraum] Organization in International Law* (1941),[25] a passage referring to "Jewish authors" Heinrich Rosin, Paul Laband, Georg Jellinek, Hans Nawiaski, Hans Kelsen, and Georg Simmel: "These

Jewish authors naturally have created prevailing territorial theory [*Raumtheorie*] to as small an extent as anything else. In fact here as well they were an important ferment in the dissolution of concrete territorial order [*ein wichtiges Ferment der Auflösung konkreter raumhafter Ordnung*]."[26]

Kempner here wished to show the falsity of Schmitt's denial of any antisemitism based on *principle*. Schmitt responded with a protest of scholarly integrity:

> I dispute that this is Goebbels style in content and form. I would like to stress the need to observe the passage's context of high scholarship [*hochwissenschaftlich*]. A pure diagnosis, in terms of intention, method, and formulation. . . . Everything I said, especially this sentence [*sic*] is meant to be scholarly [*wissenschaftlich*] in motive and intention, a scholarly thesis I will dare present before any scholarly body in the world.[27]

It is remarkable but by no means coincidental that Schmitt's students would render his insistent self-justification into a "self-condemnation."[28] In any event, not enough evidence had been assembled for a criminal indictment, and Schmitt was released into the "security of silence" in May 1947.[29]

Over the following years, Schmitt would devote a substantial portion of his energies to influencing his own historical reception.[30] This focus may have been encouraged by the fact that the "crown jurist of the Third Reich" had no chance of resuming his university career. He thus withdrew to his Sauerland birthplace, Plettenberg. From there he would present his self-interpretation in numerous postwar publications and, above all, an ever-growing correspondence. He would cultivate intensive contact with younger authors, many of them writing dissertations on him, thus naturally influencing a large portion of the work devoted to his writing. George Schwab's contact with the jurist was especially close, Bendersky's especially friendly.[31] Once again, Jewish authors were playing a decisive role for Schmitt—those who admired his legal theory could offer him at least understanding, optimally a defense of his Nazi activities and writing. Hence despite some attention to topical themes,[32] not a confrontation with the German postwar situation but his own situation stood at the center of Schmitt's reflections. The question of his own persona—*tu quis es?*—would now determine these reflections to a high degree.

Schmitt's publications appeared between 1910 and 1978, hence over nearly seventy years. In his postwar self-staging, his body of work was made to appear more unified and contradiction-free than was actually the case. To this end, he offered a series of "correlia" or "incidental remarks" on his Weimar period writings.[33] Schmitt's last book, *Political Theology II* (subtitle: *The Legend of the Termination of All Political Theology*), appropriated the title of an older text. The only extensive postwar work, *The Nomos of the Earth* (1950), did appear with a number of newly published texts; but judging from its basic arguments, much of the material appears to have been written during World War II. The preeminently self-justificatory impulse for this broadly retrospective enterprise reveals itself in certain published works, especially *Ex Captivitate Salus* (1950), as well in private notes, diary entries, and letters. The impulse is especially obvious in both the *Glossarium* (the title Schmitt gave his posthumously published notes covering the 1947–51 period, basically a collection of marginal comments on his own work), and the huge postwar correspondence, especially when it is compared to the letters from the Weimar period.[34] This is the self-exculpating context for Schmitt's emerging postwar engagement with the theme of Jews and Judaism. Although increasingly nourished by postwar events, it was focused, in the end, upon his earlier Nazi engagement.

The Jews as the Source of Salvation?

"From captivity comes salvation": *Ex Captivitate Salus.* On page 32 of his book, Schmitt refers to his "acquaintance" with and "admiration" for Léon Bloy. In the late nineteenth century Bloy had written a book titled *Le salut par les juifs (Salvation through the Jews)* that sparked considerable controversy in Catholic circles.[35] From a letter Schmitt wrote Ernst Jünger in August 1943—a letter itself containing viciously antisemitic remarks referring to the eminent art historian Erwin Panofsky—we know he reread Bloy's book at that time.[36] Bloy's titular reference, like Schmitt's, was to the influential passage from John 4:22, reading, in the King James Version, "Ye worship ye know not what: we know what we worship: for salvation is of the Jews." In the Vulgate version, the passage is rendered as follows: "Vos adoratis, quod nescitis; nos adoramus, quod scimus, quia salus ex Iudaeis est."[37] The biblical allusion is all the more evident in the title Schmitt originally planned for his book, *Salus ex Captivitate.* For Schmitt, then, salvation did *not* come from the Jews.[38]

In a letter from 1953 to Joachim Kaiser, Schmitt addresses the history of his book's inception: "Every single piece of this *Ex Captivitate Salus* originated in camp or prison as a personal letter. This dimension is increasingly vanishing from public awareness. Thus my concern, you correctly say that every word on this theme has to be placed on a gold-scale. Then every word that really has rested on the gold scale can count on its special attention."[39] Schmitt's collection thus contains six short texts written between the summer of 1945 and April 1947, in part during Allied imprisonment, along with a "song of a sixty-year-old man" dated 11 July 1948. In the period to come, not the victors, but the defeated will author history: this is one of the collection's motifs. In the *Glossarium* Schmitt observes, in a similar spirit: "We are occupied, not conquered. Only he can conquer who knows his prey better than they themselves." Where the dedication to Ahlmann proposes a proximity to the resistance, the insistence on the spiritual superiority of the defeated—the at the time widespread idea of military defeat as spiritual victory[40]—makes clear that Schmitt did not see himself as *liberated* by the Allies, but rather, precisely, as defeated by them. He developed his version of the idea with the help of Alexis de Tocqueville, an aristocrat who had been "defeated by the revolution of 1789," then emerging by virtue of this experience as the "greatest historian of the nineteenth century."[41]

Schmitt contrasts Tocqueville's triumph over adversity with the idea that "the victor authors history." In doing so, he displays, at best, carelessness regarding the grotesque nature of any comparison between the position of the French nobility and that of the "defeated," the agents and allies of a criminal regime. Such a strategic standpoint is formulated in a reserved yet personal tone. Schmitt's gesture is that of a wise bearer of secrets, issuing pronouncements out of darkness: "I am the last, conscious representative of European public law [*jus publicum Europaeum*], its last teacher and researcher in an existential sense"[42] is one example in a consistent pattern. The pronouncements were very well suited for the defensive needs of a great number of older and younger academics, Schmitt's followers and admirers in the Federal Republic. The same standpoint was strongly represented in discussions regarding a general amnesty taking place throughout West Germany. It was especially so in circles surrounding the Free Democratic Party in North Rhine-Westphalia, which was strongly under the influence of former SS and SD members. Eventually these circles made contact with Schmitt, who had himself appealed for such an amnesty as early as 1949 in an anonymously published article.[43] In particular Ernst Achenbach, a member of the North Rhine Westphalian *Landtag*, could rely on Schmitt's support in a campaign for a general amnesty that he organized in 1952. This campaign was meant above all to benefit high-ranking war criminals from the SS.[44]

In the text from *Ex Captivitate Salus* titled "Two Graves" and dated 25 August 1946, Schmitt described himself as a "victim" that an "enormous turbine" [*sic*] repeatedly tossed to Berlin. "Berlin became our fate."[45] "As things stand I'm defenseless," is the way he puts it elsewhere in the volume.[46] In Germany after the war, retroactively locating oneself among the victims was not especially original. Nor was systematic silence regarding one's own previous Nazi activities or cultivating the pose of passive and defenseless intellectual. But Schmitt upped the ante, auratically staging his postwar career as victim of *both* Hitler's security services and his Jewish enemies.[47] In this manner, the theme of the triumphant Jews, a steady presence in Schmitt's writings below the surface, took on new significance in the postwar period.

In the *Glossarium,* this motif is repeatedly evident, as part of Schmitt's rhetoric regarding the "victor's justice" at Nuremberg. The motif is directly formulated in one particular letter to Mohler: "For the Jews Christianity is an episode in their history; today they feel themselves victors, and indeed are so."[48] In one way or another, plays and films, novels and autobiographies were raising the same theme in both West Germany and France, at times crudely, at other times with intense ambivalence (as in some of the work of Rainer Werner Fassbinder).[49] Schmitt's strategy in this respect was characterized by clear distance from the Federal Republic's newborn postwar philosemites, who themselves often suffered from the problem they were trying to repudiate.[50] Schmitt, in fact, had nothing but scorn for philosemites, writing in 1952 to Mohler, whose other basic theme, alongside the "conservative revolution," would be the "morass" (literally: *Dickicht*) of "overcoming the past,"[51] as follows: "For the rest the entire German *Volk* seems to be becoming philosemitic, to be sure with this *philie* divided between Jews and Arabs. In any case some progress."[52] Schmitt displayed the same upfront stance regarding the deeds and pronouncements attributed to him, sometimes rightly and sometimes not, in various postwar publications.[53] This of course did not mean any hesitation to use his self-interpretations to counter criticism: something especially the case in regards to his compromising article "The Führer Protects the Law" ("Der Führer schützt das Recht") of 1934,[54] in which Schmitt staked his position regarding the murders committed by the SA's enemies on the "night of the long knives." But the basic strategy was as evident as it was consistent. It revealed what might be considered the basic structure of post-Holocaust political antisemitism: self-stylization into the *actual victim*.

> I am familiar with the many sorts of terror,
> The terror from above and the terror from below,
> Terror on land and terror from the air,
> Terror legal and extralegal,
> Brown, red, and checkered terror,
> And the worst kind, that no one dares name.[55]

This typical passage speaks of a taboo—a theme he will later raise masterfully in *Hamlet or Hecuba* to illuminate his situation in 1934. Nothing can be written about Hecuba—in 1934, in "The Führer Protects the Law," it is Hitler—without the author placing himself in great danger. In the quoted verse, those "initiated" into Schmitt's work would have had no trouble figuring out what "terror" he meant and what taboo he was addressing. For those less initiated, he offered the following posthumous revelation in the *Glossarium* (entry of 12 January 1948): "I was (am) discriminated against, defamed, dismantled. Terror from below and terror from above, terror on the earth and terror from the sky, terror legal and illegal, terror from Nazis and Jews, brown, red, and checkered terror."[56] Directly after the Holocaust and in the shadow of the Nuremberg trials it had been impossible to designate Jews in this way; in the posthumous work that was no longer the case. After 1945 Schmitt returned to his pre-1933 modus operandi. Once again, he refrained from openly attacking the Jews. In their resulting inability, in principle, to defend themselves, they were, as defined by Schmitt, "incapable of satisfaction" *(nie satisfaktionsfähig)*. But at the same time his insinuations designated them all the more clearly for the initiated, distinguishing them from ordinary "enemies." In 1962 Adorno would precisely define this strategy, which he termed "one of the most basic tricks of present-day antisemites": "To describe oneself as one of the persecuted; to behave as if through public opinion, which makes the utterances of antisemitism impossible at present, the antisemite was actually the one against whom society's thorn was aimed; while in reality the antisemites are, in fact, those who handle society's thorn most horribly and successfully."[57]

Schmitt's postwar antisemitism was strongly woven together with his biographical situation. In the early phase of the German Federal Republic, philosemitism (or at least the fight against antisemitism) was cultivated as part of the official self-understanding, with most people distancing themselves from both philosemitism and antisemitism on a practical level.[58] Schmitt's refusal to distance himself from his Nazi and antisemitic past thus relegated him to an outsider's role. In addition, he had so discredited himself with so many former students of Jewish origin that there was no going back. The personal and academic exchange that he had been able to cultivate in the Weimar period with Moritz Julius Bonn, Hermann Heller, Erich Kaufmann, Ludwig Feuchtwanger, Ernst Bloch, Karl Mannheim, Waldemar Gurian, Leo Strauss, Franz L. Neumann, and Hans Kelsen was now unthinkable.[59] Contacts with figures such as Alexandre Kojève and, later, Jacob Taubes were an exception. They mainly rested on inadequate knowledge of his Nazi engagement and actions—this is the case with Raymond Aron, as we know from his autobiography[60]—or else, to the contrary, on such engagement occupying the center of their interest—this is the case with Taubes, who loved the provocation of meeting, in his status as "arch Jew," with Schmitt the Nazi and antisemite, for most Germans a tabooed gesture.

Not the slightest hint exists of any apology by Schmitt for his behavior toward his Jewish colleagues. Such decency would have marked the sharpest contrast to his endlessly repeated reproaches against the "emigrants": "They're throwing us to the emigrants as feed." "The emigrants . . . are waging a just war, the most horrible sort that human obstinacy has invented. . . . I have no desire to steer the hate-affects of that type of human being, supplementing my already endured persecutions, to my poor person."[61] Similarly in the *Glossarium:* "Salus ex Judaeis? Perditio ex Judaeis?" Schmitt asks rhetorically. "First of all enough with these so-important *Judaeis!*"[62] And further:

> When we became disunited, the Jews sub-introduced [*subintroduziert*] themselves. As long as that is not understood, there is no salvation. Spinoza was the first who sub-introduced himself. Today we are experiencing a restoration of this sub-introduction with colossal claims to compensation and repayments. But the sub-introduced individuals are nevertheless even worse than the returned emigrants who are enjoying their revenge. Accepting all those dollars should make them ashamed beneath their collars [*Sie sollten sich was schämen, den Dollar anzunehmen*].[63]

Such passages themselves emerged from Schmitt's new social situation and are thus not especially surprising. For within his mind, the Jews were really "persecuting" him, as his notes from the period reveal. But they were doing so not as accusers: since his release from arrest in Nuremberg, he had had nothing to fear. Rather, they were pursuing him as his *theme* and metaphysical enemy, against whom he would struggle for the rest of his life. This is made amply clear in the Schmitt archives.[64]

The "Christian" Epimetheus and the Jews

Aura as a Means of Self-Stylization

Schmitt had considerable influence on West Germany's political and legal ideas in the postwar period.[65] This may at first seem a puzzling fact, in light of his position as the fallen "crown jurist of the Third Reich." Schmitt's Nazi collaboration symbolically condenses the collective biography of a generation of German mandarins after Hitler's rise to power. The extent and circumstances of his later influence varies from one to another academic realm (law, political science, sociology, history, theology, philosophy).[66] The same can be said for Schmitt's direct influence on the thinking of numerous West German writers, scholars, and politicians. Dirk van Laak had traced the "formative paths" of ten such persons: Ernst Forsthoff, Günther Krauss, Rolf Schroers, Armin Mohler, Rüdiger Altmann, Nicolaus Sombart, Hanno Kesting, Hermann Lübbe, Roman Schnur, and Jürgen Seifert.[67] With the notable exception of the sociologist Nicolaus Sombart, none of these authors either confronted or acknowledged Schmitt's antisemitism. In the emerging schools, circles, and groups described by van Laak, apparently no discussions of the theme took place. In other words, not the name "Carl Schmitt" but the theme of antisemitism was a taboo.[68]

This may not have always reflected consideration for the "master." Ernst Forsthoff and Günther Krauss, for example, had themselves published antisemitic texts during the Nazi years and clearly had an interest in suppressing the theme. Most likely they did not find what their colleague had written about the Jews at all disturbing.[69] But another factor was here more central. The aura Schmitt created for himself was strongly determined by his Nazi career and writings, his antisemitism at least subliminally playing an important role in this process. In order to intensify his aura, Schmitt cultivated the idea of his pronouncements emerging from a more powerful silence: "Most of what I have thought, said, and in part written for years has not been published," he at one point declared for posterity. The Schmitt archives, however, reveal no manuscripts complementing the published writings.[70] More broadly, Schmitt cultivated his image as the most *unsavory* figure in Germany's intellectual scene. One example of this tendency is the following typescript, originally meant as a publisher's blurb. Glued to the last page of his personal copy of his *Leviathan* book, the text is accompanied by Schmitt's handwritten notation "11 June 1945, confirmed June 1945 (seven years have passed)." It seems that in the postwar period Schmitt sent the text to many friends and students in order that it unfold its effect:

> Careful! Have you perhaps already heard something about the great 'Leviathan,' and do you feel an urge to take up this book? Careful, dear friend! This is a thoroughly esoteric book, and its immanent esoterics intensify to the same degree that you penetrate the book. Thus better keep your distance from it! Put it back on its shelf! Don't touch it again with your fingers, whether they're washed and cared for or bloody and colored in modern style! Wait and see whether this book meets you again, and whether you are among those to whom its esoterics reveal themselves! The *fata libellorum* and their reader's *fata* belong together in a secret manner. I say this to you in all friendship. Don't press your way into arcana but wait until you are introduced and admitted in appropriate form. Otherwise you could be seized by one of your health-damaging fits of rage and try to annihilate [*vernichten*] something that stands beyond all capacity for annihilation [*Vernichtbarkeit*]. That wouldn't be good for you. Hence keep your hands away from it and place the book back on its shelf! Sincerely your good friend, Benito Cereno.[71]

Schmitt frequently tried to link his personal biography with mythic symbols and images. Here he wishes to link his situation in the Third Reich with that of Melville's famous Benito Cereno, the prisoner of a ship's rebellious slaves whom they malevolently present to an unknowing outer world as a still-responsible captain.[72] The passage casts sharp light on Schmitt's self-staging. His highly personal address to the reader is striking: "Careful, dear friend!" (*Vorsicht, mein Lieber!*). We should here note his urging that the individual texts of *Ex Captivitate Salus* be read as personal letters.[73] Schmitt piques the curiosity of readers wishing to be initiated into his "arcana"—especially into the great state-arcana he first spoke of in *On Dictatorship* in 1921. At one point in the *Glossarium*, he describes himself as someone who was seduced by Nazism's *arcanum:* "He wished to forcibly enter into the world-ruling stratum and its *arcanum;* he did not wish to snatch it from them but only participate in it; he wanted to be accepted into the fine club, finally be a grand gentleman, a lord. But actually that *arcanum* lay in the idea of race."[74] In the above passage, Schmitt plays with the great Leviathan as does God in his *Leviathan*.[75] His "esoterics" are further intensified by the image of "modern" or "contemporary" bloody fingers. The blending of myth and supposed reality points to the entry of dry jurisprudence into the latter realm, however horrible it may be. The linkage thus underscores the difficult, indeed tragic position of a jurist entangled in a terrible reality he only wished to observe through reading and writing.

The Case of a Christian Epimetheus

In the summer of 1945, Schmitt offered the following self-interpretation: "My nature may well not be entirely transparent; but my case can be named with the help of a name that a great poet discovered. It is the bad, unworthy, yet authentic case of a Christian Epimetheus."[76] At first these cryptic words clarify nothing. Epimetheus is a relatively unknown figure in Greek mythology, one only briefly mentioned in comprehensive reference works of antiquity.[77] The "great poet" Schmitt refers to is Konrad Weiss, a Swabian antimodernist Catholic poet with whom Schmitt became acquainted in 1917.[78] Weiss authored the book *The Christian Epimetheus* (*Der christliche Epimetheus*, 1933). Like most of Schmitt's literary "discoveries," his reputation has not undergone any dramatic resuscitation.[79] Given Weiss's sheer obscurity, it is no coincidence that, as Schmitt noted with a trace of irony, "no conversation" with Eduard Spranger ensued "from this answer" to his question.[80]

The irony lay in Schmitt's view, starting with his polemic against political romanticism, of intellectual-political conversation as mainly an effort to forestall serious *decision*. Here as elsewhere, he opposes such prevarication to authoritative clarification, if necessary—to cite Meier—"between absent parties." In Greek mythology, Epimetheus, meaning "afterthought" or "he who reflects too late,"[81] is the son of the Titan Iapetos and the Oceanide Clymene. Epimetheus fails to heed the warning of his brother Prometheus, meaning "forethought" or "he who thinks ahead," not to accept any gifts from the gods. Instead, he accepts Hermes' offer of the first woman the gods created, Pandora, together with her box full of evils. Too late, he recognizes the misfortune he has thus brought upon humanity. In one mythic tradition, the misfortune lies in the nature of women (this is Hesiod's mysogenistic account in the Theogeny); in other traditions it simply springs from Pandora's box, either opened by Epimetheus (this is Philodemus's version) or by Pandora herself. Within Greek mythology, all the evils of humanity Christianity

sees collected in the Edenic narrative begin with this episode. Epimetheus is also central to Plato's version of the story of the creation of
human beings: he is responsible for equipping them for the world, but
they remain naked and defenseless until Prometheus gives them fire. In
general, Epimetheus's foolishness serves as an allegorical contrast to
Prometheus's wisdom.[82]

What, now, is a "Christian" Epimetheus? Weiss's book contains one
reference to a "Christian Pandora."[83] Schmitt remained steadily interested in the book since its inception, with notes referring to it appearing as late as 1980.[84] The book begins with a poem bearing the title
"1933."[85] The first three chapters treat the "Concepts of a Catholic in
the Hindenburg Election" of March 1932 (5–74), "Meaning beyond the
Center" (75–93), and the "German Christian Epimetheus" (94–111).
The political events transpiring in 1932–33 prompt Weiss to reflect on
their eschatological meaning. *The Christian Epimetheus* is thus simultaneously a book about Catholic politics and a confusedly esoteric, eschatological interpretation of politics and the political. The book has never
been closely examined, which is certainly tied to the difficulty in making
sense of its different levels. Andreas Koenen refers to the text as "hardly
to be overestimated from the perspective of *Reichstheologie*," hence as
speaking to Schmitt and the Reich-theologians "from the soul"; but he
does not clarify either Weiss's hermeticism in general or the nature of
the message of his "Christian Epimetheus." In any case the basis for the
importance of this "hardly to be overestimated" work remains Koenen's
secret.[86] Other approaches to the "Christian Epimetheus" and its meaning for Schmitt have been equally opaque.[87]

Without entering onto the terrain of "Weiss research,"[88] we can infer
that with his book, Weiss wished to endorse the "loosening of both the
positive-social and torpidly conservative *Volk*-forms" through the "Hitler movement" in 1933—if only with an awareness that the "danger has
increased to the strongest degree."[89] Since the passages in which Weiss
refers to his figure are even more obscure than the rest of the text, it
would seem best to focus on the context for Schmitt's strong interest in it.

In 1933 Schmitt had tried to "give meaning" to the "word National
Socialism."[90] In 1945 he tried to transfigure his previous collaboration
with the aid of Epimetheus. He certainly did not wish to announce himself as someone who, having reflected "too late," had succumbed to the
charms of a seductive Pandora. For then the unlikely point would be
that Schmitt produced all the evil on earth through his pact with the
Nazis. But Schmitt, like Konrad Weiss, interprets the "Epimetheian

idea" in a more passive manner.[91] Weiss describes the "German Christian Epimetheus" as someone "looking on from the outside," together with others: someone observing Pandora's work and hoping "for life," situated by the side of heaven-storming, overwhelmingly powerful Prometheus.[92] We should here note Hitler's designation in *Mein Kampf* of the Aryan race as the "Prometheus of humanity" and, in that capacity, as sole bearer of culture and progress.[93] Hence where Nazism struggled in promethean fashion against fate, Schmitt was passively entangled in it in an uncontrollable way. In *Ex Captivitate Salus* Schmitt writes that if a child of his should inquire about the "*arcanum* in the *fatum* of his father" and wish to touch on the "most inner core of my life," he would not be able to answer in "Promethedian" *(promethidisch)* fashion but merely as a "Christian Epimetheus," and indeed with the following strophe by Konrad Weiss: "Complete what you must, it is already / always completed and you proffer an answer [*tust Antwort*]."[94]

In this manner, Schmitt makes use of a Greek myth in withdrawing after 1945 into a position from which he can start to reinterpret his entire body of writing. Alongside the god-storming forces of the Nazis stands the Christian sufferer, steadily obeying his fate. In the myth Zeus conceives of Epimetheus's fateful gift as punishment for Prometheus's disobedience. Within this narrative framework, Schmitt, as a good Christian, declined to rebel against the *ordo* of which Weiss writes.[95] We are thus meant to understand Schmitt as a tragic witness to the destruction of the "Christian *ordo*" by the Promethean forces of—so the implication—*both* the Nazis and the Jews. We find this self-interpretation again in his *Glossarium:*

> The Christian Epimetheus would have to be correctly located in face of Bachofen's interpretation. Bachofen renders Epimetheus into a dull Hylic [in Gnosticism, entirely material, nonspiritual beings], in contrast to manly-fiery Prometheus. Why, then, is he the brother? Everyone stands on the side of Prometheus. Alongside this hero Prometheus, Epimetheus is thus a somewhat half-witted reactionary. This is the case for Carl Spitteler. In truth the two brothers are like Cain and Abel. This Abel wastes his gifts on the animals, so that nothing is left for human beings, rendering him responsible for the "biological inferiority of human beings." In the love he delivers, he opens Pandora's box; he is taken in by the deceiver sent by Hermes.[96]

Schmitt also sees "the fate of the Christian Epimetheus" depicted in a poem by Weiss that dramatically encapsulates his own situation:

Punished by ban, pursued in every word,
threatened by death is his lot from the start
and must move along the path and clear up threat.[97]

The following remark in the *Glossarium* represents a more outspoken interpretation:

> The great affirmers of 1933. Theologians like Karl Eschweiler (what a historical legitimation), poets like Konrad Weiss and Gottfried Benn (what tension of the most wide-spanning polarity!), philosophers like Martin Heidegger (what an existential documentation for both parties), and to cap it all the poem "1933" at the head of the Christian Epimetheus of Konrad Weiss.

Myths are always open to numerous interpretations. Schmitt exploits this openness by launching the myth of Christian Epimetheus to clarify his own "case." But in truth, he was not at all interested in a serious clarification of his case, at least not in public. Rather, he did his best to promote a growing number of competing interpretations. Armin Mohler's commentary on a letter Schmitt wrote him in 1951 needs to be understood against this backdrop. In the letter, Schmitt advised Mohler to inform Waldemar Gurian in a future meeting that he, Schmitt, was a "Christian Epimetheus and that Gurian, as a Christian, had to know what that is." Schmitt then remarked: "We have now arrived at our theme. For the Jews, Christianity is an episode in their history; they presently feel themselves to be victors, and indeed are so. *Le Christ est toujours dans l'agonie* [Christ is still in his agony]."[98] Since readers might not know "what that is," Mohler helps readers with the following commentary: "In the Greek myth Epimetheus is the man who 'only reflects afterwards instead of beforehand.' With his book *The Christian Epimetheus,* Konrad Weiss . . . who pushed Theodor Däubler out of the role of most intimate Schmittian poet at the end of World War II, gave the name a particular meaning in 1933: that of a Christianity that had not sprung from Judaism. Gurian was a Jew and Catholic convert."[99]

Two considerations speak against this interpretation. In the first place, the idea of a Christianity not emerging from Judaism is not found in Weiss's book. Mohler is thus either relying on conversations he had with Schmitt or offering speculation based on the passage in Schmitt's letter, not on Weiss.[100] (Mohler's interpretation is apparently not to be found in any work of Schmitt.) In the second place, regardless of whether Mohler's account of Weiss is correct, the question remains of why "Roman" Schmitt would specifically evoke a "Greek" form of Christianity.[101] Mohler himself indicates that Schmitt took "only Roman antiquity" seriously, not its Greek predecessor.[102] In our context, Mohler's interpretation is nonetheless illuminating for once basic reason: Schmitt's antisemitism, aimed especially at converted Jews as we have seen, is here furnished with a "Christian" gloss.

For Mohler, Schmitt appears as the representative of a radical pagan form of Christianity, a form struggling against the influence of Judaism and Jewish Christianity. Within this reading, Schmitt's "Christian Epimetheus" would refer to a Christianity having little in common with Roman Catholicism and far more in common with an extreme sort of Protestant political theology. A flight into religion so characteristic of postwar Germany here emerges as especially questionable, revealing as it does that Christianity did not necessarily serve as an antidote to Nazism. This contrasts sharply with the Schmitt interpretation presented at greatest length by Andreas Koenen: the Christian conservative revolutionary in strong debt to *Reichstheologie,* standing at a remove from Nazism with its anti-Christian core.[103]

Schmitt's *Glossarium:* Antisemitism with a Christian Tenor

At the center of the *Glossarium* stands Schmitt's struggle against the Jews and Judaism. Surfacing in 1933 and intensified in 1936, the struggle is now encapsulated in Schmitt's clear answer to his question concerning the most important political enemy: "The true enemy is the Jew."[104] The struggle is only conveyed in Schmitt's other postwar texts by way of the "protection through encoding" he describes as a "thoroughly recommendable method" in "times of quickly changing fronts."[105] Here a great many aspects of the struggle are revealed directly. The *Glossarium* was not intended for the 1950s when it originated but rather for posthumous publication.

In this way Schmitt's "notations for the years 1947–51" make an exhaustive analysis of the other postwar texts unnecessary. On the one hand, in itself the *Glossarium* constitutes a rich repository for decoding the basic thematic complex and message conveyed in those texts.[106] On the other hand and just as importantly, the book reveals itself as a snare, as the source of massive distortions in scholarly work on Schmitt.[107] In this regard, Micha Brumlik's assertion that "on account of its . . . nonpublic nature" Schmitt could express himself without restraint in the *Glossarium* is only qualifiedly so. In the first place, in contrast to other diaries of Schmitt, this one was certainly composed in view of eventual publication. And in the second place, it appears very unlikely that an author so intensely concerned with his own reception history would *not* wish to control the nature of his posthumous influence. While the *Glossarium* thus distorted the reception of various facets of Schmitt's work, in all its phases, the distortions are tied by a common thread: a desire to theologize previously held positions, to color them in a Christian manner. "There are not only secularizations [*Säkularisierungen*] in intellectual history [*Geistesgeschichte*]," declares Schmitt, "but also theologizations [*Theologisierungen*]."[108] As Schmitt wished to steer things, what was meant to take center stage in research on Schmitt was not the question of his position vis-à-vis Nazism but rather his roots in Catholicism.[109] The possibly "bad, unworthy, yet authentic case" of an intellectual Nazi was to be covered with a Christian hue and removed from the field of research as much as possible.

The interpretive problem generated by the *Glossarium* does not lie in Schmitt's pre-1945 antisemitism being overestimated. It lies in Schmitt's hatred of the Jews being misinterpreted as in essence Christianity-stamped anti-Judaism. But Schmitt's battle against the Jews was political, not theological, in nature. In the postwar period, he wished nothing less than to be considered an antisemite; his students and apologists have tried for many years to deny his antisemitism.[110] In the *Glossarium*, he observes, with obvious annoyance, a similar preoccupation on the part of his admired Georges Bernanos: "Visible his concern about being considered an antisemite. There the carp has already won and is no longer a carp but a pike." To avoid finding himself in a similar situation, an interest in the self-exculpating strategies of conservative intellectuals seemed called for. What certainly did not seem called for was the slightest public statement concerning the antisemitic writings of his Nazi period.

The Schmitt archives contain a typewritten text that Hans Blüher composed after the war and circulated among his friend and acquaintances. The title he gave the text was (in English translation) *Guidelines for my friends, to the extent that in conversations and especially discussions they wish to defend themselves against the reproach of antisemitism presently once more in vogue.*[111] Blüher was a popular sociologist and pedagogue whose sensational antisemitic writings had celebrated both the youth movement and the German *Volk.* The *Glossarium* contains two passages in which Schmitt refers to Blüher.[112] In one of these passages, he criticizes Blüher's "tone, a deliberate polemically Protestant self-distancing, even self-inflation [*Renommisterei*]." But in the other passage, he indicates being "very struck by H. Blüher's *Uprising*"—a reference to Blüher's book *Israel's Uprising against the Christian Gods*. In the sheer consistency of its antisemitic tenor, the *Glossarium* is more unusual from a present-day perspective than Blüher's book and other such apologetic efforts suggest was really the case. Blüher's typewritten *Guidelines* illuminate the environment in which Schmitt's reflections unfolded. The author recommends the following strategy: One should first of all make clear that "antisemitism in the vulgar sense of the word" involved "personal hatred of the Jews"; it involved a vulgar conviction "that the ostensible religion of the Jews is nothing more than a product of their race, for the sake of covering their true intentions, acquiring money." For Blüher, both these ideas are questionable. The authentic, "basic anti-Jewish stance," as he now terms his own antisemitism, is "of a theological nature." Hence as Blüher sees things, all Christian theologians, who *"ex officio"* need to take an anti-Jewish position, are *"eo ipso* defamed as 'antisemites.'"

Blüher's instrumentalizing of Christianity for the sake of battling the charge of antisemitism points to the new role assigned to the German Protestant and Catholic churches after the collapse of the Third Reich: that of the only institutions in Germany not compromised by Nazism. In effect, following the extermination of the Jews, Blüher was only willing to venture on a new attack against them after withdrawing beneath a Christian mantle. The Jews, he asserts, are the only people for which "religion and race are one and the same thing"; for this reason, "Israel" cannot allow itself to ever vanish, and can "never" abandon "its anti-Christian attitude." With the aggression thus stemming from the Jewish side, and Blüher standing on the Christian side, he must be "perforce an opponent of that which is Jewish." The problem at hand, Blüher explains, is so difficult that one cannot argue in the sense of "vulgar antisemitism." Consequently, "the two standpoints philo- and anti-semitism" are both useless: "Instead, I took up the position of determined non-Judaism."

A look at Blüher's body of antisemitic writings is enough to call the lie to that assertion.[113] He appears to have anticipated such skepticism in his indication that the "passages occasionally smacking of antisemitism" in his work had their basis "in the behavior of empirical Jewry living today, not however in essential matters [*Prinzipiellen*]"—in other words, not in antique Judaism. In his *Guidelines* Blüher now offers the following observations:

One must, however, demand from a guest that he everywhere follow the identical laws of hospitality. But when Jewry, . . . this *Volk* incapable of anything related to the state from time immemorial, attacks and overturns the constitutional forms of my own *Volk* [*die historische Verfassungen des meinigen*], and beyond that makes contemptuous remarks, that is a breach of hospitality, and Jewry should not be astonished when the German *Volk* then falls into antisemitic jargon. First they behave in such a way that antisemitism must break out, and then they complain about such a thing existing in the first place, and indeed not since yesterday but throughout the centuries. That surely must have its reasons.

In thus describing his earlier anti-Jewish writings as a forced and rational reaction to provocation, Blüher's strategically distributed apologia is a frank avowal of a radically antisemitic stance. His text contain many elements that are also found in Schmitt's postwar writings. For instance Schmitt could just as easily have formulated Blüher's inversion of the identity of victims and perpetrators, an incapacity to acknowledge guilt leading to a hardening of antisemitic affect and an effort to justify it. Schmitt, to be sure, did not distribute any self-protective guiding principles. He was too proud, and perhaps too clever to believe in the efficacy of such a measure. But he accepted and defended Blüher's argumentation, for example commenting on his own reference to "the antisemite . . . and antifeminist Blüher" with the following parenthetical remark in a letter from 1948: "he properly rejected the word ["antisemite"] because [in his case] he was too conscious an opponent of the Jews [*ein zu bewusster Judengegner*]."[114] In the *Glossarium* Schmitt condemns antisemitism, like Blücher, as something vulgar, while simultaneously demonizing the Jews, like Blücher, as themselves responsible for Nazism and antisemitism. But Schmitt actually manages to drastically upstage this strategy, formulating a postwar version of the old blood libel. He offers the formulation in the course of declaring the Jews—embodied in Isidore Isou, the Rumanian-Jewish founder of the French Lettrist movement, and Henry Morgenthau, a figure conjured by antisemites from Goebbels to the present as a mythic angel of sweeping Allied revenge on a prostrate Germany[115]—to be the true international victors of World War II: "And Nuremberg? Hiroshima? Morgenthau? / To Isidore Isou: While you talk a great deal of elites, / most people hardly suspect: / only Isra-Elites still exist / in our planet's wide-sweeping space."[116]

The initially most striking aspect of the *Glossarium* is Schmitt's suddenly emerging Christian tonality. After 1945 he tried to give all his writing such a tonality—for instance in his Christian Epimetheus and as a Catholic "intensifier" *(Verschärfer)*. This intention did not only involve confronting the Jews. But it revealed itself most clearly in this confrontation. In the *Glossarium* Schmitt identifies strongly with the figure and fate of Jesus: "Most truly poor people did not become commissars [*Volkskommissare*]; they were executed by the exploiters of the *Volk*, amidst the applause of the poor people. This happened with Jesus Christ, and I hope it does not await me."[117] For Schmitt, such an identification involves understanding Christianity "not in the first place as a doctrine, nor as a moral system, not even (my pardon) as a religion; it is a historic event."[118] This historical understanding is accompanied by a repeated raising of the classic charge of deicide. Schmitt levels this charge emphatically in the following entry from 2 December 1948:

> The crucifixion of Christ was an event *hors la loi*. Who placed the Holy One *hors la loi?* The interplay of Jews and pagans. Pilate was not active as a judge in regards to Jesus; he did not sentence Him to death, but only handed him over to the administrative measure of crucifixion, having been pressed by the Jews. I see no death-sentence tenor in the text of the Gospels. *Rex Judaeorum* is no sentencing tenor. Pilate was no judge.[119]

Schmitt seems to have placed much weight on exculpating Pilate. Rome was thus absolved of any responsibility for Jesus's crucifixion, and the Jews, in line with a classical anti-Jewish position in Christian theology, were defined as the principal guilty party.[120] Such a viewpoint is very clearly presented in a remark he attributes to a municipal politician, Franz Danzenbrink; Schmitt lays special stress on the remark, even characterizing it as brilliant: "All three peoples, the Greeks, the Romans, and the Jews, killed their greatest man: Socrates, Julius Caesar, and Jesus Christ. But the greatness and moral superiority of the Romans is revealed in their man not being killed in judicial form [*justizförmig*]."[121] The reference—on 23 April 1949—to the "murderers of Christ" who now wish to present themselves as victims, in order to "cash in on three hundred percent compensation claims," expresses the anti-Jewish reproach in the frankest possible terms.[122]

In another passage of the *Glossarium*, Schmitt formulates his general position as follows: "Our enemy repeatedly fails before the three secrets: that of the Son taking human form; that of the birth from the Virgin; and that of the resurrection of the flesh."[123] Later in the book, he argues, bizarrely, that "the murder of Christ was a ritual murder. At the center of Christian belief stands a belief that our eon was opened by a ritual murder. . . . The son is ritually slaughtered (like Isaac), the father is simply killed. . . . Beginning of Christianity: Acts of the Apostles chapter 7: You have murdered the successor."[124] Through such a fusion of two separate Christian accusations, Schmitt actually enriched Europe's antisemitic vocabulary in his posthumous writing; displaying what Martin Leutzsch has termed his "own creativity."[125] He omitted no opportunity to devise new incriminatory material to justify a hatred grounded in Christian tradition. In this respect, it is worth noting that both Christian and Protestant theology actually dropped any use of Genesis 22 as the basis for a ritual-murder charge quite early on, as the biblical passage speaks of a "binding," not of a "sacrifice."[126] In the strained nature of his efforts to place his radical antisemitism on a Christian theological basis, Schmitt revealed that his struggle against the Jews was more important, in the end, than Christianity.

16

Schmitt's Struggle
against the Theologians and Jews

Silete Theologi!

In the 320 pages of the *Glossarium*, Schmitt explicitly refers more than forty times to *die Juden, Israeliten, Judentum,* and (in English) *Jews.*[1] (Schmitt never distinguished clearly between Jews and Jewry, nor between the Jewish religion and a Jewish cultural-ethnic collective to which the nonreligious could still adhere.) There are many other less explicit allusions to the theme. Its dominant presence is best explained in terms of Schmitt's postwar approach to the problem of secularization and detheologization.

Understanding Schmitt's idea of secularization has been made difficult by the distorted image of his postwar writing at work in much of the recent scholarship. Despite his Catholic origins and indisputable ties to Bonn's Catholic circles, after the war Schmitt very emphatically viewed himself not as a theologian but (to cite again) "the last, conscious representative of European public law, its last teacher and researcher."[2] He delineated his differences with theology and theologians in various ways and to various degrees of clarity, as in the following remark: "The theologians are inclined to define the enemy as someone who must be annihilated [*vernichtet*]. But I am a jurist and no theologian."[3] He expressed his reservations regarding Catholic theology in particular in a letter to the newly converted Helmut Rumpf:

> You have become a Catholic, but not a theologian. As far as I see, you have remained a jurist. A more serious question than might first seem to be the case is here posed to a jurist who would like to become aware of his own specific academic [*wissenschaftlich*] task. As jurists we presently stand between theology and technology in a

destructive alternative, one that perhaps even supersedes [*aufheben*] us as jurists.

This self-aware distance from theology throws particular light on the radical antisemitism of Schmitt's Nazi period, since as we have seen Schmitt viewed Catholic or Protestant converts of Jewish origin as Jews, and only Jews. But after the war as well, Schmitt's relation not only to the Jews but also to the Christian theologians was extremely problematic. This was because of his political theology. On the one hand, as a jurist he believed in the need to appropriate the legitimating power of Christian theology for jurisprudence. But on the other hand he steadily and vehemently objected to any interference by the theologians in either jurisprudence or politics. But since for Schmitt the existence of a "pure" theology was as impossible as that of a "pure" jurisprudence, in other words *unpolitical* theology or jurisprudence, his approach necessarily led to a hollowing out of any theology, including that of the Catholic Church. If constitutional law *itself* was meant to preside over previously theological concepts, then theology was deprived of any autonomous domain.

A consequence of this hostility to theology was a positive assessment of secularization. Particularly after the war, Schmitt placed considerable emphasis on secularization's accomplishments: the emergence of both the modern state and European public law.[4] He tied the concept of the modern state to the "greatest rational 'progress' of mankind to the present day," a progress lying in the "distinction of friend from criminal." This distinction, he indicated, had created the basis for the "doctrine of the neutrality of one state in the wars of other states."[5] He understood the modern state as a product of the overcoming of a religious civil war—as the result of a "neutralization and secularization of the confessional fronts, i.e. detheologization."[6] For this reason, it was consistent for Schmitt to count the repression of the theologians mirrored in Albericus Gentilis' *Silete Theologi!* as belonging "for me and my political theology to the epochal turn of the modern age."[7]

For Schmitt, the withdrawal of the theologians from politics and the detheologization of the state marked the origins of its modern rationality; that, at least, was his position after the defeat of the Third Reich. (In contrast, during the Weimar Republic he fought the state with the argument that it was not in fact a state since its sovereignty was limited.[8]) He expressly defined the withdrawal of the jurists from the church as "an exodus" into the "realm of the profane," not, he indicated, as a "succession," a process of mere separation or dissociation.[9] To be sure, the jurists here had "openly or secretly taken many relics" with them, but they had not founded any new religion. They strived for neither a political theology nor a *Reichstheologie* but rather "eliminated the influence of the church's institutions."[10] As "guardians of their own tradition and authority,"[11] they created the modern state—the "new rational order" that would show itself to be the "historical vehicle" for "detheologization and rationalization."[12]

Schmitt thus now openly greeted the secularization process on a state level and wished the theologians no longer to interfere in political matters. But what was the relation between this stance and his approach to the Jews? As noted, Schmitt spoke of an "unchaining of the virulence" of "the concept of the Jews" "through detheologization": a process made possible by the transfer of the concept from a theological to a secular discourse in the writings of Hamann, Kierkegaard, Nietzsche, and, especially, Bruno Bauer. Schmitt did not explain why the "concept of the Jews" unfolded its virulence only at that particular moment or what, precisely, he meant by "virulence." At first glance it would seem that Schmitt shared the widespread view of modern antisemitism as a secularization-product of theological anti-Judaism. But this reading would make sense only if in the *Glossarium* and *Ex Captivitate Salus* Schmitt presented himself as an opponent of secularization, which is not the case. In light of Schmitt's affirmation of that process, it seems evident that he in fact viewed the "concept of the Jews" as gaining *acuity* through its removal from the Christian-theological discourse.

It was, in other words, only at this point that both the Christian-Jewish opposition and the specific peril posed by the Jews for the modern state could emerge for him in all their clarity. The Jews conformed much more readily with the laws of modernity than did the Christians. For now Schmitt saw the Jews "as a para-Christian elite; as more or less loyal placeholders when the Christian elites sink into legalism. For in any case the Jews have more expertise in the logic, tactics, and practice of a legality that has become empty than any Christian people: none of these can stop believing, counter to the law [*das Gesetz*], in love and charisma."[13]

In the *Glossarium*, Schmitt did not justify his enmity toward the Jews mainly in theological but rather in juridical terms: legality or legitimacy. The place of positive law where Jews and Christians most fundamentally part only becomes fully clear to him under the secular conditions of modernity.[14] This is the light in which we can best understand Schmitt's polemic comments in the *Glossarium* regarding positivism and Marx:

> The positivism setting in around 1840 means: transition from di-
> alectic thinking to extinction [*Vernichtung*]. Bruno Bauer still re-
> mains a dialectician. Marx reviles that as theology. Karl Marx is no
> dialectician but an eraser and destroyer [*Streicher und Vernichter*] . . .
> to that extent he is the true positivist. In 1840 the great turn took
> place: to positivism, which with dialectic necessity is negativism,
> i.e. nihilism. Despite all the leaps of the convulsive years 1840–
> 1848, Bruno Bauer steadily remained a dialectician.

In the face of this "positivist turn," after the jurists had rid the political
field of theologians, they were meant to continue the struggle against
the Jews. But now, within Schmitt's hate-filled perspective, the "concept" took on its true "virulence," for now began the decisive struggle
between Jewry and jurisprudence.

"The Enemy Gives us Laws"

> The categorical imperative is actually the law for the sake of the law.
> Judaism AD [*post Chr. N.*]
>
>   Schmitt, *Glossarium*

Schmitt supplemented the radical antisemitism of the *Glossarium* with
a massive "campaign against the law."[15] This was something like a post-
script to his extensive, much more differentiated consideration in *Constitutional Theory* of the bourgeois constitutional state's idea of law.[16]
Schmitt's long-standing struggle against the "rule of *Gesetz*" and his
"horror of laws"—what he coined as *Entsetzen vor den Gesetzen*[17]—might
seem unusual for a jurist. It is less so in light of the prevalence of antipositivist constitutional scholars in the Weimar period. But the additional
factor of Schmitt's antisemitism needs to be acknowledged in order
to fathom the depth of Schmitt's "shuddering before the 'word' and
the concept of 'law'": a frisson Schmitt saw as supported by "historical,
linguistic, and lexical-historical, conceptual-systematic, constitutional-
legal, and natural-legal" evidence, ultimately grounded in the German
upheaval of 1848 (85f.). For from the start, Schmitt's vehement antipositivism and struggle against "belief in the law" (26) did not simply stand
alongside his struggle against Judaism. To the contrary, it nourished itself
directly from that struggle. In this respect, it is striking that, as a counterpart to his theme of the Jews as Germany's postwar "victors," he appears to have chosen to more or less systematically overlook the real,
empirical destruction of European and German Jewry. He still referred,

for instance, to the collective entity of "German Jews," thus refusing to acknowledge the reality of scattered, surviving "Jews in Germany." As before the war, Schmitt thus rendered the Jews and Jewry into both real, historical and metaphysical opponents.

In numerous passages, the linkage between positivism and Judaism could base itself on the traditional Christian polemic against Judaism as a religion of laws. The manifold layers of this confrontation are mirrored in the following remark:

> My rejection of positivism came with age. Would it have made more sense in my youth? Compare the young Hegel's rejection of "positivity": Positivity = legality = Judaism = Struggle against obligation [*Sollen*] and norm. Hegel expressly and polemically juxtaposes positive Christianity with a nonpositive religiosity. Georg Lukács observes this (*The Young Hegel*, Zurich, 1948, p. 46f.), without mentioning that for the young Hegel this positive Christianity expressly signifies a legalistic religion and Judaism; the young Hegel seeks a subjective and yet public religion. He here already reveals his famous Janus-face. (209)

It is notable that Schmitt indicates only that his antipositivism came "with age," not that his struggle against the Jews did so. The remarks about Lukács are naturally directed against Lukács as a "Jewish" author who did not wish to acknowledge how perceptive the young Hegel really was in holding the Jews, and a positive Christianity still stamped by Judaism, responsible for religious depletion and pure formalization.[18]

Disseminating arguments in his postwar texts that he had at times developed years before, Schmitt tried to show how, starting with antique Judaism, human beings subjected themselves to a purely formal, empty, positive law. At various points in this development, he argued, the Jews played out their role as its agents. Here he made use of the opposition between Judaism and Christianity found in some New Testament texts to harden a position that in the end was of a juridical nature. And he did not hesitate to offer idiosyncratic—strikingly malicious and theologically untenable—variations when needed. At one point he underscored the Jewish "obsession with law" by pointing to the "judicial form" of the Jews' murder of Jesus.[19] At another point he defined this "judicial form" as "ritual slaughter."[20] The scandal in both variants lay for Schmitt in the murder being *legally* structured. In this manner, as had earlier been the case, Schmitt rendered the theological or (in his eyes even stronger) historical question of the death of Jesus into a conflict between Jewish legality and Christian legitimacy. But now a sharpening of his previous theoretical postulates, going so far as to shift them into a realm of brutal caricature, moved to the center of his juridical reflections.

In another borrowing from a particular Christian tradition, Schmitt tied the origins of the Jewish "rule of *Gesetz*," what he viewed as the Jewish effort to legalistically construct authority and sovereignty, to the Jews' biblical exile. For "open resistance" of the Jews only ended "after suppression of the Bar Kochba revolt, 135 AD," the remaining "eschatological and messianic hope" leading to an "exclusive rule of law" *(règne exclusive de la loi)*.[21] One remark in particular addresses what in his eyes is the absurdity of this effort to replace authority or sovereignty with an ever-more perfect legality: "The law is meant to replace its father. So it is conceived. . . . Legal positivism kills its father and devours its children."[22]

What might first appear to be a sudden eruption of resentment is actually an expression of Schmitt's utmost gravity. His remark occupies the center of a lifelong skepticism in face of Judaism and positivism. The skepticism had widened until the two poles finally fused with each other.

Conclusion

Schmitt's project of constructing a specifically German legal theory failed. It had to fail because legal theory cannot be grounded in particularity. The legitimacy of every modern form of such theory lies precisely in its claim to universality. This is the case even if a legal order is always limited to a specific group of persons. For this reason, all legal theory has to be "positivistic" and "abstract" in one or another manner.[1] Schmitt was aiming directly at this universality with his antipositivist, allegedly concrete doctrine, which he sometimes called "German" but that was always meant as antisemitic.

Antisemitism and Nazism stamped Schmitt's thinking in a basic way. The underlying point of reference for his analyses was the "intellectual-historical situation." But his engagement did not only involve theoretical debates. It also involved, concretely, the Nazi state's university politics. Schmitt's antisemitic and Nazi engagement was by no means simply the result of his career-related openness to seduction. Rather, it was the apogee of a historical reconstructable development carried forward by specific conceptual streams. His antisemitism was as little haphazard or coincidental as the antisemitism of German Nazism itself. It is the case that in 1933, in face of the new state's obscene brutality, Schmitt *could* have decided otherwise. But this is not relevant to consideration of the substance of his work. He was not only preoccupied with "Jewish" thinking in the Nazi state's first years. The anonymously published early writing, marked by cultural pessimism, already contains anti-Jewish comments, and the posthumously published *Glossarium* is charged with hatred of Judaism and the Jews.

Schmitt's battle against positivism was not only widely approved in both the Weimar Republic and Nazi State. At present in Europe and North America, many efforts are evident in the academic fields of legal studies, political science, history, and literary studies to make his ideas

226

fruitful by simply excising their openly racist and antisemitic dimension. One of the main arguments of the present work has been that such excision is not possible without concentrating on some banal, or at least commonplace, insights that in any case do not represent the core of his work. That work achieves its unity through ideas that take up anti-emancipatory and secularized anti-Jewish theological motifs of Catholic and Protestant origin. When Schmitt's work is studied in terms of the history of ideas, then the similarity of its various phases becomes foregrounded. The question of his attitude toward "the Jewish" can in fact never be excised, since his most important ideas originally crystallized in the historical debates of the Catholic counterrevolution and among the Young Hegelians opposed to Jewish emancipation. For this reason the question of the significance of the Jews and "the Jewish" had defining importance for Schmitt's work as a whole. As his ideas developed, his response to this question became increasingly foundational for his legal theory.

Political theology in Schmitt's sense is the effort to transmit and instrumentalize theological concepts for the sake of founding a radical doctrine of constitutional law. From theology, only the *enemy* is here taken over. The enemy's archetype is the Jew. The "substance" of anti-positivist, antinormativist, "concrete order"–based thinking can only be found in Aryanism, which itself can be defined only in terms of *not being Jewish*. "The Jewish" is composed of diverse images of the enemy that formed in Germany and France in the course of the nineteenth century. It incorporated, in the first place, the Catholic-atheistic, anti-universalistic antisemitism represented by Maurras in France; in the second place, the Protestant-atheistic, antiparticularistic antisemitism especially championed in Germany by Schmitt's paragon Bruno Bauer; and, in the third place, a widespread nineteenth- and twentieth-century German Catholic hostility to assimilated Jews, not on religious-theological grounds but as catalysts of modernity. This third stratum of Schmitt's enmity strongly informs his metaphor of "the Jewish." He steered his struggle against neutralization, desubstantialization, and depolitization by using eschatological concepts from the arsenal of both Catholic and Protestant theology. At their center was the Katechon or delayer, working against the historical acceleration pushed forward by the Jews. Schmitt increasingly viewed himself as a delayer.

The year 1945 marked a caesura for many people, including Schmitt. Since then, his main interest was not the contemporary situation but the fate of his own reception. The antisemite and Nazi now became a

Catholic diagnostician. Thus transformed, he advanced in the framework of the Schmitt renaissance to a "classic." Here, Schmitt is not
simply assessed as a superior thinker. Rather, he is seen as standing
for a specific tradition that reaches its apogee in his writing. The wide
postwar reception of his work is not coincidental but the flip side of a
laborious process of denial. The suppression and expulsion of antimetaphysical, empirical ("positivistic") theorists in both Germany and
Austria had already begun in the 1920s, particularly in the university
realm. It achieved its first highpoint with the book burnings of May
1933. In many academic circles in Europe and North America after the
war, there was no special desire to revoke this exiling and extermination
of scientific reason. The stance reflected here left its mark on the reception of Schmitt's archenemy Hans Kelsen and his school of "pure legal
studies" as well as on numerous other branches of scholarship.[2]

With the postwar renaissance of an antipositivist understanding of
law and scholarship, the concept of positivism increasingly amounted
to a defamatory slogan used negatively in scholarly, ideological, and political conflicts. But the defamation had already been initiated by the
Young Hegelian critique of religion, for instance in Feuerbach's definition of the Jewish religion of revelation as a morally indifferent faith
based on law alone: "The most complete description of positivism is Israel. In face of the Israelites the Christian is an *esprit fort,* a free spirit."[3]

In crass contrast to the actual historical connections, following the
collapse of the Nazi state the word "positivism" became a synonym for
all evils at work in the science, culture, and *Lebenswelt* (environment) of
the modern period. But in particular, it became an implicit synonym for
Nazism. Positivism was not only made responsible for the Nazis' biological racist beliefs but also for the collapse of the Weimar Republic. One
could here gratefully draw on an abundant antipositivist literature, including the exemplary writings of Schmitt. The "pure theory of law," in
other words the theory of positive law in distinction to political or religious legislation, now suddenly became a fundamentalist doctrine of
"pure" law. Whether from pure ignorance of the historical background
or under the strong influence of the aura and mystery surrounding
Schmitt, a tradition was here uncritically carried on that had close ties
to a reactionary and antisemitic intellectual history.

Carl Schmitt was an important representative of this intellectual
current. He was one of the most important jurists in the opening phase
of the Third Reich. Consequently, his work forcefully demonstrates how
unproblematically antipositivism and Nazism could harmonize with

each other. But crucially, this does not mean that all criticism of a positivistic understanding of scholarship, and, in particular, of a legal positivism taking a purely functionalistic approach to politics and morals, is not to be taken seriously or is historically tainted. Schmitt's "concrete order"-based thinking and the biologistic-Nazi idea of law represented only *one* response to a real, existing problem. It was the most radical and historically momentous response. The questions regarding modern science and culture explored by Max Weber in relation to Nietzsche and Jakob Burckhardt remain profoundly relevant.[4] But Weber offered his skeptical diagnosis of modernity and his theory of the "disenchantment of the world" in the spirit of a sober and critical scholarship. In contrast, Schmitt's diagnosis is that of a demonologist: one never capable of being satisfied with sober findings. Acknowledging the irresolvable conflicts at work between ideologies, Weber insisted on maintaining a rationally grounded discourse. He insisted (one might argue, like Wittgenstein in his own way) on adhering to both what could be expressed in its terms and its specific logic. Schmitt, on the other hand, rejected any such insight into "positive" scientific limitations, rather subjecting to ridicule all efforts to analytically separate the various scholarly spheres. His power of attraction has largely rested on pointing to real conflicts and appearing to possess true knowledge of their secret causes. But he never desired to render this knowledge discursive, and indeed could not do so. It lived from a pathos-filled contempt for "pure law" and scientific-scholarly positivism. At the same time it consisted of an endless series of intimations regarding historically potent powers secretly leading humanity into threatened disaster.

Schmitt's career is an important example of the openness to Nazi and antisemitic thinking of a very large number of German intellectuals before, during, and indeed after the Third Reich. It is an example of the way they helped form this thinking and sharpened it with their own creativity. Following the war, the approach to these thinkers was widely characterized by denial, silence, and falsification; the effect of this approach on Germany's postwar political and intellectual life needs further research. It is in any case important to recognize the great significance attached to the image of the Jews, whether a positive or negative image, in nineteenth- and twentieth-century German history. Schmitt's image of "the Jewish" was no simple negative foil. Rather, the power ascribed to the Jews and the putatively radical Jewish particularism precisely embodied Schmitt's own goals. In the desolate, distorted image of the Jewish enemy, above all his own wishful phantasms are mirrored.

Afterword

A heated controversy broke out after this book's publication in Germany.[1] To the extent they have not already been addressed in these pages, I would like to comment in this afterword on some of the objections that were raised then.[2] Over the past five years, the research on Schmitt has continued to grow on an international level.[3] Especially noteworthy in our context has been a French debate over Schmitt's Nazi and antisemitic texts, with the journals *Cités*—represented by its editor, Yves Charles Yarka—and *Le Débat* here playing a prominent role.[4] In an effort to defend Schmitt in the latter forum, Catherine Colliot-Thélène has indicated that a "good piece of historical information such as that by Raphael Gross cannot help but illuminate the interpretive work on Schmitt's oeuvre"—thus actually implying the possibility and necessity of a sharp distinction between the "historical" facts and the labor of interpretation. Following the recent appearance of the French edition of this book,[5] the debate does not appear to have reached its end.[6] But in order to further explore the question of the ties between Schmitt's work and his antisemitism, what seems more important than the evermore specialized and voluminous (above all German) literature on Schmitt is a source that had not yet been made available when I wrote this book's original version: Schmitt's diaries for the years 1912–15.[7] These texts, in fact, appear to lend strong support to my argument of Schmitt's antisemitism as representing a career-continuum.

The main point of the criticisms leveled at my book has been as follows: Although the book locates the inner unity of the Schmittian oeuvre in its antisemitism, that is actually merely one facet of the oeuvre, since there is no inner core to Schmittian theory but only an "abundance of facets." An author about whom so vast a literature has appeared, a literature representing various disciplines, is, despite my findings, "whether one likes it or not—a 'classic.'"

Very few of the critics have tried to deny Schmitt's role, following the results of this book and in the words of Friedrich Balke, as a "pioneer of the extermination." They simply have avoided spelling things out so clearly. In their view, designating Schmitt as a "classic" *despite* his role has nothing to do with repression. Rather, the designation stands opposed to a methodological narrowness that involves seeing everything from the perspective of Auschwitz, thereby neglecting other essential aspects. My reading, reducing Schmitt to his antisemitism, is consequently just as one-sided as readings that reduce him to a "political theologian," "Catholic intensifier," or "antidemocratic decisionist."

What does it mean to refine Schmitt into a classic, although his antisemitic writings are known? Why is such refinement demanded precisely in the context of works treating Schmitt's role in the Third Reich—and indeed demanded vehemently, "whether one likes it or not"? What is the sense of expressing approval for Schmitt's antisemitism being "impressively studied" while assimilating this antisemitism in the same sentence into an "abundance of facets"? Does this involve, in Clemens Jabloner's formulation, endowing Schmitt with depth even as he "lives out evil"? Or does the relativization simply serve the purpose of rescuing a corpus long *considered* classic? For many of Schmitt's admirers and defenders, such questions may simply reflect a gloomy moral absolutism. To respond to the questions from a non-Schmittian perspective, we need to recall the main arguments at work in this book.

Carl Schmitt and the Jews begins with an analysis of Schmitt's Nazi writing in the context of German anti-Jewish policies between 1933 and 1945. It is clear that the struggle against Judaism and Jewry has a central role in these texts of Schmitt, hence in his formulation of a "German legal theory." Schmitt thus views the Nuremburg laws as a "constitution of freedom." A close reading of the texts and their placement in historical context points to the highly dubious nature of the "opportunism" argument embraced by large portions of Schmitt scholarship. The jurist's assault on the Jews cannot be reduced to mere lip service to new rulers he in reality rejected. Consciously or otherwise, this widespread interpretation, I suggest, amounts to an apology.

My findings likewise point to the impossibility of reading Schmitt's antisemitic agenda as the result of a Catholic "anti-Judaism." Expressed cautiously, in the Nazi period Schmitt was not situated very closely to the Catholic Church. His Jew-hatred places precisely the "assimilated," baptized, "invisible" Jews at the heart of his struggle. In this way one of Schmitt's contributions to the period's academic politics was the demand that baptized jurists of Jewish origin such as Hans Kelsen be designated with "Jew," ergo the "Jew Kelsen." In 1936 no one made more radical demands in German legal studies. Schmitt was not one of the conservative brakemen but rather one of the accelerators and intensifiers of Nazi anti-Jewish policies.

Schmitt's phantasmagoric image of the Jews and "the Jewish" had the shape of a persistent, determined, and menacing effort he saw himself as opposing. This was an effort to postulate ostensibly *universalistic* concepts (human rights, equality, emancipation) in order to actually realize *particular* goals (Jewish law, the preservation of Jewish identity, and so forth). Through this effort, he believed, the Jews intensified an acceleration process—a negative modernization—contributing to an escalation of social conflict. This sense of "the enemy" was in full harmony with Schmitt's famous dictum: "Whoever says humanity wants to deceive."

In this light, a close connection emerges between Schmitt's work before and after 1933. For a start, it is clear that his concept of the enemy, as formulated in his best-known book from the Weimar republic period, *The Concept of the Political,* is at least grounded in the same intellectual structure as his antisemitism. Within that structure, there are in fact two concepts of the enemy. On the one hand, there is a "neutral" concept involving the distinction between enemy and friend. On the other hand, there is a concept centered on enemies of that "neutral" distinction. This second type of enemy is the focus of all the vehement aggressiveness of Schmitt's polemic. Whoever questions his friend-enemy distinction, hence his political construction, is the *true* enemy. He is so because with his universalistic vocabulary he is a deceiver or swindler.

The specific hatreds embedded in Schmitt's book are tied closely to his concept's doubleness. Schmitt proceeds to define the "swindle" as a secular continuation of the denial of Christian original sin. It thus becomes clear that even in the Weimar writings, he understands the confrontation with his opponents as amounting to a confrontation between secularized Christian theology (the side he is on) and a group of intimately connected enemies: Jews, Marxists, anarchists. The Nazi triumph in 1933 merely offered Schmitt the chance to express the confrontation in far more direct and radical terms. Its deeper roots lay in the debate over Jewish emancipation in the secular modern state that had already raged in France and Germany in the nineteenth century.

At that time the most vocal opponents of such emancipation were the very thinkers Schmitt presents as his models, the radical Young Hegelians in Germany and the conservative counterrevolutionary theorists in France.

Schmitt's antisemitism was thus as little coincidental or "opportunistic" as was German Nazism in general. But very importantly, this does not mean that his pre-1933 positions would inevitably evolve into virulent Jew-hatred and Nazism. Clearly, human beings can choose how they decide. That very freedom is what disqualifies Schmitt's political and personal behavior and exposes it as a moral problem: a problem that he shared, to be sure, with a very great portion of Germany's intellectual elite. The last chapter of my book examines Schmitt's effort to make his decision a taboo following the Nazi defeat and the revelations regarding Auschwitz.

In his hatred of the Jews, Carl Schmitt was no exception to the norms of his time and place. In Germany, the most fervent supporters and developers of Nazi antisemitism were members of Germany's intellectual elite.[8] It may well be the case that, as Christopher Browning argues, some ordinary individuals participated in horrendous crimes, for instance as participants in mobile killing units in the "eastern territories," without being convinced antisemites. But for most German intellectuals, the opposite was the case. Frequently, such intellectuals had deeply antisemitic views before opting for Nazism. And frequently, as in Schmitt's case, they maintained such views after the Third Reich's collapse.

The significance of the antisemitism in Schmitt's work should thus not be minimized. If someone were a very good cook and at the same time a committed antisemite, one might then say: I will continue to use his cookbooks, because his hatred has no effect on the recipes. But is this a serious possibility in the case of a legal thinker, a theoretician of political philosophy? It would only appear to be so if hatred of Judaism and Jewry is understood as a mere *feeling:* someone simply dislikes Jews. After Auschwitz, such personal dislike would certainly be ethically problematic, while seeming to have little additional meaning, at least on a theoretical level. To be sure, it has little to do with the Nazi antisemitism embraced by Schmitt, which was the result and intensification of a complicated, historically unfolding ideological complex. This form of antisemitism is more abstract and more dangerous than simple distaste. For one thing, it can be directed at endless images of the enemy: Bolshevism, Marxism, Liberalism, Freemasonry. For another, it can very concretely legitimate a program of murder, offering itself like a mania—an uncorrectable delusion—as the explanation and solution to every evil in this world.

There is a tendency to consider the entire question of Schmitt's antisemitism as in the end moralistic and unhistorical, hence not worthy of credit. One objection raised against this book has been that Schmitt can be studied as a historical figure without considering his antisemitism. Another objection has been that Schmitt and Hitler ought not be mentioned in one breath.[9] Apparently unifying such objections is a sense that Schmitt needs to be discussed as if Nazism had not existed, or at least as if he had not been a Nazi, or again as if we might form our scholarly judgment regarding Schmitt from a certain temporal distance, that is, without indignation. But why, in fact, should one not be indignant over Schmitt's malicious and damaging hatred of the Jews and Judaism? In this respect, many recent books on Schmitt seem to maintain a remarkably artificial distance from the object of their study. For this reason they remain oddly resistant to evaluation. In actuality, a basic element of historical scholarship is engagement with its subject to the point of forming judgments that are always *also* ethical. In the case of Schmitt, abstinence from judgment has led, I would argue, to a simple alignment of "Catholic," "atheist," "political-theological," and "aesthetic" dimensions alongside the "antisemitic" dimension—all of them to be reconstructed, then, as ingredients of a multidimensioned body of writing. As "scientific" as such a procedure claims to be, it seems to me to be historically incoherent.

Three years after this book's appearance, Carl Schmitt's diaries for the years 1912–15 were published. Although there was apparently no rush to see them published, the diaries nonetheless fill an important gap. Until the appearance in 1991 of the *Glossarium*—Schmitt's diary for the 1949–51 period—his public statements between 1933 and 1945 were all that was known of his antisemitism. This was the only reason it was possible to present opportunism as the key to these statements in the first place. But the *Glossarium* was itself permeated with antisemitic remarks and observations. In view of this fact, many Schmitt interpreters explained that he wrote in this vein only after 1933. There was, they insisted, no indication of any antisemitism beforehand. At least on a superficial level, the explanation could not be dismissed out of hand, given the manifest contents of the books Schmitt published before he became a Nazi.

The 1912–15 diaries change matters in an essential way. Two themes form the framework for the entries: Schmitt's great love for the Viennese dancer Pauline Carita von Dorotic, and his grave financial worries as a trainee lawyer. In this context, outbursts of rage and dislike against Jewish men are frequent; one typical outburst emerges from his conflict with the jurist Eduard Rosenbaum: "I am afraid of these sneaks [*Schleicher*], but not more than one is afraid of bugs and vermin [*Wanzen und Ungeziefer*]. It's difficult to defend yourself against them after they're on your body. . . . Mankind is interspersed with vermin [*Es gibt Ungeziefer unter den Menschen*]."[10]

In the course of this conflict Schmitt begins to call into question his entire (at times) friendly interaction with Jews: "I imagine how Rosenbaum would judge my book on the state: As a Jew he knows exactly which pose he needs to adapt . . . in order to be able to . . . destroy [*vernichten*] my book. He is dangerous rabble. Maybe Georg is no better" (250). Schmitt is here referring to his friend Georg Eisler, the brother, as mentioned, of Schmitt's Jewish friend Fritz Eisler, killed in the Great War in 1914. Here as in other cases, the friendship was not as steadfast as many Schmitt interpreters maintain: "Fear of the Jews, of Eisler" (140). Eisler's Jewish origins clearly played a central role for Schmitt in his friendship. This was entirely in line with his general expressions of disgust regarding Jews: "In the café, [there was] a repulsive little Jew who admired everything and laughed without stopping, but also had a pretty goat with him" (194). Or after the outbreak of war: "How nimbly the Jews have been able to adapt to the war—they're begun eagerly taking part right away, the lovely little apes" (197).

His hatred is aimed just as much at "repulsive, chatty Jewish women" (199) and Jewish arrivistes: "Pondered furiously over the fact that the *Geheimrat* title meant the nobility for the Jew Emanuel" (229). Importantly, as indicated at the beginning of this book, Schmitt interacted socially with Jews despite such sentiments, indeed was on nigh-familial terms with some. He spends Christmas 1914 with the Eisler family. It is clear that he does so above all in the hope of financial support. But he is also clearly ambivalent and openly admits that "I am starting to respect the Jews" (282). And later: "Georg is a splendid chap, a clever, intelligent, decent Jew. They can actually be wonderful fellows, which I hadn't at all suspected" (304). With Georg as later with Jacob Taubes, he discusses "the Jewish question" ("until half two at night and then we went to bed tired"); the "question" was very topical in the few years before the German army's notorious Jewish census of 1916 (318). In the diary,

Schmitt repeatedly reflects on his relation to Jews, for example in October 1914: "In addition, in the course of the day I surprisingly saw attorney Weyl twice: does that hang together with my Jewish complex? . . . There are certainly more educated people among the Jews than among the Christians, for that reason it's easier to get on with them" (226).

Alongside such fitful musing, verging on philosemitism, and beyond the far more usual expressions of a disgust that is both moral and aesthetic, Schmitt's repertoire sometimes reveals paranoid traces: "While washing I was very furious at the Jews who dally with art, the counterfeiters who falsify all authentic growth and warp human concepts [*die Begriffe der Menschen*], the mediators and nimble apes who know how to imitate everything so skillfully that one believes in it for months . . ." (245). In view of the accumulated weight of these and many similar diary entries, it is clear, at the very least, that Carl Schmitt's obsession with Jews, Jewry, and the "Jewish question" did not spring out of nowhere in 1933. Rather, it accompanied him, to large extent malignantly, throughout his adult life. This was one of the basic arguments made in this book's first edition. Naturally, there was a long road to travel from his "Jewish complex" of 1914 to his euphoria in 1935 over the Nuremberg laws as a "constitution of freedom." As indicated, the road did not necessarily have to be traveled; Schmitt could have chosen another. Naturally again, political events played a role in bringing Schmitt to express himself as he did: he would probably never have written the sorts of texts he wrote after 1933 if the Nazis had not been in power. But what this really indicates is neither that the early texts, at least, are hate-free nor that opportunism made him a Nazi. Rather—perhaps self-evidently—it indicates that without individuals like Schmitt who always saw the Jews as a problem, the Nazi triumph in 1933 would be even less easy to explain.

For this reason, it is fully appropriate and indeed necessary to ask ourselves, for example, what Schmitt liked so much about the Nuremberg laws in 1935. The 1912–15 diaries here suggest a new avenue of interpretation. In his famous *Reflections on the Jewish Question* of 1946, Jean-Paul Sartre already defined antisemitism as simultaneously a *Weltanschauung* and passion. Although as a Nazi Schmitt placed himself on the side of an "antisemitism of reason," the concept of "reason" is insufficient to clarify the contents of Nazi antisemitism. In reality such antisemitism was grounded in a passionate "moral" disgust and hatred: on a passionate disgust and hatred *understanding* itself as moral, thus legitimating the social exclusion and eventual collective murder of the Jews. Such "moral" hatred and disgust was already manifestly embedded in wide circles of German society before 1933. It is often glossed over with the notion of "reason."

The Nuremberg laws were an effort to prevent intimacy between Jews and non-Jews. They were an effort to create a social homogeneity from which Jews were absent. Above all, sexual relations between Jews and non-Jews were defined as a criminal offense. When it comes to the Jews, the predominant affect apparent in Schmitt's diary is precisely the obsessive disgust and anxiety at contact that will be, as it were, legally ratified at Nuremburg in 1935. Between 1912 and 1915 Schmitt had no political or legal answer to his own obsession, and none was planned. But the anti-Jewish euphoria increasingly permeating Germany, socially and legally, after 1933 clearly harmonized very nicely with his own long-standing needs.

The question emerges of whether a repeated use of central Schmittian concepts still reconstructs or transmits their antisemitic contents when political-moral demarcation from Schmitt's perspective has also been established. Put more simply, can we have Schmitt without his antisemitism? Neither the work of Dirk van Laak nor that of Jan-Werner Müller address this question although both treat Schmitt's reception after the war. The question did, however, emerge in the discussion of the German version of *Carl Schmitt and the Jews*. In that context, it was posed most clearly by Friedrich Balke, in a long review of the book.[11] On the one hand, Balke confirmed the book's basic finding: that Schmitt's central concepts—friend and enemy, decision and discussion, Katechon and Antichrist, nomos and law—either emerge from an antisemitic ideological tradition or were used by Schmitt in his antisemitic polemic. Hence Balke's definition of Schmitt as a "pioneer of the extermination." On the other hand, objecting to one aspect of my findings on methodological grounds, he nevertheless responds to the above question firmly in the negative. That is, for Balke it is indeed possible to save the core value of basic Schmittian concepts for other theorists. Two authors he refers to in this respect are Giorgio Agamben and Reinhart Koselleck.

In response to Balke, I would argue that with a careful empirical reading of major texts by both Agamben and Koselleck, as well as by many other authors including Ernst-Wolfgang Boeckenförde and Jan Assmann, such a salvage operation runs into difficulties. While a detailed survey of such texts would clearly overstep the boundaries of this book, I will briefly turn below to the latter author by way of example. Before doing so, I would like to return to a somewhat reformulated version of the basic question: Why should it be problematic that within the European and North American universities, central ideas of Schmitt's have become core ideas of legal, political, historical, and cultural theory? As suggested, one could hardly object if someone were to express a taste for recipes by, say, one of Hitler's dieticians. But—again as suggested—what holds true for the cook is scarcely so for a jurist— particularly one who in many ways left a stamp on the Nazi state, helping on a practical level to radicalize and realize its anti-Jewish measures. A constitutional theorist by definition grapples with fundamental political, social, and ethical problems informing a society's constitutional structure. This being so, when many books written by such a theorist and furthering the ends of the Nazi state have a strong influence on later scholarship, the fact cannot be peripheral. Rather, one might well wonder how it is possible that such books have been so widely and warmly received without anyone inquiring into the ways Nazi legal-political theory, and indeed, more recently, Nazi "international law," have thus made their way into academic theoretical discourse.

A notable exception to this tendency to turn a blind eye has been offered by Peter C. Caldwell. In his already-cited review, Caldwell has observed, referring to the traces left by Schmitt in the writing of both Agamben and Antonio Negri, that "Agamben's recent *Homo Sacer,* which uses Schmittian categories to declare that the concentration camp is 'the fundamental biopolitical paradigma of the West,' is only the most recent example of the overblown rhetoric of this [Schmittian] tradition." Here Caldwell points somewhat indirectly to one possible Schmittian legacy, an obliteration of all moral distinctions: for authors such as Negri and Agamben, we may infer, those opposing the Nazis—for instance members of the Vienna School—were peripheral to what *really* defines the Occidental tradition. He is more direct in relation to two other authors: "Balakrishnan and Blindow have rediscovered the anti-imperialist rhetoric of the Nazi empire and adopted it as their own, an enterprise of questionable value."

Such concrete examples illuminate what is actually meant when one speaks of inheriting a concept, or in this case a complex of Nazi and antisemitic ideas. Naturally, what is *not* meant is the use of a word or a term. "Political theology," "political romanticism," "state of emergency," and so forth are terms that have a meaning beyond what was stamped on them by Schmitt. Rather, what is here at stake is the postwar assimilation deep into German political and constitutional theory—and beyond that, into a great deal of contemporary cultural-theoretical speculation—of a semantic field staked out by Schmitt after the war.

The problems involved in the contemporary form of this process are at work, it seems to me, in basic ideas presented by the theoretically influential German Egyptologist Jan Assmann. Over recent years, Assmann has developed an understanding of "political theology" that reflects both a debt to and a critical distance from Schmitt. A look at the relevant texts by Assmann is worthwhile for two reasons. On the one hand, they have had a strong impact on cultural studies in Germany, especially in theoretical discourse centered on how to remember Nazism, as well as elsewhere in Europe and in North America. On the other hand, in his more recent books and essays Assmann has tried to make the concept of "political theology" useful for, precisely, an understanding of antisemitism.

The effort is apparent in two books by Assmann in particular: *Moses the Egyptian* and *Death and Salvation in Ancient Egypt* (a more literal version of the latter book's original German title is more to the point here: *Rule and Salvation: Political Theology in Ancient Egypt, Israel, and Europe*).[12] As an Egyptologist, Assmann applies the term "political theology" to another historical period than does Schmitt. Schmitt has in view the phase of *secularization* of theological concepts, Assmann the relation between "rule and salvation" in the transition between ancient Egypt to ancient Israel. Assmann speaks of a process of *theologization* of political concepts in the course of that transition. With the term "political theology," he is thus actually describing the opposite phenomenon: not a secularization of theological concepts stamping modern political discourse but a theologizing of formerly pregnant political concepts. In the course of Schmitt's increasing radicalization, the Jews play an ever-greater role in the secularization process. As we have seen, in Schmitt's writings the detheologized Jewish form becomes the embodiment of abstract positive (Jewish) law. For Assmann, not the Jews per se, but both ancient Israel and its axial "Mosaic distinction" play the decisive role. With this "distinction," he indicates, for the first time in history a difference between true and false religion, true and false gods, good and evil, stepped onto the world's stage. In a complicated narrative, Assmann thus ties ancient Israel's "Mosaic distinction" with the origins of nothing other than antisemitism and uncontrolled violence.

The manner in which Assmann takes up Schmitt's conceptual schema is naturally complex. Often he tries to establish clear distance from the jurist. At the same time, he carries over an entire spectrum of Schmittian positions intertwined with the jurist's Nazi and antisemitic engagement: an idea of the homogeneity of cultures and nations;[13] a belief that with the beginnings of Jewish history a central world-historical element had emerged that would, in a broad sense, bring misery and warfare down upon the nations; and finally, the idea that through the separation of "true" from "false," hence at the start through the Mosaic ban on idol-worship, humanity was endowed with a moral discourse that was in the end destructive. The idea of homogeneity emerges with particular clarity in Assmann's concept of cultural memory: "In every single member of the group a knowledge of the priority of the entirety is constructed; the wishes, drives, and goals of the individual are subordinated to this knowledge." Each cell of an organism, he writes, subordinates itself "normally to the interests of the entire organism" thus seeing to it that it is "in harmony with the rest of the organism." Likewise in society, he indicates: a "network of controls" sees to it "that in the group a common spirit prevails over individual spirit [*Gemeinsinn/Eigensinn*]."[14]

Clearly such a necessarily brief overview cannot exhaustively address the issue of Schmitt's legacy to modern theory. The discussion of Assmann would itself need far greater nuancing, far more attention to detail. It in any event seems important that the issue be examined by the very theorists involved in transmitting Schmitt's ideas. None of the above-cited authors has done so—and it appears called for on the part of each.

London, March 2005

NOTES

Foreword

1. See in particular Franz L. Neumann and Otto Kirchheimer, *The Rule of Law Under Siege: Selected Essays of Franz L. Neumann and Otto Kirchheimer*, ed. William E. Scheuerman (Berkeley: Univ. of California Press, 1996), and Ernst Fraenkel, *The Dual State: A Contribution to the Theory of Dictatorship*, trans. E. A. Shils (New York: Oxford Univ. Press, 1941).

2. Jürgen Habermas, *The Structural Transformation of the Public Sphere: An Inquiry into a Category of Bourgeois Society* (Cambridge, Mass.: MIT Press, 1989).

3. See the collection of Ernst-Wolfgang Böckenförde's essays: *State, Society, and Liberty: Studies in Political Theory and Constitutional Law*, trans. J. A. Underwood (New York: Berg, 1991).

4. On Koselleck and Schmitt, as well as in general on Schmitt in the Federal Republic: Jan-Werner Müller, *A Dangerous Mind: Carl Schmitt in Post-War European Thought* (New Haven, Conn.: Yale Univ. Press, 2003).

5. *Homo Sacer: Sovereign Power and Bare Life*, trans. Daniel Heller-Roazen (Stanford: Stanford Univ. Press, 1998), 172, 174.

6. By way of comparison, note how Jacob Taubes, while engaged in a similar reading of Schmitt, insists on reading him in his specific context as an anti-semite in *The Political Theology of Paul*, trans. Dana Hollander (Stanford: Stanford Univ. Press, 2005), 104–5.

7. Eberhard Freiherr von Medem, ed., *Glossarium: Aufzeichnungen der Jahre 1947–1951* (Berlin: Duncker & Humblot, 1991).

8. Ibid., 255.

9. Ibid., 290.

10. Ibid., 290.

11. Ibid., 276.

12. Spinoza plays a central role throughout Schmitt's *Der Leviathan in der Staatslehre des Thomas Hobbes: Sinn und Fehlschlag eines politischen Symbols* (Hamburg: Hanseatischer Verlag, 1938): while, according to Schmitt's highly questionable reading, Hobbes remained within the "Volk" and its set of beliefs

241

while formulating the idea of the Leviathan, Spinoza, operating from the perspective of "Jewish existence," "switched" Hobbes's thoughts on conscience in order to deprive the state of its soul (87–89; see also 92–94). The *Glossarium* (162–63) paints a similar picture of Spinoza as an indifferent, soulless outsider, enjoying the battle of extermination between a spider and a fly as his only respite from his thinking.

13. Taubes, *The Political Theology of Paul*, 51.

14. See the excellent collection edited by David Dyzenhaus, *Law as Politics: Carl Schmitt's Critique of Liberalism* (Durham, N.C.: Duke Univ. Press, 1998).

15. See Hans Mommsen's reading of Schmitt's actions in *The Rise and Fall of Weimar Democracy*, trans. Elborg Forster and Larry Eugene Jones (Chapel Hill: Univ. of North Carolina Press, 1996); but compare the readings of Schmitt as seeking a way out of constitutional paralysis in Joseph Bendersky, *Carl Schmitt: Theorist for the Reich* (Princeton, N.J.: Princeton Univ. Press, 1983) and Lutz Berthold, *Carl Schmitt und der Staatsnotstandsplan am Ende der Weimarer Republik* (Berlin: Duncker & Humblot, 1999).

16. For an overview, see Dirk Blasius, *Carl Schmitt: Preussischer Staatsrat in Hitlers Reich* (Göttingen: Vandenhoeck & Ruprecht, 2001).

17. Articles collected in Schmitt, *Staat, Grossraum, Nomos: Arbeiten aus den Jahren 1916–1969* [State, Grossraum, Nomos: Work from the Years 1916–1969], ed. with a foreword and notes by Günter Maschke (Berlin: Duncker & Humblot, 1995).

18. Müller, *A Dangerous Mind;* Dirk van Laak, *Gespräche in der Sicherheit des Schweigens: Carl Schmitt in der politischen Geistesgeschichte der frühen Bundesrepublik*, 2nd ed. (Berlin: Akademie, 2002).

19. Published as "Die Tyrannei der Werte," in *Säkularisierung und Utopie: Ernst Forsthoff zum 65. Geburtstag* (Stuttgart: Kohlhammer, 1967), 37–62.

20. *Nomos of the Earth in the International Law of Jus Publicum Europaeum* (New York: Telos Press, 2003); for a variety of appraisals of this book see the special issue of *South Atlantic Quarterly* 104:2 (Spring 2005), "World Orders: Confronting Carl Schmitt's *The Nomos of the Earth*," ed. William Rasch.

21. *Theorie des Partisanen: Zwischenbemerkung zum Begriff des Politischen* (Berlin: Duncker & Humblot, 1963).

22. William Scheuerman, "Carl Schmitt and the Road to Abu Ghraib," *Constellations* 13:1 (2006): 108–24.

23. Schmitt, *Political Theology: Four Chapters on the Concept of Sovereignty*, trans. George Schwab (Cambridge, Mass.: MIT Press, 1985), 36.

24. Karl Löwith, "The Occasional Decisionism of Carl Schmitt," in *Martin Heidegger and European Nihilism*, ed. Richard Wolin, trans. Gary Steiner (New York: Columbia Univ. Press, 1995), 137–59.

25. Schmitt, *Der Leviathan*.

26. See Heinrich Meier, *Carl Schmitt and Leo Strauss: The Hidden Dialogue*, trans. J. Harvey Lomax (Chicago: Univ. of Chicago Press, 1995); *The Lesson of*

Carl Schmitt: Four Chapters on the Distinction between Political Theology and Political Philosophy, trans. Marcus Brainard (Chicago: Univ. of Chicago Press, 1998).

27. Mosse, "Culture, Civilization, and German Anti-Semitism," in *Germans and Jews: The Right, the Left, and the Search for a "Third Force" in Pre-Nazi Germany* (New York: Grosset & Dunlap, 1970), 60.

Introduction

1. Important studies appearing before the first German edition of this book (2000): George Schwab, *The Challenge of the Exception: An Introduction to the Political Ideas of Carl Schmitt between 1921 and 1936*, 2nd ed. with a new introduction (1970; repr., New York: Greenwood, 1989); Ingeborg Maus, *Bürgerliche Rechtstheorie und Faschismus: Zur sozialen Funktion und aktuellen Wirkung der Theorie Carl Schmitts* (Munich: Fink, 1976); Volker Neumann, *Der Staat im Bürgerkrieg: Kontinuität und Wandlung des Staatsbegriffs in der politischen Theorie Carl Schmitts* (Frankfurt a.M.: Campus Verlag, 1980); Bendersky, *Carl Schmitt, Theorist for the Reich*; Reinhard Mehring, *Pathetisches Denken, Carl Schmitts Denkweg am Leitfaden Hegels: Katholische Grundstellung und antimarxistische Hegelstrategie* (Berlin: Duncker & Humblot, 1989); Nicolaus Sombart, *Die deutschen Männer und ihre Feinde: Carl Schmitt—ein deutsches Schicksal zwischen Männerbund und Matriarchatsmythos* (Munich: Hanser, 1991); Reinhard Mehring, *Carl Schmitt zur Einführung* (Hamburg: Junius, 1992); Hasso Hofmann, *Legitimität gegen Legalität: Der Weg der politischen Philosophie Carl Schmitts*, 2nd ed. with new preface (1962; repr., Berlin: Duncker & Humblot, 1992); Dirk van Laak, *Gespräche in der Sicherheit des Schweigens: Carl Schmitt in der politischen Geistesgeschichte der frühen Bundesrepublik;* van Laak, *Die Lehre Carl Schmitts: Vier Kapitel zur Unterscheidung Politischer Theologie und Politischer Philosophie* (Stuttgart: Metzler, 1994); Günter Meuter, *Der Katechon: Zu Carl Schmitts fundamentalistischer Kritik der Zeit* (Berlin: Duncker & Humblot, 1994); Andreas Koenen, *Der Fall Carl Schmitt: Sein Aufstieg zum "Kronjurist des Dritten Reiches"* (Darmstadt: Wissenschaftliche Buchgesellschaft, 1995); Helmut Quaritsch, *Positionen und Begriffe Carl Schmitts*, 3rd rev. ed. (Berlin: Duncker & Humblot, 1995); Friedrich Balke, *Der Staat nach seinem Ende: Die Versuchung Carl Schmitts* (Munich: Fink, 1996). Some recent overviews of the literature: Peter Römer, "Tod und Verklärung Carl Schmitts," *Archiv für Rechts- und Sozialphilosophie* 76 (1990): 373ff.; Uwe Justus Wenzel, "Zur Carl Schmitt-Forschung," *Philosophisches Jahrbuch* 97 (1990): 395ff.; Herfried Münkler, "Carl Schmitt in der Diskussion," *Neue Politische Literatur* 35 (1990): 289ff.; Reinhard Mehring, "Vom Umgang mit Carl Schmitt: Zur neueren Literatur," *Geschichte und Gesellschaft* 19 (1993): 388–407; polemically distorted: Günter Maschke, "Carl Schmitt in den Händen der Nicht-Juristen: Zur neueren Literatur," *Der Staat* 34 (1995): 104–29.

2. Of these titles, the following have not been published in English translation: *Die Diktatur, Verfassungslehre*, and *Theorie des Partisanen*. For the sake of ease of understanding, the following procedure has been adopted throughout this

book: following a first reference to both the original German title of a work and the title's English-language translation (either as published, or in the present translator's version when not published), all titles will be furnished in the English alone.

3. See Carl Schmitt, *Die Diktatur, Von den Anfängen des modernen Souveränitäts-gedankens bis zum proletarischen Klassenkampf,* 5th ed. (1921; repr. based on 2nd ed. of 1928; Berlin: Duncker & Humblot, 1989), 13–15.

4. This is reported by Hofmann in the introduction (x) to the 1992 edition of his work *Legitimität gegen Legalität.*

5. But see now the recently published diaries for the years 1912–15: Carl Schmitt, *Carl Schmitt Tagebücher: Oktober 1912 bis Februar 1915,* ed. Ernst Hüsmert (Berlin: Akademie, 2003); see my afterword, 234–37.

6. See Ernst Hüsmert, "Die letzten Jahre von Carl Schmitt," in *Schmittiana,* ed. Piet Tommissen (Brussels: Economica Hogeschool Sint-Aloysius, 1990), 1: 40–54, 50. Apparently Fritz Eisler was in the process of converting when he and Schmitt were friends—possibly one source of Schmitt's interest in him. I thank Jerry Z. Muller for personally communicating this information to me in Jerusalem in 1994.

7. See Koenen, *Der Fall Carl Schmitt,* 88. After World War II Bonn looked back on Schmitt as "without a doubt" the most gifted colleague he had "helped get started." See Moritz Julius Bonn, *So macht man Geschichte? Bilanz eines Lebens* [Thus One Makes History: The Balance of a Life] (Munich: List, 1953), 330. In contrast Bonn was bitter about Schmitt's postwar behavior: "He survived the Third Reich and the war and is now busy trying to break through into the golden light of publicity. He regrets the lack of success of the misdeeds he supported, not the misdeed itself. He excuses himself where he should feel ashamed and indulges himself in complaints where he should remain silent" (331). Manifestly furious at this characterization, Schmitt made several emendations in hand on the title page of his copy of Bonn's book, so that the title now read as follows: *So verkauft man Geschichte: Verkaufs-Bilanz eines Lebens* [Thus History is Sold: The Sales-Balance of a Life]. Carl Schmitt archives, Düsseldorf, RW 265. (All material in the Schmitt archives will be designated hereafter by the catalogue letters "RW" followed by the catalogue number.) See also Dirk van Laak and Ingeborg Villinger, eds., *Nachlass Carl Schmitt: Verzeichnis des Bestandes im Nordrhein-Westfälischen Hauptstaatsarchiv* (Siegburg: Respublica Verlag, 1993), 392. The prewar dialogue between Bonn and Schmitt was reflected in Schmitt's text of 1924, *The Intellectual-Historical Situation of Present-Day Parliamentarianism;* no study of this dialogue has yet appeared.

8. On Gurian and Schmitt see below, 90–93. On Broch and Schmitt, see Wolfgang Graf Vitzthum, "Hermann Broch und Carl Schmitt," in *Wege in die Zeitgeschichte: Festschrift zum 65. Geburtstag von Gerhard Schulz,* ed. Gerhard Hufnagel, Jürgen Heideking, and Franz Knipping (Berlin: Walter de Gruyter, 1989), 69–100.

9. RW 265-399, letter nos. 1–6. Upon becoming convinced of the deep radicalism in Schmitt's 1927 essay "Concept of the Political" (later published as a book [Munich: Duncker & Humblot, 1932]), Heller saw Schmitt and not Hans Kelsen as his chief opponent.

10. RW 265-272, letter no. 40 (typescript), Schmitt to Jakobi, 18 July 1933. See Raphael Gross, "Carl Schmitts Nomos und die 'Juden,'" *Merkur: Zeitschrift für europäisches Denken* 47 (1993): 410–20; Koenen, *Der Fall Carl Schmitt*, 381f.

11. See *Preussen contra Reich vor dem Staatsgerichtshof: Stenogrammbericht der Verhandlungen vor dem Staatsgerichtshof in Leipzig vom 10. bis 14. und vom 17. Oktober 1932* (Berlin: Dietz, 1933); Carl Schmitt, "Schlussrede vor dem Staatsgerichtshof in Leipzig in dem Prozess Preussen contra Reich" (1932) in Carl Schmitt, *Positionen und Begriffe im Kampf mit Weimar-Genf-Versailles 1923–1939* (Berlin: Duncker & Humblot, 1994), 204–10. Cf. Dan Diner, "On the Brink of Dictatorship: Carl Schmitt and the Weimar Constitution," in Diner, *Beyond the Conceivable: Studies on Germany, Nazism, and the Holocaust* (Berkeley: Univ. of California Press, 2000), 11–25.

12. See letters from Hensel to Schmitt, RW 265-93 and RW 265-206. Schmitt even intervened for Hensel after 1933 when it came to an academic appointment in Berlin. However, the reason for this was probably to keep another jurist, Poetzsch-Heffter, from being appointed. See Koenen, *Der Fall Carl Schmitt*, 383.

13. See Horst Göppinger, *Juristen jüdischer Abstammung im "Dritten Reich": Entrechtung und Verfolgung*, 2nd. rev. ed. (Munich: C.H. Beck, 1990), 225, 386f., and Heinrichs et al., eds., *Deutsche Juristen jüdischer Herkunft* (Munich: C.H. Beck, 1993), 185. In 1935, after appealing fruitlessly to Schmitt on 3 July 1933 (letter and Schmitt's negative response of 10 July 1933 in RW 265-206), Lassar committed suicide out of despair at his situation. See Koenen, *Der Fall Carl Schmitt*, 388.

14. After becoming aware in "lightening-like" fashion of Schmitt's "basic nihilistic-relativistic stance" as a result of Schmitt's 1936 antisemitic conference, Leibholz distanced himself from the jurist. See Gerhard Leibholz, "Die Haltung Carl Schmitts—Leserbrief," *Frankfurter Allgemeine Zeitung*, 24 July 1973, cited from van Laak, *Gespräche in der Sicherheit des Schweigens*, 156. On Leibholz, see Ernst Benda, "Hugo Preuss and Gerhard Leibholz: Von der Weimarer Verfassung zum Grundgesetz," *Zeitschrift für Religions- und Geistesgeschichte* 48 (1996): 291–392.

15. See Karl Löwith, *My Life in Germany Before and After 1938: A Report* (London: Athlone, 1994); Reinhard Mehring, "Karl Löwith, Carl Schmitt, Jacob Taubes und das 'Ende der Geschichte,'" *Zeitschrift für Religions- und Geistesgeschichte* 48 (1996): 231–48.

16. Schmitt was particularly concerned with Mannheim. See "Antwortende Bemerkungen zu einem Rundfunkvortrag von Karl Mannheim," in Carl Schmitt, *Ex Captivitate Salus: Erfahrungen der Zeit 1945/47* (Cologne: Greven, 1950), 13–24.

17. A specialist in international law, Rosenstiel was the author of an obscure book, *Der Sieg des Opfers: Jüdische Anfragen* [The Triumph of the Victim: Jewish Enquiries] (Stuttgart: Klett-Cotta, 1980). Multiple copies of the book are found in the Schmitt archives.

18. Schmitt first met Aron in 1954. The archive has eleven letters from Aron to Schmitt for the 1954–79 period; see van Laak and Villinger, *Nachlass Carl Schmitt*, 29. In his autobiography Aron explains that "Carl Schmitt did not belong to the National Socialist party at any time. As a highly educated man [*als Mann von hoher Bildung*] he could not have been a follower of Hitler and actually was not." Raymond Aron, *Erkenntnis und Verantwortung: Lebenserinnerungen*, trans. Kurt Sontheimer (Munich: Piper, 1985), 418. A deep confusion on Aron's part regarding the nature of Nazism is here apparent. The confusion seems to have kept him from asking with whom he had been corresponding for a quarter of a century. References to the contacts between Aron and Schmitt are found in Schmitt, *Staat, Grossraum, Nomos*, 638.

19. On Kojève, Strauss, and Schmitt, see Martin Meyer, *Ende der Geschichte?* (Munich: Hanser, 1993), 179–92; Mehring, "Karl Löwith, Carl Schmitt, Jacob Taubes und das 'Ende der Geschichte,'" 231–48; Jacob Taubes, *Ad Carl Schmitt: Gegenstrebige Fügung* (Berlin: Merve, 1987).

20. On Kirchheimer and Neumann, see Rolf Wiggershaus, *Die Frankfurter Schule: Geschichte-Theoretische Entwicklung-Politische Bedeutung*, 3rd ed. (Munich: Hanser, 1991), 251–65, 524. (As Wiggershaus suggests, Kirchheimer's visit to his former teacher Schmitt in 1949 led to a conflict with Adorno. The Schmitt archives contain twelve letters and a postcard from Kirchheimer for the 1931–61 period; see van Laak and Villinger, *Nachlass Carl Schmitt*, 89.)

21. According to Derrida, Benjamin received "congratulations from Carl Schmitt" for his famous essay on violence ("Zur Kritik der Gewalt," *Archiv für Sozialwissenschaft und Sozialpolitik* 47, no. 3 [1921]: 809–32). As Derrida describes it, this was "a letter from this great conservative, Catholic thinker, who was at that time still a constitutionalist; you will be aware [?] of his strange conversion to Hitlerism in 1933 and his correspondence with Benjamin (but also with Heidegger)." Jacques Derrida, "Force of Law: The 'Mystical Foundation of Authority,'" in *Deconstruction and the Possibility of Justice*, ed. Drucilla Cornell, Michael Rosenfeld, and David Gray Carlson (New York: Routledge, 1992), 29–30. As indicated, there is no evidence of a correspondence between Schmitt and Benjamin. Nor is there any evidence of a congratulatory letter from Schmitt. See Taubes, *Ad Carl Schmitt*, 27. Benjamin's letter is found in the Schmitt archives, RW 265-125; letter no. 5/1, typewritten copy: "Dear honored Herr Professor, you will soon receive my book 'The Origin of German Tragic Drama' from the publishers. With these lines I not only wish to let you know of this but also to express my joy that I can have it sent to you, on the prompting of Herr Albert Salomon. You will see very quickly how much the book owes its

description of the doctrine of sovereignty in the 17th century to you. Perhaps I may let you know, in addition, that in your approach by way of philosophy of state, especially in 'On Dictatorship,' I have sensed a confirmation of my own approach to art-philosophical research. If a reading of my book makes this feeling seem understandable to you, then my wishes in mailing it to you will be fulfilled. With the expression of special esteem / yours very loyally / [signed] Walter Benjamin."

22. Helmut Quaritsch, "Einleitung: Über den Umgang mit Person und Werk Carl Schmitts," in Quaritsch, ed., *Complexio Oppositorum — Über Carl Schmitt: Vorträge und Diskussionsbeiträge des 28. Sonderseminars 1986 der Hochschule für Verwaltungswissenschaften Speyer* (Berlin: Duncker & Humblot, 1988), 13.

23. See for instance Maschke, "Carl Schmitt in den Händen der Nicht-Juristen: Zur neueren Literatur," 127.

24. See especially Norbert Frei, *Adenauer's Germany and the Nazi Past: The Politics of Amnesty and Integration*, trans. Joel Golb, foreword by Fritz Stern (New York: Columbia Univ. Press, 2002).

25. Martin Broszat describes the approach of representatives of the Hitler Youth generation to Nazism after the war as one of "holy sobriety." Martin Broszat and Saul Friedländer, "Um die 'Historisierung' des Nationalsozialismus: Ein Briefwechsel," *Vierteljahrshefte für Zeitgeschichte* 37 (1988): 361.

26. In this respect see Ulrich Herbert's masterful case history of Werner Best, *Best: Biographische Studien über Radikalismus, Weltanschauung und Vernunft, 1903–1989* (Bonn: Wietz, 1996).

27. Martin Broszat, "Plädoyer für die Historisierung des Nationalsozialismus," in Broszat, *Nach Hitler: Der Schwierige Umgang mit unserer Geschichte*, ed. Hermann Graml and Klaus-Dietmar Henke (Munich: Oldenbourg, 1986), 159–73.

28. For this and below see the chapter on "Taboo and Emotional Ambivalence" in Sigmund Freud, *Totem and Taboo: Some Points of Agreement between the Mental Lives of Savages and Neurotics*, trans. James Strachey (New York: Norton, 1950), 18–74.

29. See Jean Solchany, "Vom Antimodernismus zum Antitotalitarismus: Konservative Interpretationen des Nationalsozialismus in Deutschland 1945–1949," *Vierteljahreshefte für Zeitgeschichte* 44 (1996): 373–95.

30. Heinz Bude, *Bilanz der Nachfolge: Die Bundesrepublik und der Nationalsozialismus* (Frankfurt a.M.: Suhrkamp, 1992), 13.

31. See Werner Bergmann and Reiner Erb, eds., *Antisemitismus in der politischen Kultur nach 1945* (Opladen: Westdeutscher Verlag, 1990); *Antisemitismus in der Bundesrepublik Deutschland: Ergebnisse der empirischen Forschung von 1946–1989* (Opladen: Leske & Budrich, 1991).

32. Broszat and Friedländer, "Um die 'Historisierung' des Nationalsozialismus," 372.

33. For academic history, see Winfried Schulze, _Deutsche Geschichtswissenschaft nach 1945_ (Munich: Oldenbourg, 1989). The theme of "historians in the Nazi period" was given its own section at the Conference of German Historians for the first time in 1998.

34. See Ingeborg Villinger, _Carl Schmitts Kulturkritik der Moderne: Texte, Kommentar und Analyse der "Schattenrisse" des Johannes Negelinus_ (Berlin: Akademie, 1995); Carl Schmitt, _Theodor Däublers "Nordlicht": Drei Studien über die Elemente, den Geist und die Aktualität des Werkes_ (Berlin: Duncker & Humblot, 1991); Schmitt, _Glossarium: Aufzeichnungen der Jahre 1947–1951_ (Berlin: Duncker & Humblot, 1991); Schmitt, _Carl Schmitt Tagebücher: Oktober 1912 bis Februar 1915_ (Berlin: Akademie, 2003). Original texts of Schmitt are included in Piet Tommissen, ed., _Schmittiana_, vols. 1–3 (Brussels: Economica Hogeschool Sint-Aloysius, 1988–91), and vols. 4–8 (Berlin: Duncker & Humblot, 1994–2003).

35. Franz Blei, _Briefe an Carl Schmitt, 1917–1933_, ed. with notes by Angela Reinthal in collaboration with Wilhelm Kühlmann (Heidelberg: Manutius, 1995); R. Nagel, ed., "Briefe von Ernst Robert Curtius an Carl Schmitt (1921/1922)," _Archiv für das Studium der neueren Sprachen und Literaturen_ 218 (1981): 1–15; Ernst Jünger and Carl Schmitt, _Briefe 1930–1983_, ed. Helmuth Kiesel (Stuttgart: Klett-Cotta, 1999); Armin Mohler, Irmgard Huhn, and Piet Tommissen, eds., _Carl Schmitt—Briefwechsel mit einem seiner Schüler_ (Berlin: Akademie, 1995) (correspondence with Mohler); Joachim Schickel, _Gespräche mit Carl Schmitt_ (Berlin: Merve, 1993) (of special biographical interest, see "Gespräch über Hugo Ball," 31–59); Hansjörg Viesel, ed., _Jawohl, der Schmitt: Zehn Brief aus Plettenberg_ (Berlin: Support Edition, 1988). The edition of the Schmitt-Mohler correspondence is highly problematic for both historians and a general readership. Passages and entire letters are omitted without this being made clear; one of the editors has shortened and commented on his own letters. Such editorial practice may reflect editorial modesty, but it may have entirely other motives, reflected in the all but impartial bibliography of secondary literature.

36. Gary L. Ulmen, _Politischer Mehrwert: Eine Studie über Max Weber und Carl Schmitt_ (Weinheim: VCH, Acta Humaniora, 1991); Jean-François Kervégan, _Hegel, Carl Schmitt: Le politique entre spéculation et positivité_ (Paris: Presses Universitaires de France, 1992); Hartmuth Becker, _Die Parlamentarismuskritik bei Carl Schmitt und Jürgen Habermas_ (Berlin: Duncker & Humblot, 1994); Rüdiger Kramme, _Helmuth Plessner und Carl Schmitt: Eine historische Fallstudie zum Verhältnis von Anthropologie und Politik in der deutschen Philosophie der zwanziger Jahre_ (Berlin: Duncker & Humblot, 1989); Susanne Heil, _Gefährliche Beziehungen: Walter Benjamin und Carl Schmitt_ (Stuttgart: Metzler, 1996); Mathias Eichhorn, _Es wird regiert! Der Staat im Denken Karl Barths und Carl Schmitts in den Jahren 1919–1938_ (Berlin: Duncker & Humblot, 1994); Heiner Bielefeldt, _Kampf um Entscheidung: Politischer Existenzialismus bei Carl Schmitt, Helmuth Plessner und Karl Jaspers_ (Würzburg: Königshausen & Neumann, 1994); Heinrich Meier, _Carl Schmitt, Leo Strauss und_

"Der Begriff des Politischen": Zu einem Dialog unter Abwesenden: Mit Leo Strauss' Aufsatz über den "Begriff des Politischen" und drei unveröffentlichten Briefen an Carl Schmitt aus den Jahren 1932/33 (Stuttgart: Metzler, 1988).

37. Paul Noack, *Carl Schmitt: Eine Biographie* (Frankfurt a.M.: Propyläen, 1993), 13. For a good overview of Schmitt's work that pays attention to context see Mehring, *Carl Schmitt zur Einführung.* The absence of any critical distance from the sources renders Noack's own book into a source of confusion. Typical, unfortunately, is the following platitude: "Carl Schmitt—that was and continues to be ourselves." Noack proudly indicates that he has "knowingly refrained" from using Sombart's book on Schmitt. He bases this on a citation from an in his opinion "well founded" review by Andreas Raithel (appearing under the pseudonym Kentaro Moto, "Konservativ-revolutionäres coming-out," *Neunte Etappe* [1993], ed. Heinz-Theo Homann and Günter Maschke), to the effect that Sombart's book is merely "the occult, sultry jockeying of an almost 70 years old pathetic pipsqueak." Such remarks are naturally more a comment on their source—or those who praise them—than their object. The glaring factual errors in Noack's study are discussed in Raphael Gross, "Politische Polykratie 1936: Die legendenumwobene SD-Akte Carl Schmitt," *Tel Aviver Jahrbuch für deutsche Geschichte* 23 (1994): 115–43; Koenen, *Der Fall Carl Schmitt,* 20–22; and Manfred H. Wiegandt, "Buchbesprechung, Paul Noack: Carl Schmitt. Eine Biographie," *Kritische Justiz* 28 (1995): 97–103.

38. Nicolaus Sombart, *Jugend in Berlin, 1933–1945: Ein Bericht* (Munich: Hanser, 1984).

39. Sombart, *Die deutschen Männer und ihre Feinde: Carl Schmitt, ein deutsches Schicksal zwischen Männerbund und Matriarchatsmythos,* 107, 278. In light of the book's importance, its weaknesses are regrettable. In particular, using a rhetorical device he admires in Schmitt, Sombart offers apodictic assertions that often do not stand up to scrutiny. He thus refers to "Columbus the Jew" (264); we suddenly learn that "Wagner is by far the most important sociologist of the nineteenth century" (92). What is more problematic is that Sombart tends to torpedo his sometimes very convincing analysis through bizarre arguments. His analysis of fantasies of Schmitt centered around the "secret" (the *arcanum*) have their echo, remarkably, in Sombart's own interests: "If one wishes to fathom the secret of the German-Jewish relation" (271) or "There is no access to the secret of Carl Schmitt for those who try to judge him in terms of the role that he allegedly or actually played in the Third Reich" (12). Sombart's psychoanalytic approach, his insistence on the role of the "unconscious," might have offered grounds for pointing to aspects of Schmitt's texts remaining beyond Schmitt's own grasp, thus revealing the jurist's auratic self-staging. Schmitt of course saw secrets everywhere and tried to create them—a basic element of his aura, as Sombart observes.

40. Schmitt, *Glossarium,* 131.

41. Thus for example Noack, *Schmitt*, 17.

42. This episode emerges in an interview held by Dieter Groh and Klaus Figge with Schmitt on 6 February 1972, published in Piet Tommissen, "Over en zake Carl Schmitt," *Eclectia* 5 (1975): 93.

43. For Catholic doctrine during the Weimar Republic, see Karl Adam, *Das Wesen des Katholizismus* (Augsburg: Haas & Grabherr, 1924); Peter Lippert, *Die Weltanschauung des Katholizismus* (Leipzig: Reinicke, 1927); Lippert, *Das Wesen des katholischen Menschen: Drei Vorträge* (Munich: Theatiner Verlag, 1923). The last book was the fifth volume in the series *Der katholische Gedanke* [The Catholic Idea], in which the second edition of Schmitt's *Roman Catholicism and Political Form* (Munich: Theatiner-Verlag, 1925) would appear two years later.

44. The existence of a Catholic "inferiority complex" is an important but partial explanation for nineteenth- and twentieth-century German Catholic antisemitism. The situation in Austria suggests the need for caution: Austrian Catholicism was equally stamped by antisemitism, although the Catholics did not constitute a social minority. Olaf Blaschke, "Katholizismus und Antisemitismus im Deutschen Kaiserreich" (Ph.D. diss., Bielefeld, 1995; a wide-ranging study, examining social, religious, and political sources), thus points to the following functions as being fulfilled in the German Catholic framework: counter-modernization (antisemitism as an appeal for all Catholics to actively fight against the steady growth of modernism); minimalization of complexity (a function of nearly all highly politicized ideologies); maximalization of coherence (antisemitism for the sake of solidifying the Catholic milieu); compensation (the "inferiority complex" thesis); overcoming of competition (antisemitism as a means to assure the Catholic Center Party a broad electorate by discrediting the "Jewish liberal" competition).

45. See Villinger, *Carl Schmitts Kulturkritik*, 69.

46. See Reinhard Rürup and Thomas Nipperdey, "Antisemitismus: Entstehung, Funktion und Geschichte eines Begriffs," in *Geschichtliche Grundbegriffe: Historisches Lexikon zur politisch-sozialen Sprache in Deutschland*, ed. Otto Brunner, Werner Conze, and Reinhart Koselleck (Stuttgart: Klett, 1975), 1:129–53; Olaf Blaschke, "Wider die 'Herrschaft des modernen-jüdischen Geistes': Der Katholizismus zwischen traditionellem Antijudaismus und modernem Antisemitismus," in *Deutscher Katholizismus im Umbruch zur Moderne*, ed. Wilfried Loth (Stuttgart: Kohlhammer, 1991); Blaschke, "Kontraste in der Katholizismusforschung: Das antisemitische Erbe des 19. Jahrhunderts und die Verantwortung der Katholiken," *Neue Politische Literatur* 40 (1995): 411–20.

47. See the texts collected in Ernst Rudolf Huber and Wolfgang Huber, *Staat und Kirche im 19. und 20. Jahrhundert: Dokumente zur Geschichte des deutschen Staatskirchenrechts* (Berlin: Duncker & Humblot, 1976), 2:395–406. On the context see Blaschke, "Wider die 'Herrschaft des modernen-jüdischen Geistes,'" 241.

48. Ibid., 257.

49. Ibid., 241.

50. See, e.g., Albert Stöckel, *Das Christentum und die modernen Irrthümer: Apologetisch-philosophische Meditationen* (Mainz, 1886), 323.

51. See Steven Aschheim, "'The Jew Within': The Myth of 'Judaization' in Germany," in *The Jewish Response to German Culture: From Enlightenment to the Second World War*, ed. Jehuda Reinharz and Walter Schatzberg (Hanover, N.H.: Univ. Press of New England, 1985), 212–41.

52. On the following see Amos Funkenstein, "Interpretations théologiques de l'holocauste: Un bilan," in *L'Allemagne Nazie et le Génocide Juif* (colloquium proceedings, Paris, 1985), 465–95; Funkenstein, "Changes in Christian Anti-Jewish Polemics in the Twelfth Century," in *Perceptions of Jewish History*, ed. Amos Funkenstein (Berkeley: Univ. of California Press, 1993), 172–201.

53. See the many documentary references in Heinz Schreckenberg, *Die christlichen Adversus-Judaeos-Texte (11.–13. Jh.): Mit einer Ikonographie des Judenthemas bis zum 4. Laterankonzil* (Frankfurt a.M.: Lang, 1991).

54. Funkenstein, *Perceptions of Jewish History*, 320. On the accompanying reproach of nonsensically overly literal biblical interpretation (the incapacity for allegorical reading), see Adolf Leschnitzer, *Das Judentum im Weltbild Europas* (Berlin: Im Schocken Verlag, 1935), 18; Pierre Legendre, "Les Juifes se livrent à des interprétations insensées," in *La psychanalyse, Est-elle une histoire Juive?* ed. Adélie and Jean-Jacques Rassial (Paris: Seuil, 1981).

55. Funkenstein, *Perceptions of Jewish History*, 321.

56. Schmitt, *Die Diktatur*, 13–15.

57. Dan Diner, *Weltordnungen: Über Geschichte und Wirkung von Recht und Macht* (Frankfurt a.M.: Fischer, 1993), 131–32.

58. Carl Schmitt, "Der Neubau des Staats- und Verwaltungsrechts," in *Deutscher Juristentag 1933*, vol. 4: *Reichstagung des Bundes Nationalsozialistischer Deutscher Juristen e.V., Ansprachen und Sachvorträge*, ed. Rudolf Schraut (Berlin: Deutsche Rechts- & Wirtschafts-Wissenschaftliche Verlags-Gesellschaft, 1934), 251.

Chapter 1. The Jews in Schmitt's Early Work

1. For example Schwab, *Challenge of the Exception*, 137f; Bendersky, *Carl Schmitt, Theorist for the Reich*, 207f., 227f., 234ff.; Helmut Ridder, "Ex oblivione malum: Randnoten zum deutschen Partisanenprogress," in *Gesellschaft, Recht und Politik*, ed. Heinz Maus (Neuwied: Luchterhand, 1968), 319; Bernd Rüthers, *Entartetes Recht: Rechtslehren und Kronjuristen im Dritten Reich* (Munich: C.H. Beck, 1988), 125f., 129f., 133–41, 148. Arguing against Rüthers: Gross, "Politische Polykratie 1936" and (referring to that article) Günter Meuter, "Blut oder Boden? Anmerkungen zu Carl Schmitts Antisemitismus," *Deutsche Vierteljahresschrift für Literaturwissenschaft und Geistesgeschichte* 70 (1996): 227–55, here 234.

2. Volker Neumann, "Schatten und Irrlichter: Zur Neuauflage der Schrift von Carl Schmitt: Der Leviathan in der Staatslehre des Thomas Hobbes (1938)," *Leviathan* 1 (1984): 34. Neumann says: "In his *Leviathan* Schmitt

tried belatedly to put his antisemitic attacks from 1933 to 1936 on a scholarly foundation."

3. Blaschke, "Katholizismus und Antisemitismus im Deutschen Kaiserreich," 269, arrives at the following conclusion (taking in both the Weimar Republic and the Third Reich): "That the Catholics were antisemitic was not despite their being Christians and not because they were simply Christians without character or bad Catholics. Rather, the Catholics were antisemitic precisely because they wanted to be good Catholics." Cf. David Blackbourn, "Roman Catholics, the Center Party and Anti-Semitism in Imperial Germany," in *Nationalist and Racist Movements in Britain and Germany before 1914*, ed. Paul Kennedy and Anthony Nicholls (London: Macmillan, 1981); and (on the level of local history) Blackbourn, *Marpingen: Apparitions of the Virgin Mary in Bismarckian Germany* (Oxford: Clarendon, 1993).

4. Schmitt, *Glossarium*, 45. Schmitt's concept of "the enemy" will be examined at various points below.

5. Ibid., 290 ("Erst einmal Schluss mit diesen vordringlichen Judaeis!").

6. Translator's note: I have here used the Revised English Bible but modified the closing phrase—"comes the Messiah"—to correspond to Luther's German translation, cited by Taubes.

7. Taubes, *Ad Carl Schmitt*, 25.

8. Koenen points in his book to Schmitt's "Reich Theology" background; but he stresses the theme unduly, placing it at the center of Schmitt's thinking. Cf. Klaus Breuning, *Die Vision des Reiches: Deutscher Katholizismus zwischen Demokratie und Diktatur (1929–1934)* (Munich: Hueber, 1969). It is striking that Waldemar Gurian already identified this context at an early point: Walter Gerhart [Waldemar Gurian], *Um des Reiches Zukunft: Nationale Wiedergeburt oder politische Reaktion?* (Freiburg im Breisgau: Herder, 1932).

9. See Hermann Greive, *Theologie und Ideologie: Katholizismus und Judentum in Deutschland und Österreich 1918–1935* (Heidelberg: Schneider, 1969), 37.

10. On the socio-historical significance of this antisemitic encoding see Dietz Bering, *Kampf um Namen: Bernhard Weiss gegen Joseph Goebbels* (Stuttgart: Klett-Cotta, 1991).

11. Carl Schmitt [under the pseudonym Johannes Negelinus, Mox Doctor], *Schattenrisse* (Leipzig: Skiamacheten-Verlag, 1913); see also Villinger, *Carl Schmitts Kulturkritik*, 14.

12. Schmitt, 20.

13. Ibid., 69. In 1912 Schmitt had published a review of Rathenau's *Kritik der Zeit* (Berlin: Fischer, 1912) in a journal edited by W. Schäfer, *Die Rheinlande*. In this context Balke, *Der Staat nach seinem Ende*, 76f., has pointed to "Schmitt's antisemitism" as playing a role in the "intensive conversation" the jurist had with Robert Musil in December 1930. It is the case that the figure of Paul Arnheim in Musil's *Man Without Qualities*, known to have been based partly on Walther Rathenau, possesses qualities attributed to Rathenau in *Silhouettes*.

14. Schmitt [Negelinus], *Schattenrisse*, 61.

15. Ibid., 52–54 (Mauthner); 45–47 (France).

16. Ibid., 7.

17. See the detailed commentary in Villinger, *Carl Schmitts Kulturkritik*, 117. Sombart, *Die deutschen Männer*, 240–47, applies Freud's analysis of the role of circumcision in anti-Jewish fantasies to Schmitt. Regrettably, Sombart himself contributes to a related mystification: in order to expound on a supposed difference between Christian (uncircumcised) and Jewish (circumcised) sexual behavior, he indicates (244) that "the woman's physical satisfaction is part of the Sabbath ritual [*sic*]," thus being "sacralized and even actionable." This is apparently a mistaken description of a well-known Talmudic good deed.

18. Cf. Carl Schmitt, "Der Wahnmonolog und eine Philosophie des Als-Ob," *Bayreuther Blätter*, June 1912, 240f. Sombart, *Die deutschen Männer*, 277, points to this article, which he understands as a sign of Schmitt's early antisemitism.

19. Schmitt, *Carl Schmitt Tagebücher: Oktober 1912 bis Februar 1915;* Van Laak and Villinger, eds., *Nachlass Carl Schmitt*, 368. For more remarks on these diaries—which appeared after publication of this book's first German edition—see my afterword, 234–37.

20. RW 265, *Kasernen-Tagebuch*, 25 February 1915–5 May 1915, entry for 8 April 1915. Alexander Kojève, who came into contact with Schmitt in the postwar years, wrote a dissertation about Solovyev (a friend of Dostoevsky) in Heidelberg under Karl Jaspers. Cf. Taubes, *Ad Carl Schmitt*, 25.

21. RW 265, *Kasernen-Tagebuch*, 25 February 1915–5 May 1915, entry for 16 April 1915.

22. Blaschke, *Katholizismus und Antisemitismus*, 79–81, and (under the title "Double Antisemitism") 58ff. An explicit reference to such "double antisemitism," the "good" sort being directed against Judaism's "pernicious influence" on society, is found in the widely distributed *Kirchliches Handlexikon* published by the Catholic Herder-Verlag in 1907 (257f.).

23. Ernst Troeltsch used the expression *Welle von rechts* in an observation made in December 1919, cited in Eberhard Kolb, *Die Weimarer Republik*, 3rd rev. ed. (Munich: Oldenbourg, 1993), 37. Until now, I have not been able to locate any direct comments by Schmitt concerning antisemitism in the Weimar Republic. In this regard his letters responding to those of the antisemitism researcher Fritz Bernstein would be of great interest. (Under the name Peretz Bernstein, Fritz Bernstein [1890–1971] would be trade and economics minister in Israel between 1948 and 1949 and again between 1952 and 1955). These letters are located neither in the Schmitt archives nor those of Bernstein, located in the World Zionist Archive in Jerusalem. In two letters to Schmitt (both extant), Bernstein discusses his book *Der Antisemitismus als Gruppenerscheinung* and tries to persuade Schmitt to write a review of the book. The letters make clear that Schmitt has until then refused that request. Fritz Bernstein to Carl Schmitt, Rotterdam, 31 October 1927, and 8 December 1927 (RW 265-35, letter nos. 15 and 13).

24. RW 265-196, letter no. 3. Laak and Villinger, *Nachlass Carl Schmitts*, 43, erroneously identifies Georg Schmitt as Carl Schmitt's brother; I took over the identification in the first German-language edition of this book.

25. RW 265-206, letter no. 166. Dietrich Schaefer to Carl Schmitt, Stettin, 30 December 1932.

26. Schmitt, *Glossarium*, 65; 151; 210. Schmitt's dedication of his *Verfassungslehre* [Constitutional Theory] (Munich: Duncker & Humblot, 1928) "to the memory of my friend Dr. Fritz Eisler from Hamburg, fallen on 27 September 1914" is often cited as proof of his open-mindedness. But it is in fact anything but open-minded. Even for radical antisemites, in the Weimar period and for a time after, a heroic death for the fatherland could render a Jew into an "exception," i.e., into an honorary German. (Compare the Nazi "front-soldiers' clause" exempting Jewish participants in World War I from certain antisemitic laws.)

27. This "Jewish antisemitism" was mainly evident in Germany and Austria in the years before World War I. As Shulamit Volkov has suggested in *Jüdisches Leben und Antisemitismus im 19. und 20. Jahrhundert* (Munich: Beck, 1990), it cannot simply be explained in psychological terms centered on a specific phenomenon termed "Jewish self-hatred."

28. I am aware of no documentary evidence of such co-authorship. It is nevertheless likely, since Schmitt indicated as much to some friends.

29. Meuter, "Blut oder Boden?" 226.

Chapter 2. Schmitt's Position in 1933

1. Cf. Majer, *Grundlagen des nationalsozialistischen Rechtssystems: Führerprizip, Sonderrecht, Einheitspartei* (Stuttgart: Kohlhammer, 1987), 23. On the Nazi "racial idea" or "racial principle," see ibid., 117–200.

2. Cf. ibid., 23; Michael Stolleis, "Nationalsozialistisches Recht," in *Handwörterbuch zur deutschen Rechtsgeschichte*, vol. 3, ed. Adalbert Erler and Ekkehard Kaufmann (Berlin: Schmidt, 1984), cols. 873–892, here col. 887. This was already recognized by Fraenkel in *The Dual State* (1941) and by Franz Neumann in *Behemoth: The Structure and Practice of National Socialism* (London: Gollancz, 1942). Majer, *Grundlagen*, offers an overview and comprehensive bibliography. Cf. Bernd Rüthers, *Die unbegrenzte Auslegung* (Tübingen: Mohr, 1969). In contrast, see Rottleuthner, "Substantieller Dezisionismus: Zur Funktion der Rechtsphilosophie im Nationalsozialismus," *Archiv für Rechts- und Sozialphilosophie*, Beiheft 18, *Recht, Rechtsphilosophie und Nationalsozialismus* (1983): 20–35. For Rottleuthner, Nazi law justified all possible political decisions as the expression of a "folk substance" *(völkischen Substanz)*. For this "substantial decisionism," every decision of the Führer was simply an expression of the murmurings of blood and land.

3. Also arguing for the existence of various doctrines and theories: Michael Stolleis, "Staatsrechtslehre zwischen Monarchie und Führerstaat," in

Wissenschaft und Nationalsozialismus, ed. Steffen Harbordt (Berlin: Technical Univ. Berlin, 1983), 30; Peter Caldwell, "National Socialism and Constitutional Law: Carl Schmitt, Otto Koellreutter, and the Debate Over the Nature of the Nazi State, 1933–1937," *Cardozo Law Review* 16 (1994): 399–427. For an overview of more recent and older literature on the subject, see Michael Ruck, "Führerabsolutismus und polykratisches Herrschaftsgefüge — Verfassungsstrukturen des NS-Staates," in *Deutschland 1933–1945: Neue Studien zur nationalsozialistischen Herrschaft,* ed. Karl Dietrich Bracher, Manfred Funke, and Hans-Adolf Jacobsen (Düsseldorf: Droste, 1993), 32–56.

4. Cf. Martin Broszat, *Der Staat Hitlers: Grundlegung und Entwicklung seiner inneren Verfassung,* 9th ed. (Munich: Deutscher Taschenbuch Verlag, 1981), 403–22; Volker Epping, "Die Lex van der Lubbe: Zugleich ein Beitrag zur Bedeutung des Grundsatzes 'nullum crimen, nulla poena sine lege,'" *Der Staat* 34 (1995): 243–67.

5. Hermann Weinkauff, *Die deutsche Justiz und der Nationalsozialismus: Ein Überblick* (Stuttgart: Deutsche Verlags-Anstalt, 1968) furnishes an overview and problematic interpretation. More precise and probing, focusing on one individual as an example: Herbert, *Best.*

6. On Schmitt and the Third Reich, alongside Koenen's study and the other literature already cited see Karl Graf Ballestrem, "Carl Schmitt und der Nationalsozialismus: Ein Problem der Theorie oder des Charakters?" in *Der demokratische Verfassungsstaat: Theorie, Geschichte, Probleme: Festschrift für Hans Buchheim zum 70. Geburtstag,* ed. Oscar W. Gabriel et al. (Munich: Oldenbourg, 1992), 115–32; Hasso Hofmann, "Die deutsche Rechtswissenschaft im Kampf gegen den jüdischen Geist," in *Geschichte und Kultur des Judentums: Eine Vorlesungsreihe an der Julius-Maximilians-Universität, Würzburg,* ed. Klaus Wittstadt and Karlheinz Müller (Würzburg: Kommissionsverlag F. Schöningh, 1988), 223–40; Gerhard Hufnagel, *The Escape from Freedom: Carl Schmitt and the Allure of Fascism* (Siegen: Forschungsschwerpunkt HiMon, Univ.-GH, 1990); Manfred Lauermann, "Versuch über Carl Schmitt im Nationalsozialismus," in *Carl Schmitt und die Liberalismuskritik,* ed. Klaus Hansen and Hans Lietzmann (Opladen: Leske & Budrich, 1988), 37–51; Günter Maschke, "Im Irrgarten Carl Schmitts," in *Intellektuelle im Bann des Nationalsozialismus,* ed. Karl Corino (Hamburg: Hoffman & Campe, 1980), 204–41; Ingeborg Maus, "Zur 'Zäsur' von 1933 in der Theorie Carl Schmitts," *Kritische Justiz* 2 (1969): 113ff.; Bernd Rüthers, *Carl Schmitt im Dritten Reich, Wissenschaft als Zeitgeist-Verstärkung?* 2nd exp. ed. (Munich: C.H. Beck, 1991); Dian Schefold, "Carl Schmitt: Auf dem Weg der Staatsrechtslehre in den Nationalsozialismus und zurück," in Steffen Harbordt, *Wissenschaft und Nationalsozialismus,* 35–53.

7. On Hitler's contempt for intellectuals, see Marlis Steinert, *Hitler* (Munich: C.H. Beck, 1994), 614. According to Steinert, Hitler believed that the jurists were (in Lenin's words) "useful idiots," indispensable in the short term but eventually to be discarded. On Hitler's "ideas" in general, see ibid., esp. 175–220.

8. Most convincing in this respect: Herbert, *Best*. Also Raul Hilberg, *The Destruction of the European Jews*, 3rd ed., 3 vols. (New Haven, Conn.: Yale Univ. Press, 2003), 3:1013–27.

9. Extensive adherence to Schmitt's self-interpretation is evident, for example, in the twenty-nine conference-talks in Quaritch, ed., *Complexio Oppositorum*. This problem is discussed at greater length in part 5.

10. Cf. Koenen, *Der Fall Carl Schmitt*, 313ff.

11. See Majer, *Grundlagen*, 137.

12. See Rapp, *Die Stellung der Juden in der nationalsozialistischen Staatsrechtslehre: Die Emanzipation der Juden im 19. Jahrhundert und die Haltung der deutschen Staatsrechtslehre zur staatsrechtlichen Stellung der Juden im Nationalsozialismus* (Baden-Baden: Nomos, 1990), 145–76. Rapp is referring here to Gerhard Anschütz, Richard Thoma, Willibald Apelt, Ernst Friesenhahn, and Heinrich Triepel.

13. Biographical information on Anschütz in Dagmar Drüll, *Heidelberger Gelehrtenlexikon, 1803–1932* (Berlin: Springer-Verlag, 1986), 4. Citations from the application for emeritus status of 31 March 1933, in Rapp, *Die Stellung der Juden*, 146–47, and Ilse Staff, ed., *Justiz im Dritten Reich: Eine Dokumentation*, 2nd ed. (Frankfurt a.M.: Fischer, 1978), 147. Against the still-widespread myth that "legal positivism" (meaning Thoma, Anschütz, and Kelsen) undermined possible resistance to the Nazis (Weinkauff's argument, *Die deutsche Justiz und der Nationalsozialismus*, 30), see Peter Caldwell, "Legal Positivism and Weimar Democracy," *American Journal of Jurisprudence: An International Forum for Legal Philosophy* 39 (1994): 273–301.

14. Cf. Drüll, *Heidelberger Gelehrtenlexikon*, 212.

15. Cf. Herbert A. Strauss and Werner Röder, eds., *International Biographical Dictionary* (Munich: Sauer, 1980), s.vv. "Heller," "Kaufmann," and "Kelsen"; Heinrichs et al., eds., *Deutsche Juristen jüdischer Herkunft*. For an extensive overview clarifying the wider context, see Göppinger, *Juristen jüdischer Abstammung*, 219–373.

16. On Heller, see entry by Christoph Müller in Heinrichs et al., eds., *Deutsche Juristen jüdischer Herkunft*, 767–80.

17. RW 265-196, letter no. 67. See Wilhelm Stapel, "Zum Fall Cohn-Breslau," *Deutsches Volkstum* 15 (1933): 87–88; Wilhelm Stapel, "Herr Professor Hermann Heller," ibid., 351–52 ("in order to educate Herr Professor Heller in how to behave with Germans, we will not allow him to get away with it [i.e., with his gloss on Stapel's article]"); Wilhelm Stapel, "Hermann Heller in heller Wut," ibid., 2nd half-year volume (1933): 793.

18. RW 265-399, letter no. 6, 17 July 1933.

19. On Forsthoff's short occupation of Heller's chair see Koenen, *Der Fall Carl Schmitt*, 378.

20. Frank Golczewski, *Kölner Universitätslehrer und der Nationalsozialismus* (Cologne: Böhlau, 1988). Quaritsch, *Positionen und Begriffe Carl Schmitts*, 105, somehow concludes from Schmitt's refusal to help Kelsen that Schmitt could not have been an opportunist.

21. All citations: RW 265-459, letter no. 8, unsigned. For an extensive analysis of this letter see Gross, "Politische Polykratie 1936," 138f.; additional comments on the "case of Kaufmann" in Koenen, *Der Fall Carl Schmitt*, 633ff.

22. The cited phrase is Schwab's in *Challenge of the Exception*, 101.

23. Quaritsch, *Positionen und Begriffe Carl Schmitts*, 109.

24. Cf. esp. Schmitt's diary entries in Noack, *Carl Schmitt*, 160–61.

25. On Schmitt's plan see Dan Diner, "Constitutional Theory and 'State of Emergency' in the Weimar Republic: The Case of Carl Schmitt," *Tel Aviver Jahrbuch für Deutsche Geschichte* 17 (1988): 303–21, here 318.

26. On Schmitt's "Katechon" see below, part 4. The possible association is found in Schmitt's *Glossarium*, 80. But this passage quite likely contains a writing or transcription error, "1932" being properly read as "1942." This would correspond precisely to the emergence of the term "Katechon" in Schmitt's work from the 1940s.

27. Cf. Ralf Dahrendorf, *Gesellschaft und Demokratie in Deutschland* (Munich: Piper, 1965), 245–60.

28. On the question of Hitler's modernity and that of his movement, see the selective bibliography in Michael Prinz and Rainer Zitelmann, eds., *Nationalsozialismus und Modernisierung* (Darmstadt: Wissenschaftliche Buchgesellschaft, 1991).

29. See Peter Caldwell, "Ernst Forsthoff and the Legacy of Radical Conservative State Theory in the Federal Republic of Germany," *History of Political Thought* 15 (1994): 615–41, here 623. At the time the Nazis took power not even Koellreuter was a party member; see Jörg Schmidt, *Otto Koellreutter, 1883–1972: Sein Leben, sein Werk, seine Zeit* (Frankfurt a.M.: Lang, 1995).

30. See Hubert Schorn, *Der Richter im Dritten Reich: Geschichte und Dokumente* (Frankfurt a.M.: Klostermann, 1959), 23.

31. Compare Quaritsch's opinion, *Positionen und Begriffe Carl Schmitts*, 83–120 ("Der Konvertit").

32. On Hohn see Shlomo Aronson, *Reinhard Heydrich und die Frühgeschichte von Gestapo und SD* (Stuttgart: Deutsche Verlagsanstalt, 1971). The anonymously published articles of Forsthoff and Huber from the period are listed in various festschrifts published in Germany since 1945 in their honor. Cf. also Yuji Ishida, *Jungkonservative in der Weimarer Republik: Der Ring-Kreis 1928–1933* (Frankfurt a.M.: Lang, 1988).

33. Rapp, *Die Stellung der Juden*, 100–144, shows this in relation to Ernst Forsthoff, Theodor Maunz, Ernst Rudolf Huber, Günther Küchenhoff, and Carl Hermann Ule—the "Young Right" of German constitutional theory.

34. In a telephone interview with the author held on 23 March 1994, Höhn denied ever having opposed Schmitt in any way.

35. Cf. Dieter Grimm, "Die 'Neue Rechtswissenschaft'—Über Funktion und Formation nationalsozialistischer Jurisprudenz," in Grimm, *Recht und Staat der bürgerlichen Gesellschaft* (Frankfurt a.M.: Suhrkamp, 1987), 373–95.

36. Gottfried Salomon already noted in 1938 that "aside from the young arrivistes, only one significant publicist has spoken up for the new regime." See Salomon, "Staatsrecht in Deutschland," in *Freie Wissenschaft,* ed. Emil J. Gumbel (Strasbourg: Brant, 1938), 174–89, here 182.

37. In this regard cf. Lutz Hachmeister, *Der Gegnerforscher: Die Karriere des SS-Führers Franz Alfred Six* (Munich: C.H. Beck, 1998).

38. Cf. Werner Jochmann, *Gesellschaftskrise und Judenfeindschaft in Deutschland, 1870–1945,* 2nd ed. (Hamburg: Christians, 1991), 13–29.

39. Hitler's reference to "antisemitism of reason" is found in an edited letter to Adolf Gemlich in *Hitler: Sämtliche Aufzeichnungen, 1905–1924,* ed. Eberhard Jäckel and Axel Kuhn (Stuttgart: Deutsche Verlagsanstalt, 1980), 89. See also Wolfram Meyer, "Wann wurde Hitler zum Antisemiten? Einige Überlegungen zu einer strittigen Frage," *Zeitschrift für Geschichtswissenschaft* 43 (1995): 687–697.

40. See Bendersky, *Carl Schmitt, Theorist for the Reich,* 208: "By the autumn of 1933, he had also gradually begun to pay lip service to Nazi views by inserting the odd anti-Semitic remark into his publications. . . . By doing so he might also avoid embarrassing questions about his past close professional and personal involvements with Jews. But he never became an ideological convert to Nazism." This argument appears to follow Schmitt's postwar self-staging, and to reflect Bendersky's personal contact with Schmitt. The Schmitt archive contains twenty letters and four postcards from Bendersky to Schmitt between 1972 and 1981; see van Laak and Villinger, eds., *Nachlass Carl Schmitt,* 33.

41. Bendersky, *Carl Schmitt, Theorist for the Reich,* 227.

42. Ibid., 228.

43. The argument is examined in Gross, "Politische Polykratie 1936."

44. Bendersky, *Carl Schmitt, Theorist for the Reich,* 269, cites one remark of Schmitt from the interrogation that would appear to suggest remorse: "It is definitely horrible. Nothing else can be said about it." But in fact Schmitt is here only rather vaguely renouncing what his interrogators referred to as his "thesis" that "legislation should be National Socialist." Cited in Claus-Dietrich Wieland, "Carl Schmitt in Nürnberg" (1947), *1999* 2 (1987): 111.

45. Citations in Claus-Ekkehard Bärsch, "Der Jude als Antichrist in der NS-Ideologie: Die kollektive Identität der Deutschen und der Antisemitismus unter religionspolitologischer Perspektive," *Zeitschrift für Religions- und Geistesgeschichte* 47 (1995): 161–88, here 172. Cf. Bärsch, *Erlösung und Vernichtung: Dr. phil. Joseph Goebbels: Zur Psyche und Ideologie eines jungen Nationalsozialisten 1923–1927* (Munich: Boer, 1987).

46. See Wilhelm Stuckart and Rolf Schiedermair, *Rassen- und Erbpflege in der Gesetzgebung des Dritten Reiches* (Leipzig: Kohlhammer, 1938), 10: "For the German Volk the problem of race is [the same as] the Jewish question, since only the Jews carry weight among members of foreign races [*fremde Rassen*] in Germany."

47. The work of Jacob Katz and Léon Poliakov has demonstrated this in different ways. On the theological roots of "secular antisemitism" in connection with the Pauline conception of law, see Gesine Palmer's extensive study, *Ein*

Freispruch für Paulus: John Tolands Theorie des Judenchristentums (Berlin: Institut Kirche und Judentum, 1996), esp. 149ff.

48. Cf. Dagmar Pöpping, "Blut oder die Metaphysik des Wirklichen— über einige Grundannahmen rassistischer Theorie," in *Blut*, ed. Regina Nössler and Petra Flocke (Munich: Urban & Schwarzenberg, 1977), 91–105.

49. Stuckart and Schiedermair, *Rassen- und Erbpflege*, 10.

50. Cf. George L. Mosse, "Die deutsche Rechte und die Juden," in *Entscheidungsjahr 1932: Zur Judenfrage in der Endphase der Weimarer Republik*, ed. Werner E. Mosse (Tübingen: Mohr, 1966), 183–246.

51. The phrase is Schwab's in *Challenge of the Exception*.

52. Cf., as a persistent theme, Koenen, *Der Fall Carl Schmitt*. For many plausible arguments to the contrary, see Rainer Walz, "Der vormoderne Antisemitismus: Religiöser Fanatismus oder Rassenwahn?" *Historische Zeitschrift* 260 (1995): 719–48.

53. See Reinhard Rürup, "Das Ende der Emanzipation: Die antijüdische Politik in Deutschland von der 'Machtergreifung' bis zum Zweiten Weltkrieg," in *Die Juden im Nationalsozialistischen Deutschland, 1933–1943*, ed. Arnold Paucker (Tübingen: Mohr, 1986), 97–114, here 102.

Chapter 3. Schmitt's Assault on the "Jewish Legal State"

1. Cf. Koenen, *Der Fall Carl Schmitt*, 227, n.252.

2. "Nach wiederholten Ansätzen und Umkreisungen." Schmitt, *Positionen und Begriffe*, 5.

3. On this law cf. Hermann Wagner's 1936 Munich dissertation, "Das Berufsbeamtentum im nationalsozialistischen Reich"; Hans Mommsen, *Das Beamtentum im Dritten Reich* (Stuttgart: Deutsche Verlagsanstalt, 1966), 505ff; Koenen, *Der Fall Carl Schmitt*, 227.

4. One year after his essay's publication, Schmitt cites a remark of Hölderlin's that, torn entirely from its proper historical context, has affinities with the essay's vocabulary: "The nomos, the law, is here the discipline [*Zucht*] . . . in which, with time, a people meets and has met itself." In Schmitt, *Über die drei Arten des rechtswissenschaftlichen Denkens* (repr., Berlin: Duncker & Humblot, 1993), 17; Carl Schmitt, *On the Three Types of Juristic Thought*, trans. Joseph W. Bendersky (Westport, Conn.: Greenwood, 2004), 51. Throughout these notes, references to English translations of Schmitt's books will be furnished immediately following the original German texts when parallel pages or page-ranges are available; because Schmitt's books often appeared in various editions, this is not always the case.

5. Carl Schmitt, *Staat, Bewegung, Volk: Die Dreigliederung der politischen Einheit*, 2nd ed. (Hamburg: Hanseatische Verlagsanstalt, 1933) (henceforth *State, Movement, Volk*), 45; *State, Movement, People: The Triadic Structure of the Political Unity* and *The Question of Legality*, edited, trans., and with a preface by Simona Draghici (Corvallis, Ore.: Plutarch, 2001), 51. ("Ein Artfremder mag sich noch so kritisch

gebärden und noch so scharfsinnig bemühen, mag Bücher lesen und Bücher schreiben, er denkt und versteht anders, weil er anders geartet ist, und bleibt in jedem entscheidenden Gedankengang in den existentiellen Bedingungen seiner eigenen Art. Das ist die objektive Wirklichkeit der 'Objektivität.'")

6. Cf. Majer, *Grundlagen*, 148. On Schmitt's concept of *Artgleichheit* cf. Werner Hill, *Gleichheit und Artgleichheit* (Berlin: Duncker & Humblot, 1966), 264–72. Hill's discussion of Schmitt (also on 182–203) does not examine what he is attacking with the concept. In general, despite all Hill's jabs at Schmitt's opportunism, he negates the jurist's radicalism by declaring his ideas "within the tradition of Western thought" (271), in contrast to authentic Nazism.

7. Paul de Lagarde, *Deutsche Schriften*, 4th ed. (Göttingen: Horstmann, 1903), 408f. Before this passage on the same page Lagarde argues: "If, for Prussia's sake, Prussia's conservatives . . . are able to solve the problem of destroying Judaism, then the problem is solved for Europe. And it must be solved if Europe is not to become a field of corpses."

8. Schmitt, "Das gute Recht der deutschen Revolution," *Westdeutscher Beobachter* 9, no. 108 (12 May 1933): 1–2.

9. Carl Schmitt, "Fünf Leitsätze für die Rechtspraxis," *Deutsches Recht* 3 (1933): 201–2. Two texts of Schmitt published in 1935 treat the idea of the *Rechtsstaat* at length: "Der Rechtsstaat," in *Nationalsozialistisches Handbuch für Recht und Gesetzgebung*, ed. Hans Frank (Munich: Zentralverlag der NSDAP, 1935), 3–10, and "Was bedeutet der Streit um den 'Rechtsstaat'?" *Zeitschrift für die gesamte Staatswissenschaft* 95 (1935): 189–201.

10. Günther Krauss, "These: Der Begriff des Rechtsstaats ist an die verfassungsrechtliche Lage des 19. Jahrhunderts gebunden; für den Staat des 20. Jahrhunderts hat er keine Berechtigung mehr," in Günther Krauss and Otto von Schweinichen, *Disputation über den Rechtsstaat*, ed. with an intro. and epilogue by Carl Schmitt (Hamburg: Hanseatische Verlagsanstalt, 1935), 32.

11. Cf. Hans Mommsen, "Der Reichstagsbrand und seine politischen Folgen," in *Der Nationalsozialismus und die deutsche Gesellschaft: Ausgewählte Aufsätze*, ed. Lutz Niethammer and Bernd Weisbrod (Reinbeck: Rowohlt, 1991), 102–83; Epping, "Die 'Lex van der Lubbe.'" On Schmitt's attitude toward the principle of *nulla poena sine lege*, see Koenen, *Der Fall Carl Schmitt*, 481–89. Also important here: Schmitt's essay "Kodifikation oder Novelle? Über die Aufgabe und Methode der heutigen Gesetzgebung," *Deutsche Juristen-Zeitung* 40 (1935): 919–25, concerning the "Law on Alterations to the Penal Code," which instructed judges to impose punishments "according to healthy popular feelings [*Volksempfinden*]."

12. Schmitt, "Das gute Recht der deutschen Revolution."

13. Ibid.

14. In *Der totale Staat* (Hamburg: Hanseatische Verlagsanstalt, 1933), 38, Ernst Forsthoff addresses the same problem of telling friend from enemy; and he also does so in terms of *Artgleichheit* and *Artverschiedenheit* (difference of kind).

15. Schmitt, "Das gute Recht der deutschen Revolution."

16. Meier, *Carl Schmitt, Leo Strauss und der "Begriff des Politischen."*

17. Cf. Siegfried Lokatis, *Die Hanseatische Verlagsanstalt: Politisches Buchmarketing im "Dritten Reich"* (Frankfurt a.M.: Buchhändler-Vereinigung, 1992), 51.

18. Carl Schmitt, *Der Begriff des Politischen: Text von 1932 mit einem Vorwort und drei Corollarien* (Berlin: Duncker & Humblot, 1963), 8.

19. Stuckart and Schiedermair, *Rassen- und Erbpflege*, 12.

20. See already Majer, *Grundlagen*, 159: "Nazi special law was only born through this deduction" (i.e., the projection of the racially "alien" into Schmitt's idea of the "enemy"); Majer's observation is based on Fraenkel, *The Dual State*. Cf. Schmitt, *Staat, Bewegung, Volk*, 5f.; *State, Movement, People*, 11f.

21. Cf. Koenen, *Der Fall Carl Schmitt*, 315. Schmitt presents his views on the *Preussenschlag* in *Positionen und Begriffe*, 180–84 ("Schlussrede vor dem Staatsgerichtshof in Leipzig") and 185–90 ("Weiterentwicklung des totalen Staats in Deutschland").

22. Franz Blei, "Der Fall Carl Schmitt: Von einem der ihn kannte," *Der christliche Ständestaat*, 25 December 1936, 1217–20. Cf. the Schmitt portrait in Blei, *Zeitgenössische Bildnisse* (Amsterdam: Allert de Lange, 1940), 21–29.

23. Cf. Koenen, *Der Fall Carl Schmitt*, 227, n.252.

24. Schmitt, "Der Neubau des Staats- und Verwaltungsrechts," 251.

25. Cf. Göppinger, *Juristen jüdischer Abstammung*, 16.

26. Schmitt, "Der Neubau des Staats- und Verwaltungsrechts," 250f.

27. Ibid., 251.

28. Ibid.

29. Schmitt, *Staat, Bewegung, Volk*, 42; *State, Movement, People*, 49. For an interesting review of the book see Hugo Marx, "Schmitt, Carl, Staat Bewegung, Volk. Die Dreigliederung der politischen Einheit," *Zeitschrift für Sozialforschung* 3 (1934): 272. The review ends as follows: "It remains completely unclear what kind of *Artgleichheit* is considered absolutely necessary. The proof for the exigency of *Artgleichheit* is limited to a simple 'hence' that, as the above citation shows, is directly joined to the postulate. As far as can be seen, Schmitt has joined the followers of a faith-oriented science."

30. Schmitt, *Staat, Bewegung, Volk*, 32; *State, Movement, People*, 36. Schmitt owed Göring his appointment as Prussian state councillor.

31. Schmitt, "Das gute Recht der deutschen Revolution."

32. Schmitt, *Staat, Bewegung, Volk*, 44; *State, Movement, People*, 50.

33. Ibid., 52; ibid., 58.

34. Ibid., 45; ibid., 51.

35. Ibid., 41; ibid., 46–47.

36. In contrast, Schmitt's doctoral student Günther Krauss is clear and direct in a 1934 review of Schmitt's book: "In Germany a Jew cannot be Führer. But *Artgleichheit* is not only required for political leadership [*Führung*]; it must also be realized in all other realms of the life of the state and *Volk*. This is also

the case for justice and administration. Judicial independence immediately becomes caprice when someone who is *artfremd* replaces the concept of law and morality held by the German *Volk* with his own concept of loyalty and belief, good manners, public order, unjust hardness." See Krauss, "Staat, Bewegung, Volk," *Deutsches Recht* 4 (1934): 23–24, here 24.

37. Schmitt, *Staat, Bewegung, Volk,* 14–16; *State, Movement, People,* 15ff. The first edition of Jellinek's *Allgemeine Staatslehre* (Berlin: O. Häring) appeared in 1900; Kelsen's own *Allgemeine Staatslehre* (Berlin: J. Springer) appeared in 1925.

38. Schmitt, *Staat, Bewegung, Volk,* 42; *State, Movement, People,* 48.

39. On the concept of homogeneity see Hofmann, *Legitimität gegen Legalität,* 131–41; Thomas Vesting, *Politische Einheitsbildung und technische Realisation: Über die Expansion und die Grenzen der Demokratie* (Baden-Baden: Nomos, 1990), 23ff.; and the early analysis of Hermann Heller, "Autoritärer Liberalismus?" (1933), in Heller, *Gesammelte Schriften,* vol. 2 (Leiden: Sijthoff, 1973). In regards to the concept, the following sentence from Schmitt's *Verfassungslehre* (1928), 230, is rich in resonance: "In smaller organizations whose members consider themselves to be elected, holy, or redeemed, the state of being elected, hence external inequality, is an especially firm basis for equality within the society."

40. For an outstanding example of this systematic elision, see the article: "Passed on the same day as the law on representatives of the Reich, the law of 7 April 1933 concerning officials (*Reichsgesetzblatt,* 1:175) is of special importance in that it removes elements from officialdom that are *artfremd.* In this manner the principle of *Artgleichheit,* which is decisive for the National Socialist *Weltanschauung,* has been realized in one of the most important locations of public life" (29).

41. Schmitt, "Nationalsozialistisches Rechtsdenken," *Deutsches Recht* 4 (1934): 225 and 229.

42. Ibid.

43. Ibid., 225.

44. Ibid.

45. Schmitt, *Über die drei Arten des rechtswissenschaftlichen Denkens,* 16; *On the Three Types of Juristic Thought,* 50. On this book see Koenen, *Der Fall Carl Schmitts,* 470ff.

46. *Jüdisches Lexikon: Ein enzyklopädisches Handbuch des jüdischen Wissens in vier Bänden,* ed. Georg Herlitz and Bruno Kirschner (Berlin: Jüdischer Verlag, 1927), s.v. "Bodenbesitz" (by Mordechei Sew-Wolf Rapaport). Cf. *Encyclopaedia Judaica: Das Judentum in Geschichte und Gegenwart,* ed. Jakob Klatzkin et al. (Berlin: Eschkol, 1929), s.v. "Boden" (by S. Krauss), esp. col. 902 ("Wertschätzung").

47. Cf. Carl Schmitt, *Der Nomos der Erde im Völkerrecht des Jus Publicum Europaeum* (Cologne: Greven, 1950).

48. See Schmitt, *Über die drei Arten des rechtswissenschaftlichen Denkens,* 5; *On the Three Types of Juristic Thought,* 6.

49. Ibid., 7ff.

50. Ibid., 52. On the development in England and France, see 52–57; on the situation in Germany, 42–52. For France, Schmitt especially stresses the institutional doctrine of Maurice Hauriou (1856–1929).

51. Ibid., 9f.

52. This concern becomes clear in Schmitt's correspondence with the Hanseatische Verlagsanstalt: "My work on the three sorts of jurisprudential thinking is becoming too scholarly to still be considered for the brochure-series. I wish to bring it out either with the Academy for German Law or with Duncker & Humblot." (*Nachlass Carl Schmitt*, 472, Schmitt to the Hanseatische Verlagsanstalt, 3 March 1934; cited from Lokatis, *Die Hanseatische Verlagsanstalt*, 59.)

53. Schmitt, *Über die drei Arten des rechtswissenschaftlichen Denkens*, 7ff.; *On the Three Types of Juristic Thought*, 44.

54. Ibid., 15; ibid., 50.

55. Ibid. On the concept of *Gesetz* see Rolf Grawert, "Gesetz," in Brunner et al., *Geschichtliche Grundbegriffe*, 2:863–922. Grawert proposes the following definition (p. 863): "From its origins in the sacral realm as an explication of the divine and world order to its meaning as a falsifiable hypothesis in the modern natural sciences, the concept takes in a field of significations whose only common denominator is the ordering function, mainly a statement concerning regularities." Cf. *Deutsches Wörterbuch*, vol. 4, ed. Jakob Grimm and Wilhelm Grimm (Leipzig: Göschen, 1897), s.v. "Gesetz."

56. Carl Schmitt, *Staatsgefüge und Zusammenbruch des zweiten Reiches: Der Sieg des Bürgers über den Soldaten* (Hamburg: Hanseatische Verlagsanstalt, 1934), 12.

57. Schmitt, *Über die drei Arten des rechtswissenschaftlichen Denkens*, 9; *On the Three Types of Juristic Thought*, 45.

58. Ibid., 9–10. Cf. the chapter "Ghosts from the Past: The Wandering Jews," in *The History of Anti-Semitism*, 3 vols., ed. Léon Poliakov, trans. Miriam Kochan (New York: Vanguard, 1975), 3:349–64, and Joshua Trachtenberg, *The Devil and the Jews: The Medieval Conception of the Jew and Its Relation to Modern Anti-semitism* (1943; 2nd ed., Philadelphia: Jewish Publication Society of America, 1983).

59. Schmitt, *Über die drei Arten des rechtswissenschaftlichen Denkens*, 14; *On the Three Types of Juristic Thought*, 50.

60. Schmitt, *Der Wert des Staates, und die Bedeutung des Einzelnen*, 2nd ed. (Hellerau: Hellerauer Verlag, 1917), 85.

61. Schmitt, *Über die drei Arten des rechtswissenschaftlichen Denkens*, 12; *On the Three Types of Juristic Thought*, 48.

62. Carl Schmitt, *Politische Theologie: Vier Kapitel zur Lehre von der Souveränität* (1922, 2nd ed. 1934; repr., Berlin: Duncker & Humblot, 1985), 22; Schmitt, *Political Theology: Four Chapters on the Concept of Sovereignty*, trans. George Schwab, foreword by Tracy B. Strong (Chicago: Univ. of Chicago Press, 2005), 15. This passage shows that for Schmitt the "exception" does not merely represent a limiting concept but a political, existential, and mental state that he supports.

63. Schmitt, *Über die drei Arten des rechtswissenschaftlichen Denkens*, 10; *On the Three Types of Juristic Thought*, 46.

64. Ibid., 14; ibid., 50.

65. Schmitt, *Verfassungslehre*, 138–57.

66. Ibid., 146–47.

67. Ibid., 142.

68. Ibid., 16.

69. Various suggestions to this effect in Heinrich Kessler, *Wilhelm Stapel als politischer Publizist: Ein Beitrag zur Geschichte des konservativen Nationalismus zwischen den beiden Weltkriegen* (Nuremberg: Spindler, 1967), 148f., 187, 219; Klaus Scholder, *Die Kirchen und das Dritte Reich*, vol. 2 (Frankfurt a.M.: Ullstein, 1986), 16f., 19ff., 26f., 29f., 32, 43, 87, 128, 130f., 240; Lokatis, *Die Hanseatische Verlagsanstalt*; Heiner Faulenbach, *Ein Weg durch die Kirche: Heinrich Josef Oberheid* (Cologne: Rheinland-Verlag, 1992), 2f., 3, 14, 16, 21, 26ff., 42, 49, 91ff., 100, 126, 144, 155, 185, 215, 222, 223, 226, 227, 240; Koenen, *Der Fall Carl Schmitt*; and Raphael Gross, "Jesus oder Christus? Überlegungen zur 'Judenfrage' in der politischen Theologie Carl Schmitts," in *Metamorphosen des Politischen: Grundfragen politischer Einheitsbildung seit den 20er Jahren*, ed. Andreas Göbel, Dirk van Laak, and Ingeborg Villinger (Berlin: Akademie, 1995), 75–94. On Stapels' situation after 1945, see van Laak, *Gespräche in der Sicherheit des Schweigens*, 99–100.

70. Cf. Scholder, *Die Kirchen und das Dritte Reich*, vol. 1 (Frankfurt a.M.: Ullstein, 1977), 124–50. For a critique of Scholder, in particular regarding his excessively positive assessment (influenced by his admiration for Karl Barth) of the Confessional Church and his tendency to see even regime-true Christians as victims, cf. Susannah Heschel and Robert P. Ericksen, "The German Churches Face Hitler: Assessment of the Historiography," *Tel Aviver Jahrbuch für deutsche Geschichte* 23 (1994): 433–59.

71. Cf. Scholder, *Die Kirchen und das Dritte Reich*, 1:144. For documentary material on the "Jewish question" in German Protestantism in 1933 see Günther van Norden, *Der deutsche Protestantismus im Jahr der nationalsozialistischen Machtergreifung* (Gütersloh: Gütersloher Verlagshaus Mohn, 1979), 313–92. Cf. Bernard Raymond, "Die Konzepte einiger protestantischer deutscher Theologen zur 'Judenfrage,'" in *Protestantismus und Antisemitismus in der Weimarer Republik*, ed. Kurt Nowak and Gérard Raulet (Frankfurt a.M.: Campus Verlag, 1994), 127–46.

72. Schmitt would describe Ball's early essay as one of the finest he ever received. Cf. Schickel, *Gespräche mit Carl Schmitt*, 31–59.

73. Schmitt, *Politische Theologie*, 7; *Political Theology*, 2.

74. Brauweiler was a Catholic theorist of the corporatist state; see Armin Mohler, *Die Konservative Revolution in Deutschland 1918–1932: Ein Handbuch*, 3rd ed. (with additional volume), vol. 2 (Darmstadt: Wissenschaftliche Buchgesellschaft, 1989), 407.

75. Wilhelm Stapel, *Der christliche Staatsmann: Eine Theologie des Nationalismus*, 2nd ed. (Hamburg: Hanseatische Verlagsanstalt, 1932), 9. On Stapel cf. Hans

G. K. Sieh, "Der Hamburger Nationalistenklub: Ein Beitrag zur Geschichte der christlich-konservativen Strömungen in der Weimarer Republik" (PhD diss., Mainz, 1963); Wolfgang Tilgner, *Volksnomostheologie und Schöpfungsglaube: Ein Beitrag zur Geschichte des Kirchenkampfes* (Göttingen: Vandenhoeck & Ruprecht, 1966); Kessler, *Wilhelm Stapel als politischer Publizist;* Lokatis, *Die Hanseatische Verlagsanstalt;* Louis Dupeux, "Der Kulturantisemitismus von Wilhelm Stapel," in Nowak and Raulet, *Protestantismus und Antisemitismus,* 167–76. Eschweiler underscores a similar tie to Schmitt in his own article, itself entitled "Politische Theologie," *Der Ring* 4 (1931): 903–4.

76. See Georg Denzler and Volker Fabricius, *Christen und Nationalsozialismus: Darstellung und Dokumente,* 2nd ed. (Frankfurt a.M.: Fischer, 1993), 40.

77. Cf. Scholder, *Die Kirchen und das Dritte Reich,* 1:110–23.

78. For a general study of the topic see Uriel Tal, "On Structures of Political Theology and Myth in Germany Prior to the Holocaust," in *The Holocaust as Historical Experience: Essays and a Discussion,* ed. Yehuda Bauer and Nathan Rotenstreich (New York: Holmes & Meier, 1981), 43–74. More extensively: Scholder, *Die Kirchen und das Dritte Reich,* 1:124–50.

79. Ernst-Wolfgang Boeckenförde (both a former student of Schmitt and a retired member of the West German Constitutional Court) has offered a positive, liberal reception of Schmitt along these lines. See, e.g., his article "Politische Theorie und Politische Theologie," in *Der Fürst dieser Welt: Carl Schmitt und die Folgen,* ed. Jacob Taubes (Munich: Fink, 1983), 16–25.

80. For instance, as articulated by Stapel, *Der christliche Staatsmann,* 6.

81. Cf. one of the movement's key works, Friedrich Gogarten, *Politische Ethik: Versuch einer Grundlegung* (Jena: Diederichs, 1932).

82. On this aspect of the movement see Scholder, *Die Kirchen und das Dritte Reich,* 1:130.

83. See in this regard Robert Hepp, "Politische Theologie und theologische Politik. Studien zur Säkularisierung des Protestantismus im Weltkrieg und in der Weimarer Republik" (PhD diss., Erlangen, 1967), and Domenico Losurdo, *Heidegger and the Ideology of War: Community, Death, and the West,* trans. Jon Morris (Amherst, N.Y.: Humanity Books, 2001).

84. See Dupeux, "Der Kulturantisemitismus von Wilhelm Stapel," 167; Dietrich Braun, "Carl Schmitt und Friedrich Gogarten: Erwägungen zur 'eigentlich katholischen Verschärfung' und ihrer protestantischen Entsprechung im Übergang von der Weimarer Republik zum Dritten Reich," in *Die eigentlich katholische Verschärfung—: Konfession, Theologie und Politik im Werk Carl Schmitts,* ed. Bernd Wacker (Munich: Fink, 1994), 203–27.

85. Cf. Scholder, *Die Kirchen und das Dritte Reich,* 1:125.

86. Wilhelm Stapel, "Volk und Volkstum," in *Die neue Front,* ed. H. von Gleichen, Moeller van den Bruck, and M. H. Boehm (Berlin: Paetel, 1922), 81. Stapel, *Volk: Untersuchung über Volkheit und Volkstum,* 4th rev. ed. (Hamburg: Hanseatische Verlagsanstalt, 1942) (original title: *Volksbürgerliche Erziehung* [Jena:

Diederichs, 1917]). See Reinhart Koselleck, "Volk, Nation, Nationalismus, Masse," in *Geschichtliche Grundbegriffe: Historisches Lexikon zur politisch-sozialen Sprache in Deutschland*, vol. 7, ed. Otto Brunner, Werner Conze, and Reinhart Koselleck (Stuttgart: Klett-Cotta, 1992), 141–431.

87. Cf. ibid., 409.

88. This is the subtitle of Stapel's *Der christliche Staatsmann*.

89. Cf. Koselleck, "Volk, Nation, Nationalismus, Masse," 407.

90. Scholder, *Die Kirchen und das Dritte Reich*, 1:124–50.

91. Cf. "Die 5. Richtlinie der Glaubensbewegung Deutsche Christen," in Denzler and Fabricius, *Christen und Nationalsozialismus*, 257.

92. Scholder, *Die Kirchen und das Dritte Reich*, 1:146.

93. Stapel, "Versuch einer praktischen Lösung der Judenfrage," in *Was wir vom Nationalsozialismus erwarten: Zwanzig Antworten*, ed. Albrecht Erich Günther (Heilbronn: Salzer, 1932), 186–91, here 190. On the fate of the so-called Christian Jews in the Nazi state, see Raul Hilberg, *Täter, Opfer, Zuschauer: Die Vernichtung der Juden 1933–1945* (Frankfurt a.M.: Fischer, 1992), 168–77.

94. The German Christians favored the Nazi "euthanasia" program directed at psychically and physically disabled persons for similar "self-protective" reasons. See Denzler und Fabricius, *Christen und Nationalsozialismus*, 56.

95. Tilgner, *Volksnomostheologie und Schöpfungsglaube;* Denzler und Fabricius, *Christen und Nationalsozialismus*, 40–42.

96. Stapel, "Versuch einer praktischen Lösung der Judenfrage," 186, 189.

97. Stapel, *Die Kirche Christi und der Staat Hitlers*, 4th ed. (Hamburg: Hanseatische Verlagsanstalt, 1933). See Kessler, *Wilhelm Stapel als politischer Publizist*, 187–94.

98. See Scholder, *Die Kirchen und das Dritte Reich*, 1:536. On the backdrop to the *Volksnomos* conception in Protestant political theology of the Weimar Republic, see Tilgner, *Volksnomostheologie und Schöpfungsglaube*. On the Nazi linkage between the *Volksnomos* and "the Jews," see the example of Paul Althaus, "Nomos und Erlösung," *Deutsches Volkstum* 15 (1933): 49–53.

99. Faulenbach, *Ein Weg durch die Kirche*, 26, suggests this date. Although Faulenbach fails to confront the question of the etiology of Oberheid's antisemitism, he does show (181) that already in 1937, the cleric pushed for establishment of an institute devoted to research on the influence of Judaism on German religious life. Cf. Heschel and Ericksen, *The German Churches Face Hitler*, 444.

100. Cf. Scholder, *Die Kirchen und das Dritte Reich*, 2:13ff., 26ff., 38, 43, 45f., 48, 50f., 53f., 63f., 66, 70, 72, 82, 87ff., 96, 108, 111, 126, 159, 164, 205, 207, 213, and 276; and Faulenbach, *Ein Weg durch die Kirche*. Koenen, *Der Fall Carl Schmitt*, does not explore this connection. He does indicate (379) that in the summer of 1933 Schmitt hoped to offer Oberheid a "convenient starting position" and "the greatest possible influence"; but he views this as simply a continuation of Schmitt's ties with the Weimar Republic's "conservative-revolutionary" camp.

101. Cf. Mohler, Huhn, and Tommissen, *Carl Schmitt—Briefwechsel*, 24.

102. Faulenbach, *Ein Weg durch die Kirche*, 14.

103. It is thus remarkable that in Tommissen, *Schmittiana*, 1:65, Günther Krauss maintains that Oberheid had never been an antisemite. This assertion was then taken over uncritically by Noack, *Carl Schmitt*, 88.

104. Faulenbach, *Ein Weg durch die Kirche*, 25. For information in the previous paragraph see 16 and 24.

105. Ibid., 16, 24, 25, 26, 41, and 53.

106. Scholder, *Die Kirchen und das Dritte Reich*, 2:16.

107. Ibid. On Ludwig Müller see Thomas Martin Schneider, *Reichsbischof Ludwig Müller: Eine Untersuchung zu Leben, Werk und Persönlichkeit* (Göttingen: Vandenhoeck & Ruprecht, 1993).

108. Scholder, *Die Kirchen und das Dritte Reich*, 2:29.

109. Ibid. On the Schmitt-Popitz relation see Lutz-Arwed Bentin, *Johannes Popitz und Carl Schmitt: Zur wirtschaftlichen Theorie des totalen Staates in Deutschland* (Munich: C.H. Beck, 1972); Gerhard Schulz, "Johannes Popitz," in *20. Juli: Portraits des Widerstands*, ed. Rudolf Lill (Dusseldorf: Econ Verlag, 1984), 237–51, here 245.

110. See Scholder, *Die Kirchen und das Dritte Reich*, 2:11–36.

111. Ibid.

112. Ibid.

113. This in a letter to the publisher Friedrich Vorwerk. He continues as follows: "The effort to construct a real state on the basis of present-day confessional divisions finishes itself off in the end." Cited in Faulenbach, *Ein Weg durch die Kirche*, 40.

114. He first used the term at the end of 1930 in a talk called "The Woman in the State." Information on the term in Schmitt based on Koenen, *Der Fall Carl Schmitt*, 120f. See also Maus, *Bürgerliche Rechtstheorie und Faschismus*, 152–59; Schmitt, *Staat, Grossraum, Nomos*, 58, 66f. (note of Günter Maschke).

115. Koenen, *Der Fall Carl Schmitt*, 120f.

116. Ibid., 198.

117. Ibid., 201.

118. Carl Schmitt, "Gesunde Wirtschaft im starken Staat," *Mitteilungen des Vereins zur Wahrnehmung der gemeinsamen Interessen in Rheinland und Westfalen (Langnamenverein)*, no. 1 (1932): 13–32, 17.

119. Scholder, *Die Kirchen und das Dritte Reich*, 17.

120. Ibid., 19.

121. Schmitt, *Staat, Bewegung, Volk*, 7; *State, Movement, People*, 6.

122. Ibid., 32. Cf Walter Grundmann, *Totale Kirche im totalen Staat* (Dresden: Günther, 1933).

123. Scholder was the first to address the influence, although only in relation to the impact of Schmitt's ideas on the German Christian political representatives, especially Oberheid, between 1933 and 1934. Robert Hepp was the first author to focus on the background to Schmitt's nomos concept. He indicates that it was already anchored "in the German language" as a "firm topos"

at the time Schmitt introduced it to characterize a "concrete order"-based theory as opposed to normativism and decisionism. See Hepp, "Nomos," in *Historisches Wörterbuch der Philosophie,* ed. Joachim Ritter and Karlfried Gründer (Darmstadt: Wissenschaftliche Buchgesellschaft, 1984), 6:893–95, here 894.

124. H. Schmidt, "Der Nomos-Begriff bei Carl Schmitt," *Der Staat* 2 (1963): 81–108, does not consider this semantic field. The concept thus loses a basic dimension of its polemic thrust.

125. Although published after the war, Schmitt's *Nomos of the Earth* is a synthesis of reflections on the nomos concept largely stemming from the 1933–45 period. The nomos also appears in two essays from his *Staat, Grossraum, Nomos:* "Der neue Nomos der Erde" (518–22) and "Nomos-Nahme-Name" (573–91).

126. Cited in Sieh, "Der Hamburger Nationalistenklub," 83.

127. Hans Bogner, *Die verwirklichte Demokratie: Die Lehren der Antike* (Hamburg: Hanseatische Verlagsanstalt, 1930); Bogner, "Die Zersetzung des griechischen Nomos," *Deutsches Volkstum* 13 (1931): 854–61.

128. Sieh, "Der Hamburger Nationalistenklub," 82f.

129. Tilgner, *Volksnomostheologie und Schöpfungsglaube,* 13.

130. Albrecht Erich Günther, "Ein afrikanischer Nomos," *Deutsches Volkstum* 12 (1930): 142–48.

131. Wilhelm Stapel, *Sechs Kapitel über Christentum und Nationalsozialismus* (Hamburg: Hanseatische Verlagsanstalt, 1931), 12.

132. Ibid., 12–16; Stapel, "Versuch einer praktischen Lösung der Judenfrage," 186–91.

133. Stapel, *Sechs Kapitel über Christentum und Nationalsozialismus,* 12.

134. Ibid., 13. Stapel notes that his discussion of the "nomos" is in debt to Bogner.

135. Ibid., 13.

136. Ibid., 13f.

137. Tilgner, *Volksnomostheologie und Schöpfungsglaube,* 13.

138. Ibid.

139. See esp. Gurian [Gerhart], *Um des Reiches Zukunft,* 62–111, 150–208. On the enormously popular "metaphysical"-racial antisemitism of this political current, grounded on the exclusion of "the Jew" from the *Volksgemeinschaft,* see esp. 76–77.

140. Stapel, *Sechs Kapitel über Christentum und Nationalsozialismus,* 14.

141. Steven T. Katz, *Jewish Ideas and Concepts* (New York: Schocken, 1977), 183.

142. Amos Funkenstein, *Jüdische Geschichte und ihre Deutungen* (Frankfurt a.M.: Jüdischer Verlag, 1995).

143. Stapel, *Sechs Kapitel über Christentum und Nationalsozialismus,* 14ff.

144. Adolf von Harnack, *Marcion: Das Evangelium vom fremden Gott* (Leipzig: Hinrichs, 1921), 254.

145. Ernst Jünger to Carl Schmitt, 10 February 1945, in Kiesel, *Briefe 1930–1983,* 189–90. Filling more than four hundred pages, the commentary on this

correspondence considers this passage unworthy of comment. On the other hand we are informed that Flavius Josephus was a "Jewish historian."

146. See Jacob Taubes, "Die Streitfrage zwischen Judentum und Christentum," in Taubes, *Vom Kult zur Kultur: Bausteine zu einer Kritik der historischen Vernunft: Gesammelte Aufsätze zur Religions- und Geistesgeschichte*, ed. Aleida Assmann, Jan Assmann, Wolf-Daniel Hartwich, and Winfried Menninghaus (Munich: Fink, 1996), 68–98.

147. Wilhelm Stapel, "Das Verhältnis des Alten Testamentes zum Neuen: Eine Aussprache zwischen Friedrich Baumgärtel und Wilhelm Stapel," *Deutsches Volkstum* 15 (1933): 50–62, here 61.

148. Karl Barth, *Gottes Wille und unsere Wünsche* (Munich: Kaiser, 1934), 34f.; Barth, *Theologische Existenz heute* (Munich: Kaiser, 1933), 33: "I say 'no' to the spirit and letter of this doctrine absolutely and without reservation." See Tilgner, *Volksnomostheologie und Schöpfungsglaube*, 232.

149. Stapel, *Der christliche Staatsmann*, 7.

150. Stapel, "Versuch einer praktischen Lösung der Judenfrage," 187.

151. Albrecht Erich Günther, "Die politische Seite der Judenfrage," *Europäische Revue* 8 (1932): 489–97.

152. On the relationship between Schmitt and Günther see Lokatis, *Die Hanseatische Verlagsanstalt*. The Schmitt archives contain four letters from Günther and one letter to him from the 1930–34 period.

153. Günther, "Die politische Seite der Judenfrage," 493. Like Stapel, Günther relies on Hans Bogner's *Die verwirklichte Demokratie* for his understanding of the "nomos."

154. Ibid. On the controversy over military service for Jews and its meaning for the emancipation debate see Horst Fischer, *Judentum, Staat und Heer in Preussen im frühen 19. Jahrhundert: Zur Geschichte der staatlichen Judenpolitik* (Tübingen: Mohr, 1968).

155. Günther, "Die politische Seite der Judenfrage," 493.

156. Ibid.

157. The following is based on Schmitt, *Der Nomos der Erde*, 36–48; the two above-cited essays from his *Staat, Grossraum, Nomos*, and Schmitt, *Verfassungsrechtliche Aufsätze* [Essays in Constitutional Law] (Berlin: Duncker & Humblot, 1958), 489–504 ("Take-Divide-Graze: An Effort to Correctly Pose the Basic Question of any Social and Economic Order in Terms of the Nomos").

158. Schmitt *Politische Theologie*, 49; *Political Theology*, 36.

159. Schmitt, *Staat, Grossraum, Nomos*, 187.

160. Schmitt, *Der Nomos der Erde*, 39.

161. Ibid.

162. See Gerhard O. Forde, *The Law-Gospel Debate: An Interpretation of Its Historical Development* (Minneapolis: Augsburg, 1969). On Paul, see Jacob Taubes, *Die Politische Theologie des Paulus: Vorträge gehalten an der Forschungsstätte der evangelischen Studiengemeinschaft in Heidelberg, 23.–27. Februar 1987*, ed. Aleida Assmann

and Jan Assmann with the assistance of Horst Folkers, Wolf-Daniel Hartwich, and Christoph Schulte (Munich: Fink, 1995).

163. Schmitt, *Der Nomos der Erde*, 37–42. Cf. Gross, "Carl Schmitt's Nomos und die 'Juden.'"

164. See *Historisches Wörterbuch der Philosophie*, s.v. "Konkretes Ordnungsdenken" (by Ernst-Wolfgang Böckenförde), 6:1312–15. Boeckenförde addresses neither the connection between Schmitt's idea of the "nomos" and this sort of thinking nor the broader context discussed in these pages.

165. Carl Schmitt, *Der Neubau des Staats- und Verwaltungsrechts*, 251.

166. RW 265-65. As spelled out in a letter dated 14 May 1939 from Schmitt to Hans Niedermeyer (professor of Roman and civil law at Göttingen), Schmitt "carefully avoided" philological study of the "nomos" concept, not being able to undertake his "own deep research."

167. Schmitt, *Der Nomos der Erde*, 39.

168. Schmitt, *Über die drei Arten des rechtswissenschaftlichen Denkens*, 9f.; *On the Three Types of Juristic Thought*, 45.

169. Ibid., 7ff.; ibid., 44f.

170. Heinrich Triepel, "Law of the State and Politics," in *Weimar: A Jurisprudence of Crisis*, ed. Arthur J. Jacobson and Bernhard Schlink (Berkeley: Univ. of California Press, 2000), 176–88, here 188.

171. Schmitt, *Verfassungslehre*, 142.

172. Ibid., 138.

173. See for instance Carl Schmitt, "Nomos—Nature—Name," in Schmitt, *Der Beständige Aufbruch: Festschrift für Erich Przywara*, ed. Siegfried Behm (Nuremberg: Glock & Lutz, 1959), 92–105.

174. Schmitt, *Über die drei Arten des Rechtswissenschaftlichen Denkens*, 15 and 17; *On the Three Types of Juristic Thought*, 51.

175. *Das Gesez, / Von allen der König, Sterblichen und / Unsterblichen; das führt eben / darum gewaltig / Das gerechteste Recht mit allerhöchster Hand.*

176. The role played by the circle around Stefan George in helping to shape the "Nietzsche-Hölderlin apotheosis" is discussed in Stefan Breuer, *Ästhetischer Fundamentalismus: Stefan George und der deutsche Antimodernismus* (Darmstadt: Wissenschaftliche Buchgesellschaft, 1995), passim.

177. Schmitt's most extensive comments on this rootlessness are in *Staat, Grossraum, Nomos*, 578–80.

178. Schmitt, *Über die drei Arten des rechtswissenschaftlichen Denkens*, 65; *On the Three Types of Juristic Thought*, 96f.

179. Schmitt, *Verfassungsrechtliche Aufsätze*, 502, points to a study written during the war years by Martin Noth, "Das Gesetz im Pentateuch"; see Noth, *Gesammelte Studien zum Alten Testament* (Munich: Kaiser, 1957).

180. The following discussion is in debt to the fourth chapter ("Definition") of Hilberg, *Destruction of the European Jews*, 1:61–77.

181. Joseph Walk, ed., *Das Sonderrecht für die Juden im NS-Staat: Eine Sammlung der gesetzlichen Massnahmen und Richtlinien, Inhalt und Bedeutung* (Heidelberg: Müller Juristischer Verlag, 1981), 11, 16. There also the many additional decrees related to "Jewish names," in chronological order: 1:2, 3, 34, 45, 103, 328, 410; 2:342, 400, 405, 439, 452; 3:79, 101; 4:156.

182. Cf. Hellmut von Gerlach, *Von Rechts nach Links* (Hildesheim: Gerstenberg, 1978), 111–13, cited in Hilberg, *Destruction of the European Jews*, 62; Peter Pulzer, *The Rise of Political Anti-Semitism in Germany and Austria*, 2nd rev. ed. with new introduction and bibliography (London: Halban, 1988).

183. See Walther Hofer, *Der Nationalsozialismus, Dokumente 1933–1945* (Munich: Fischer, 1960), 28ff. On Nazi racial legislation, see the official juridical commentary by Stuckart and Schiedermair, *Rassen- und Erbpflege*.

184. On Stuckart, see Uwe Dietrich Adam, *Judenpolitik im Dritten Reich*, 2nd ed. (Düsseldorf: Droste, 1979); Dieter Rebentisch, *Führerstaat und Verwaltung im Zweiten Weltkrieg: Verfassungsentwicklung und Verwaltungspolitik 1939–1945* (Stuttgart: Steiner Verlag Wiesbaden, 1989).

185. *Reichsgesetzblatt*, 1:175.

186. Ibid., 195, "Erste Verordnung zur Durchführung des Gesetzes zur Wiederherstellung des Berufsbeamtentums vom 11. April 1933"; §2 (on §3). Italics in original.

187. All "Nuremberg laws": *Reichsgesetzblatt*, 1:1145–47.

188. Ibid., 1147.

189. Ibid.

190. Hilberg, *Destruction of the European Jews*, 62.

191. Ibid., 69–70. Hilberg's commentary in this respect: "a task they performed as a matter of course."

192. On the problem of definition, cf. H. G. Adler, *Der verwaltete Mensch* (Tübingen: Mohr, 1974). In his preface to *Das Sonderrecht für die Juden im NS-Staat*, xi, Joseph Walk distinguishes between four phases of Nazi anti-Jewish legislation: (1) from attainment of power to the Nuremberg Laws (31 Jan. 1933–15 Sept. 1935); (2) from the Nuremberg Laws to the November pogrom-night (15 Sept. 1935–9 Nov. 1938); (3) from the pogrom to the outbreak of World War II (10 Nov. 1938–1 Sept. 1939); (4) from the war's outbreak to the extermination of the Jews.

193. "Die Verfassung der Freiheit," *Deutsche Juristen-Zeitung* 40 (1935): 1133–35. The term "constitution of freedom" appears three times (including title) in this one and one-half-page article, without Schmitt ever clarifying what he means by "freedom."

194. Schmitt, "Die Verfassung der Freiheit," 1135. Hereafter cited in text.

195. Carl Schmitt, "Die nationalsozialistische Gesetzgebung und der Vorbehalt des 'ordre public' im Internationalen Privatrecht," *Zeitschrift der Akademie für Deutsches Recht* 3 (1936): 204–11.

196. Schmitt, "Die Verfassung der Freiheit," 1134.
197. *Reichsgesetzblatt,* 1:1146.
198. Schmitt, "Die Verfassung der Freiheit," 1134.
199. Ibid., 1134.

Chapter 4. "Judaism in Legal Studies"

1. The most important source of material on the conference is the published collection of talks in Carl Schmitt, *Das Judentum in der Rechtswissenschaft: Ansprachen, Vorträge und Ergebnisse der Tagung der Reichsgruppe Hochschullehrer des NSRB am 3. und 4. Oktober 1936* (Berlin: Deutscher Rechts-Verlag, n.d. [1936]). Schmitt spoke twice at the conference: "Eröffnung der wissenschaftlichen Vorträge durch den Reichsgruppenwalter Staatsraat Professor Dr. Carl Schmitt," ibid., 14–17; "Schlusswort des Reichsgruppenwalters Staatsrat Prof. Dr. Carl Schmitts," ibid., 28–34. The latter, closing talk was published in altered form as "Die deutsche Rechtswissenschaft im Kampf gegen den jüdischen Geist: Schlusswort auf der Tagung der Reichsgruppe Hochschullehrer des NSRB vom 3. und 4. Oktober 1936," *Deutsche Juristen-Zeitung* 41 (1935): cols. 1193–99. On the function of the antisemitic conferences held in Germany between 1936 and 1938 see Göppinger, *Juristen jüdischer Abstammung,* 17–18. On the conference organized by Schmitt, cf. ibid., 153–82, Hofmann, "Die deutsche Rechtswissenschaft im Kampf gegen den jüdischen Geist"; Rapp, *Die Stellung der Juden in der nationalsozialistischen Staatsrechtslehre,* 176–85; Gross, "Politische Polykratie 1936"; and Koenen, *Der Fall Carl Schmitt,* 387, 708–23. Both Hugo Sinzheimer, *Jüdische Klassiker der deutschen Rechtswissenschaft* (Amsterdam: Hertzberger, 1938) and Salomon, *Staatsrecht in Deutschland,* already considered the nature and meaning of this conference during the Third Reich. See also Max Weinreich, *Hitler's Professors: The Part of Scholarship in Germany's Crimes against the Jewish People* (New York: Yiddish Scientific Institute, 1946), 36–40.

2. Schmitt, *Das Judentum in der Rechtswissenschaft,* 5. Koenen, *Der Fall Carl Schmitt,* 709, suggests that the number of participants reflected Schmitt's "increasing isolation," as in the preceding two years he could mobilize up to three hundred teachers for other conferences.

3. Ibid., 5.

4. Ibid., 5. It thus seems improbable that Hans Frank was a co-initiator of the conference, as surmised by Göppinger, *Juristen jüdischer Abstammung,* 17, on the basis of the proceedings.

5. See Koenen, *Der Fall Carl Schmitt,* 651–764, and Gross, "Politische Polykratie 1936." Koenen places strong emphasis on what he views as a substantive conflict between the conservative-revolutionary Schmitt and the National Socialist SD people. Against such a reading, I argue for a concept of "political polycracy." What speaks for Koenen's approach is his very convincing embedding of Schmitt's 1936 "neutralization" within his interpretation of the

"crown jurist" as the most important representative of "Reich theology." The Nazis (Höhn, Eckhardt, Koellreutter, and so on), he suggests, somehow recognized that Schmitt was not really one of them, rather being in the Catholic camp. My argument is supported by the fact that all Schmitt's opponents in the SD (Höhn and Eckhardt, but also Koellreutter) themselves lost their power within a few years. Had they themselves come into conflict with "the" Nazis? At least in the realm of legal theory, there was no closed corpus of obligatory interpretive guidelines running through the history of the Nazi state. If we allow those who managed to prevail in the jungle of hard power struggles to set the basic standard for "authentic" Nazi views, then the standard is stretched ad absurdum. After their own "neutralization," were Höhn, Koellreutter, and Eckhardt no longer Nazis? This appears to be the suggestion of Michael Stolleis, "Otto Koellreutter," in *Neue Deutsche Biographie,* ed. Historischen Kommission bei der Bayerischen Akademie der Wissenschaften (Berlin: Duncker & Humblot, 1980), 12:324–25: "The progressive destruction of the constitutional state in Germany and a stay in Japan (1938–39) made him an opponent of National Socialism" (325). But Koellreutter had played an essential role in the destruction of the constitutional state; he was now simply responding to the failure to accord him the power he desired in the Nazi state. For a very different assessment of Koellreutter's visit to Japan from a more direct perspective, see Löwith, *My Life in Germany,* 114f. After the war Koellreutter worked on behalf of persons who came to be known in Germany as *Entnazifizierungsgeschädigte*— "those damaged by denazification." See Otto Koellreutter, *Die Entnazifizierung eine Sünde wider Recht und Ehre* (Landau, 1954).

6. Heinrich Oberheid to Duska Schmitt, 4 October 1936, Bad Godesberg, RW 265-459 (letter no. 17).

7. The fanatical antisemite Johann van Leers was the author of, among many similar works, *Juden sehen dich an,* 4th ed. (Berlin: NS.-Druck & Verlag, 1933), *14 Jahre Judenrepublik: Die Geschichte eines Rassenkampfes* (Berlin: NS.-Druck & Verlag, 1933), and *Wie kam der Jude zum Geld* (Berlin: Fritsch, 1939). In 1933 he had collaborated on an at the time extremely radical "draft for a law to regulate the employment of Jews." This envisioned the dismissal of all Jews without exception from the civil service and a prohibition of any employment as editors, artists, and doctors. See Jochmann, *Gesellschaftskrise und Judenfeindschaft,* 239. A page from Schmitt's guestbook published in Noack, *Carl Schmitt,* indicates that in 1938 Leers still counted as one of his close acquaintances.

8. Schmitt, *Das Judentum in der Rechtswissenschaft,* 6.

9. Ibid., 6.

10. Koenen, *Der Fall Carl Schmitt,* 710.

11. In relation to these two texts, Martin Leutzsch, "Der Bezug auf die Bibel und ihre Wirkungsgeschichte bei Carl Schmitt," in Wacker, *Die eigentliche katholische Verschärfung,* 174–202, has criticized the thesis of Schmitt's "anti-Judaism" and supported that of his "antisemitism." Leutzsch directs his remarks

mainly against Maschke (in his afterword to *Carl Schmitt, Der Leviathan in der Staatslehre des Thomas Hobbes: Sinn und Fehlschlag eines politischen Symbols* [2nd ed. (Cologne: Hohenheim, 1982), 209]); and Quaritsch (*Positionen und Begriffe Carl Schmitts* [3rd ed., 85–87]).

12. Schmitt, *Das Judentum in der Rechtswissenschaft*, 14 and 34. Cf. Bärsch, *Der Jude als Antichrist*, 182–85.

13. Göppinger, *Juristen jüdischer Abstammung*, 17.

14. Cf. Friedrich Heer, *Der Glaube des Adolf Hitler: Anatomie einer politischen Religiosität* (Frankfurt a.M.: Ullstein, 1989); and Heer, *Gottes erste Liebe: Die Juden im Spannungsfeld der Geschichte* (Frankfurt a.M.: Ullstein, 1986).

15. Cited in Göppinger, *Juristen jüdischer Abstammung*, 17, from *Deutscher Juristentag 1933: 4. Reichstagung des Bundes Nationalsozialistischer Deutscher Juristen e.V., Ansprachen und Fachvorträge*, ed. Rudolf Schraut (Berlin: Deutscher Rechts-Verlag, 1934), 43.

16. See Susanne Meinl, "Nationalsozialisten gegen Hitler: Die Entwicklung der Nationalrevolutionäre am Beispiel der politischen Karriere des Friedrich Wilhelm Heinz" (PhD diss., Bochum, 1997), 124; Joachim Fest, *Hitler: Eine Biographie* (Frankfurt a.M.: Zeitgeschichte, 1983), 273.

17. Schmitt, *Das Judentum in der Rechtswissenschaft*, 14.

18. See above, 258n39.

19. Schmitt, *Das Judentum in der Rechtswissenschaft*, 15–16; 35.

20. Ibid., 16.

21. Schmitt discusses Wagner in his *Glossarium*, 255.

22. See Jakob Katz, *The Darker Side of Genius: Richard Wagner's Anti-Semitism* (Hanover, N.H.: Univ. Press of New England, 1986).

23. Richard Wagner, *Sämtliche Schriften und Dichtungen*, 5th ed., vol. 5 (Leipzig: Breitkopf & Härtel, 1911).

24. This is the thrust, however, of Koenen's interpretation of precisely this passage; see *Der Fall Carl Schmitt*, 710.

25. This is the argument in Gross, "Politische Polykratie 1936."

26. Schmitt, *Das Judentum in der Rechtswissenschaft*, 16. Hereafter cited in text.

27. Schmitt repeatedly concerned himself with Stahl (whom he often called Stahl-Jolson), usually for the sake of exposing his Jewish origins. See for example his letter to Ernst Jünger, 24 May 1935, in Kiesel, *Briefe 1930–1983*, 48: "Dear Herr Jünger, tomorrow (Saturday) I wanted to use a surprisingly free day to once more corner Joel Jolson in Wolfenbüttel."

28. Ibid., 29f.

29. Schmitt, *Das Judentum in der Rechtswissenschaft*, 30.

30. Ibid., 29 (note).

31. Published on 15 October 1936 by the Deutscher Reichsverlag, the 188-page catalogue contained no indication of an editor. We learn of the work's withdrawal from circulation from the foreword to the second edition. See

Göppinger, *Juristen jüdischer Abstammung*, 166. The catalogue is now very difficult to locate, but one copy is in the possession of the Wiener Library, Tel Aviv.

32. Schmitt, *Das Judentum in der Rechtswissenschaft*, 28.

33. Text here cited from Schmitt, "Die deutsche Rechtswissenschaft im Kampf gegen den jüdischen Geist," col. 1193 (italics are Schmitt's). The word "remarkable" (or "odd"—*merkwürdig*) is absent from the version of the text published in the conference proceedings (Schmitt, *Das Judentum in der Rechtswissenschaft*, 28); the use of italics is also different in the two versions.

34. Cf.: Léon Poliakov, *The Aryan Myth: A History of Racist and Nationalist Ideas in Europe*, trans. Edmund Howard (London: Chatto & Windus, 1974), 4.

35. Ibid.

36. Volkov, *Jüdisches Leben und Antisemitismus*, 146–65.

37. Schmitt, *Das Judentum in der Rechtswissenschaft*, 28.

38. Schmitt, "Die deutsche Rechtswissenschaft im Kampf gegen den jüdischen Geist," col. 1198.

39. Schmitt, *Das Judentum in der Rechtswissenschaft*, 28.

40. Ibid., 33.

41. Ibid., 14, 33. At the start of the conference: "Again and again, we must impress on both our memory and that of our students what the Führer has said about Jewish dialectics, in order to escape the great danger of ever-new masking and debased formulations [*Tarnungen und Zerredungen*]." At the end of the conference: "Again and again, I repeat the urgent request to read that passage [*Satz*] in Adolf Hitler's *Mein Kampf* about the Jewish Question, especially his exposition of 'Jewish dialectics.' Here we find the same thing stated, simply and exhaustively, in a manner understandable to every *Volksgenosse*, that has been presented by specialists at our conference in many lectures of the highest scholarly quality."

42. Ibid., 34. The text is slightly altered in the *Deutsche Juristen-Zeitung* version (col. 1198).

Chapter 5. The French Revolution and the Catholic Reaction

1. On modern German constitutional theory with a focus on Heller, Neumann, Kirchheimer, Max Adler, and Schmitt, cf. Ilse Staff, "Zur Rezeption der Ideen der Französischen Revolution von 1789 in der deutschen Staatslehre des 20. Jahrhunderts," in *Die Ideen von 1789 in der deutschen Rezeption*, ed. Forum für Philosophie Bad Homburg (Frankfurt a.M.: Suhrkamp, 1989), 223–58.

2. Cf. Carl Schmitt, *Die Geistesgeschichtliche Lage des heutigen Parlamentarismus* (Berlin: Duncker & Humblot, 6th ed. 1986 [=2nd ed. 1926]); Schmitt, *The Crisis of Parliamentary Democracy*, trans. Ellen Kennedy (Cambridge, Mass.: MIT Press, 1985).

3. Cf. Waldemar Gurian, *Die politischen und sozialen Ideen des französischen Katholizismus 1789/1914* (Mönchen-Gladbach: Volksvereins-Verlag, 1929); Isaiah

Berlin, "The Counter-Enlightenment," in Berlin, *Selected Writings*, vol. 3: *Against the Current: Essays in the History of Ideas*, ed. Henry Hardy (London: Hogarth, 1979), 1–24; Berlin, "Joseph de Maistre and the Origins of Fascism," in Berlin, *The Crooked Timber of Humanity: Chapters in the History of Ideas*, ed. Henry Hardy (London: John Murray, 1990), 91–175; Richard A. Lebrun, *Joseph de Maistre: An Intellectual Militant* (Kingston, Ont.: McGill-Queen's Univ. Press, 1988).

4. Schmitt, *Die Diktatur*, 130–53.

5. Carl Schmitt, *Politische Romantik* (Berlin: Duncker & Humblot, 1982), 42; Schmitt, *Political Romanticism*, trans. Guy Oakes (Cambridge, Mass.: MIT Press, 1986), 29.

6. Pierre Lasserre, *Le Romantisme Français: Essai sur la révolution dans les sentiments et dans les idées au XIXe siècle* (Paris: Hachette, 1907). Schmitt cites this book in *Politische Romantik*, 39; *Political Romanticism*, 25f, which contains a reference to Maurras' criticism of romanticism (Charles Maurras, *Romantisme et Révolution* [Paris: Nouvelle Librairie Nationale, 1922]).

7. See Julius Anthony, *T.S. Eliot, Anti-Semitism, and Literary Form* (Cambridge: Cambridge Univ. Press, 1996). On the broader context, see Louis Menand, "Eliot and the Jews," *New York Review of Books*, 6 June 1996, 34–41.

8. Characteristically Schmitt's debt was to the late romanticism of Adam Müller, not to the early Jena Romanticism that was so influential in the German and European literary context. Cf. Karl Heinz Bohrer, *Die Kritik der Romantik: Der Verdacht der Philosophie gegen die literarische Moderne* (Frankfurt a.M.: Suhrkamp, 1989), 284–311.

9. On modern literary decisionism, see Karl Heinz Bohrer, *Die Ästhetik des Schreckens: Die pessimistische Romantik und Ernst Jüngers Frühwerk* (Munich: Hanser, 1978). While focusing on Jünger, Bohrer places him in a tradition, which he examines closely, extending from Poe and Baudelaire to Walter Benjamin, Heidegger, and Carl Schmitt.

10. Viktor Klemperer, "Romantik und französische Romantik," in *Idealistische Neuphilologie, Festschrift für Karl Vossler*, ed. Viktor Klemperer and Eugen Lerch (Heidelberg: Winter, 1922), 10–32, 20. Only a few years before, in his *Nordlicht* book, Schmitt had glowingly praised a befriended author by indicating that "in its contents the work's roots lie in Romanticism" (Schmitt, *Theodor Däublers "Nordlicht,"* 17). Klemperer is unlikely to have known this work since Schmitt had it pulped a few years after its appearance. Cf. Schmitt, *Glossarium*, 171.

11. Schmitt discussed postrevolutionary France and the thinkers of the Catholic counterrevolution in the chapter "The Philosophy of State of the Counterrevolution (de Maistre, Bonald, Donoso Cortés)," in his *Politische Theologie* (67–84); *Political Theology*, 53–66. He also included this text in his post–World War II collection *Donoso Cortés in gesamteuropäischer Interpretation: Vier Aufsätze* (Cologne: Greven, 1950).

12. Cf. Karl Mannheim, *Konservatismus: Ein Beitrag zur Soziologie des Wissens*

(1927; repr., Frankfurt a.M.: Suhrkamp, 1984); Martin Greiffenhagen, *Das Dilemma des Konservatismus in Deutschland* (Munich: Piper, 1971).

13. Louis Gabriel Ambroise Vicomte de Bonald, *Oeuvres complètes*, 3 vol. (Paris: Migne, 1864), vol. 1, 338.

14. Joseph de Maistre, *Betrachtungen über Frankreich*, ed. and with an afterword by Günter Maschke (Vienna: Karolinger-Verlag, 1991), cited in Stephen Holmes, *Die Anatomie des Antiliberalismus* (Hamburg: Rotbuch-Verlag, 1995), 36.

15. Cited in Poliakov, *History of Anti-Semitism*, 3:217.

Chapter 6. The Counterrevolution in the Weimar Republic

1. Robert Spaemann has pointed to a line stretching from Bonald to Maurras in his important study *Der Ursprung der Soziologie aus dem Geist der Restauration: Studien über L.G.A. de Bonald* (Munich: Kösel-Verlag, 1959).

2. Joseph de Maistre, *Die spanische Inquisition* (Vienna: Karolinger, 1992), 11.

3. Ibid.

4. Ibid., 11–12.

5. See Jacob Katz, "A State within a State: The History of an Anti-Semitic Slogan," in Katz, *Zur Assimilation und Emanzipation der Juden: Ausgewählte Schriften* (Darmstadt: Wissenschaftliche Buchgesellschaft, 1982), 124–53. Katz (129) locates the first anti-Jewish use of the slogan in an anonymously published tractate by François Hell about the Jews in Alsace (*Observations d'un Alsacien sur l'affaire présente des Juifs d'Alsace* [Strasbourg, 1779]).

6. Schmitt, *Politische Theologie*, 74; *Political Theology*, 57. As early as 1935, Karl Löwith ("Der okkasionelle Dezisionismus von C. Schmitt," in Löwith, *Sämtliche Schriften*, vol. 8: *Heidegger—Denker in dürftiger Zeit, Zur Stellung der Philosophie im 20. Jahrhundert*, ed. Klaus Stichweh [Stuttgart: Metzler, 1960], 42), cited this phrase as revealing "what impressed [Schmitt] so strongly in Donoso Cortés." The merits of José Rafael Hernández's book *Donoso Cortés und Carl Schmitt: Eine Untersuchung über die staats- und rechtsphilosophische Bedeutung von Donoso Cortés im Werk Carl Schmitts* (Paderborn: Schöningh, 1998) are diminished by a startling sympathy it appears to display with the views of Donoso Cortés and the perspective on the Jews of Schmitt.

7. Carl Schmitt, "Donoso Cortés in Berlin, 1849" (1927), in *Positionen und Begriffe*, 84–96, 91.

8. Schmitt, *Geistesgeschichtliche Lage*, 83; *Crisis of Parliamentary Democracy*, 70; *Römischer Katholizismus und politische Form*, 2nd ed. (1925; repr., Stuttgart: Klett-Cotta, 1984), 5; *Roman Catholicism and Political Form*, trans. and annotated by G. L. Ulmen (Westport, Conn.: Greenwood, 1996), 3.

9. Cf. Robert Lemm, *Die Spanische Inquisition: Geschichte und Legende* (Munich: Deutscher Taschenbuch-Verlag, 1996), 137; R. W. Dove, s.v. "Inquisition," in *Deutsches Staats-Wörterbuch*, vol. 5, ed. J. C. Bluntschli (Stuttgart: Expedition des Staats-Wörterbuchs, 1860), 326–41; G. Schnürer, "Inquisition," in *Staatslexikon:*

Unter Mitwirkung von Fachmännern herausgegeben im Auftrag der Görres-Gesellschaft zur Pflege der Wissenschaft im katholischen Deutschland, ed. Julius Bachem (Freiburg: Herder, 1909), 2:1390–98; Henry Kamen, "Inquisition," in *Theologische Realenzyklopädie,* ed. Gerhard Müller (Berlin: Walter de Gruyter, 1987), 16:189–96; Jocelyn Nigel, *The Spanish Kingdoms, 1250–1516,* 2 vols. (Oxford: Clarendon, 1978).

10. Poliakov, ed., *History of Anti-Semitism,* vol. 2, ch. 9, "The Impasse—Marranism," 170–82; ch. 10, "The Inquisition," 183–203; appendix b, "The Moors and Their Expulsion," 328–57.

11. Yosef Hayim Yerushalmi, *Ein Feld in Anatot: Versuch über jüdische Geschichte* (Berlin: Wagenbach, 1993), 54.

12. Kamen, "Inquisition," 189; more exhaustively: Henry Kamen, *The Spanish Inquisition* (London: Weidenfeld & Nicolson, 1965), 137–61.

13. Kamen, "Inquisition," 194.

14. On the Spanish cult of "blood purity," see David Nirenberg, "Les juifs, la violence et le sacré," *Annales: Histoire, Sciences Sociales* 50 (1995): 109–31.

15. Poliakov, ed., *History of Anti-Semitism,* 2:226.

16. Kamen, "Inquisition," 193.

17. Schnürer, "Inquisition," 1396.

18. Kamen, "Inquisition," 194.

19. Heidegger conveyed as much to Otto Pöggeler by word of mouth. See Otto Pöggeler, "Von Nietzsche zu Hitler? Heideggers politische Optionen," in *Annäherungen an Martin Heidegger: Festschrift für Hugo Ott zum 65. Geburtstag,* ed. Hermann Schäfer (Frankfurt a.M.: Campus Verlag, 1996), 94.

20. Schmitt, *Römischer Katholizismus und politische Form,* 5; *Roman Catholicism and Political Form,* 3.

21. Jacob Taubes, *Ad Carl Schmitt,* 15. Taubes offers the following information: "In fact, in a stormy conversation held in Plettenberg in 1980, Carl Schmitt told me that whoever failed to see that, in face of all the effusions of Jesuitical piety, the 'Grand Inquisitor' simply was right, neither grasped the meaning of the church nor what Dostoyevsky 'actually conveyed, forced by the power of the problem' and against his own sensibility." Eichhorn, *Es wird regiert!* (82–86) points to this passage, backing up Taubes in the process: "Much suggests . . . that Carl Schmitt needs to be seen less as a believing Christian than as a Grand Inquisitor" (83). But in contrast to what is argued in these pages, Eichhorn sees in Schmitt a "Grand Inquisitor as restrainer [*Aufhalter*]," like his Dostoyevskian model "not without humanity." This approach appears to reflect fidelity to Schmitt's late self-stylization.

22. Schmitt, *Politische Theologie,* 73; *Political Theology,* 57.

23. Ibid., 72; ibid., 56. Here, Schmitt is in debt to Helmuth Plessner, who had already tied his political anthropology to the figure of the Grand Inquisitor in *Grenzen der Gemeinschaft: Eine Kritik des sozialen Radikalismus* (Bonn: Cohen, 1924); Plessner's book ends with a paean to the conversation Dostoyevsky presents between Christ and that figure: "The law of this world, remaining

subject to the gravity of the public sphere even when the savior appears in its midst, demands the inquisitor's paradoxical self-negation. For the sake of order, he must render existence impossible for the heart of order; it is a terrible thing to contemplate that because he believes in Christ, in He who has appeared, he is determined to sacrifice Christ, He who is appearing. For there is no greater danger for God's rule on earth than an uprising of the heart for His sake." See Helmuth Plessner, *Gesammelte Schriften*, vol. 5, ed. Günter Dux (Frankfurt a.M.: Suhrkamp, 1981), 126ff.

24. Schmitt, *Politische Theologie*, 83; *Political Theology*, 66.

25. Schmitt, *Glossarium*, 243.

26. See for example Meier, *Die Lehre Carl Schmitts*.

27. See Scholder, *Die Kirchen und das Dritte Reich*, 1:3ff.

28. See Karl-Egon Lönne, "Carl Schmitt und der Katholizismus der Weimarer Republik," in Wacker, *Die eigentlich katholische Verschärfung*, 11–35. Lönne locates Schmitt on the far right of Weimar Catholicism. He argues that he exercised no decisive influence on the latter but simply strengthened already-present authoritarian, antiparliamentary and antidemocratic leanings present within it. Cf. more generally, Karl-Egon Lönne, *Politischer Katholizismus im 19. und 20 Jahrhundert* (Frankfurt a.M.: Suhrkamp, 1986).

29. Ernst-Wolfgang Böckenförde, "Der Zusammenbruch der Monarchie und die Entstehung der Weimarer Republik," in *Die Weimarer Republik, 1918–1933: Politik, Wirtschaft, Gesellschaft*, ed. Karl Dietrich Bracher, Manfred Funke, and Hans-Adolf Jacobsen (Düsseldorf: Droste, 1987), 42. For a contrary perspective, see Peter C. Caldwell, "Constitutional Theory in the Weimar Republic: Positivists, Anti-positivists, and the Democratic Welfare State" (PhD diss., Cornell University, 1993), 84ff.

30. *Grundsätze der Deutschnationalen Volkspartei vom Jahre 1920*, Article 11. Cited from Helmut Berding, *Moderner Antisemitismus in Deutschland* (Frankfurt a.M.: Suhrkamp, 1988), 213.

31. See Pierre Sorlin, "Katholizismus nach 1848, Die Entwicklung in Frankreich nach 1850," in *Kirche und Synagoge: Handbuch zur Geschichte von Christen und Juden: Darstellung mit Quellen*, ed. Karl Heinrich Rengstorf and Siegfried von Kortzfleisch (Munich: Deutscher Taschenbuch, 1988), 421–52, here 422.

32. Typical in this respect is the following remark (in *Das neue Reich* 32 [1920]: 512) about the constitution by the Center Party delegate Martin Spahn (1875–1945): "Its author, the Berlin Jew Preuss, lives and moves exclusively in the conceptual corridors of West-enthused [*westlerisch*] constitutionalism." Cited from Rudolf Lill, "Die deutschen Katholiken und die Juden in der Zeit von 1850 bis zur Machtübernahme Hitlers," in Rengstorf and von Kortzfleisch, *Kirche und Synagoge*, 370–420, here 401.

33. Cf. Eberhard Kolb, "Vom Kaiserreich zur Republik: Politische Neuordnung im Zeichen von militärischer Niederlage und Staatssumsturz," in *Ploetz, Weimarer Republik: Eine Nation im Umbruch*, ed. Gerhard Schulz (Freiburg: Ploetz, 1987), 18–31, here 21.

34. See especially Hans Kelsen, *Vom Wesen und Wert der Demokratie*, 2nd ed. (Tübingen: Mohr, 1929).

35. On Schmitt's attitude toward the Center Party see Koenen, *Der Fall Carl Schmitt*, 45ff.

36. Ulrich Bröckling has convincingly argued as much in his *Katholische Intellektuelle in der Weimarer Republik: Zeitkritik und Gesellschaftstheorie bei Walter Dirks, Romano Guardini, Carl Schmitt, Ernst Michel und Heinrich Mertens* (Munich: Fink, 1993); see esp. 36.

37. See also remarks in ch. 1, 20, and notes 43 and 44. On Schmitt's battle against the morality and practical reason associated with modernism, see Jürgen Habermas, "Kants Idee des ewigen Friedens—aus dem historischen Abstand von 200 Jahren," *Kritische Justiz* 2 (1995): 293–319, here 309.

Chapter 7. Catholic Atheism

1. Carl Schmitt, *Politische Theologie*, 75; *Political Theology*, 55.

2. Clemens Lang [Günther Krauss], "Die Ideologie des Widerstandes: Bemerkungen zu Carl Schmitts 'Begriff des Politischen,'" *Deutsches Volkstum* 14 (1932): 963.

3. Hermann Greive, *Geschichte des modernen Antisemitismus in Deutschland*, 2nd ed. (Darmstadt: Wissenschaftliche Buchgesellschaft, 1988), 53.

4. Julien Benda, *The Treason of the Intellectuals*, trans. Richard Aldington (1st French ed. 1927; 1st American ed. 1928; reprint, New York: Norton, 1969).

5. See René Rémond, *Les droites en France* (Paris: Aubier Montaigne, 1982), 410.

6. Gurian was followed up on by the West German philosopher Robert Spaemann, whose work on de Bonald, *Der Ursprung der Soziologie aus dem Geist der Restauration*, extends to the Action Française. On Gurian see Heinz Hürten, *Waldemar Gurian: Ein Zeuge der Krise unserer Welt in der ersten Hälfte des 20. Jahrhunderts* (Mainz: Matthias-Grünewald-Verlag, 1972); Hannah Arendt, "Waldemar Gurian 1903–1954," in *Menschen in finsteren Zeiten*, ed. Ursula Ludz, 2nd ed. (Munich: Piper, 1989), 310–23; Breuning, *Die Vision des Reiches*, 73, 162–64, 247, 319, 345, 362, 366–69, 372, 377; Wacker, *Die eigentlich katholische Verschärfung*, 17, 27, 68f., 71, 74, 82, 87, 128f., 131, 139, 276f., 281; Barbara Nichtweiss, *Erik Peterson: Neue Sicht auf Leben und Werk* (Freiburg: Herder, 1992), 723ff. See also Koenen, *Der Fall Carl Schmitt*, 520; Manfred Dahlheimer, *Carl Schmitt und der deutsche Katholizismus* (Paderborn: Schoningh, 1998), 526–36.

7. Hürten, *Waldemar Gurian*, 3.

8. Modern Russian and French political history were two of Gurian's points of interest; he approached both from a distinctly Catholic perspective. See Waldemar Gurian, *Der Bolschewismus, Einführung in Geschichte und Lehre* (Freiburg: Herder, 1931); Gurian, *Der Integrale Nationalismus in Frankreich* (Frankfurt a.M.: Klostermann, 1931).

9. At the time Schmitt was discussing Bernanos with various colleagues; in the Schmitt archives, one eight-page letter, from Ludwig Oppenheimer, is concerned solely with that author (RW 265-196, letter no. 39). That Schmitt had extensive discussions with Hermann Heller about Bernanos is strongly suggested by a passage in one letter from the German-Jewish jurist: "Dear Herr Schmitt! Today, on Easter Monday, I can finally take a pause and thank you warmly for the happy days spent in your house. I cannot express how joyful and productive this time was for me. Alongside having gotten to know an amiable man, I've left with the conviction and satisfaction that you have very much to say to the Germany that is arriving—the Germany still lying under a thin cover, taut to the point of tearing. . . . I take your having just sent me Bernanos as an answer to the questions in my last letter. Religiously and aesthetically it is the greatest book of our age. I now thoroughly agree with everything you said to your wife then about the nature of the holy. In addition the heading 'On the Holy' is justified; for we who live in the present cannot imagine another sort of holiness than that of Bernanos." RW 265-339; letter no. 1, Hermann Heller to Carl Schmitt, Berlin-Schlachtensee, 17 April 1927.

10. Waldemar Gurian, *Die politischen und sozialen Ideen des französischen Katholizismus, 1789–1914* (Mönchen-Gladbach: Volksvereins-Verlag, 1929).

11. Ibid., viii. For the period between 12 June 1924 and 30 April 1932 Gurian's archives contain twenty-nine letters from Schmitt (Hürten, *Waldemar Gurian,* 12). The Schmitt archives contain four letters from Gurian (RW 265-460), all dated between 1927 and 1929.

12. Gurian to Schmitt, Godesberg, 7 June 1929 (RW 265-460; letter no. 58): "Dear esteemed Herr Professor, after much reflection I have decided to write this letter. It is meant as a direct statement that I very much regret the incident of December 1927. / If you wish you can forward my letter to Herr Prof. Eschweiler, who is the only one to know of this incident on account of his presence. / Yours most faithfully / Waldemar Gurian." A transcript of this letter of apology is located in the Schmitt archives; Schmitt appears to have sent the letter to at least five individuals (three copies being mailed in 1970): Tommissen (22 Nov. 1970), Ernst-Wolfgang Böckenförde (27 Nov. 1970), George Schwab (12 Dec. 1970), Hans-Dietrich Sander, and Walter Petwaidic. It seems that at this late date Schmitt wished to show his friends and acquaintances that Gurian's eventual turn against him had nothing to do with his Nazism but rather reflected conflicts already emerging in the Weimar period.

13. Paul Müller [Waldemar Gurian], "Entscheidung und Ordnung: Zu den Schriften von Carl Schmitt," *Schweizerische Rundschau: Monatsschrift für Geistesleben und Kultur* 34 (1939): 566–76.

14. See [Waldemar Gurian and Otto Michael Knap,] *Deutsche Briefe 1934–1938: Ein Blatt der katholischen Emigration,* ed. Heinz Hurten, 2 vols. (Mainz: Matthias-Grünewald-Verlag, 1969).

15. Müller [Gurian], "Entscheidung und Ordnung," 566–76, 567–68.

16. See Alfons Söllner, "'Kronjurist des Dritten Reiches': Das Bild Carl Schmitts in den Schriften der Emigranten," *Jahrbuch für Antisemitismusforschung* 1 (1992): 191–216; Gross, "Politische Polykratie 1936."

17. RW 265-262 (letter no. 16, typewritten transcript), Oberheid to Schmitt (31 Oct. 1964). Repeatedly, Gurian's devastating critique of Hugo Ball's *Folgen der Reformation* was referred to as responsible for that author's break with Schmitt. In this regard Bernd Wacker, "Die Zweideutigkeit der katholischen Verschärfung—Carl Schmitt und Hugo Ball," in *Die eigentlich katholische Verschärfung* (123–45, here 131), has observed that "even if [Schmitt] had no direct influence on the contents and placement of his student Gurian's review of *Folgen der Reformation* . . . Gurian was expressing Schmitt's innermost thoughts." Whether Gurian published his review with Schmitt's blessings in any case seems unimportant, and assigning sole "guilt" to Gurian for Ball's break with his teacher seems extremely dubious.

18. On Schmitt's relation with Erik Peterson, see Nichtweiss, *Erik Peterson*, 727–62. For criticism of Nichtweiss's lack of distance from Peterson's ideas, see Gregor Ahn, "Buchbesprechung," *Zeitschrift für Religions- und Geistesgeschichte* 48 (1996): 90–93.

19. Letter from Berlin, 18 March 1929, published in Barbara Nichtweiss, "'Die Zeit ist aus den Fugen': Auszüge aus den Briefen von Paul Adams an Erik Peterson," in Wacker, *Die eigentlich katholische Verschärfung*, 65–87, 82.

20. Waldemar Gurian, "Das Judentum und die Aufklärung des 19. Jahrhunderts," *Erfüllung* 1 (1934/35): 26–34; and after World War II: Waldemar Gurian, "Antisemitism in Modern Germany," in *Essays on Antisemitism*, 2nd. ed., ed. Koppel Shub Pinson (New York: Conference on Jewish Relations, 1946), 218–65.

21. Gurian to Peterson, September 1926, cited from Nichtweiss, *Erik Peterson*, 728–29.

22. Ibid., 728–29.

23. Müller [Gurian], "Entscheidung und Ordnung," 566–76, 567–68.

24. Ibid., 575.

25. Ibid.

26. For a detailed description of the Catholic critique of Schmitt, see Karl-Egon Lönne, "Carl Schmitt und der Katholizismus der Weimarer Republik," in Wacker, *Die eigentlich katholische Verschärfung*, 11–35, 27–35.

27. Heinrich Getzney, "Katholizismus des Seins oder Katholizismus des Geltenwollens," *Schildgenossen* 7 (1927): 341–46.

28. *Je suis catholique, mais je suis athéiste.* Cited from Lönne, *Carl Schmitt und der Katholizismus der Weimarer Republik*, 29.

29. François Georges Dreyfus, "Antisemitismus in der Dritten Französischen Republik," in *Die Juden als Minderheit in der Geschichte*, ed. Bernd Martin and Ernst Schulin (Munich: Deutscher Taschenbuch, 1981), 231–48; Villinger, *Carl Schmitts Kulturkritik der Moderne*, 119.

30. Schmitt, *Politische Theologie*, 20; *Political Theology*, 13.

31. Schmitt, *Geistesgeschichtliche Lage*, 83; *Crisis of Parliamentary Democracy*, 70.

32. Schmitt, *Politische Theologie*, 20; *Political Theology*, 13.

33. Ibid., 72; ibid., 55f.

34. Ibid., 75; ibid., 59.

35. For an illuminating study of the meaning of the Great War for German intellectuals see Losurdo, *Heidegger and the Ideology of War.*

36. Carl Schmitt, *Politische Theologie*, 44; *Political Theology*, 33. In the 1922 edition, Schmitt mistakenly refers to chapter 19 of Hobbes's *Leviathan*, "Of the Several Kinds of Commonwealth by Institution, and of Succession to the Sovereign Power," instead of chapter 26, "Of Civil Laws."

37. Joseph de Maistre, *Les Soirées de Saint-Pétersbourg* (Paris: Maisnie, 1980), 1:34.

38. Schmitt, *Politische Theologie*, 43; *Political Theology*, 32.

39. Ibid., 44; ibid., 33.

40. Ibid., 43; ibid., 32.

41. Schmitt, *Geistesgeschichtliche Lage*, 77–90; *Crisis of Parliamentary Democracy*, 65–76; *Positionen und Begriffe*, 11–21.

42. Schmitt, *Politische Theologie*, 20; *Political Theology*, 13. Hereafter cited in text.

43. Schmitt, *Geistesgeschichtliche Lage*, 52f.; *Crisis of Parliamentary Democracy*, 42.

44. Schmitt, *Politische Theologie*, 71; *Political Theology*, 55.

45. Since the Enlightenment, Bodin's reputation has been based on his *Demonomanie des Sorciers* (1580), an introduction to legal procedure in the trials of witches that was based on the German *Hexenhammer* (1487). In his *Six livres de la République*, he presented a concept of unlimited sovereignty. But in contrast to Machiavelli or Hobbes, he stipulated that the monarch was subject to the laws of religion, nature, and nations—without, to be sure, naming the authority that could control this. Cf. Roman Schnur, *Die französischen Juristen im konfessionellen Bürgerkrieg des 16. Jahrhunderts* (Berlin: Duncker & Humblot, 1962).

46. Hermann Josef Pottmeyer, *Unfehlbarkeit und Souveränität: Die päpstliche Unfehlbarkeit im System der ultramontanen Ekklesiologie des 19. Jahrhunderts* (Mainz: Matthias-Grünewald-Verlag, 1975), 1.

47. Ibid., 78.

48. Staff, "Zur Rezeption der Ideen der Französischen Revolution," 223.

49. Schmitt, *Politische Theologie*, 65; *Political Theology*, 51.

50. Cf. Carl Schmitt, *Politische Theologie II: Die Legende von der Erledigung jeder politischen Theologie*, 2nd ed. (Berlin: Duncker & Humblot, 1984), 113. On Schmitt's concept of representation see his *Verfassungslehre*, 216–20, and the following detailed critiques: Margit Kraft-Fuchs, "Prinzipielle Bemerkungen zu Carl Schmitts Verfassungslehre," *Zeitschrift für öffentliches Recht* 9 (1930): 511–41; Eric Voegelin, "Die Verfassungslehre von Carl Schmitt: Versuch einer konstruktiven

Analyse ihrer staatstheoretischen Prinzipien," *Zeitschrift für öffentliches Recht* 11 (1931): 89–109; and Hofmann, *Legitimität gegen Legalität*, 151f.

51. Schmitt, *Römischer Katholizismus und politische Form*, 35; *Roman Catholicism and Political Form*, 25.

52. Herbert Krüger, *Allgemeine Staatslehre* (Stuttgart: Kohlhammer, 1966), 235, taking up Max Weber's definition in *Wirtschaft und Gesellschaft*, 2nd ed. (Tübingen: Mohr, 1925), 1:171.

53. Schmitt, *Verfassungslehre*, 209.

54. Ibid., 210.

55. Schmitt, *Römischer Katholizismus und politische Form*, 29; *Roman Catholicism and Political Form*, 21.

56. Ibid., 11; ibid., 7.

57. Schmitt, *Geistesgeschichtliche Lage*, 53; *Crisis of Parliamentary Democracy*, 42.

58. Spaemann, *Der Ursprung der Soziologie aus dem Geist der Restauration*, 184.

59. In a letter written in 1815, the same period as the writing of *Du Pape* (Lyon: Rusand, 1819), de Maistre explained to the Viennese Nuntius Severoli that he approached papal infallibility as a technical device meant to maintain peace in the realm. See Joseph de Maistre, *Oeuvres complètes* (Lyon: E. Vitte, 1884–1893), 13:185; the letter is referred to by Pottmeyer, *Unfehlbarkeit und Souveränität*, 62.

60. Ibid., 29.

61. De Maistre, *Du Pape*, xii.

62. See Vincent Duclert, *Die Dreyfus-Affäre: Militärwahn, Republikfeindschaft, Judenhass* (Berlin: Wagenbach, 1994); Günther Fuchs and Eckhardt Fuchs, *"J'accuse!": Zur Affäre Dreyfus* (Mainz: Decaton Verlag, 1994); Eric Cahm, *L'affaire Dreyfus: Histoire, politique et société* (Paris: Le Livre de Poche, 1994). In most detail: Jean-Denis Bredin, *L'affaire* (Paris: Julliard, 1993); Norman Kleeblatt, ed., *The Dreyfus Affair: Art, Truth, and Justice* (Berkeley: Univ. of California Press, 1987) (catalog of 1987 exhibition, Jewish Museum of New York).

63. Edouard Drumont, *La France juive* (Paris: Flammarion, 1943), 1:322.

64. In Germany, Ernst Robert Curtius recognized Barrès's historical importance several years before the Great War; cf. Curtius, *Maurice Barrès und die geistigen Grundlagen des französischen Nationalismus* (Bonn: Cohen, 1921), 128. On Barrès see Jean-Marie Domenach, *Barrès par lui-meme* (Paris: Seuil, 1954); Robert Soucy, *Fascism in France: The Case of Maurice Barrès* (Berkeley: Univ. of California Press, 1972); Zeev Sternhell, *Maurice Barrès et le nationalisme français*, preface by Raoul Girardet (Paris: Colin, 1972); Philip Ouston, *The Imagination of Maurice Barrès* (Toronto: Univ. of Toronto Press, 1974). In 1921 the Dada movement in Paris planned a "trial" of Barrès; this led to serious conflicts within the movement. See Wolfram Kiepe, ed., *Dada gegen Dada: Die Affaire Barrès* (Hamburg: Nautilus, 1996). On integralism see Eduard Hegel, "Integralismus," in *Staatslexikon: Recht, Wirtschaft, Gesellschaft*, 7th ed., vol. 3, ed. Görres-Gesellschaft (Freiburg: Herder, 1987); compare Otto B. Roegele, "Integralismus," ibid., 4th ed. (1959).

Philologically the concept takes in a series of theological and historical negations; within theology, it addresses the state of humankind before the Fall.

65. Ernst Nolte, *Der Faschismus in seiner Epoche* (Munich: Piper, 1963), 103.

66. Ibid., 193.

67. Zeev Sternhell, *Maurice Barrès et le nationalisme français;* Sternhell, *La droite révolutionnaire, 1885–1914: Les origines françaises du fascisme* (Paris: Seuil, 1978); Sternhell, *Ni droite, ni gauche: L'idéologie fasciste en France* (Brussels: Complexe, 1987). The 1987 book has sparked the most intense controversy.

68. Ernst Nolte, *Der Faschismus in seiner Epoche,* 344. In this context, I cannot discuss Nolte's general phenomenological thesis regarding the origins of Nazism, including the later apologetic location of fascism in the horizon of a European civil war. For a detailed bibliography of work concerned with Nolte's discussion of the Action Française, see Winfried Becker, "Charles Marie Photius Maurras," in *Biographisch-Bibliographisches Kirchenlexikon,* vol. 5, ed. Traugott Bautz and Friedrich Wilhelm Bautz (Herzberg: Traugott Bautz, 1993), 1063–71.

69. See Victor Nguyen, *Aux Origines de l'Action française: Intelligence et politique vers du XXe siècle* (Paris: Fayard, 1991); critical of this book and with an extensive bibliography on Maurras: Christophe Prochasson, "Sur le cas Maurras: Biographie et Histoire des idées politiques (note critique)," *Annales: Histoire, Sciences Sociales* 50 (1995): 579–87; Michel Sutton, *Charles Maurras et les catholiques français, 1890–1914: Nationalisme et positivisme* (Paris: Beauchesne, 1994).

70. Above all Richard Faber has focused on Schmitt's relationship with the Action Française. See Faber, *Roma Aeterna: Zur Kritik der "Konservativen Revolution"* (Würzburg: Königshausen & Neumann, 1981); Faber, "Carl Schmitt, der Römer," in Wacker, *Die eigentlich katholische Verschärfung,* 257–78. On Schmitt's relationship with Italian Fascism, see Ilse Staff, *Staatsdenken im Italien des 20. Jahrhunderts: ein Beitrag zur Carl Schmitt-Rezeption* (Baden-Baden: Nomos, 1991), and Wolfgang Schieder, "Carl Schmitt und Italien," *Vierteljahrshefte für Zeitgeschichte* 37 (1989): 1–22.

71. The following observations rely heavily on Ernst Nolte, *Der Faschismus in seiner Epoche,* 165–73.

72. Cf. Gurian, *Der Integrale Nationalismus in Frankreich,* 44.

73. Sternhell, *La droite révolutionnaire,* 214.

74. Cited from C. Capitan Peter, *Charles Maurras et l'idéologie d'Action française: Etude soiologique d'une pensée de droite* (Paris: Seuil, 1972), 75. Importantly, in fin-de-siècle France antisemitism did not play an important role for the radical right only. Rather, it was an essential element of both revolutionary and antirevolutionary ideologues opposed to the spirit of liberalism, from syndicalists and followers of Sorel and Berth to the extreme left around Hervé and Lagardelle. See the chapter "L'antisémitisme de gauche" (which also discusses right-wing antisemites) in Sternhell, *La droite révolutionnaire,* 177–214.

75. Schmitt, *Der Nomos der Erde,* 129–31.

76. Schmitt, *Der Begriff des Politischen*, 55; *The Concept of the Political*, 54. Heinrich Forsthoff used this idea for his theology in *Das Ende der humanistischen Illusion* (Berlin: Furche-Verlag, 1933).

77. See, for example, "Die Literatur der Staats-Arcana," in Schmitt, *Die Diktatur*, 16–19; *Positionen und Begriffe*, 51f. and 314f.

78. See George L. Mosse, *Toward the Final Solution: A History of European Racism*, 2nd ed. (Madison: Univ. of Wisconsin Press, 1985), 117ff.; extensively: Norman Cohn, *Warrant for Genocide* (New York: Harper & Row, 1967).

79. See Mosse, *Toward the Final Solution*, 117.

80. See Léon Poliakov, *Aryan Myth*. The *Protocols* had been published in German translation in Berlin by an antisemitic press under the title *Die Geheimnisse der Weisen von Zion* [The Secrets of the Elders of Zion] and had then been reprinted a number of times. In 1923 Alfred Rosenberg (influential Nazi racial "philosopher" and author of *The Myth of the Twentieth Century* [1930]) had published it with his own commentaries, explaining that what mattered was not its authenticity but "inner truth." See Friedrich Battenberg, *Das Europäische Zeitalter der Juden: Zur Entwicklung einer Minderheit in der nichtjüdischen Umwelt Europas* (Darmstadt: Wissenschaftliche Buchgesellschaft, 1990), 2:236. See also Hans Sarkowicz, "Die Protokolle der Weisen von Zion," in *Gefälscht! Betrug in Politik, Literatur, Wissenschaft, Kunst und Musik*, ed. Kurt Corino (Frankfurt a.M.: Eichborn, 1990); Will Eisner, *The Plot: The Secret Story of The Protocols of the Elders of Zion*, introduction by Umberto Eco (New York: Norton, 2005) (comic strip with pedagogic intent).

81. See Jacob Rogozinski's extraordinary essay "Hell on Earth: Hannah Arendt in the Face of Hitler," *Philosophy Today* 37 (1993): 257–74, here 262.

82. Schmitt, *Positionen und Begriffe*, 333.

83. Reinhart Koselleck, *Kritik und Krise: Eine Studie zur Pathogenese der bürgerlichen Welt*, 6th edition (Frankfurt a.M.: Suhrkamp, 1989); *Critique and Crisis: Enlightenment and the Pathogenesis of Modern Society* (Cambridge, Mass.: MIT Press, 1988). Interestingly, Koselleck appears to have taken the phrase from his teacher Schmitt, who uses it in the context of Bruno Bauer (see part 3).

84. See chap. 4, "Judaism in Legal Studies."

85. Sigmund Freud, *Moses and Monotheism*, trans. Katherine Jones (New York: Vintage, 1967), 133–36.

86. On this "New Jurisprudence" see Dieter Grimm, *Recht und Staat der bürgerlichen Gesellschaft* (Frankfurt a.M.: Suhrkamp, 1987), 347–72.

87. Schmitt, "Der Führer schützt das Recht," in Schmitt, *Positionen und Begriffe*, 227–32.

88. This understanding of Judaism has of course had many modern philosophical-theoretical ramifications; it has for instance been a basis for Emmanuel Levinas's effort to emend Husserlian and Heideggerian phenomenology.

89. Schmitt, "Die Formung des französischen Geistes durch den Legisten," *Deutschland-Frankreich, Vierteljahresschrift des deutschen Instituts Paris* 1/2 (1942): 1–30, 4.

90. Ibid., 24.

91. Carl Schmitt in a "conversation with Eduard Spranger" taking place in summer 1945, in Schmitt, *Ex Captivitate Salus*, 11.

Chapter 8. Political Theology as a Festschrift for Max Weber

1. Carl Schmitt, "Die Soziologie des Souveränitätsbegriff und politische Theologie," in *Hauptprobleme der Soziologie: Erinnerungsgabe für Max Weber*, ed. Melchior Palyi (Munich: Duncker & Humblot, 1923), 2:3–35.

2. Schmitt, *Politische Theologie*, 19. Focused on Erich Kaufmann, the paragraph containing this phrase was removed from the book's 1934 edition.

3. Karl Löwith already pointed to the common elements and differences between Weber and Schmitt in 1938. In regards to Schmitt, his concluding judgment is devastating: "Weber's historical 'relativism' was born by a firm ethos, not subject to negotiation; Schmitt's dictatorial decisionism has its explanation in what he himself revealed as 'occasionalism' in regards to Adam Müller— striking a bargain as the opportunity arises. Part of the tragedy of German political life is that a perceptive man like Weber could never bring himself to act during the crisis of Bismarck's founding, while a talented eager beaver like Schmitt could win an influence on the Third Reich's political thinking and legislation that can hardly be overestimated." Karl Löwith, "Max Weber und seine Nachfolger" (1939–40), in Löwith, *Sämtliche Schriften: Hegel und die Aufhebung der Philosophie im 19. Jahrhundert—Max Weber*, 5th ed. (Stuttgart: Metzler, 1988), 408–18, here 418. For extensive—if broadly uncritical—discussions of Weber and Schmitt, see Ulmen, *Politischer Mehrwert*; Gary L. Ulmen, "Politische Theologie und politische Ökonomie—Über Carl Schmitt und Max Weber," in Quaritsch, *Complexio Oppositorum*, 341–65; Reinhard Mehring, "Politische Ethik in Max Webers 'Politik als Beruf' und Carl Schmitts 'Der Begriff des Politischen,'" *Politische Vierteljahresschrift* 3 (1990): 608–26; Fritz Loos, "Exkurs: Max Weber und Carl Schmitt," in Loos, *Zur Wert- und Rechtslehre Max Webers* (Tübingen: Mohr, 1970), 87–92.

4. Schmitt, *Politische Theologie*, 11; *Political Theology*, 5 (italics mine). See Wolfgang J. Mommsen, *Max Weber und die deutsche Politik 1890–1920*, 2nd ed. (Tübingen: Mohr, 1974), 380, n.3.

5. Max Weber, *Wirtschaft und Gesellschaft: Grundriss der Verstehenden Soziologie* (1922), 5th ed. (Tübingen: Mohr, 1980), 166. Weber is here borrowing from a remark made by Bismarck to the liberal opposition in parliament during the constitutional crisis: English circumstances, he indicated, did not prevail in Prussia. See Wolfgang J. Mommsen, *Das Ringen um den nationalen Staat: Die Gründung und der innere Ausbau des Deutschen Reiches unter Otto von Bismarck 1850–1890* (Berlin: Propyläen, 1993), 130.

6. Schmitt, *Politische Theologie*, 8; preliminary remark to 2nd ed.: "This last epoch of German jurisprudence is characterized by not offering an answer, in the framework of constitutional law, to the decisive case—namely, an answer to

the Prussian constitutional conflict with Bismark, and as a result an answer to all further decisive cases." Later Schmitt would comment at length on the conflict in *Staatsgefüge und Zusammenbruch,* 10–36.

Bismarck resolved this question by invoking so-called *Lückentheorie* ("gap theory"). He disposed of the conflict politically by submitting an indemnity bill to the Prussian Landtag that retroactively approved the spent funds without the agreement of parliament. See Mommsen, *Das Ringen um den nationalen Staat,* 137. For a convincing description of the constitutional conflict and efforts to interpret it see Hans Boldt, "Verfassungskonflikt und Verfassungshistorie: Eine Auseinandersetzung mit Ernst-Rudolf Huber," in *Probleme des Konstitutionalismus im 19. Jahrhundert,* ed. Ernst-Wolfgang Böckenförde (Berlin: Duncker & Humblot, 1975), 75–102.

7. See Jacob Taubes, "Die Entstehung des jüdischen Pariavolkes: Ideologiekritische Noten zu Max Webers 'Gesammelte Aufsätze zur Religionskritik,' Bd. III, 'Das Antike Judentum,'" in *Max Weber: Gedächtnisschrift der Ludwig-Maximilians-Universität München zur 100. Wiederkehr seines Geburtstages 1964,* ed. Johannes Winckelmann (Berlin: Duncker & Humblot, 1966), 185–94.

8. See Giacomo Marramao, *Die Säkularisierung der westlichen Welt,* trans. Günter Memmert (Frankfurt a.M.: Insel Verlag, 1996), 19–53.

9. Ibid., 57–64; see Max Weber, *Die protestantischen Ethik und der Geist des Kapitalismus* (Tübingen: Mohr, 1976), 212.

10. Hans Liebeschütz, *Das Judentum im deutschen Geschichtsbild von Hegel bis Max Weber* (Tübingen: Mohr, 1967), 329.

11. Cf. Villinger, *Carl Schmitts Kulturkritik,* 131–42.

12. Schmitt, *Römischer Katholizismus und politische Form,* 20; *Roman Catholicism and Political Form,* 14f. Cf. Mehring, *Pathetisches Denken,* 62.

13. See Jeffrey Herf, *Reactionary Modernism: Technology, Culture, and Politics in Weimar and the Third Reich* (Cambridge: Cambridge Univ. Press, 1984).

14. Schmitt, *Römischer Katholizismus und politische Form,* 19; *Roman Catholicism and Political Form,* 13f.

15. Werner Sombart, *Die Juden und das Wirtschaftsleben* (Leipzig: Duncker & Humblot, 1911); see 242: "Rationalism is the basic characteristic of both Judaism and capitalism."

16. See in general: Gary A. Abraham, *Max Weber and The Jewish Question: A Study of the Social Outlook of His Sociology* (Urbana: Univ. of Illinois Press, 1992), here 180. See also Karl-Siegbert Rehberg, "Das Bild des Judentums in der frühen deutschen Soziologie: 'Fremdheit' und 'Rationalität' als Typusmerkmale bei Werner Sombart, Max Weber und Georg Simmel," in *Judentum, Antisemitismus und europäische Kultur,* ed. Hans Otto Horch (Tübingen: Francke, 1988), 151–86.

17. Max Weber, *Gesammelte Aufsätze zur Religionssoziologie* (Tübingen: Mohr, 1920), 1:15. For a strong criticism of Weber's stance, see Eugène Fleischmann, "Max Weber, die Juden und das Ressentiment," in *Max Webers Studie über das*

antike Judentum: Interpretation und Kritik, ed. Wolfgang Schluchter (Frankfurt a.M.: Suhrkamp, 1981), 263–86.

18. W. Sombart, *Die Juden und das Wirtschaftsleben*, 293.

19. Liebeschütz, *Das Judentum im deutschen Geschichtsbild von Hegel bis Max Weber*, 313; Abraham, *Max Weber and The Jewish Question*, 230.

20. See Wolfgang Schluchter, *Die Entwicklung des okzidentalen Rationalismus: Eine Analyse von Max Webers Gesellschaftsgeschichte* (Tübingen: Mohr, 1979), 8.

21. Shulamit Volkov, *Die Juden in Deutschland 1780–1918* (Munich: Oldenbourg, 1994), 114; Avraham Barkai, *Jüdische Minderheit und Industrialisierung: Demographie, Berufe und Einkommen der Juden in Westdeutschland 1850–1914* (Tübingen: Mohr, 1988).

22. Weber, *Gesammelte Aufsätze zur Religionssoziologie*, 11.

23. Carl Schmitt, *Politische Theologie*, 49ff.; *Political Theology*, 45.

24. See Norbert Bolz, *Auszug aus der entzauberten Welt: Philosophischer Extremismus zwischen den Weltkriegen* (Munich: Fink, 1989); Bolz, "Charisma und Souveränität," in Taubes, *Der Fürst dieser Welt*, 249–62.

25. Friedrich Gogarten, *Verhängnis und Hoffnung der Neuzeit: Die Säkularisierung als theologisches Problem* (Stuttgart: Friedrich Vorwerk Verlag, 1953), 138–41.

26. Schmitt, *Politische Theologie*, 21; *Political Theology*, 18.

27. See for example Hans Kelsen, *Der soziologische und der juristische Staatsbegriff: Kritische Untersuchung des Verhältnisses von Staat und Recht* (Tübingen: Mohr, 1922).

28. See Leo Strauss, "Anmerkungen zu Carl Schmitts Begriff des Politischen," in Meier, ed., *Carl Schmitt, Leo Strauss und der "Begriff des Politischen,"* 97–128, 102, 105.

Chapter 9. Jewish Emancipation or a "Christian State"

1. For general material informing the following discussion see Ernst-Ludwig Ehrlich, "Emanzipation und christlicher Staat," in *Christen und Juden: Ihr Gegenüber vom Apostelkonzil bis heute*, ed. Wolf-Dieter Marsch and Karl Thieme (Mainz: Matthias-Grünewald-Verlag, 1961), 147–81; Jacob Toury, *Die politischen Orientierungen der Juden in Deutschland: Von Jena bis Weimar* (Tübingen: Mohr, 1966); Michael Stolleis, *Geschichte des öffentlichen Rechts in Deutschland*, vol. 2, *Staatsrechtslehre und Verwaltungswissenschaft, 1800–1914* (Munich: C.H. Beck, 1992), 121–86; Hans Boldt, *Deutsche Staatslehre im Vormärz* (Düsseldorf: Droste, 1975); Hermann Lübbe, *Die Hegelsche Rechte* (Stuttgart: Frommann, 1962).

2. See Jacob Katz, "The Term 'Jewish Emancipation': Its Origin and Historical Impact," in Katz, *Zur Assimilation und Emanzipation der Juden*, 115; Katz, "Die Anfänge der Judenemanzipation," in ibid., 83; David Sorkin, "Emancipation and Assimilation: Two Concepts and Their Application to German-Jewish History," *Leo Baeck Institute Yearbook* 35 (1990): 18. The most extensive study of the Jews in the *Vormärz* period is Annegret H. Brammer,

Judenpolitik und Judengesetzgebung in Preussen 1812–1847 (Berlin: Schelzky & Jeep, 1987).

3. Wilhelm Traugott Krug, *Über das Verhältnis verschiedener Religionsparteien zum Staate und über die Emanzipation der Juden* (Leipzig: Brockhaus, 1828); Krug, *Die Politik der Christen und die Politik der Juden im mehr als tausendjährigen Kampfe* (Leipzig: Brockhaus, 1832).

4. Fischer, *Judentum, Staat und Heer*, 2.

5. Ibid., 30; Hans-Ulrich Wehler, *Deutsche Gesellschaftsgeschichte* (Munich: C.H. Beck, 1989), 1:408.

6. Amos Funkenstein, *Jüdische Geschichte und ihre Deutungen* (Frankfurt a.M.: Jüdischer Verlag, 1995), 154.

7. Manfred Botzenhart, *Reform, Restauration, Krise: Deutschland 1789–1847* (Frankfurt a.M.: Suhrkamp, 1985), 58.

8. Fischer, *Judentum, Staat und Heer*, 156.

9. See Ernst Rudolf Huber, *Deutsche Verfassungsgeschichte seit 1789*, vol. 2, *Der Kampf um Einheit und Freiheit 1830 bis 1850* (Stuttgart: Kohlhammer, 1960), 482–483.

10. Thomas Nipperdey, *Deutsche Geschichte 1800–1866: Bürgerwelt und starker Staat* (Munich: C.H. Beck, 1983), 250. On the idea of a "Christian state," see the article "Christentum," in Brunner et al., *Geschichtliche Grundbegriffe*, 1:801–07. On Friedrich Wilhelm IV, see Dirk Blasius, *Friedrich Wilhelm IV., 1795–1861: Psychopathologie und Geschichte* (Göttingen: Vandenhoeck & Ruprecht, 1992).

11. Ibid., 158–66.

12. The text is included in Gabriel Riesser, *Gabriel Riessers Gesammelte Schriften* (Frankfurt a.M.: Verlag der Riesser-Stiftung, 1867), 416–506.

13. In this respect the author thanks Manfred Jehle, Berlin, for access to his unpublished "Edition zweier Enqueten preussischer Verwaltungsbehörden von 1842 und 1843" (1997).

14. Ibid., 2.

15. Fischer, *Judentum, Staat und Heer*, 205. Written shortly after the revolution, Karl Hermann Scheidler's long article on "Judenemancipation" in the *Allgemeine Encyklopädie der Wissenschaften und Künste in alphabetischer Folge von genannten Schriftstellern bearbeitet und herausgegeben von Ersch und Gruber* (Leipzig: Brockhaus, 1850), 253–315, clearly expresses emancipatory ideals.

16. See Eleonore Sterling, *Er ist wie du: Aus der Frühgeschichte des Antisemitismus in Deutschland (1815–1850)* (Munich: Kaiser, 1956), 83–143; Hans-Wolf Jäger, *Politische Metaphorik im Jakobinismus und im Vormärz* (Stuttgart: Metzler, 1971).

17. Schmitt, *Politische Romantik*, 217; *Political Romanticism*, 154f.

18. On Stahl, see Hugo Sinzheimer, *Jüdische Klassiker der deutschen Rechtswissenschaft* (Amsterdam: Hertzberger, 1938), 19–65; Dieter Grosser, *Grundlagen und Struktur der Staatslehre Friedrich Julius Stahls* (Cologne: Westdeutscher Verlag, 1963); Hanns-Jürgen Wiegand, *Das Vermächtnis Friedrich Julius Stahls: Ein Beitrag zur Geschichte konservativen Rechts- und Ordnungsdenkens* (Königstein/Ts.: Athenäum,

1980); Christoph Link, "Friedrich Julius Stahl (1802–1861), 'Christlicher Staat und Partei der Legitimität,'" in Heinrichs et al., *Deutsche Juristen jüdischer Herkunft*, 59–83; Robert A. Kann, "Friedrich Julius Stahl: A Reexamination of his Conservatism," *Leo Baeck Institute Yearbook* 12 (1967): 55–74. An antisemitic study is often cited: Johannes Heckel, "Der Einbruch des jüdischen Geistes in das deutsche Staats- und Kirchenrecht durch Friedrich Julius Stahl," *Historische Zeitschrift* 155 (1937): 506–41.

19. Friedrich Julius Stahl, *Der christliche Staat und sein Verhältnis zu Deismus und Judenthum*, first published in the *Evangelische Kirchen-Zeitung*, 1847, nos. 64–68.

20. Fischer, *Judentum, Staat und Heer*, 185.

21. On the various groupings within Prussian conservatism see Huber, *Deutsche Verfassungsgeschichte seit 1789*, vol. 2, 331–45.

22. The term "Young Hegelians" is often used synonymously with the term "Left Hegelians." But since the individuals involved, writing and acting in a Hegelian framework, can only superficially be divided into "left" and "right" wings, the term "Young Hegelians" (in contrast to the "Old Hegelians" who Hegel influenced personally) is preferable. See Zvi Rosen, *Bruno Bauer and Karl Marx: The Influence of Bruno Bauer on Marx's Thought* (The Hague: Nijhoff, 1977), 34f.

23. The Young Hegelian attack on the roots of Christian thought was initiated with the appearance of David Friedrich Strauss's book *Das Leben Jesu* (1835).

24. On Bauer's theological development see Martin Kegel, *Bruno Bauer und seine Theorien über die Entstehung des Christentums* (Leipzig: Quelle & Meyer, 1908).

25. See the account in Wolfgang Essbach, *Die Junghegelianer: Soziologie einer Intellektuellengruppe* (Munich: Fink, 1988).

26. On the general context see Eleonore Sterling, *Judenhass: Die Anfänge des politischen Antisemitismus in Deutschland (1815–1850)*, 2nd ed. (Frankfurt a.M.: Europäische Verlagsanstalt, 1969). On Bauer's life, see Ernst Barnikol, s.v. "Bruno Bauer," in *Die Religion in Geschichte und Gegenwart: Handwörterbuch für Theologie und Religionswissenschaft*, 3rd ed., ed. Kurt Galling (Tübingen: Mohr, 1957), cols. 922–24.

27. Bauer, *Das Judenthum in der Fremde* (Berlin: Heinicke, 1863), 620–21.

28. See Bauer's letters to his brother Edgar referring to his loss of faith: *Briefwechsel zwischen Bruno Bauer und Edgar Bauer während der Jahre 1838–1842 aus Bonn und Berlin* (Charlottenburg: Bauer, 1844).

29. Bauer, *Die Judenfrage* (Braunschweig: Otto, 1843), 1f. Hereafter cited in text.

30. Bauer, "Die Fähigkeit der heutigen Juden und Christen, frei zu werden" [The Capability of Today's Jews and Christians to Become Free], in Bauer, *Einundzwanzig Bogen aus der Schweiz: Erster Teil* (Zurich: Verlag des Literarischen Comptoirs, 1843; new ed., ed. Ingrid Pepperle, Leipzig: Reclam, 1989), 140.

31. Cf. Nathan Rotenstreich, "For and against Emancipation: The Bruno Bauer Controversy," *Leo Baeck Institute Yearbook* 4 (1959): 3–36.

32. Bruno Bauer, *Kritik der Geschichte der Offenbarung, Die Religion des Alten Testaments in der geschichtlichen Entwicklung ihrer Principien dargestellt*, 2 vols. (Berlin: Dümmler, 1838).

33. Ibid., x.

34. Bauer, "Die Fähigkeit der heutigen Juden und Christen, frei zu werden," 136–54.

35. Georg Wilhelm Friedrich Hegel, "Der Geist des Judentums" [The Spirit of Judaism], in Hegel, *Werke*, 2nd ed. (Frankfurt a.M.: Suhrkamp, 1990), 1:282–83. On Hegel's incorporation of this early approach into his philosophical system see Reinhard Sonnenschmidt, "Zum philosophischen Antisemitismus bei G. W. F. Hegel," *Zeitschrift für Religions- und Geistesgeschichte* 44 (1992): 289–302 (with further references). For the most extensive discussion of Hegel's critique of Judaism, see Reinhard Leuze, *Die ausserchristlichen Religionen bei Hegel* (Göttingen: Vandenhoeck und Ruprecht, 1975), 144–80.

36. Hegel, "Der Geist des Christentums und sein Schicksal" [The Spirit of Christianity and Its Fate] (1798–1800), in Hegel, *Werke*, 1:336.

37. Bauer, *Die Judenfrage*, 13.

38. Cf. Rom. 11.

39. Hegel, "Der Geist des Christentums," 299.

40. Bauer, *Die Judenfrage*, 12.

41. Ibid.

42. Ibid., 30, subtitle *Die Haltungslosigkeit und Starrheit des jüdischen Volksbewusstseyns* [roughly "The Lack of Bearing and Rigidity of the Jewish Nation's Consciousness"]; the word *Haltungslosigkeit* appears in Hegel's *Science of Logic*, pt. 1, bk. 1, ch. 3 ("Repulsion and Attraction").

43. Baruch de Spinoza, *Theologisch-politischer Traktat*, ed. Carl Gebhardt, 3rd ed. (Leipzig: Dürr, 1908), 93ff.

44. Bauer, *Die Judenfrage*, 9. Hereafter cited in text.

45. In *Rasse und Staat* (Tübingen: Mohr, 1933), 197, Eric Voegelin draws attention to the fact that Bauer and Kierkegaard developed their ideas of "landlessness" at approximately the same time.

46. Bauer, *Die Judenfrage*, 5.

47. Ibid., 9.

48. Ibid., 11.

49. Liebeschütz, *Das Judentum im deutschen Geschichtsbild*, 39; Hegel, *Vorlesungen über die Philosophie der Geschichte* (Leipzig: Reclam, 1907), 262–65. Hegel's biographer Karl Rosenkranz emphatically criticized this historical construction, indicating that "the main controversy between Hegel and myself" turned on "the world-historical position of the Jews." See Karl Rosenkranz, "Hegel als deutscher Nationalphilosoph," in Rosenkranz, *Neue Studien*, vol. 1, *Studien zur Culturgeschichte* (Leipzig: Roschny, 1875), xiv.

50. Bauer, *Die Judenfrage*, 11.

51. Ibid.

52. "The Jewish people [*Volk*] is in itself already the goal towards which the nations [*Völker*] of the world are only advancing." In Franz Rosenzweig, *Der Stern der Erlösung*, intro. Reinhold Mayer (1921; rev. ed., Frankfurt a.M.: Suhrkamp, 1988), 368.

53. Bauer, *Die Judenfrage*, 19.

54. Ibid., 19.

55. Bauer, "Die Fähigkeit der heutigen Juden und Christen, frei zu werden," 139.

56. Ibid., 139 (italics mine).

57. Bauer, *Die Judenfrage*, 19.

58. Ibid., 17.

59. Ibid., 20.

60. Bauer, "Die Fähigkeit der heutigen Juden und Christen, frei zu werden," 154.

61. Bauer, *Die Judenfrage*, 21.

62. Bauer, "Die Fähigkeit der heutigen Juden und Christen, frei zu werden," 137.

63. See Rotenstreich, "For and Against Emancipation," 6.

64. Bauer, *Die Judenfrage*, 73.

65. Bauer, "Die Fähigkeit der heutigen Juden und Christen, frei zu werden," 154.

66. See Rosen, *Bruno Bauer and Karl Marx*, 223. On Marx's concept of religion, Ernst Benz, "Hegels Religionsphilosophie und die Linkshegelianer (Zur Kritik des Religionsbegriffes von Karl Marx)," *Zeitschrift für Religions- und Geistesgeschichte* 7 (1955): 247–71; Helmut Hirsch, "Karl Marx zur 'Judenfrage' und zu Judenfragen—Eine weiterführende Metakritik?" in *Juden im Vormärz und in der Revolution von 1848*, ed. Walter Grab and Julius H. Schoeps (Stuttgart: Burg Verlag, 1983), 199–215.

67. Rosen, *Bruno Bauer and Karl Marx*, 171.

68. Ibid., 171.

69. See for example Edmund Silberner, *Kommunisten zur Judenfrage: Zur Geschichte von Theorie und Praxis* (Opladen: Westdeutscher Verlag, 1983), 16–42.

70. Karl Marx to Arnold Ruge, 13 March 1843, in *Die Hegelsche Linke: Dokumente zu Philosophie und Politik im deutschen Vormärz*, ed. Heinz Pepperle and Ingrid Pepperle (Frankfurt a.M.: Röderberg, 1986), 872.

71. Jürgen Gebhardt, "Karl Marx und Bruno Bauer," in *Politische Ordnung und menschliche Existenz: Festgabe für Eric Voegelin zum 60. Geburtstag*, ed. Alois Demf, Hannah Arendt, and Friedrich Engel-Janosi (Munich: C.H. Beck, 1962), 216.

72. Essbach, *Die Junghegelianer*, 369.

73. Rosen, *Bruno Bauer and Karl Marx*, 238.

74. Marx, *Zur Judenfrage*, ed. Stefan Grossmann (Berlin: Ernst Rovohlt Verlag), 298.

75. See Tamar Bermann, *Produktivierungsmythen und Antisemitismus: Eine soziologische Studie* (Vienna: Europaverl, 1973), 25.

76. Marx, *Zur Judenfrage*, 293.

77. Silberner, *Kommunisten zur Judenfrage*, 41.

78. Marx, *Zur Judenfrage*, 270. Hereafter cited in text.

79. On the misreading see most recently Essbach, *Junghegelianer*, 370.

80. Marx, *Zur Judenfrage*, 275.

81. All citations below are from Hegel, "Grundlinien der Philosophie des Rechts oder Naturrecht und Staatswissenschaft im Grundrisse" (1821) in Hegel, *Werke*, 7:421. On the question of power and tolerance, cf. the addition to paragraph 268, which Hegel refers to in connection with Jewish emancipation: "A widespread idea is that the state adheres because of power; but what causes such adhesion is only a basic feeling of order shared by all" (414). Cf. Shlomo Avineri, "A Note on Hegel's Views on Jewish Emancipation," *Jewish Social Studies* 25 (April 1963): 145–51; on the entire complex: Ernst Wolfgang Böckenförde, "Bemerkungen zum Verhältnis von Staat und Religion bei Hegel," in Böckenförde, ed., *Recht, Staat, Freiheit* (Frankfurt a.M.: Suhrkamp, 1991), 115–42.

82. Marx, *Zur Judenfrage*, 276. Hereafter cited in text.

83. Karl Marx and Friedrich Engels, *Die heilige Familie: Oder Kritik der kritischen Kritik. Gegen Bruno Bauer und Konsorten* (Frankfurt a.M.: Literarische Anstalt, 1845), esp. ch. 6, 1.b ("Die Judenfrage Nr. I: Die Stellung der Fragen"), 208–10; 2.b ("Die Judenfrage Nr. II: Kritische Entdeckungen über Sozialismus, Jurisprudenz und Politik [Nationalität]"), 213–19; 3.b ("Die Judenfrage Nr. III"), 229–45. In this work Marx defends the pioneers of Jewish emancipation Gustav Philippson (1814–80), Samuel Hirsch (1809–89), and Gabriel Riesser (1806–63) in their conflict with Bauer.

84. Marx, *Zur Judenfrage*, 290.

85. On Jewish emancipation and freedom to practice a trade see Fischer, *Judentum, Staat und Heer in Preussen im frühen 19. Jahrhundert. Zur Geschichte der staatlichen Judenpolitik*, 22.

86. Marx, *Zur Judenfrage*, 13.

87. Bauer, *Die Judenfrage*, 19–20.

88. Essbach, *Die Junghegelianer*, 371.

89. See Silberner, *Kommunisten zur Judenfrage*, 21–39.

90. Marx, *Zur Judenfrage*, 292.

91. Ibid., 293.

92. Thoughts on the "proletariat" were first expressed in "Introduction to a Critique of the Hegelian Philosophy of Law," written shortly afterward.

93. Marx, *Zur Judenfrage*, 293. Hereafter cited in text.

Chapter 10. Protestant Atheism

1. Schmitt, *Glossarium*, 192.

2. Hans Kelsen, "Gott und Staat," *Logos* 11 (1922–23): 261–84; reprinted in

Die Wiener Rechtstheoretische Schule: Schriften von Hans Kelsen, Adolf Merkel, Albert Verdross, ed. Hans Klecatsky, René Marcic, and Herbert Schambeck (Vienna: Europa-Verlag, 1968), 1:171–93, here 179. Cf. the extensive critique of Kelsen's text by W. Pohl, "Kelsens Parallele: Gott und Staat. Kritische Bemerkungen eines Theologen," *Zeitschrift für öffentliches Recht* 4 (1925): 571–609.

3. Kelsen, "Gott und Staat," 178f.

4. Schmitt, *Politische Theologie*, 1st ed., 39.

5. Carl Schmitt, *Politische Theologie II*, 22. For a lengthy response to this text see Hans Blumenberg, "Politische Theologie I und II" in Blumenberg, *Säkularisierung und Selbstbehauptung* (rev. and exp. ed. of Blumenberg, *Die Legitimität der Neuzeit*, pts. 1 and 2) (Frankfurt a.M.: Suhrkamp, 1974), 103–18; and Blumenberg, *Arbeit am Mythos* (Frankfurt a.M.: Suhrkamp, 1979), 567–604.

6. Böckenförde, "Politische Theorie und Politische Theologie," 19. In more detail: José María Beneyto, *Politische Theologie als politische Theorie: Eine Untersuchung zur Rechts- und Staatstheorie Carl Schmitts und zu ihrer Wirkungsgeschichte in Spanien* (Berlin: Duncker & Humblot, 1983), 72–77.

7. Hans Kelsen, *Reine Rechtslehre: Einleitung in die rechtswissenschaftliche Problematik* (1934; repr., Aalen: Scientia-Verlag, 1994), iii.

8. Hans Kelsen, "Der Staatsbegriff und die Psychoanalyse," *Almanach für das Jahr 1927*, repr. in Klecatsky, Marcic, and Schambeck, *Die Wiener Rechtstheoretische Schule*, 214. Important observations on the theme of God and state are found in the following works of Kelsen: *Der soziologische und der juristische Staatsbegriff*, 219–53; *Allgemeine Staatslehre*, 76–80; *Staatsform und Weltanschauung* (Tübingen: Mohr, 1933), 29f.

9. "Kein anderer war wie Bruno Bauer der Vollstrecker und Zu-Ende-Führer der theologisch-philosophischen Kritik, im vollen Sinne und in aller Schicksalhaftigkeit, die für die deutsche Geistesgeschichte der beiden letzten Jahrhunderte mit den Worten Kritik und Krise verbunden ist." Schmitt, *Donoso Cortés in gesamteuropäischer Interpretation*, 100.

10. See van Laak and Villinger, *Nachlass Carl Schmitt*.

11. Ibid., 93.

12. Carl Schmitt to Ernst Jünger, 26 April 1939, in Kiesel, *Briefe 1930–1983*, 84.

13. Ernst Jünger to Carl Schmitt, 26 March 1944, RW 265-64, letter no. 136.

14. Schmitt, *Die Diktatur*, xiii.

15. Schmitt, "Versuch eines Berichtes an P. Erich Przywara," RW 265-93, typescript Carl Schmitt, 4 leaves, convolute no. 6, dated February 1946 by Przywara, Schmitt. The document reveals that Schmitt never sent it off. See, among other works on the theme by Erich Przywara, "Jude, Heide, Christ," *Europäische Revue* (August 1932): 470–76. Schmitt writes on Przywara in *Staat, Grossraum, Nomos*, 590f.

16. In the original handwritten version of the typescript, the words *des Emigranten* (of the emigrant) are here crossed out and replaced by *von* (by).

17. In a long note by the editor of Schmitt's essay "Die Stellung von Steins in der Geschichte des 19. Jahrhunderts" (1940), in which Schmitt refers at one point to Bruno Bauer as the "author of some daring 'Christian attacks on Christianity,'" excerpts are cited from the *Depositum* (Schmitt, *Staat, Grossraum, Nomos*, 162). But no passages are printed that clarify either the context of Schmitt's remarks in particular or his antisemitism in general, leading to an inadequate picture of the basic problems. We are, however, offered some useful information, to the effect that Schmitt was already in contact with the Bauer researcher Ernst Barnikol (1892–1968) in 1927. In the 1960s and 1970s Schmitt made efforts to publish his extensive scattered writings on Bauer. On Schmitt and Löwith see Reinhard Mehring, "Karl Löwith, Carl Schmitt, Jacob Taubes und das 'Ende der Geschichte.'"

18. See Katz, "Die Anfänge der Judenemanzipation," 83–98.

19. Marx, *Zur Judenfrage*, 294.

20. Schmitt, *Glossarium*, 61.

21. Benjamin Disraeli, *Tancred, or, The New Crusade* (London: Colburn, 1847), 6:4. In *Tancred, oder, der neue Kreuzzug* (Berlin, 1936), the German version translated and edited by Julius Elbau for the *Jüdische Buchvereinigung*, Elbau reported (13) that Bismarck had portraits of his wife, of the Kaiser, and of Disraeli in his study—an anecdote also told about Schmitt; see Sombart, *Jugend in Berlin, 1933–1943*. In his *Die deutschen Männer*, esp. 282–94, Sombart closely considers the interesting constellations Disraeli-Schmitt and Victoria-Disraeli vs. Schmitt.

22. Schmitt, *Glossarium*, 268.

Chapter 11. "Pure Legal Theory" as Secularized Theology of the Enemy

1. The Gospel according to John, *The Revised English Bible: With the Apocrypha; The New Testament* (Oxford: Oxford Univ. Press, 1989). Hereafter *REB*. For exegetical literature on this passage, see George R. Beasley-Murray, *John* (Waco, Tex.: Word Books, 1987) and Raymond E. Brown, *The Gospel According to John (XII–XXI)* (Garden City, N.Y.: Doubleday, 1970), 787–897. The commentary of Rudolf Bultmann, *Das Evangelium des Johannes*, 17th ed. (Göttingen: Vandenhoeck & Ruprecht, 1964), has been especially influential.

2. John 18:38. David Flusser, "What Was the Original Meaning of Ecce Homo?" in Flusser, *Judaism and the Origins of Christianity* (Jerusalem: Magnes Press, 1988), 593–603, has clarified the irony contained in this phrase in terms of its historical context.

3. John 18:38.

4. Ibid., 18:39.

5. Ibid., 18:40.

6. For a theoretical overview see Caldwell, "Constitutional Theory in the Weimar Republic."

7. Fritz Bauer, "Der Prozess Jesu," in Bauer, *Die Humanität der Rechtsordnung: Ausgewählte Schriften*, ed. Joachim Perels and Irmtrud Wojak (Frankfurt a.M.: Fritz-Bauer-Inst., 1998), 411–26.

8. Ibid., 32.

9. "*(Arch. .f. Soz.-W. 1920, S. 84).*"

10. Hans Kelsen, "Vom Wesen und Wert der Demokratie," *Archiv für Sozial-wissenschaft und Sozialpolitik* 47 (1920–21), then published separately in expanded form as *Vom Wesen und Wert der Demokratie* (Tübingen: Mohr, 1929).

11. Schmitt, *Politische Theologie*, 55; *Political Theology*, 42.

12. Kelsen, "Vom Wesen und Wert der Demokratie," 84.

13. Cf. Dieter Grimm, "Die 'Neue Rechtswissenschaft'—Über Funktion und Formation nationalsozialistischer Jurisprudenz," 373–95.

14. Otto Koellreutter, "Rezension von Hans Kelsens, Vom Wesen und Wert der Demokratie, 2. umgearbeitete Aufl., 1929," *Archiv des öffentlichen Rechts* 56 (1929): 138–41, here 140.

15. Kelsen, "Vom Wesen und Wert der Demokratie," 85.

16. Ibid.

17. Hans Kelsen, *Die philosophischen Grundlagen der Naturrechtslehre und des Rechtspositivismus* (Charlottenburg: Pan-Verlag, 1928), 74f.

18. John 19:12–15.

19. Cf. Bultmann, *Das Evangelium des Johannes*, 508; Beasley-Murray, *John*, 343. Cf. also Schmitt, *Der Nomos der Erde*, 33.

20. Flusser, "What Was the Original Meaning of Ecce Homo?" 595, suggests that the historical Pilate would have wished to free Jesus, who posed no danger, lacking political ambitions regarding Roman rule.

21. Kelsen, "Vom Wesen und Wert der Demokratie," 85.

22. Rudolf Aladár Metall, *Hans Kelsen: Leben und Werk* (Vienna: Deuticke, 1969), confirms that Kelsen was religiously indifferent.

23. Ibid., 84.

24. Ibid., 85.

25. Plato, *Politics*, 3, cited in Kelsen, "Vom Wesen und Wert der Demokratie," 77. "Border" can here be understood as a political border or a border between life and death.

26. Kelsen, "Vom Wesen und Wert der Demokratie," 83.

27. Horst Dreier, "Hans Kelsen (1881–1973): 'Jurist des Jahrhunderts'?" in Heinrichs et al., *Deutsche Juristen jüdischer Herkunft*, 711, notes the antiparliamentary message Schmitt reads into the episode from John.

28. Schmitt, *Politische Theologie* (1st ed.), 54.

29. Schmitt, *Der Begriff des Politischen*, 121–23.

30. See Schmitt, *Politische Romantik*, 40; *Political Romanticism*, 27. Cf. Karl Heinz Bohrer, "Carl Schmitts Polemik gegen die Romantik als das moderne Bewusstsein," in Bohrer, *Die Kritik der Romantik*, 284–311. Carl Schmitt, *Geistesgeschichtliche Lage*, 46; *Crisis of Parliamentary Democracy*, 35f.

31. Ibid.

32. Donoso Cortés, *Der Staat Gottes* (Darmstadt: Wissenschaftliche Buchge-sellschaft, 1966), 37.

33. Ibid., 12 (Donoso Cortés cites this phrase in English).

34. Ibid., 37.

35. Schmitt, *Politische Theologie* (1st ed.), 54.

36. Ibid., 54.

37. Schmitt reproaches Jellinek for making a "discovery" already obvious for Donoso Cortés and Marx, to the effect that human rights are not innate. Remarkably, Marx already attacks Bruno Bauer on precisely the same point. See Karl Marx and Friedrich Engels, *Die Heilige Familie und andere philosophische Frühschriften*, 204.

38. See "Edikt betreffend die bürgerlichen Verhältnisse der Juden in dem Preussischen Staate vom 11. März 1812," in *Dokumente zur deutschen Verfassungsge-schichte*, ed. Ernst Rudolf Huber (Stuttgart: Kohlhammer, 1961), 1:49–51.

39. See Schmitt, *Disputation über den Rechtsstaat*, 84–88; Albrecht Wagner, re-view in *Deutsche Juristen-Zeitung*, 15 June 1935, on the connection between the "victory of the concepts *Staatsbürger* and *Rechtsstaat*" and Jewish emancipation. In the Schmitt archives, RW 265-449, there is a newspaper clipping from *Ger-mania*, 23 July 1935, in which Schmitt marked off the following passage: "Ori-gins of the concept *Staatsbürger:* It is well known that Kant introduced the con-cept of the *Staatsbürger* into legal theory. But the word only took on positive meaning in the 19th century. In Prussian legislation, it appears for the first time in the edict on Jewish emancipation of 1812."

40. Similarly Donoso Cortés, *Der Staat Gottes*, 17–18, who juxtaposes indeci-sive Pilatus with a decisive Jewish high priest.

41. Kelsen, *Reine Rechtslehre*, x–xi.

42. Kelsen, *Der soziologische und der juristische Staatsbegriff*. For the following discussion see Horst Dreier, "Die Parallele von Gott und Staat," in Dreier, *Rechtslehre, Staatssoziologie und Demokratietheorie bei Hans Kelsen*, 2nd ed. (Baden-Baden: Nomos, 1990); Hans Georg Schenk, "Die Emanzipation des Jus huma-num vom Jus divinum: Ein Beitrag zur Geschichte des Rechtspositivismus," *Internationale Zeitschrift für Theorie des Rechts, Neue Folge* 1 (1939): 56–67; Wolfgang Mantl, "Hans Kelsen und Carl Schmitt," in *Ideologiekritik und Demokratietheorie bei Hans Kelsen*, ed. Werner Krawietz, Ernst Topitsch, and Peter Koller (Berlin: Duncker & Humblot, 1982), 185–99; Manfred Prisching, "Hans Kelsen und Carl Schmitt: Zur Konfrontation zweier staatstheoretischer Modelle," in *Reine Rechtslehre im Spiegel ihrer Fortsetzer und Kritiker*, ed. Ota Weinberger and Werner Krawietz (Vienna: Springer-Verlag, 1988), 77–116; Werner Krawietz, "Die Lehre vom Stufenbau des Rechts—Eine säkularisierte Politische Theologie?" in *Rechtssystem und gesellschaftliche Basis bei Hans Kelsen*, ed. Werner Krawietz and Hans Schelsky (Berlin: Duncker & Humblot, 1984), 255–71.

43. Schmitt, *Politische Theologie* (1st ed.), 39.

44. Kelsen, *Reine Rechtslehre*, iii.

45. Kelsen himself points to this heritage: *Reine Rechtslehre*, iv. But as was the case with Gerhard Anschütz and Richard Thoma as well, he does not carry forward the variety of *Kaiserreich* legal positivism stamped by Laband. See Peter C. Caldwell, *Popular Sovereignty and the Crisis of German Constitutional Law* (Durham, N.C.: Duke Univ. Press, 1997), 186–237.

46. Kelsen, *Der soziologische und der juristische Staatsbegriff*, 250.

47. Ibid., 251. See also Kelsen, "Der Staatsbegriff und die Psychoanalyse," 209.

48. Ibid.

49. Kelsen, "Gott und Staat," 178. Hereafter cited in text.

50. Kelsen, *Der soziologische und der juristische Staatsbegriff*, 219f. Hereafter cited in text.

51. See Hans Kelsen, "Der Staat als Gott," in Kelsen, *Der soziologische und der juristische Staatsbegriff*, 249–250.

52. See Hans Kelsen, "Das Wesen des Staates," *Revue internationale de la théorie du droit* 1 (1926–27): 9.

53. Kelsen, *Der soziologische und der juristische Staatsbegriff*, 86–91. Hereafter cited in text.

54. Hans Kelsen, *Über Grenzen zwischen juristischer und soziologischer Methode* (1911; repr., Aalen: Scientia Verlag, 1970), 5. The talk is based on the first major work of Kelsen, *Hauptprobleme der Staatsrechtslehre entwickelt aus der Lehre vom Rechtssatze* (Tübingen: Mohr, 1911).

55. See Kelsen, *Die philosophischen Grundlagen der Naturrechtslehre und des Rechtspositivismus*.

56. Ibid., 30–31.

57. Ibid., 75f.

58. I thank Kelsen's student Dr. Gerhard M. Riegner for personally offering this interpretation in Berlin on 10 March 1997.

59. Kelsen, *Die philosophischen Grundlagen der Naturrechtslehre und des Rechtspositivismus*, 66.

60. Ibid., 77.

61. Kelsen, *Staatsform und Weltanschauung*, 29f.

62. Carl Schmitt, *Der Hüter der Verfassung* (Tübingen: Mohr, 1931); Hans Kelsen, "Wer soll der Hüter der Verfassung sein?" (1931), in Klecatsky, Marcic, and Schambeck, *Die Wiener Rechtstheoretische Schule*. See Caldwell, *Popular Sovereignty*, 85–119.

63. Schmitt, *Verfassungslehre*, 3; Schmitt, *Der Hüter der Verfassung*, 70.

64. See Hans Kelsen, "Die Funktion der Verfassung," in *Hans Kelsen, oder, die Reinheit der Rechtslehre*, ed. Friedrich Koja (Vienna: Böhlau, 1988), 89–99, 98.

65. Schmitt, *Römischer Katholizismus und politische Form*, 11; *Roman Catholicism and Political Form*, 7.

66. See Kelsen, "Gott und Staat," 189.

67. Ibid., 14.

68. Ibid., 14.

69. This is the subtitle of Kelsen, *Der soziologische und der juristische Staatsbegriff.* Section 42 (245–47) is devoted to "the theological and juridical belief in miracles."

70. Ibid., 247.

71. Schmitt, *Politische Theologie* (1st ed.), 10. Hereafter cited in text.

72. The concept of legal irrationalism has been widely neglected; on the concept see Ralf Dreier, "Irrationalismus in der Rechtswissenschaft," in Dreier, *Recht-Staat-Vernunft, Studien zur Rechtstheorie,* vol. 2 (Frankfurt a.M.: Suhrkamp, 1991), 120–41.

73. Caldwell, "Constitutional Theory in the Weimar Republic," 267ff.

74. Schmitt, *Römischer Katholizismus und politische Form,* 11; *Roman Catholicism and Political Form,* 7.

75. Schmitt, *Politische Theologie,* 69; *Political Theology,* 53. See Ian Ker, "Papal Infallibility," in Ker, *John Henry Newman: A Biography* (Oxford: Clarendon, 1988), 651–93.

76. Schmitt, *Politische Theologie* (1st ed.), 49; *Political Theology,* 53.

77. Schmitt, *Der Begriff des Politischen,* 122; cf. *Politische Theologie* (1st ed.), 33.

78. Ibid.

79. Ibid., 8. Schmitt first refers to the *Entartung* of law by the "normativists" in the foreword to the new edition of 1934.

80. Ibid., 35. In *Die deutschen Männer und ihre Feinde,* 277, Nicolaus Sombart has pointed to this passage, suggesting that *Political Theology* marked the opening of Schmitt's battle with "Jewish legal studies." On Hugo Preuss, see Detlev Lehnert, "Hugo Preuss als moderner Klassiker einer kritischen Theorie der 'verfassten' Politik: Vom Souveränitätsproblem zum demokratischen Pluralismus," *Politische Vierteljahresschrift* 33 (1992): 33–54.

81. Hugo Krabbe, *Die Lehre der Rechtssouveränität: Beitrag zur Staatslehre* (Groningen: Wolters, 1906).

82. See Christoph Schönberger, "Das Parlament im Anstaltsstaat: Zur Theorie parlamentarischer Repräsentation in der Staatsrechtslehre des Kaiserreichs (1870–1918)" (PhD diss., Humboldt University of Berlin, 1996), 64–232.

83. Kelsen, *Der soziologische und der juristische Staatsbegriff,* 253.

84. Schmitt, *Politische Theologie* (1st ed.), 21f.

85. Ibid., 56.

86. Ibid., 22; Hans Kelsen, *Das Problem der Souveränität und die Theorie des Völkerrechts* (Tübingen: Mohr, 1920), 320.

87. Schmitt, *Politische Theologie* (1st ed.), 22.

88. Cf. Kelsen, *Allgemeine Staatslehre,* 285–301; also *Reine Rechtslehre.*

89. Schmitt, *Politische Theologie* (1st ed.), 58f.

90. See Mehring, *Pathetisches Denken*, 79. Mehring stresses Schmitt's orientation towards Hegel and his dictum concerning the reality of the rational from the preface to the *Philosophy of Right*.

91. Schmitt, *Politische Theologie*, 58f. Hereafter cited in text.

92. Schmitt, *Römischer Katholizismus und politische Form*, 10; *Roman Catholicism and Political Form*, 7.

93. Sombart, *Die deutschen Männer und ihre Feinde*, 61. In 1934 Schmitt nuanced his position as follows: "The Roman Catholic dogma of the infallibility of papal decision itself has strong juridical-decisionistic elements; but the infallible decision of the Pope does not ground the order and institution of the church, but rather presumes them: the Pope is only infallible by virtue of his office; the infallible one is not, inversely, the Pope."

94. Carl Schmitt, "Der unbekannte Donoso Cortés," in *Positionen und Begriffe*, 118. In *Political Theology* Schmitt designated "atheistic-anarchistic socialism" as Donoso Cortés's mortal enemy.

95. See Schmitt's talk "Das Zeitalter der Neutralisierungen und Entpolitisierungen" (1932), included in *Der Begriff des Politischen*, 79–95, here 73.

96. Kelsen, *Der soziologische und der juristische Staatsbegriff*, 253.

97. Carl Schmitt, "Neutralität und Neutralisierungen (1939)," in Schmitt, *Positionen und Begriffe*, 334.

Part 4. Acceleration: Katechon and Antichrist

1. Jacob Taubes had discussed this eschatological concept and its impact on the German philosophical tradition in *Abendländische Eschatologie: Mit einem Anhang* (1947, repr., Munich: Matthes & Seitz, 1991) and *Die Politische Theologie des Paulus*. For an interesting discussion of Paul, see Daniel Boyarin, *A Radical Jew: Paul and the Politics of Identity* (Berkeley: Univ. of California Press, 1994), esp. 136–57 on the question of Paul's attitude toward the Jews.

Chapter 12. The Jews in the Christian History of Salvation

1. Thomas Hobbes of Malmesbury, *Leviathan or the Matter, Forme, & Power of a Common-Wealth Ecclesiastical and Civill. Printed for Andrew Crooke, at the Green Dragon in St. Paul's Churchyard* (London, 1651). For the words cited above, see Schmitt, *Der Leviathan in der Staatslehre des Thomas Hobbes*, 18; *The Leviathan in the State Theory of Thomas Hobbes: Meaning and Failure of a Political Symbol*, foreword and introduction by George Schwab; trans. George Schwab and Erna Hilfstein (Westport, Conn.: Greenwood, 1996), 9. See Paul Bookbinder, "Carl Schmitt, *Der Leviathan*, and the Jews," *International Social Science Review* 66, no. 3 (1991): 99–109; Helmut Rumpf, *Carl Schmitt und Thomas Hobbes: Ideelle Beziehungen und aktuelle*

Bedeutung mit einer Abhandlung über: Die Frühschriften Carl Schmitts (Berlin: Duncker & Humblot, 1970).

2. See Otfried Höffe, "Widersprüche im Leviathan: Zur Aktualität der Staatsphilosophie von Thomas Hobbes," *Merkur, Zeitschrift für europäisches Denken* 33 (1979): 1186–1203. On modern research concerning Hobbes's *Leviathan*, see Quentin Skinner, "Hobbes's Leviathan," *Historical Journal* 7 (1964): 321–33; Skinner, "The Ideological Context of Hobbes's Political Thought," *Historical Journal* 9 (1966): 286–317.

3. See Joseph Vialatoux, *La cité de Hobbes: Théorie de l'état totalitaire; Essai sur la conception naturaliste de la civilisation* (Paris: Lecoffre, 1935); R. Capitant, "Hobbes et l'Etat totalitaire," *Archives de Philosophie de droit et de Sociologie iuridique*, 1936, 46ff.

4. Schmitt, *Der Hüter der Verfassung*, 78ff. Schmitt's discussion itself generated an intense debate in Nazi Germany extending well beyond the narrow group of Schmitt's followers. See H. O. Ziegler, *Autoritärer oder totaler Staat* (Tübingen: Mohr, 1932), Ernst Forsthoff, *Der totale Staat* (Hamburg: Hanseatische Verlagsanstalt, 1933); Paul Ritterbusch, *Der totale Staat bei Thomas Hobbes* (Kiel, 1938); G. D. Daskalakis, "Der totale Staat als Moment des Staates," *Archiv für Rechts- und Sozialphilosophie* 31 (1938): 194–201; Alfred Rosenberg "Totaler Staat?" *Völkischer Beobachter*, 9 January 1934; Roland Freisler, "Totaler Staat? Nationalsozialistischer Staat!" *Deutsche Justiz*, 1934, 43ff. See also the discussion by Schmitt's opponent Otto Koellreutter, "Leviathan und totaler Staat," *Reichsverwaltungsblatt*, 17 September 1938.

5. Franz Neumann, *Behemoth: The Structure and Practice of National Socialism*, 2nd ed. (London: Frank Cass, 1967), 3. Letters from Neumann now part of the Schmitt archive (RW 265-339, letter no. 5, Berlin, 21 November 1930, Franz Neumann to Carl Schmitt; RW 256-217, letter no. 81, Berlin, 7 September 1932, Franz Neumann to Carl Schmitt) show that he participated in Schmitt's seminars.

6. Schmitt, *Leviathan*, 94; *Leviathan*, 61.

7. Schmitt, *Ex Captivitate Salus*, 21.

8. On the different Leviathan interpretations see Günter Meuter, "Die zwei Gesichter des Leviathan: Zu Carl Schmitts abgründiger Wissenschaft vom 'Leviathan,'" in van Laak, Göbel, and Villinger, eds., *Metamorphosen des Politischen*, 95–118.

9. Schmitt's words in a talk delivered on 8 February 1941 at a historians' conference in Nuremberg. See Carl Schmitt, "Staatliche Souveränität und freies Meer: Über den Gegensatz von Land und See im Völkerrecht der Neuzeit," in *Das Reich und Europa*, Fritz Hartung et al., eds., 2nd rev. ed. (Leipzig: Koehler & Amelang, 1941), 91–117.

10. Schmitt, *Leviathan*, 23; *Leviathan*, 11.

11. See the relevant texts in Schmitt, *Staat, Grossraum, Nomos*; Lothar Gruchmann, *Nationalsozialistische Grossraumordnung: Die Konstruktion einer "deutschen*

Monroe-Doktrin" (Stuttgart: Deutsche Verlagsanstalt, 1962); Dan Diner, "Norms for Domination: Nazi Legal Concepts of World Order," in Diner, *Beyond the Conceivable*, 49–77.

12. Schmitt, *Ex Captivitate Salus*, 67.

13. See Schmitt, *Leviathan*, 131; *Leviathan*, 85. "The intellectual [*geistig*] weapons Hobbes created did not help his cause. But as Hegel rightly indicates, the weapons are the essence of the warrior himself." On Schmitt's leaning toward "conspiracy theory" in a wider context, see Groh, *Anthropologische Dimensionen der Geschichte*, 267–304.

14. Schmitt, *Leviathan*, 21, 96, 23; *Leviathan*, 10, 62, 11.

15. Ibid., 131; ibid., 86.

16. See George Mosse, *German Jews beyond Judaism* (Cincinnati: Hebrew Union College Press, 1985), 50.

17. Schmitt, *Geistesgeschichtliche Lage des heutigen Parlamentarismus* (1st ed., Munich: Duncker & Humblot, 1923), 65; Schmitt, *The Crisis of Parliamentary Democracy*, 68; *Positionen und Begriffe*, 17.

18. Schmitt, *Leviathan*, 6; *Leviathan*, 1.

19. Carl Schmitt, "Der Staat als Mechanismus bei Hobbes und Descartes," *Archiv für Rechts- und Sozialphilosophie* 30 (1937): 622–32, 627.

20. Ibid., 625.

21. Schmitt, *Leviathan*, 16; *Leviathan*, 8.

22. Schmitt, "Staat als Mechanismus bei Hobbes und Descartes," 626. Schmitt referred in this text to Friedrich von Bezold, "Jean Bodin als Okkultist und seine Démonomanie," *Historische Zeitschrift* 105 (1910): 1–64; and J. Guttmann, *Jean Bodin in seinen Beziehungen zum Judentum* (Breslau: Marcus, 1906). First appearing in the *Monatsschrift für Geschichte und Wissenschaft des Judentums*, Guttmann's essay was a detailed refutation of the idea that Bodin was of Jewish origin. Schmitt insisted this was the case, defending this view with a reference to an essay by Emile Pasqué, in *Revue d'histoire de l'Eglise de France* 19 (1933): 457–62. See Richard Tuck, "Hobbes and Descartes," in *Perspectives on Thomas Hobbes*, ed. Alan Ryan and G. A. J. Rogers (Oxford: Clarendon, 1988), 11–41. On Bodin, see S. Goyard-Fabre, *Jean Bodin et le droit de la république* (Paris: Presses Universitaires de France, 1989).

23. Schmitt, "Staat als Mechanismus bei Hobbes und Descartes," 626. Schmitt added the following: "All of this is very interesting and could be the mythic primal image for many communist doctrines of the state and for the condition of a stateless and classless society emerging with the abolition of the state. Such things are not discussed in Hobbes."

24. Louis Ginzberg, *The Legends of the Jews: Bible Times and Characters from the Creation to Jacob*, trans. Henrietta Szold (Philadelphia: Jewish Publication Society of America, 1909), 5:27.

25. See Schmitt, *Leviathan*, 17, n.1; *Leviathan*, 8, n.10: "Joh. Andreas

Eisenmenger's *Entdecktes Judenthum* has been used in the edition appearing with Royal Prussian license, Königsberg 1711 (vol. 1, p. 401; vol. 2, pp. 873ff.).''

26. Carl Schmitt, *Land und Meer: Eine weltgeschichtliche Betrachtung* (1942; 3rd ed., Cologne: Hohenheim, 1981), 17; *Land and Sea*, trans. and with a foreword by Simona Draghici (Washington, D.C.: Plutarch, 1997), 6.

27. Schmitt, *Leviathan*, 18; *Leviathan*, 9.

28. Schmitt, *Land und Meer*, 17; *Land and Sea*, 6.

29. Ibid.

30. Heinrich Heine, *Historisch-kritische Gesamtausgabe der Werke* (Hamburg: Hoffmann & Campe, 1992), 3:1, 158–72, here 167–68. The relevant passage begins as follows: *Leviathan heisst der Fisch, / Welcher haust im Meeresgrunde: / Mit ihm spielet Gott der Herr / Alle Tage eine Stunde*—(lines 293–96: "The fish is called Leviathan / It has its house in the ocean's depths: / With him plays God our lord / Every day for just an hour—"); Heine devotes considerable space to the pungent recipe—including garlic and raisins—for preparing Leviathan's "delicate flesh"; the recipe is designed by the rabbi to tempt the monk (lines 305ff.).

31. Heine had a traditional Jewish education and certainly was familiar with the hymn, found for instance in *Sepher Kruwot: Machsor Lechag Haschawuot* (Hamburg, 5599 [=1838]), 108–19 (Hebrew with German translation). The poet comes to speak of Leviathan in the course of describing the happiness of a future life at the end of all times: "Now begins the aerial scuffle between Leviathan and the wild mountain animal; they attack one another and have an entertaining battle. The animal uses his horns for deadly thrusts; the sea-monster whips death at him with his fins of iron. They succumb and are cut up by the creator's huge sword and prepared for the blessed ones' delicious meal. Here they sit in rows . . . alongside balsam-streaming brooks, quaffing from full beakers the most delicious wine, preserved in berries from the beginning. . . . You've understood it, o pious one, the worth of this hymn, o, let you also once be accepted into this happy company!" (117–19). This concluding moral appeal to the pious was perhaps taken up by Heine ironically at the close of his lyric disputation: after the rabbi softens the monk through his description of the future feast, he declares, "What God cooks is well cooked / dear monk, now take my advice / and sacrifice your old foreskin " (168).

32. The essay appeared in *Das Reich*, 9 March 1941.

33. There is no reference to the myth Schmitt cites in connection with Abravanel in any of the standard German-language Jewish encyclopedias, nor in Ginzberg, *The Legends of the Jews* or *The Jewish Encyclopedia* (New York and London: Funk & Wagnall, 1904). The latter reference work (vol. 9, 38) does indicate that "Kimih, Abravanel and others consider the expressions [i.e. various symbolical interpretations of the Leviathan myth, including that of the Leviathan feast] to be allusions to the destruction of the powers which are hostile to the Jews."

34. Meier, *Die Lehre Carl Schmitts*, 238.

35. Schmitt, *Land und Meer*, 17, 95; *Land and Sea*, 6, 52. The same parallel is drawn in Schmitt's essay "The Sea against the Land."

36. Bauer, *Disraelis romantischer und Bismarcks sozialistischer Imperialismus* (Chemnitz: Schmeitzner, 1882), 32–62. See the preliminary remark to the first edition of *On Dictatorship*.

37. See for example Abraham Heschel, *Don Jizchak Abravanel* (Berlin: Reiss, 1937); Erwin I. J. Rosenthal, "Don Isaac Abravanel: Financier, Statesman and Scholar, 1437–1937," *Bulletin of the John Rylands Library* 21, no. 2 (1937): 3–36; and Leo Strauss, "On Abravanel's Philosophical Tendency and Political Teaching," in *Isaac Abravanel; Six Lectures*, ed. John Brande Trend and H. Loewe (Cambridge: Cambridge Univ. Press, 1937), 95–129.

38. See Rahel Wischnitzer-Bernstein, ed., *Gedenkausstellung Don Jizchaq Abravanel* (Jüdisches Museum in Berlin, 1937) (exhibition catalog).

39. On 23 August 1933 Marcu wrote from French exile to Ernst Jünger concerning this book project; see Valeriu Marcu, "Briefwechsel mit Ernst Jünger, 1933–1937," *Der Pfahl: Jahrbuch aus dem Niemandsland zwischen Kunst und Wissenschaft* 5 (1991): 119–27. On Marcu see Koenen, *Der Fall Carl Schmitt*, 372, nn. 52 and 53.

40. See *Jewish Encyclopedia*, 1:127.

41. Schmitt, *Leviathan*, 207.

42. Bookbinder, "Carl Schmitt, *Der Leviathan*, and the Jews," 101.

43. In contrast, Ernst Jünger was pleased above all by Schmitt's "prose" in this text: "A piece that shows nerves and muscle." In his note of thanks of 20 October 1938 (RW 265-182; letter no. 43, typescript), he thus advised Schmitt as follows: "I thus have the feeling that when the occasion arises you ought to write a work without a note-apparatus, as it were with a second naiveté that would suit you well." It seems Schmitt took up Jünger's suggestion in *Land und Meer*, which was written shortly after.

44. RW 265-345, letter no. 34.

45. See in this respect Arnaldo Momigliano, "The Disadvantages of Monotheism for a Universal State," in Momigliano, *On Pagans, Jews, and Christians* (Middletown, Conn.: Wesleyan Univ. Press, 1987), 142–58.

46. See Fraenkel, *Dual State*.

47. RW 265-182, letter no. 35.

48. RW 265-182, letter no. 42, typescript, Munich, 20 October 1938, Dr. Jur. Gottfried Neesse to Carl Schmitt.

49. See Johann Gottlieb Fichte, *Beitrag zur Berichtigung der Urtheile des Publikums über die Französischen Revolution* (Berlin, 1793); Katz, "A State within a State," 124–53.

50. Schmitt, *Leviathan*, 110; *Leviathan*, 70.

51. Ibid., 5; ibid., 1.

52. Ibid., 7; ibid., 3.

53. Ibid., 86, 88f.; ibid., 57f.

54. "Dear Herr Schmitt . . . I believe you are entirely right when you say that Pilate did not condemn as a judge, but I am not orientated regarding jurid. things, e.g. I don't know whether Jesus was subject to the accusation of *perduellio* [=high treason] & if any sort of trial was needed for that. I also think that one has to speak of an interplay between occupying power, collaborationists, & Jewish groups. But have no competence at all to treat these questions" (RW 265-345, letter no. 39, Erik Peterson to Carl Schmitt; 25 June 1939).

55. Schmitt, *Leviathan*, 66–67; *Leviathan*, 44. Hereafter cited in text.

56. The talk was delivered in 1929 and would be placed at the end of the second edition of *The Concept of the Political* in 1932.

57. Carl Schmitt, *Die Wendung zum diskriminierenden Kriegsbegriff* (Munich: Duncker & Humblot, 1938); Schmitt, *War/Non-War? A Dilemma*, ed., trans., and with a preface by Simona Draghici (Corvallis, Ore.: Plutarch, 2004).

58. See Bielefeldt, *Kampf um Entscheidung*, 63–66. In his *Verfassungslehre*, 83, Schmitt defines such proscription, as expressed in the Kellogg-Briand Pact of 1928, as merely an ideology masking political reality.

59. Schmitt, *Leviathan*, 84; *Leviathan*, 56f. Hereafter cited in text.

60. Ibid. Schmitt here cites from chap. 19 of Spinoza's *Tractatus theologico-politicus* (Leipzig: Meiner, 1922). Ironically, in the 3rd 1933 edition of the *Concept of the Political*, Schmitt had cited Spinoza's dictum "in suo esse perseverare," whose true meaning had been entirely unpolitical, in order to justify the struggle for one's own, specific form of political existence.

61. Schmitt, *Leviathan*, 87; *Leviathan*, 57. Hereafter cited in text.

62. The most comprehensive collection of sources documenting the history of the interpretation of 2 Thess. 2:1–12 and of the concept of the Katechon is found in W. Bornemann, *Die Thessalonicherbriefe* (Göttingen: Vandenhoeck & Ruprecht, 1894), 400–59 (the later revisions of this volume are substantially shortened and contain fewer sources). On the political influence of the New Testament passage see Werner Goez, *Translatio Imperii: Ein Beitrag zur Geschichte des Geschichtsdenkens und der politischen Theorien im Mittelalter und in die frühen Neuzeit* (Tübingen: Mohr, 1958). See also Ernst von Dobschütz, *Die Thessalonicher-Briefe* (1909; repr., Göttingen: Vandenhoeck & Ruprecht, 1974); Oscar Cullmann, *Vorträge und Aufsätze, 1925–1962*, ed. Karlfried Fröhlich (Tübingen: Mohr, 1966); Willy Böld, "Die antidämonischen Abwehrmächte in der Theologie des Spätjudentums" (PhD diss., University of Bonn, 1938; partial printing: *Das Bollwerk wider die Chaosmächte: Eine problemgeschichtliche Studie zur Staatstheologie von 2. Thess. 2.6 ff.*).

On the Katechon concept see Wilhelm Stählin, "Die Gestalt des Antichristen und das Katechon," in *Festgabe Joseph Lortz*, vol. 2, *Glaube und Geschichte*, ed. E. Iserloh and P. Manns (Baden-Baden: Grimm, 1957), 1–12; Otto Betz, "Der Katechon," *New Testament Studies: An International Journal* 9 (1963): 276–91. On the concept in Schmitt, see Lutz Berthold, "Wer hält zur Zeit den Satan auf? Zur Selbstglossierung Carl Schmitts," *Leviathan: Zeitschrift für Sozialwissen-schaft* 21 (1993): 285–99. Günter Meuter, *Der Katechon* (Berlin: Duncker & Humblot, 1994), is an effort to reconstruct Schmitt's ideas as "political theology" on the basis of earlier discussions. The ideas are thus placed in the context of the so-called conservative revolution, with extensive discussion of the relationship with Romanticism. Meuter offers little new information on the Katechon concept itself.

On the connection between the Katechon and the Antichrist see Wilhelm Bousset, *Der Antichrist in der Überlieferung des Judentums, des Neuen Testaments und der alten Kirche: Ein Beitrag zur Auslegung der Apokalypse* (Göttingen: Vandenhoeck & Ruprecht, 1895); Josef Ernst, *Die eschatologischen Gegenspieler in den Schriften des Neuen Testaments* (Regensburg: Pustet, 1967); Wolfgang Trilling, "Antichrist und Papsttum, Reflexionen zur Wirkungsgeschichte von 2 Thess. 2,1/10a," in *Begegnung mit dem Wort, Festschrift für Heinrich Zimmermann,* ed. Josef Zwijewski and Ernst Nellessen (Bonn: Hanstein, 1980), 251–71, here 253. Neil Forsyth reviews various antichrist-concepts in *The Old Enemy: Satan and the Combat Myth* (Princeton, N.J.: Princeton Univ. Press, 1987); on Paul, see 279f.

63. On the theological dispute over the question of the incorporation of eschatology into Christian salvational history, see Oscar Cullmann, *Christus und die Zeit: Die urchristliche Zeit- und Geschichtsauffassung,* 3rd ed. (Zurich: Evangelischer Verlag, 1962), 14f.

64. *REB*, 186.

65. See the chapter "Antichrist" in Ernst Kantorowicz, *Kaiser Friedrich der Zweite* (Berlin: Bondi, 1927).

66. Schmitt, *Theodor Däublers "Nordlicht,"* 61f.

67. Generating fierce scholarly and scholarly-political controversy, the numerous early Jewish texts discovered in the Dead Sea region starting in the mid-twentieth century reveal that very similar ideas (messiah/anti-messiah) were present in antique Judaism. See Norman Golb, *Who Wrote the Dead Sea Scrolls? The Search for the Secret of Qumran* (New York: Scribner, 1995), 79ff. and 361–85.

68. *REB*, 186. For an extensive discussion of the problem of messianic delay and delay of Christ's second coming, see A. Strobel, *Untersuchungen zum eschatologischen Verzögerungsproblem auf Grund der spätjüdisch-urchristlichen Geschichte von Habakuk 2,2 ff.* (Leiden: Brill, 1961); on the Katechon concept, see 98–116, 194–98.

69. See Trilling, "Antichrist und Papsttum."

70. Ibid.

71. See Rosenzweig, *Der Stern der Erlösung,* 461ff., and Taubes, *Abendländische Eschatologie.*

72. On the concept of accommodation see Amos Funkenstein, *Heilsplan und natürliche Entwicklung: Formen der Gegenwartsbestimmung im Geschichtsdenken des hohen Mittelalters* (Munich: Nymphenburger Verlanshandlung, 1965), 51–54.

73. Trilling, "Antichrist und Papsttum," 253.

74. Bousset, *Der Antichrist,* 16.

75. Schmitt, *Theodor Däublers "Nordlicht,"* 70.

76. See Karlfried Gründer in Quaritsch, ed., *Complexio Oppositorum*, 230: "Schmitt presumably gets the Katechon . . . from Peterson . . . or else from Protestant exegesis. For as far as I know Catholic theology of the sort at Donoso Cortés's disposal in the nineteenth century made use of New Testament concepts according to the Vulgata, not from the Greek."

77. Cited from Nichtweiss, *Peterson*, 481.

78. Schmitt, *Politische Theologie*, 2:81.

79. Nichtweiss, *Peterson*, 489. For early passages concerning the "Jewish origin of the Antichrist," see Bousset, *Der Antichrist*, 84–86; on the medieval image: Norman Cohn, *Warrant for Genocide* (New York: Harper & Row, 1967), 254.

80. See Schmitt, *Die Diktatur*, 5th ed. (2nd ed., 1928, repr., Berlin: Duncker & Humblot, 1989), 1–42 (dictatorship of the commissar) and 130–52 (sovereign dictatorship).

81. See for example John Day, *God's Conflict with the Dragon and the Sea: Echoes of a Canaanite Myth in the Old Testament* (Cambridge: Cambridge Univ. Press, 1985).

82. Ernst, *Gegenspieler*, x.

83. Schmitt, *Leviathan*, 79; *Leviathan*, 53.

84. Ernst Forsthoff, *Der Staat der Industriegesellschaft. Dargestellt am Beispiel der Bundesrepublik Deutschland*, 2nd ed. (Munich: C.H. Beck, 1971), 25.

85. Carl Schmitt, *Hugo Preuss, sein Staatsbegriff und seine Stellung in der deutschen Staatslehre* (Tübingen: Mohr, 1930), 5. Jacques Derrida intended his own highly influential concept of deferral, *différance*, to be located beyond any teleological or eschatological horizon. Nevertheless, throughout his writing there are interesting parallels with Schmitt's concept. See, for instance, Derrida's essay "Freud and the Scene of Writing," in Derrida, *Writing and Difference*, trans. Rodolphe Gasché, with introd. and additional notes by Alan Bass (Chicago: Univ. of Chicago Press, 1978), 198.

86. Schmitt, *Hugo Preuss*, 5. Schmitt continues as follows: "[Preuss] has a political enemy in sight and is defined in his spiritual [*geistig*] rank, intellectual strength, and historical significance by his enemy. . . . At least for a scholarly commentary this should be taken into account."

87. Schmitt, *Leviathan*, 124; *Leviathan*, 82.

88. This notion is expressed even more drastically at the close of Schmitt's article "Das Meer gegen das Land": "With this the time of Leviathan, i.e. the historical segment of a rule built on the element of the sea, face to face with the land, is at an end."

89. In Carl Schmitt, *Verfassungsrechtliche Aufsätze aus den Jahren 1924–1954: Materialien zu einer Verfassungslehre* (Berlin: Duncker & Humblot, 1958), 375–85.

90. Carl Schmitt, *Völkerrechtliche Grossraumordnung mit Interventionsverbot für raumfremde Mächte: Ein Beitrag zum Reichsbegriff im Völkerrecht* [Organization of Greater Territory in International Law, with a Ban on Intervention for Alien Powers], 1st ed. (Berlin: Deutscher Rechtsverlag, 1939), 87.

91. Ibid.

92. Schmitt, *Positionen und Begriffe*, 354.

93. Stefan Breuer, *Anatomie der konservativen Revolution* (Darmstadt: Wissenschaftliche Buchgesellschaft, 1993), 104–14.

94. Schmitt, *Der Nomos der Erde*, 29.

95. Ibid., 16. This sentence was deleted from the Maschke edition without any indication this had been done. Hereafter cited in text.

96. Wolfgang Abendroth, *Ein Leben in der Arbeiterbewegung* (Frankfurt a.M.: Suhrkamp, 1976), 212.

97. Carl Schmitt, "Beschleuniger wider Willen oder: Problematik der westlichen Hemisphäre," *Das Reich*, 19 April 1942.

98. Ibid.

99. Schmitt, "Drei Stufen historischer Sinngebung," *Universitas* 5 (1950): 927–31.

100. Schmitt, *Der Nomos der Erde*, 28–32.

101. See Bousset, *Der Antichrist*, 16.

102. Ibid. and in general Trachtenberg, *Devil and the Jews*.

103. Otto Brunner to Carl Schmitt, 25 June 1942, RW 265-193, letter no. 7.

104. Hans Körniken to Carl Schmitt, 25 June 1942, RW 265-249, letter no 1.

105. See Martin Dibelius, "Rom und die Christen im ersten Jahrhundert," meeting minutes, Heidelberger Akademie der Wissenschaften, Philosophisch-historische Klasse, 1941–42 (2nd lecture, Heidelberg, 1942).

106. Carl Schmitt to Martin Dibelius, 4 June 1942, RW 265-193, convolute no. 1, letter no. 5. Dibelius's text is heavily underlined: RW 265-193, library.

107. Berthold, "Wer hält zur Zeit den Satan auf?" stresses the influence of Oscar Cullmann's work on the Katechon. But whether Schmitt had any knowledge of these texts remains uncertain in the absence of any references to them. This does not diminish the importance of Berthold's interesting observations for understanding Schmitt's own idea of the Katechon.

108. Adolph Zahn, *Über den biblischen und kirchlichen Begriff der Anrechnung: Ein Beitrag zur Rechtfertigungslehre* (Amsterdam: Scheffer, 1899). See also Zahn, *Das Gesetz Gottes nach der Lehre und der Erfahrung des Apostels Paulus* (Halle: Mühlmann, 1876).

109. Zahn, *Über den biblischen und kirchlichen Begriff*, x.

110. Berthold, "Wer hält zur Zeit den Satan auf?" 291.

111. Zahn, *Über den biblischen und kirchlichen Begriff*, foreword, v. Hereafter cited in text.

Chapter 13. Depolitization

1. Meuter, *Der Katechon*, esp. 211–91. For the most part Felix Grossheutschi's book *Carl Schmitt und die Lehre vom Katechon* (Berlin: Duncker & Humblot, 1996) adheres to Schmitt's own intentions, thus neglecting the concept's systematic location in his oeuvre. Neither Meuter nor Grossheutschi refer to Adolph Zahn.

2. Schmitt, *Der Begriff des Politischen*, 80.

3. Schmitt's strongest expression of a will to form was in *Roman Catholicism and Political Form*.

4. Schmitt, *Der Begriff des Politischen*, 27; *The Concept of the Political*, 26.

5. Ibid., 88.

6. Ibid.

7. Ibid. On the reality of this historical caesura see Amos Funkenstein, *Theology and the Scientific Imagination from the Middle Ages to the Seventeenth Century* (Princeton, N.J.: Princeton Univ. Press, 1986).

8. Cf. Meier, *Die Lehre Carl Schmitts*.

9. The theme of "pathetic thinking" (Mehring) never leaves Schmitt completely. The battle against play and for seriousness extends from *Northern Light* (1916) to *Hamlet oder Hekuba, Der Einbruch der Zeit in das Spiel* (Düsseldorf: Diederichs, 1956); *Hamlet or Hecuba: The Interruption of Time into Play*, trans. Simona Draghici (Corvallis, Ore.: Plutarch, 2006).

10. Quaritsch, ed., *Complexio Oppositorum*, 317.

11. Ibid.

12. Cf. Schmitt, *Der Begriff des Politischen*, 70: "If need be the political unit must demand the sacrifice of life." Hereafter cited in text.

13. Evoking Hegelian dialectic, these gnomic sentences of Schmitt stem from Theodor Däubler, *Hymne an Italien*, 2nd ed. (Leipzig: Insel-Verlag, 1919), 65, and are addressed to the city of Palermo: "The enemy is our own question as form / And he will hunt us, we him, to the same end."

14. Schmitt, *Theorie des Partisanen: Zwischenbemerkung zum Begriff des Politischen*, 87f.

15. Ibid., 89.

16. Schmitt, *Begriff des Politischen*, 3rd ed., 7.

17. Ibid., 26.

18. Ibid., 31.

19. Reinhart Koselleck in particular has described Schmitt's friend-enemy distinction in terms of symmetry. By symmetry, he means that the vocabulary used in the distinction is neutral in that the terms can be reversed. See *Vergangene Zukunft: Zur Semantik geschichtlicher Zeiten* (Frankfurt a.M.: Suhrkamp, 1989), 211–59, 258.

20. Schmitt, *Begriff des Politischen*, 26.

21. Ibid., 27; 1st ed. (1927), 4; 3rd ed. (1933), 8.

22. For the entire citation see chap. 1, 36, and 261n18.

23. Dan Diner, "Nationalstaat und Migration: Zu Begriff und Geschichte," in *Schwierige Fremdheit: Über Integration und Ausgrenzung in Einwanderungsländern*, ed. Friedrich Balke, Rebekka Habermas, Patrizia Nanz, and Peter Sillem (Frankfurt a.M.: Fischer, 1993), 37. In contrast in his "Exkurs über den Fremden" [Excursus on the Stranger] Georg Simmel designated the European Jews as "the classical example" of his concept of the foreigner. See Simmel, *Soziologie: Untersuchungen über die Formen der Vergesellschaftung* (Leipzig: Duncker & Humblot,

1908), 685–91. See also Friedrich Balke, "Die Figur des Fremden bei Carl Schmitt und Georg Simmel," *Sociologia Internationalis: Internationale Zeitschrift für Soziologie, Kommunikations- und Kulturforschung* 30 (1992): 35–59. Balke here argues that the foreigner, not the enemy, is the key concept in Schmitt's political theory.

24. On the "modernization" debate see Ian Kershaw, *Der NS-Staat: Geschichtsinterpretationen und Kontroversen im Überblick* (Hamburg: Rowohlt, 1989), 258–88; Mommsen, "Nationalsozialismus als vorgetäuschte Modernisierung," 405–27.

25. See Michael Ley and Julius H. Schoeps, eds., *Der Nationalsozialismus als politische Religion* (Bodenheim b. Mainz: Philo, 1997).

26. Hegel, *Schriften zur Politik und Rechtsphilosophie*, ed. Georg Lasson (Leipzig: Meiner, 1913), 470–71; Schmitt, *Begriff des Politischen*, 62 (without indication of source).

27. Ibid, 29; 1st ed., 6; 3rd ed., 11.

28. Ibid., 30. In the 3rd ed., p. 11, Schmitt becomes more precise, referring twice to "political" enemies.

29. In this respect see Martin Leutzsch, "Der Bezug auf die Bibel," 183: "Schmitt, who does not stand alone in relegating love for one's enemy to the private sphere, philologically ignores the framework for understanding the admonition to love one's enemy made by Jesus of Nazareth, the Jew: Israelite-Jewish society and Jewish linguistic usage. This insight was by no means rare at the time *Der Begriff des Politischen* was written. That Schmitt elsewhere points to the distinction between public and private as having only being 'driven forward to an ever-sharper separation and antithesis' in the eighteenth century is another argument against the accuracy of his privately focused reading of love for one's enemy."

30. Schmitt, *Begriff des Politischen*, 29.

31. Ibid., 20; 1st ed., 1. Hereafter cited in text.

32. Ibid., 90. Generally denoting public proclamation, preconization is chiefly an ecclesiastical term for the pope's nomination of a church dignitary.

33. See James Tully, ed., *Meaning and Context: Quentin Skinner and his Critiques* (Cambridge: Polity Press, 1988).

34. Schmitt, *Positionen und Begriffe*, 198, cited in Mehring, *Carl Schmitt zur Einführung*, 7.

35. Schmitt, *Begriff des Politischen*, 94.

36. Ibid., 59.

37. Schmitt, *Politische Theologie*, 79; *Political Theology*, 62.

38. Cf. Meier, *Carl Schmitt, Leo Strauss und "Der Begriff des Politischen."*

39. Schmitt's remarks in *Disputation über den Rechtsstaat*, 87. See also a widely neglected review of this book by Hans Mayer, in *Zeitschrift für Sozialforschung* 5 (1936): 460–61.

40. Schmitt, *Glossarium*, 18.

41. Ibid., 9.

42. Schmitt, *Begriff des Politischen*, 75.

43. Franz Oppenheimer, *Der Staat* (Frankfurt a.M.: Rütten & Loening, 1912), 168. For a closer evaluation of Schmitt's critique of Oppenheimer see Hanno Kesting, *Geschichtsphilosophie und Weltbürgerkrieg: Deutungen der Geschichte von der Französischen Revolution bis zum Ost-West-Konflikt* (Heidelberg: Winter, 1959), 156–64.

44. All citations are from Schmitt, *Begriff des Politischen*, 3rd ed., 59.

45. Ibid., 2nd ed., 37–45; 1st ed., 9–14; 3rd ed., 20–28. Schmitt discusses Laski in the following works as well: "Das Reichsgericht als Hüter der Verfassung," (1929) in *Verfassungsrechtliche Aufsätze*, 63–109, 76; "Zu Friedrich Meineckes 'Idee der Staatsräson,'" (1926) in *Positionen und Begriffe*, 45–52, 52; and, most extensively, in "Staatsethik und pluralistischer Staat," (1930) in ibid., 133–45.

46. Schmitt, *Begriff des Politischen*, 1st ed., 12. In "Zu Friedrich Meineckes 'Idee der Staatsräson,'" 52, Schmitt describes Laski's theory as "more interesting and topical" than the "clichés found in compendia of constitutional law or indeed the products of methodological inflation."

47. Schmitt, "Das Reichsgericht als Hüter der Verfassung." This assessment is absent from the revised version of this text, *Der Hüter der Verfassung* (Tübingen: Mohr, 1931).

48. Sombart, *Die deutschen Männer und ihre Feinde*, 278–79.

49. Schmitt, *Begriff des Politischen*, 39.

50. Schmitt, "Staatsethik und pluralistischer Staat," in Schmitt, *Positionen und Begriffe*, 141. Also in *Begriff des Politischen*, 38f.; 3rd ed., 21.

51. See Harold J. Laski, *A Grammar of Politics* (1925; 4th ed., London: Allen & Unwin, 1941), x–xi.

52. Schmitt, *Begriff des Politischen*, 41, 43.

53. This rhetorical pattern begins in his early book *Gesetz und Urteil* (Berlin: Liebmann, 1912), 120, where Schmitt writes that "in reality" it is not Ferdinand Lassalle's "juridical sharpness that matters." On Marxist "sharpness" see Schmitt, *Geistesgeschichtliche Lage*, 75; *Crisis of Parliamentary Democracy*, 63.

54. Schmitt, *Begriff des Politischen*, 44–45.

55. Ibid., 3rd ed., 23. In the second edition, G. D. H. Cole is mentioned alongside Laski.

56. Schmitt's essay "Staatsethik und pluralistischer Staat," in Schmitt, *Positionen und Begriffe*, 135, offers some clarification by underscoring the place of Laski's idea of the state in a series of intellectual-historical "phenomena that I defined as 'political theology.'"

57. Schmitt, *Begriff des Politischen*, 43.

58. See Heinz Hürten, "Deutscher Katholizismus am Ende des Kaiserreichs: Strukturen, Traditionen, Tendenzen," in Hürten, *Deutsche Katholiken, 1918–1945* (Paderborn: Schöningh, 1992), 13–34, 27.

59. Schmitt, *Begriff des Politischen*, 3rd ed., 24.

60. Ibid., 25, n.12.

61. Schmitt, "Staatsethik und pluralistischer Staat," in Schmitt, *Positionen und Begriffe*, 135.

62. Schmitt, *Begriff des Politischen*, 64. For a critique of Schmitt's misleading idea of the miracle in *Political Theology*, see Panajotis Kondylis, "Jurisprudenz, Ausnahmezustand und Entscheidung: Grundsätzliche Bemerkungen zu Carl Schmitts 'Politische Theologie,'" *Der Staat* 34, no. 3 (1995): 325–57.

63. Schmitt, *Begriff des Politischen*, 64. See also *Politische Romantik*, 5–6; *Political Romanticism*, 3: "The life of many sects, for whom Ernst Troeltsch (in his *Soziallehren der christlichen Kirchen*) came up with the formula 'absolute natural law,' springs from a fanaticism whose anarchic power lies in a denial of original sin."

64. Schmitt, *Politische Theologie*, 79; *Political Theology*, 62.

65. Schmitt, *Begriff des Politischen*, 64.

66. RW 265-193, nos. 12–13.

67. Ernst Forsthoff, "Über Gerechtigkeit," *Deutsches Volkstum* 16 (1934): 969–74, 971.

68. Schmitt, *Begriff des Politischen*, 92.

69. *Arthur Schopenhauers sämtliche Werke*, ed. Julius Frauenstädt (Leipzig: Brockhaus, 1930), vol. 6, *Parerga und Paralipomena*, 412.

70. Wilhelm Stapel, "Deutschtum und Christentum," *Deutsches Volkstum* 14 (1932): 794.

71. For this ideational complex see Hubert Cancik, "Augustin als constantinischer Theologe," in Taubes, *Der Fürst dieser Welt*, 136–52; Elaine Pagels, *Adam, Eve, and the Serpent* (New York: Random House, 1988), ch. 5; Pagels, "The Politics of Paradise: Augustine's Exegesis of Genesis 1–3 versus that of John Chrystostomos," *Harvard Theological Review* 78, nos. 1–2 (1985): 67–95.

72. Jan Assmann, *Politische Theologie zwischen Ägypten und Israel* (Munich: Carl Friedrich von Siemens Stiftung, 1992), 35ff., has thus noted that Schmitt's *Political Theology* does not confront a process of secularization, but of resecularization.

73. Pagels, *Adam, Eve, and the Serpent*, xxv. Hereafter cited in text.

74. See Adolf von Harnack, "Der pelagianische Kampf: Die Lehre von der Gnade und Sünde," in von Harnack, *Dogmengeschichte*, 7th ed. (Tübingen: Mohr, 1931), 314–24.

75. See the article "Sünde und Schuld," in *Die Religion in Geschichte und Gegenwart*, vol. 6, cols. 476–505; "Erbsünde," in *Historisches Wörterbuch der Philosophie*, ed. Joachim Ritter (Darmstadt: Wissenschaftliche Buchgesellschaft, 1972), 2:604–7.

76. See *Die Religion in Geschichte und Gegenwart*, vol. 6, col. 491.

77. St. Augustine, *Civitas Dei*, 21, 12.

78. Pagels, *Adam, Eve, and the Serpent*, xxvi.

79. On Augustine's view of world history see Karl Jaspers, *Die grossen Philosophen* (Munich: Piper, 1957), 369–73.

80. Decree on original sin, 17 June 1546; text in Heinrich Denziger, *Enchiridion symbolorum, definitionum et declarationum de rebus fidei et morum* (Freiburg: Herder, 1858).

81. Harnack, *Dogmengeschichte*, 322.

82. Pagels, *Adam, Eve, and the Serpent*, 98.

83. In 1546 the Council of Trent retroactively declared Paul to have recognized the doctrine, on the basis of Rom. 5:12–21 and 1 Cor. 15:21f.—an interpretation maintained to this day. On the doctrine of original sin see the article "Erbsünde," in *Lexikon für Theologie und Kirche*, ed. Josef Höfer and Karl Rahner (Freiburg: Herder, 1959), 3:965–73.

84. Schmitt, *Der Begriff des Politischen*, 64. Hereafter cited in text.

85. *Jüdisches Lexikon, Ein enzykopädisches Handbuch des jüdischen Wissens in fünf Bänden* (Berlin: Jüdischer Verlag, 1928), s.v. Max Dienemann, "Erbsünde," 2: 456–59, with many examples.

86. See "Sünde und Schuld," in *Die Religion in Geschichte und Gegenwart*, vol. 6, cols. 476–505.

87. Jacob Jervell, *Imago Dei: Gen. 1,26f. im Spätjudentum, in der Gnosis und in den paulinischen Briefen* (Göttingen: Vandenhoeck & Ruprecht, 1960), 40–41.

88. Julius Gross, *Entstehungsgeschichte des Erbsündendogmas: Von der Bibel bis Augustinus* (Munich: Reinhart, 1960), 31 and 375.

89. Schmitt, *Begriff des Politischen*, 64.

90. Ibid., 60. See Kramme, *Helmuth Plessner und Carl Schmitt*.

Chapter 14. Desubstantialization

1. Dreier, *Rechtslehre*, 16.

2. Hans Kelsen, "Wer soll der Hüter der Verfassung sein?" (1931), in Klecatsky, Marcic, and Schambeck, eds., *Die Wiener Rechtstheoretische Schule*, 1876 and 1917. Hereafter cited in text.

3. Ibid., 1917. See Michel Troper, "'The Guardian of the Constitution': Hans Kelsen's Evaluation of a Legal Concept," trans. Joel Golb, in *Hans Kelsen and Carl Schmitt: A Juxtaposition*, ed. Dan Diner and Michael Stolleis (Gerlingen: Bleicher, 1999), 81–100.

4. Caldwell, *Constitutional Theory in the Weimar Republic*, 304.

5. See Gross, "Carl Schmitts Nomos und die 'Juden.'"

6. Kelsen, "Gott und Staat," 193.

7. Kelsen, "Der Staatsbegriff und die Psychoanalyse," 212.

8. Schmitt, *Begriff des Politischen*, 70.

9. Ibid. I thank Michael Reiter for drawing my attention to the importance of the concept of sacrifice, and in particular to that of the society's founding through blood sacrifice, i.e., war. Reiter focuses on sacrifice in a 1996 dissertation for the Free University of Berlin.

10. Kelsen, *Allgemeine Staatslehre*, 76.

11. Ibid.

12. See Gross, "Jesus oder Christus?"

13. Kelsen, *Hauptprobleme der Staatsrechtslehre*, 401–12.

14. Kelsen, "Wer soll der Hüter der Verfassung sein?" 1890.

15. Müller [alias Gurian], "Entscheidung und Ordnung," 575.

16. *Meyers Lexikon von 1939*, s.v. "Kelsen, Hans," cited from Izhak Englard, "Nazi Criticism Against the Normativist Theory of Hans Kelsen: Its Intellectual Basis and Post-Modern Tendencies," in Diner and Solleis, *Hans Kelsen and Carl Schmitt*, 133–88, here 188.

Chapter 15. The Flight into Religion

1. Schmitt, *Glossarium*, 229.

2. Schmitt, *Glossarium*, 20. Cf. Herbert, *Best*, 498–501. Herbert shows how Werner Best successfully maneuvered along those lines to protect himself and other high-ranking SS and SD officials against legal proceedings in West Germany after the war.

3. Following her visit to West Germany in 1950, Arendt, "Besuch in Deutschland," 44, wrote of a "general lack of feeling" and "apparent heartlessness" in face of the Jewish victims. She interpreted this as the reflection of a deep-rooted, stubborn, and "occasionally brutal" refusal to confront what actually had taken place and accept any responsibility for it. Her diagnosis seems to apply perfectly to Schmitt. On the postwar myth of an all-encompassing, indiscriminate Allied accusation of "collective guilt," see Norbert Frei, "Von deutscher Erfundungskraft oder: Die Kollektivschuldthese in der Nachkriegszeit," *Rechtshistorisches Journal* 16 (1997): 621–34.

4. This process of repression has perhaps been described most precisely in a historical sense by Herbert, *Best* and Frei, *Adenauer's Germany*.

5. See Christoph Klessmann, *Die doppelte Staatsgründung: Deutsche Geschichte 1945–1955*, 5th rev. ed. (Bonn: Bundeszentrale für Politische Bildung, 1991).

6. See the chapter "The Churches and the 'Jewish Question'" in Frank Stern, *Im Anfang war Auschwitz: Antisemitismus und Philosemitismus im deutschen Nachkrieg* (Gerlingen: Bleicher, 1991), 269–98.

7. See the critical overview in Heschel and Ericksen, "The German Churches Face Hitler." On the Vatican's attitude, see Saul Friedländer, *Pius XII und das Dritte Reich: Eine Dokumentation*, afterword by Alfred Grosser (Reinbek: Rowohlt, 1965).

8. See Shlomo Aronson, *Reinhard Heydrich und die Frühgeschichte von Gestapo und SD* (Stuttgart: DVA, 1971). On a number of occasions the same charge was leveled against Schmitt by the SD. See Gross, "Politische Polykratie 1936."

9. See "Studien zum Mythus des XX. Jahrhunderts," in *Kirchlicher Anzeiger für die Erzdiözese Köln: Amtliche Beilage* (Cologne: Bachem, 1934).

10. Frank Stern, *Im Anfang war Auschwitz*, 158, describes the incapacity of the German professorial caste to reflect on its relationship with the Jews, rather opting for a "flight into the religious," as one of its typical traits after 1945. On the role played by the church in undermining Allied efforts at denazification, see also Ulrich Herbert, "Als die Nazis wieder gesellschaftsfähig wurden: Vom raschen Wiederaufstieg der NS-Eliten und von der Frage: Wie konnte aus der Bundesrepublik dennoch eine stabile Demokratie werden?" *Die Zeit*, January 10, 1997, 34. On the determining role played by both the German Evangelical and Catholic churches in gaining clemency for condemned Nazi criminals, see Frei, *Adenauer's Germany*, 93–233.

11. See Jeffrey Herf, *Reactionary Modernism: Technology, Culture, and Politics in Weimar and the Third Reich* (Cambridge: Cambridge Univ. Press, 1984); Stefan Breuer, "'Konservative Revolution': Kritik eines Mythos," *Politische Vierteljahresschrift* 31 (1990): 585–607; Breuer, *Anatomie der konservativen Revolution* (Darmstadt: Wissenschaftliche Buchgesellschaft, 1993); Rolf Peter Sieferle, *Die Konservative Revolution: Fünf biographische Skizzen (Paul Lensch, Werner Sombart, Oswald Spengler, Ernst Jünger, Hans Freyer)* (Frankfurt a.M.: Fischer, 1995). Ulrich Herbert, *Arbeit, Volkstum, Weltanschauung: Über Fremde und Deutsche im 20. Jahrhundert* (Frankfurt a.M.: Fischer, 1995), 238; and *Best*, 549, reject the term "conservative revolution." On Mohler, see van Laak, *Gespräche in der Sicherheit des Schweigens*, 256–62.

12. Sieferle, *Die Konservative Revolution*, 21.

13. Mohler, *Die Konservative Revolution in Deutschland*, 4.

14. Schmitt, *Ex Captivitate Salus*, 9. Schmitt wrote an introduction with information on the questionnaire's origins for the book's Spanish translation. A German translation of the questionnaire is found in Tommissen, *Schmittiana*, 2: 140–42.

15. Schmitt respectfully refers to Ahlmann's suicide in *Ex Captivitate Salus*, 42. On Ahlmann, see Schulz, "Johannes Popitz," 245 (with the first name erroneously given as Werner instead of Wilhelm); Koenen, *Der Fall Carl Schmitt* (Darmstadt: Wissenschaftliche Buchgesellschaft, 1995), 352, 360, 366, 367, 378, 450, 639, 829; and *Tymbos für Wilhelm Ahlmann: Ein Gedenkbuch hrsg. von seinen Freunden* (Berlin: Walter de Gruyter, 1951).

16. Maschke "Im Irrgarten Carl Schmitts," 231.

17. See van Laak, *Gespräche in der Sicherheit des Schweigens*, 31–41. Accurate information on Schmitt and the questionnaire on 31, n.67. More comments on the questionnaire by Schmitt in the *Glossarium*, 181, 226. Prepared by the Americans, the questionnaire consisted of 132 rubrics focused on the recipients' personal and political pasts. For Ernst von Salomon, the questionnaire served as the basis for a notorious autobiographical book, one of the best-selling books in Germany after the war. During the Weimar Republic period, Salomon spent several years in prison for his participation in the murder of Walther Rathenau; he was one of the republic's *völkisch*, far right-wing destroyers. At the end of his book he presented himself as a rescuer of Jews, unjustly placed in the dock by

vengeful occupiers. See Markus Josef Klein, *Ernst von Salomon: Eine politische Biographie* (Limburg: San Casciano, 1994). The duplicitous effort by Werner Best, a key official in the execution of the "final solution," to establish a reputation as a rescuer of Denmark's Jews was similarly cynical but even more scandalous. See Ulrich Herbert, "Die deutsche Besatzungspolitik in Dänemark im 2: Weltkrieg und die Rettung der dänischen Juden," *Tel Aviver Jahrbuch für deutsche Geschichte* 23 (1994): 93–114, here 100f.

18. See van Laak, *Gespräche in der Sicherheit des Schweigens,* 31f.

19. Ibid., 32.

20. See Tommissen, *Schmittiana,* 1:51.

21. RW 265-424. By the end of 1945, 117,512 persons had been arrested in the American Zone in the course of denazification, 68,500 in the British Zone, 18,963 in the French Zone, and 67,179 in the Russian Zone. See Klessmann, *Die doppelte Staatsgründung,* 86f.

22. Laak, *Gespräche in der Sicherheit des Schweigens,* 32. The references are found in RW 265-469, mat. no. 4.

23. Ibid., 33. Cf. Schmitt, *Staat, Grossraum, Nomos,* 477; Tommissen, *Schmittiana,* 2:140.

24. Schmitt, *Glossarium,* 264. Remarks on Kempner on 205, 259, and 314. On Flechtheim and Kempner, see the short biographies in Walter Tetzlaff, *2000 Kurzbiographien bedeutender deutscher Juden des 20. Jahrhunderts* (Lindhorst: Askania, 1982), 79f., 173. More extensively on Kempner: Friedhelm Kröll, *Das Verhör: Carl Schmitt in Nürnberg* (Nuremberg: Bildungszentrum Stadt Nürnberg, 1995), 22–26. The protocols of Kempner's three interrogations of Schmitt are reprinted and extensively commentated in that book. See Schmitt, *Staat, Grossraum, Nomos,* 453–77, for Schmitt's written response to Kempner's questions: "To what extent did you advance Hitler's greater-territory policies?" and "To what extent did you reinforce the theoretical underpinnings of Hitler's greater-territory policies?" There are three separate versions of Flechtheim's interrogation of Schmitt. The earliest of these is included in the memoirs of Ernst Niekisch, *Gewagtes Leben* (Cologne: Kiepenheuer & Witsch, 1958), 244–45; a second version is offered by Tommissen in her edition of *Schmittiana,* vol. 2; and a last version is found in a letter of Flechtheim to C. Wieland, 24 February 1983 (ibid., 143; here as well the reference to Niekisch). All three versions seem skewed. Flechtheim writes: "As an attorney on the staff of the American prosecutor for war crimes, Telford Taylor, I interrogated Schmitt in Berlin. . . . I informed him that in 1933 I hoped to write a dissertation in Cologne on Donoso Cortés under his direction, and that after initially reacting very positively, he then wrote me a letter that read roughly like this: 'Dear Sir, the theme you propose can only be worked on in circumstances that I must assume are not present in your case. Yours sincerely. . . .' (That could only refer to my so-called racial origins). He insisted he knew nothing about such a letter." In line with Schmitt's self-stylization, Tommissen's version depicts him as superior in defeat.

25. The passage from the interrogation cited by Bendersky, *Carl Schmitt, Theorist for the Reich,* 269: "It is definitely horrible. Nothing else can be said about it," does not refer to Schmitt's antisemitism but to his "thesis" that legislation was meant to be National Socialist. Cf. Wieland, "Carl Schmitt in Nürnberg" (1947), 111. Even if, in the context of the interrogation, Schmitt's remark had indeed referred to his antisemitic statements—which, as indicated, is not the case—it would still remain incomprehensible why historians could then say "nothing more" about it.

26. Carl Schmitt, *Völkerrechtliche Grossraumordnung,* 78f; also in Schmitt, *Staat, Grossraum, Nomos,* 317f.

27. Cited after Wieland, "Carl Schmitt in Nürnberg," 112.

28. Thus Quaritsch, foreword to *Complexio Oppositorum,* 5.

29. The term is Kempner's, in his recounting of his last conversation with Schmitt; Robert M. W. Kempner, *Das Dritte Reich im Kreuzverhör* (Munich: Bechtle, 1969), 300.

30. Cf. ibid., 71f.

31. The extent of this correspondence emerges in van Laak and Villinger, *Nachlass Carl Schmitt.*

32. See, for example, Schmitt's *Theory of the Partisan* (Berlin: Duncker & Humblot, 1963).

33. See Tommissen, *Schmittiana,* 1:12.

34. The difference becomes clear in Schmitt's correspondence with his "pupil" Armin Mohler. See Mohler, Huhn, and Tommissen, *Carl Schmitt—Briefwechsel mit einem seiner Schüler.*

35. Léon-Henri-Marie Bloy, *Le salut par les juifs* (Paris: Demay, 1892). On Bloy, see also note of Maschke in Schmitt, *Staat, Grossraum, Nomos,* 398f.; and numerous comments (few going beyond general attestations of admiration) scattered through Mohler, Huhn, and Tommissen, *Carl Schmitt—Briefwechsel mit einem seiner Schüler.*

36. See Kiesel, *Briefe 1930–1983,* 164, Carl Schmitt to Ernst Jünger, 4 August 1943: "A Jewish art historian, Panofsky, was in Hamburg; in 1933, referring to a street demonstration marching under the cry 'death to Judah!' [*Judah verrecke*] he opined 'more likely the heroes will turn Jewish' [*eher werden die Recken verjuden*], upon which he was correctly [*mit Recht*] arrested. I was reminded of this when reading L. Bloy."

37. See Mohler, Huhn, and Tommissen, *Carl Schmitt—Briefwechsel mit einem seiner Schüler,* 24, Carl Schmitt to Armin Mohler, 29 August 1948.

38. On the interpretive history of the passage from John, see the recently republished article of Jacob Taubes, "Die Streitfrage zwischen Judentum und Christentum," in Taubes, *Vom Kult zur Kultur,* ed. Assmann, Assmann, Hartwich, and Menninghaus. The most extensive Catholic commentary on the St. John Gospel, Rudolf Schnackenburg, *Das Johannesevangelium,* 2nd ed., 3 vols. (Freiburg: Herder, 1967), 470f., devotes little space to John 4:22. It indicates that the

"salvational role of Israel" is not meant to be denied here, but is rather meant to be "considered superseded"—this the proper interpretation "despite purported anti-Judaism." The older commentary by Bultmann, *Das Evangelium des Johannes*, 139, suggests that the passage has to be understood as an "editorial gloss," and that it is "impossible" that it stems from John.

39. Carl Schmitt to Joachim Kaiser, 3 October 1953; RW 265-126, letter no. 6.

40. See Schmitt, *Ex Captivitate Salus*, 31 and 25. On this idea and its effect on West German historiography, see van Laak, *Gespräche in der Sicherheit des Schweigens*, 79, 103f. There also, 269, is a citation of Nicolaus Sombart (from "Patriotische Betrachtungen über die geistesgeschichtliche Bedeutung von Ernst Jüngers 'Arbeiter,' anlässlich der Neuauflage 1964," *Frankfurter Hefte* [1965]: 390–400, esp. 390) that lays bare the weaknesses of Schmitt's argumentation: "We know that chiliasm flourishes in times of need and that finally all philosophy of history rests on an effort to convert defeat into victory. This when all that truly matters is understanding the causes of the defeat." In contrast, Hans-Joachim Arndt, *Die Besiegten von 1945* (Berlin: Duncker & Humblot, 1978), has positive comments on Schmitt's way of seeing things.

41. Schmitt, *Ex Captivitate Salus*, 31, 27.

42. Ibid., 75.

43. [Carl Schmitt,] "Amnestie—Urform des Rechts," *Christ und Welt*, 10 November 1949, 2. (Also under the title "Amnestie oder die Kraft des Vergessens," in Schmitt, *Staat, Grossraum, Nomos*, 218–21.) See also Schmitt, *Glossarium*, 257: "But amnesty is a two-sided, mutual process. That's something different from mercy and pardon [*Gnade und Begnadigung*]."

44. Ernst Achenbach, "Generalamnestie!" *Zeitschrift für Geopolitik* 23 (1952): 321f.; cited in van Laak, *Gespräche in der Sicherheit des Schweigens*, 102. On the amnesty laws, see Joachim Perels, "Amnestie für NS-Täter in der Bundesrepublik," *Kritische Justiz* 28 (1995): 382–89. This was the context for the "amnesty campaign" of Heydrich-deputy Werner Best; see Herbert, *Best*, 454–57. On this context see also Frei, *Adenauer's Germany*, 5ff.

45. Schmitt, *Ex Captivitate Salus*, 35.

46. Ibid., 12.

47. On the self-stylization of a philosopher himself entwined—albeit less strongly than Schmitt—with Nazism see Reinhard Mehring, *Heideggers Überlieferungsgeschick: Eine dionysische Selbstinzenierung* (Würzburg: Königshausen & Neumann, 1992). On the interpretation of the SD files aimed at Schmitt, see Gross, "Politische Polykratie 1936."

48. Mohler, Huhn, and Tommissen, *Carl Schmitt—Briefwechsel mit einem seiner Schüler*, 95.

49. Saul Friedländer has examined this phenomenon in *Reflections of Nazism: An Essay on Kitsch and Death* (New York: Harper & Row, 1984). On the idea of the "victorious" return of the Jews in postwar Germany see esp. 109f. In

general on German antisemitism after 1945, see Stern, *Im Anfang war Auschwitz;* Poliakov, *History of Anti-Semitism,* esp. articles on German antisemitism by Klaus von Münchhausen and Rudolf Pfister, both with extensive bibliographies; Werner Bergmann and Rainer Erb, *Antisemitismus in der Bundesrepublik Deutschland: Ergebnisse der empirischen Forschung von 1946–1989* (Opladen: Leske & Budrich, 1991), esp. ch. 11 on antisemitism in the context of "overcoming National Socialism," 231–73; Werner Bergmann, "Die Reaktion auf den Holocaust in Westdeutschland von 1945 bis 1989," *Wissenschaft und Unterricht* 43 (1992): 327–50; Alphons Silbermann and Julius H. Schoeps, eds., *Antisemitismus nach dem Holocaust: Bestandsaufnahme und Erscheinungsformen in deutschsprachigen Ländern* (Cologne: Verlag Wissenschaft & Politik, 1986); Werner Bergmann and Rainer Erb, eds., *Antisemitismus in der politischen Kultur nach 1945* (Opladen: Westdeutscher Verlag, 1990).

50. On philosemitism see Stern, *Im Anfang war Auschwitz,* esp. 241–65.

51. See Armin Mohler, *Der Nasenring: Im Dickicht der Vergangenheitsbewaeltigung* (Essen: Heitz & Höffkes, 1989).

52. Mohler, Huhn, and Tommissen, *Carl Schmitt—Briefwechsel mit einem seiner Schüler,* 133.

53. Charges leveled by the Marxist and former National Bolshevist (and antisemite) Ernst Niekisch (1889–1967) appear to fall into the latter category. Niekisch tried to link Schmitt's antisemitism to statements of the Nazi propagandist Johannes van Leers (1902–65). Mohler and Schmitt corresponded over this case for a long time, without ever addressing the question of what Schmitt actually did say. Mohler's main motive appears to have been obtaining "justice" for his master, in the form of correct citation. This is, to be sure, a justified expectation; but in this case the main intent was to evade any confrontation with Schmitt's talks and other activities at the conference "Judaism in Legal Studies." See ibid., 159, 160, 162, 165, 169, and 455. Schmitt made no public statement regarding Niekisch's reproaches.

54. The article first appeared in the *Deutsche Juristenzeitung,* then in *Positions and Concepts.*

55. "Song of the Sixty-Year-Old," in Schmitt, *Ex Captivitate Salus,* 92, and as entry of 8 July 1948, in Schmitt, *Glossarium,* 177.

56. Ibid., 81.

57. Theodor W. Adorno, "Zur Bekämpfung des Antisemitismus heute," in Adorno, *Vermischte Schriften,* vol. 1, ed. Rolf Tiedemann (Frankfurt a.M.: Suhrkamp, 1962), 359–83, here 363.

58. See the polemic text by Ernst Bloch, "Die sogenannte Judenfrage" (1963), in Bloch, *Literarische Aufsätze* (Frankfurt a.M.: Suhrkamp, 1965), 9:549–554.

59. On the impression Schmitt made within emigants' circles see Alfons Söllner, "'Kronjurist des Dritten Reiches': Das Bild Carl Schmitts in den Schriften der Emigranten," *Jahrbuch für Antisemitismusforschung* 1 (1992): 191–216.

60. Aron, *Erkenntnis und Verantwortung*, 418; cf. introduction, n.28.

61. See Schmitt, *Glossarium*, 59, 115, 252.

62. Ibid., 290.

63. Ibid.

64. See the relevant entries under "Judentum" in van Laak and Villinger, *Nachlass Carl Schmitt*, 329.

65. Van Laak, *Gespräche in der Sicherheit des Schweigens*. See also the review by Herfried Münkler, "Carl Schmitt in der frühen Bundesrepublik," *Neue politische Literatur* 40 (1995): 467–69; and on Schmitt's influence on German neoconservatism: Mehring, *Carl Schmitt zur Einführung*, 11–30. Van Laak focuses mainly on West Germany's early phase. As the ever-rising number of publications on Schmitt shows, the interest in him has only increased since then, with no end to the Schmitt renaissance in sight.

66. See van Laak, *Gespräche in der Sicherheit des Schweigens*, 209–30.

67. Ibid., 240–93.

68. For an opposing view see Nicolaus Sombart, "Gruppenbild mit zwei Damen: Zum Verhältnis von Wissenschaft, Politik und Eros im wilhelminischen Zeitalter," *Merkur, Zeitschrift für europäisches Denken* 30 (1976): 972–90. As indicated, Sombart would later concern himself intensely, in both *Die deutschen Männer und ihre Feinde* and *Jugend in Berlin*, with Schmitt's "aura," which included an essential element of stylization as a person placed under a taboo.

69. Cf. Forsthoff, *Der totale Staat*; Forsthoff, "Über Gerechtigkeit," 969–74, 971; Forsthoff, ed., *Deutsche Geschichte seit 1918 in Dokumenten*, 2nd rev. and exp. ed. (Stuttgart: Kröner, 1938); Günther Krauss [Clemens Lang], "Das jüdische Frankreich," *Deutsches Volkstum* 1 (1933), 370–74.

70. Schmitt, *Glossarium*, 182; van Laak and Villinger, *Nachlass Carl Schmitt*.

71. RW 265-346. It is unclear who added the note "(so-called) blurb of Carl Schmitt for the Leviathan book, not used by the publisher." Schmitt mailed this text to Armin Mohler, who made it accessible to the less "initiated" through publication of their correspondence. See Mohler, Huhn, and Tommissen, *Carl Schmitt—Briefwechsel mit einem seiner Schüler*, 38–39.

72. See Ruth Groh, *Arbeit an der Heillosigkeit der Welt: Zur politisch-theologischen Anthropologie Carl Schmitts* (Frankfurt a.M.: Suhrkamp, 1988), 115–55. Groh carefully analyzes Schmitt's "myth-work." Perhaps as a reflection of her strong debt to Heinrich Meier, she does not adequately consider questions of historical context: she focuses on Schmitt as political theologian, not as a political commentator and jurist insisting on politics. She thus exaggerates both the originality of Schmitt's political strategies and the consistency of his political theology.

73. See the prologue to the book's Spanish edition in Tommissen, *Schmittiana*, 2:140–42.

74. Schmitt, *Glossarium*, 157.

75. See above, 155–65, and Schmitt, *Ex Captivitate Salus*, 12.

76. Ibid.

77. *Paulys Real-Encyclopädie der classischen Altertumswissenschaft*, s.v. "Epimetheus" (Stuttgart: Metzler, 1907), vol. 11, cols. 181–82; *Ausführliches Lexikon der griechischen und römischen Mythologie*, s.v. "Epimetheus" (Leipzig: Teubner, 1884–90), vol. 1, col. 1284, *Reclams Lexikon der antiken Mythologie*, s.v. "Epimetheus" (Stuttgart: Reclam, 1974), 177.

78. Piet Tommissen, "Bausteine zu einer wissenschaftlichen Biographie (Periode 1888–1933)," in Quaritsch, *Complexio Oppositorum*, 71–100, esp. 80.

79. In *Ex Captivitate Salus* Schmitt mentions Konrad Weiss on the following pages: 40, 45, 51f., 91. On the life and work of the Swabian author, see *Marienlexikon*, s.v. "Konrad Weiss," ed. Remigius Bäumer and Leo Scheffczyk, 6th ed. (St. Ottilien: EOS, 1994), 703–5; Friedhelm Kemp, *Der Dichter Konrad Weiss: 1880–1940* (Marbach: Deutsche Schillergesellschaft, 1980). On Weiss and Schmitt, see Wilhelm Kühlmann, "Im Schatten des Leviathan: Carl Schmitt und Konrad Weiss," in Wacker, *Die eigentliche katholische Verschärfung*, 89–114; Wilhelm Nyssen, "Carl Schmitt 'Der schlechte, unwürdige und doch authentische Fall eines christlichen Epimetheus,'" in Quaritsch, *Complexio Oppositorum*, 181–92. Koenen offers an assessment in *Der Fall Carl Schmitt*, 406–10.

80. Schmitt, *Ex Captivitate Salus*, 12.

81. Weiss himself offers another translation: Epimetheus does not think too late, but as someone who "observes together with others," he is a witness to the work of the Christian Pandora.

82. Wilhelm Vollmer, *Wörterbuch der Mythologie aller Völker*, 3rd ed. (Stuttgart: Hoffmann, 1874), 189.

83. Konrad Weiss, *Der christliche Epimetheus* (Berlin: Runge, 1933), 95.

84. On the precise holdings regarding Konrad Weiss in the Schmitt archives, see Kühlmann, "Im Schatten des Leviathan," 112–14.

85. Weiss, *Der christliche Epimetheus*, 3.

86. Koenen, *Der Fall Carl Schmitt*, 406.

87. See Kühlmann, "Im Schatten des Leviathan," 89–114. Even Kühlmann does not clarify the concept.

88. Ibid., 99.

89. Weiss, *Der christliche Epimetheus*, 90.

90. See interrogation by Kempner, 29 April 1947, in Wieland, "Carl Schmitt in Nürnberg," 120f.

91. Ibid., 110.

92. Ibid., 94, 110.

93. Adolf Hitler, *Mein Kampf* (Munich: F. Eher Nachf, 1941), 317.

94. Schmitt, *Ex Captivitate Salus*, 53 *(Vollbringe, was du musst, es ist schon / Immer vollbracht und du tust Antwort)*.

95. See Weiss, *Der christliche Epimetheus*, 5, 6ff.

96. Schmitt, *Glossarium*, 238.

97. Ibid., 211 *(Bestraft mit Bann, verfolgt in jedem Wort, / bedroht zum Tode ist sein Los von Anfang / und muss den Weg gehn und Drohung klären)*.

98. Mohler, Huhn, and Tommissen, *Carl Schmitt—Briefwechsel mit einem seiner Schüler*, 95.

99. Ibid.

100. Mohler does not furnish any page numbers in his commentary, making it hard to verify. In contrast to his interpretation, Weiss, *Der christliche Epimetheus*, 88, offers the following "conceptual definition": "In order to find the crucified interiority [*Innenheit*] of [the term's] meaning, the Germanic human being further increases the burden of the earth through the burden of history. This is the propagation of Christianity through premonition within history, and that is the Christian German Epimetheus." The correspondence seems to suggest that Schmitt's follower Armin Mohler was intimidated by the hardly readable *Christliche Epimetheus*. The Plettenberg master thus sent him the following imprecation: "I must ask you (for the umpteenth time) to read K. on the conservative revolution (Christl. Epimetheus pp. 83–94); K. Weiss does not appear in your dissertation!" In Mohler, Huhn, and Tommissen, *Carl Schmitt—Briefwechsel mit einem seiner Schüler*, 311.

101. See Faber, "Carl Schmitt, der Römer," in Wacker, *Die eigentliche katholische Verschärfung*, 257–78.

102. Mohler, Huhn, and Tommissen, *Carl Schmitt—Briefwechsel mit einem seiner Schüler*, 153.

103. See Raphael Gross, "Katholischer Reichstheologe oder Nazi? Andreas Koenens Studie zum 'Fall Carl Schmitt,'" Beilage Literatur und Kunst, *Neue Zürcher Zeitung*, 3–4 Feb. (1996): 52.

104. Schmitt, *Glossarium*, 18.

105. Ibid., 280.

106. So also Reinhard Mehring, "Carl Schmitts Dämonologie—nach seinem Glossarium," *Rechtstheorie* 23 (1992): 258–71.

107. Micha Brumlik, "Carl Schmitts theologisch-politischer Antijudaismus," in Wacker, *Die eigentlich katholische Verschärfung*, 247–56, 249.

108. Schmitt, *Glossarium*, 277. Martin Leutzsch, "Der Bezug auf die Bibel und ihre Wirkungsgeschichte bei Carl Schmitt," 174–202, esp. 201, also refers to a theologization process.

109. The anthology *Die eigentlich katholische Verschärfung*, ed. Bernd Walker, can be criticized along these lines. On the one hand, most of the volume's contributions are skeptical regarding Schmitt's "Catholicism." On the other hand, the basic orientation of the volume is strongly tied to Schmitt's own premises.

110. Schmitt, *Glossarium*, 253.

111. Hans Blüher, *Richtlinien für meine Freunde, sofern sie mich in Gesprächen und besonders in Besprechungen gegen den augenblicklich wieder einmal im Schwange befindlichen Vorwurf des Antisemitismus verteidigen wollen.* RW 265-263, no. 4. Located in a file named "Judaica": *Die Erhebung Israels gegen die christlichen Güter* (Hamburg: Hanseatische Verlagsanstalt, 1931). RW 265-249: copy of Martin Buber,

"Nachkriegsbriefe, Hans Blüher an Martin Buber, Berlin 1953," *Neue Deutsche Hefte* 2 (1979): 247ff.

112. For here and the following, see Schmitt, *Glossarium*, 22.

113. See Hans Blüher, *Secessio Judaica: Philosophische Grundlegung der Historischen Situation des Judentums und der Antisemitschen Bewegung* (Berlin: Ritter, 1922); Hans Blüher, *Deutsches Reich, Judentum und Sozialismus* (Prien: Anthropos Verlag, 1920).

114. Mohler, Huhn, and Tommissen, *Carl Schmitt—Briefwechsel mit einem seiner Schüler*, 30.

115. See Bernd Greiner, *Die Morgenthau-Legende: Zur Geschichte eines umstrittenen Plans* (Hamburg: Hamburger, 1995).

116. Schmitt, *Glossarium*, 255 (*Zu Isidore Isou: Sie reden zwar viel von Eliten, / doch ahnen die meisten es kaum: / es gibt nur noch Isra-Eliten / im grossplanetarischen Raum*). Reinhard Mehring points to this passage in "Geist gegen Gesetz: Carl Schmitts Destruktion des positiven Rechtsdenkens," in Wacker, *Die eigentliche katholische Verschärfung*, 229–45, esp. 242.

117. Schmitt, *Glossarium*, 9.

118. Carl Schmitt to Pierre Linn, in Schmitt, *Glossarium*, 283 (original text in French).

119. Ibid., 208. The parallelization is clear down to details: "I'm always only treated unjustly; I'm *hors la loi*. . . ."; ibid., 59.

120. Leutzsch, *Der Bezug auf die Bibel und ihre Wirkungsgeschichte bei Carl Schmitt*, 193.

121. *Glossarium*, 227. Schmitt was openly pleased to be acknowledged as the author of this remark; see Mohler, Huhn, and Tommissen, *Carl Schmitt—Briefwechsel mit einem seiner Schüler*, 52.

122. Schmitt, *Glossarium*, 232.

123. Ibid., 269.

124. Ibid., 313. The original passage refers to "descendents," in the plural; through an inaccurate paraphrase, Schmitt thus implies that the New Testament passage contains a reference to the killing of Jesus.

125. See Leutzsch, *Der Bezug auf die Bibel und ihre Wirkungsgeschichte bei Carl Schmitt*, 195.

126. Ibid., 201.

Chapter 16. Schmitt's Struggle against the Theologians and Jews

1. See pp. 4, 9, 17, 18, 45, 57, 61, 81, 91, 94, 142, 150, 153, 154, 156, 169, 176, 192, 208, 209, 215, 227, 240, 241, 249, 253, 254, 255, 256, 258, 259, 262, 264, 267, 268, 280, 287, 290, 298, 300, 306, 307, and 308.

2. Schmitt, *Ex Captivitate Salus*, 75. Cf. Schmitt, *Der Nomos der Erde*.

3. Schmitt, *Ex Captivitate Salus*, 89.

4. See the talk "Der Zeitalter der Neutralisierungen und Entpolitisierungen," in Schmitt, *Der Begriff des Politischen*, 79–95.

5. Schmitt, *Politische Theologie 2*, 110f. See also Schmitt, *Der Nomos der Erde*.

6. Schmitt, *Glossarium*, 19.

7. Schmitt, *Politische Theologie 2*, 110f. (italics in original). For Schmitt's confrontation with Gentilis, see Schmitt, *Der Nomos der Erde*, 129–31.

8. Schmitt, *Staat, Grossraum, Nomos*, 44–54 ("The Bourgeois Constitutional State").

9. Schmitt, *Ex Captivitate Salus*, 70.

10. Ibid., 72.

11. Ibid.

12. Schmitt, *Der Nomos der Erde*, 131.

13. Schmitt, *Glossarium*, 154.

14. Ibid., 189.

15. For the subtitle citation: Karl Marx, "Manifest der Kommunistischen Partei," in Karl Marx and Friedrich Engels, *Werke*, ed. Institut für Marxismus-Leninismus, 40 vols. (Berlin: Dietz, 1957–89), 4:459–93; cited in Schmitt, *Glossarium*, 213. For the epigraph, ibid., 57.

16. Schmitt, *Verfassungslehre*, 138–57.

17. Schmitt, *Glossarium*, 162. Hereafter cited in text.

18. Cf. the following passage from the *Glossarium* (200): "Fine definition of law in the young Hegel: the law is a fragment of human nature. Before the law a criminal is nothing but a criminal; but the law is precisely only a fragment of human nature and only applies to fragments."

19. Ibid., 313.

20. Ibid., 313; 227.

21. Ibid., 300. Schmitt is here referring to Marcel Simon, *Verus Israel: Étude sur les relations entre chrétiens et juifs dans l'empire romain* (Paris: Boccard, 1948), 13.

22. Ibid., 234.

Conclusion

1. See Niklas Luhmann, "Positivität des Rechts als Voraussetzung einer modernen Gesellschaft," in Luhmann, *Ausdifferenzierung des Rechts: Beiträge zur Rechtssoziologie und Rechtstheorie* (Frankfurt a.M.: Suhrkamp, 1981), 113–53.

2. Friedrich Stadler shows this for the Vienna Circle with which Kelsen was aligned in his *Studien zum Wiener Kreis: Ursprung, Entwicklung und Wirkung des Logischen Empirismus im Kontext* (Frankfurt a.M.: Suhrkamp, 1997); on Kelsen, 607–19.

3. Ludwig Feuerbach, "Das Wesen des Christentum" (1841) in Feuerbach, *Gesammelte Werke*, vol. 5, ed. Werner Schuffenhauer (2nd rev. ed., Berlin: Akademie, 1984), 74.

4. See Detlev J. K. Peukert, *Max Webers Diagnose der Moderne* (Göttingen: Vandenhoeck & Ruprecht, 1989), 5–10.

Afterword

1. Friedrich Balke, "Kreuzzug und Kartei: Carl Schmitt und die Juden," *Neue Rundschau* 111 (2000): 168–79; Uwe Pralle, "Der unsichtbare Feind: Raphael Gross unternimmt eine erste umfassende Erkundung des Antisemitismus bei Carl Schmitt," *Frankfurter Rundschau*, 17 June 2000, 20; Jürgen Busche, "Wie die meisten: Neue Anmerkungen zu Carl Schmitts Antisemitismus," *Badische Zeitung*, 3 June 2000, 37; Thomas Wirz, "Ein Fall von reiner Rechtsleere: Einfach unklug: Raphael Gross über 'Carl Schmitt und die Juden,'" *Frankfurter Allgemeine Zeitung*, 31 July 2000, 51; Heinz Dieter Kittsteiner, "Das entdeckte Arcanum: Raphael Gross über 'Carl Schmitt und die Juden,'" *Neue Zürcher Zeitung*, 2 August 2000, 36; Herfried Münkler, "Feinde des Politischen: Raphael Gross über Carl Schmitts Antisemitismus," *Die Zeit*, 14 September 2000, 67; Jürgen Zarusky, "Opportunistischer Held" Der Staatsrechtler Carl Schmitt hinterliess ein zwiespältiges Werk," *Süddeuche Zeitung*, 30 October 2000, 11; Wilfried Nippel, "Raphael Gross: Carl Schmitt und die Juden," *H-Soz-u-Kult*, 27 October 2000; Günter Maschke, "Der subventionierte Amoklauf—Raphael Gross: Carl Schmitt und die Juden," *Junge Freiheit*, 20 October 2000, 16; Guido Kalberer, "Der frühe Fall des Juristen Carl Schmitt," *Tages Anzeiger*, 1 December 2000, 65; Thomas Meyer, "Eine Studie von Raphael Gross: 'Carl Schmitt und die Juden,'" www.hagalil.com/archiv/2000/12/schmitt.htm, 10 December 2000; Tobias Korenke, "'. . . nur Isra-eliten.' Raphael Gross, Carl Schmitt und die Juden. Eine deutsche Rechtslehre," *Sociologia Internationalis* 2 (2000): 260–63; Axel Schmitt, "Raphael Gross demaskiert Carl Schmitts theologisch-politischen Antisemitismus," *literaturkritik.de*, no. 10 (October 2000); Michael Rumpf, "Raphael Gross, Carl Schmitt und die Juden; Ernst Jünger and Carl Schmitt, *Briefe 1930–1983*," *zeno: Zeitschrift für Literatur und Sophistik* (November 2000): 95–97; Markus Schwering, "Studie über Carl Schmitt: Ein unversöhnlicher Antisemit. Raphael Gross untersucht die Haltung des Staatsrechtlers zum Judentum," *Kölner Stadt-Anzeiger*, 9 November 2000, 27; Ulrike Hermann, "Der Jude als Feind," *die tageszeitung*, 27 February 2001, 16; Astrid Deuber-Mankowsky, "Flucht aus der Geschichte und ihre Folgen," *Die Wochenzeitung*, 8 February 2001, 24; Ulrich Sieg, "Carl Schmitt und die Juden," *Zeitschrift für Geschichtswissenschaft* 49 (2001): 268–70; Manfred Kuhn, Carl Schmitt und die Juden," *Schweizerische Juristen-Zeitung*, 1 July 2001; Susanne Benöhr, "'Die Vertrauten Eigenen Anderen': Rezension des Buches von Raphael Gross 'Carl Schmitt und die Juden,'" *Forum Recht* 3 (2001): 91–93; Clemens Jabloner, *Tel Aviver Jahrbuch für Deutsche Geschichte* 30 (2002): 434–41. Most recently: Roger-Pol Droit, "Carl Schmitt, un antisémite trop respecté," *Le Monde*, supplement, "Le Monde des Livres," 18 November 2005, 9.

2. I here draw on my response for the Internet review forum *H-Soz-u-Kult*, sent on 23 October 2001.

3. For a broad overview and convincing critique of recent work on Schmitt appearing in Germany and the United States, see Peter C. Caldwell, "Controversies over Carl Schmitt: A Review of Recent Literature," *Journal of Modern History* 77 (June 2005). Caldwell discusses the following more recent publications: Gopal Balakrishnan, *The Enemy: An Intellectual Portrait of Carl Schmitt* (London: Verso, 2000); Berthold, *Carl Schmitt und der Staatsnotstandsplan am Ende der Weimarer Republik;* Dirk Blasius, *Carl Schmitt: Preussischer Staatsrat in Hitlers Reich* (Göttingen: Vandenhoeck & Ruprecht, 2001); Felix Blindow, *Carl Schmitts Reichsordnung: Strategie für einen europäischen Grossraum* (Berlin: Akademie, 1999); Renato Cristi, *Carl Schmitt and Authoritarian Liberalism: Strong State, Free Economy* (Cardiff: Univ. of Wales Press, 1998); David Dyzenhaus, ed., *Law as Politics: Carl Schmitt's Critique of Liberalism* (Durham, N.C.: Duke Univ. Press, 1998); Richard Faber, *Lateinischer Faschismus: Über Carl Schmitt, den Römer und Katholiken* (Berlin: Philo, 2001); Christoph Möllers, *Staat als Argument* (Munich: C.H. Beck, 2000); Chantal Mouffe, ed., *The Challenge of Carl Schmitt* (London: Verso, 1999); Wolfgang Pircher, ed., *Gegen den Ausnahmezustand: Zur Kritik an Carl Schmitt* (Vienna: Springer, 1999); Helmut Quaritsch, *Carl Schmitt: Antworten in Nürnberg* (Berlin: Duncker & Humblot, 2000); Gabriel Seiberth, *Anwalt des Reiches: Carl Schmitt und der Prozess "Preussen contra Reich" vor dem Staatsgerichtshof* (Berlin: Duncker & Humblot, 2001); Jeffrey Seitzer, *Comparative History and Legal Theory: Carl Schmitt in the First German Democracy* (Westport, Conn.: Greenwood, 2001); Rüdiger Voigt, ed., *Mythos Staat: Carl Schmitts Staatsverständnis* (Baden-Baden: Nomos, 2001). In addition, much attention has been paid in the United States to the book by Ellen Kennedy, *Constitutional Failure: Carl Schmitt in Weimar* (Durham, N.C.: Duke Univ. Press, 2004). Ellen Kennedy was active several years ago in the debate over Schmitt's influence on Jürgen Habermas. In her book she attempts to introduce the antidemocrat Schmitt as a theorist of democracy on the same level as John Rawls.

4. Yves Charles Yarka, "Carl Schmitt, le nazi," *Cités* 14:161–65, followed by two translations: Carl Schmitt, *Le Führer protège le droit*, 165–72; Schmitt, *La science allemande du droit dans sa lutte contre l'esprit juif*, 173–81. The debate is continued in *Cités* 17, "Analyses et Documents: Contre le Blanchiment du Nazi, Carl Schmitt," with a French translation by Denis Trierweiler of the most important antisemitic passages in the *Glossarium*. *Le Débat* furnishes another perspective in its 2004 September/October issue, under the title "Y a-t-il un bon usage de Carl Schmitt?" with the following articles: Catherine Colliot-Thélène, "Carl Schmitt à l'Index?" 128–37; Giuseppe Duso, "Pourquoi Carl Schmitt?" 138–46; Jean-François Kervégan, "Questions sur Carl Schmitt," 147–59; Philippe Raynaud, "Que faire de Carl Schmitt?" 160–67.

5. Raphael Gross, *Carl Schmitt et les juifs*, trans. Denis Trierweiler, preface by Yves Charles Zarka (Paris: Presses Universitaires de France, 2005).

6. Published as of April 2005: Yves Charles Zarka, *Un détail nazi dans la pensée de Carl Schmitt: La justification des lois de Nuremberg du 15 septembre 1935*, trans. Denis Trierweiler (Paris: Presses Universitaires de France, 2005); Théodore Paléologue, *Sous l'œil du grand Inquisiteur: Carl Schmitt et l'héritage de la théologie politique* (Paris: Cerf, 2004) (focusing on the alleged "Catholic intensification" in Schmitt's work); David Cumin, *Carl Schmitt: Biographie politique et intellectuelle* (Paris: Cerf, 2005). For various reasons, the foreword by Étienne Balibar to the French translation of Schmitt's *Leviathan* has been sharply criticized. Most likely, in evaluating Schmitt's text Balibar was unaware of the depth of its antisemitism; possibly, he did not consider it an important aspect of Schmitt's argument.

7. Schmitt, *Carl Schmitt Tagebücher: Oktober 1912 bis Februar 1915*.

8. Yehuda Bauer, *Rethinking the Holocaust* (New Haven, Conn.: Yale Univ. Press, 2001), 93–119, Herbert, *Best*.

9. On this argument (in the context of a discussion of Nietzsche's anti-egalitarianism), see Ernst Tugendhat, *Aufsätze 1992–2000* (Frankfurt a.M.: Suhrkamp, 2001), 225.

10. Schmitt, *Carl Schmitt Tagebücher*, 47. Hereafter cited in text. More on Rosenbaum appears on pages 48, 49, 50. In London I received kind permission from the granddaughter of Eduard Rosenbaum to view the Schmitt-Rosenbaum correspondence, which extended from 22 June 1912 to 24 November 1932. The correspondence consists of nineteen letters and a marriage notice from Schmitt to Rosenbaum and eleven letters from Rosenbaum to Schmitt. During that period the relationship between Schmitt and Rosenbaum had clearly improved.

11. Balke, "Kreuzzug und Kartei," 174.

12. Jan Assmann, *Moses the Egyptian: The Memory of Egypt in Western Monotheism* (Cambridge, Mass.: Harvard Univ. Press, 1997); Assmann, *Death and Salvation in Ancient Egypt*, trans. David Lorton (Ithaca, N.Y.: Cornell Univ. Press, 2005); Assmann, *Herrschaft und Heil: Politische Theologie in Altägypten, Israel und Europa* (Munich: Hanser, 2000).

13. Jan Assmann, *Das kulturelle Gedächtnis: Schrift, Erinnerung und politische Identität in frühen Hochkulturen* (Munich: C.H. Beck, 1992), 140f.

14. See esp.: Werner Konitzer, "Die mosaische Unterscheidung: Zwei Erzählungen zur Erklärung antisemitischer Affekte," *Mittelweg* 13 (2004): 49–60.

INDEX

GEORGE L. MOSSE SERIES
IN MODERN EUROPEAN CULTURAL AND
INTELLECTUAL HISTORY

Series Editors

Stanley G. Payne, David J. Sorkin, and John S. Tortorice

Collected Memories: Holocaust History and Postwar Testimony
Christopher R. Browning

Carl Schmitt and the Jews: The "Jewish Question," the Holocaust, and German Legal Theory
Raphael Gross; Translated by Joel Golb

Confronting History: A Memoir
George L. Mosse

Nazi Culture: Intellectual, Cultural, and Social Life in the Third Reich
George L. Mosse

What History Tells: George L. Mosse and the Culture of Modern Europe
Stanley G. Payne, David J. Sorkin, and John S. Tortorice

The Jews in Mussolini's Italy: From Equality to Persecution
Michele Sarfatti; Translated by John and Anne C. Tedeschi